Transfer on Trial:

Intelligence, Cognition, and Instruction

edited by

Douglas K. Detterman
Case Western Reserve University

Robert J. Sternberg
Yale University

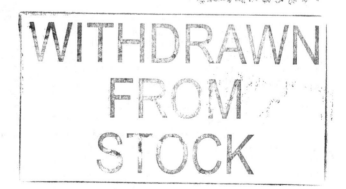

ABLEX PUBLISHING CORPORATION
NORWOOD, NEW JERSEY

Library of Congress Cataloging-in-Publication Data

Transfer on trial : intelligence, cognition, and instruction / edited
 by Douglas K. Detterman, Robert J. Sternberg.
   p.   cm.
  Includes bibliographical references and index.
  ISBN 0-89391-825-3 (cl.). — ISBN 0-89391-826-1 (ppb)
  1. Transfer of training.   I. Detterman, Douglas K.
 II. Sternberg, Robert J.
 LB1059.T74   1992
 370.15—dc20   92-33487
                                                   CIP

Ablex Publishing Corporation
355 Chestnut Street
Norwood, New Jersey 07648

Contents

List of Contributors

(Numbers in parentheses indicate the pages on which the authors' contributions begin.)

Miriam Bassok, Department of Psychology, University of Chicago, 5848 South University Avenue, Chicago, Illinois 60637. (68)

Earl C. Butterfield, Bureau of Educational Development and Research, 322 Miller DQ-12, University of Washington, Seattle, Washington 98195. (192)

Stephen J. Ceci, Department of Human Development and Family Studies, College of Human Ecology, Cornell University, Ithaca, New York 14853-4401. (168)

Douglas K. Detterman, Department of Psychology, Case Western Reserve University, 10900 Euclid Avenue, Cleveland, Ohio 44106-7123. (1)

Emily Dibble, Department of Psychology, University of Washington, Seattle, Washington 98195. (258)

Peter A. Frensch, Department of Psychology, 210 McAlester Hall, University of Missouri at Columbia, Columbia, Missouri 85211. (25)

Robert Glaser, Learning Research and Development Center, University of Pittsburgh, 3939 O'Hara Street, Pittsburgh, Pennsylvania 15260. (258)

Sherrie P. Gott, Basic Job Skills Function, Air Force Human Resources Laboratory (AFHRL/MOMJ), Brooks Air Force Base, Texas 78235-5601. (258)

James G. Greeno, School of Education, Stanford University, Stanford, California 94305. (99)

Ellen Parker Hall, Basic Job Skills Function, Air Force Human Resources Laboratory (AFHRL/MOMJ), Brooks Air Force Base, Texas 78235-5601. (258)

Keith J. Holyoak, Department of Psychology, University of California, Los Angeles, 405 Hilgard Avenue, Los Angeles, California 90024-1563. (68)

Joyce L. Moore, School of Education, Stanford University, Stanford, California 94305. (99)

Gregory D. Nelson, Bureau of Educational Development and Research, 322 Miller DQ-12, University of Washington, Seattle, Washington 98195. (192)

Robert A. Pokorny, Basic Job Skills Function, Air Force Human Resources Laboratory (AFHRL/MOMJ), Brooks Air Force Base, Texas 78235-5601. (258)

Stephen K. Reed, Center for Research in Mathematics and Science Education, College of Sciences, San Diego State University, San Diego, California 92182-0315. (39)

Ana Ruiz, Department of Human Development and Family Studies, College of Human Ecology, Cornell University, Ithaca, New York 14853-4401. (168)

Timothy A. Slocum, Bureau of Educational Development and Research, 322 Miller DQ-12, University of Washington, Seattle, Washington 98195. (192)

David R. Smith, Department of Psychology, University of California, Santa Cruz. (99)

Robert J. Sternberg, Department of Psychology, Yale University, Box 11A Yale Station, New Haven, Connecticut 06520-7447. (25)

Chapter 1

The Case for the Prosecution: Transfer as an Epiphenomenon*

Douglas K. Detterman

Case Western Reserve University

Santayana (1905–1906/1982) implied that previous experience can transfer to new situations when he said, "Those who cannot remember the past are condemned to repeat it" (p. 423). Hegel (1832/1982) was closer to the truth saying, "What experience and history teach are this—that people and governments never have learned anything from history, or acted on principles deduced from it" (p. 703).

These two quotes are good summaries of positions concerning transfer of training. The question raised in this chapter is if things people learn can be used by them in new but similar situations. On the one hand, represented by Santayana, is the belief that a major adaptive mechanism of the human species is

* Parts of this work were supported by Grants No. HD07176, HD15516, and HD21947 from the National Institute of Child Health and Human Development, Office of Mental Retardation, the Air Force Office of Scientific Research, and the Brooks Air Force Base Human Resources Laboratory, Project LAMP. Requests for reprints may be sent to D. K. Detterman, Department of Psychology, Case Western Reserve University, Cleveland, OH 44106.

the ability to profit from experience. Humans do this by using previous experiences to advantage in new situations. They *transfer* knowledge to new situations. Santayana is careful not to say that people do profit from history. He only says that, if they don't profit, they will repeat history. The implication of the statement is that transfer is an important human capability.

On the other hand, Hegel is clear. He doesn't believe that anyone ever applied previously learned lessons from history. People, he claims, simply don't transfer what they learn in one situation to another. At first, this proposition is astounding. The progress of human civilization seems a history of transfer where new inventions arise regularly from the application of old principles to new situations. It is hard to believe that people don't transfer learning on a regular basis. It also is hard to believe that transfer is not an important explanatory mechanism for intelligence, cognition, and education, but that is exactly what I will argue.

The argument against transfer becomes more believable when one realizes that universities are full of people who are attempting to make one significant transfer. They are called professors. If a professor can apply what he or she has learned to one new, novel situation, he or she will have earned his keep. The truth is that most professors pass their entire academic careers without a single important novel insight. Novel insights as cases of transfer are probably rarer than volcanic eruptions and large earthquakes. Like any other rare event, important cases of transfer are difficult to study because no one knows exactly when or where they will occur.

Many students of human achievement think the magnificent transfers that advance human civilization really never occur. They argue that all such cases of important transfers are just many cases of smaller advances. The public never notices the smaller advances. The landmark occurs when an entire line of discoveries gets widespread recognition by singling out one link in the chain of discoveries as most significant. That single link gets the credit for all the work that has gone before. One piece of evidence supporting this position is the high frequency of major multiple discoveries, where two people discover the same thing simultaneously.

It is possible to take this line of argument one step further. It can be argued that it is not transfer we want to achieve in the solution of important problems but freedom from transfer. The creative solution to an important problem may depend on freeing the problem solver from interference from old solutions. So the question is, if we want to build creative problem solvers, should we teach people to transfer or teach them to avoid transfer? Two experiences I had illustrate that the answer to that question depends on your point of view.

The first paper I ever heard at a convention was about the operant training of a mentally retarded woman to use money. By using extensive and elaborate methods, trainers taught her to give the correct amount of money to a clerk when she bought something. She acquired these skills and could use them in the token economy in the institution. The staff decided to see if she could use the skills in a 'real' situation. They took the woman shopping in a store where she selected an item she wanted to buy. She approached the clerk to pay for it and became confused. Instead of carefully counting out the amount for the purchase, she simply took all the money from her pocket and handed it to the clerk. The clerk carefully counted out the money for the purchase, showing the retarded woman how to do it. The authors of the paper concluded that the clerk was doing the trainer's job and that additional attention would have to be given to transfer of training. They resolved to conduct at least part of the training in settings where the behavior would be used. To this day, whenever I think of transfer of training, a picture of a retarded woman handing all of her money to a clerk comes to mind.

But when most people talk of transfer of training, they are talking of headier matters, things like the solution of important scientific problems, new insights in philosophy, and drawing important lessons from history. All these are often attributed to transfer of training. I like to think of the following story as a small example of how a lack of transfer can lead to a creative solution to a problem.

Several years ago I found myself on a bus in Germany going from the rail station to my hotel. The bus driver spoke no English, and I spoke no German. This was apparent to me but it must not have been apparent to the bus driver, because he continued to speak in German. His only concession to my ignorance was that, as I looked more confused, he talked louder. Guessing that he was trying to collect the bus fare, I hit on what I considered a highly creative solution to the problem. I reached in my pocket and pulled out all the German money I had and held it out toward him. He smiled approvingly. As he took one coin at a time, he carefully explained to me, in German and pantomime, the denomination of each coin and how the coins added up to the total fare. I have used this technique frequently, and, invariably, I get a lesson in the denomination of the countries currency and the rudiments of simple math. The lesson is always given in the native language of the country that I don't speak or understand. To the best of my knowledge nobody has ever cheated me. People are always helpful and make an effort to be sure I understand what is happening. The method is one I recommend if you find yourself in a country where you don't know the currency and you don't speak the language.

My behavior is obviously similar to the behavior of the retarded woman. I must confess that, until I wrote this, the similarity never occurred to me. I was proud of my creative solution to a difficult problem and have even taught others how to use my method. Why is one case of failure of transfer considered unfortunate while the same behavior in a very similar situation is considered novel and creative? There are probably those who would argue that my behavior really consisted of appropriate transfer of some previously learned skill. The retarded woman's behavior, they would say, was simply a failure of training to transfer. Other than I am writing about these situations, I cannot discover anything that really makes one different from the other.

The point of these two stories is that it is possible to make as strong a case for failure of transfer as it is to build a case for the importance of transfer. As additional evidence, mathematicians generally make their most significant contributions early in life, often in their early 20s. Some even claim that a mathematician will not make a major contribution if he hasn't done it by 30. The explanation of the importance of youth in mathematical achievement is that, by 30, a person has so overlearned standard mathematics it is impossible to see things in a fresh or new way. That is, it is impossible to have a transfer failure. Of course, there are many other examples of people making discoveries because of transfer. Both failure to transfer and appropriate transfer are equally important in major human accomplishment.

I think there is little doubt that major transfers of training important to the future of humanity are rare events, if it is transfer that is important at all. Very little human behavior is novel and of great significance to the future of humanity. For the moment, the question of transfer's importance in human affairs will be ignored. Instead the question is how difficult it is to produce any kind of transfer and whether it is possible to increase the frequency of transfer. If people don't transfer the training they receive to new situations very often, it is reasonable to ask if they can be made to do so. If people seldom transfer skills and if they cannot be taught to transfer, then transfer can have no importance as an explanation of individual differences in everyday behavior. The role of transfer in individual differences would be irrelevant if transfer never occurs. Before considering if transfer occurs, a formal definition of transfer is presented, followed by a brief review of what is already known about transfer.

A DEFINITION OF TRANSFER

Transfer is the degree to which a behavior will be repeated in a new situation. This definition seems simple. How the concept applies to each real situation is what is difficult to specify. In a trivial sense, all repeated behavior must be transferred. Each occasion the behavior occurs is different than the last, even if it only differs in the moment it is performed. Discussions of transfer are usually not concerned with nearly identical situations. If the situations studied are nearly identical, differing only by a short temporal interval, then interest is said to be in learning. If two situations where the same behavior occurs are obviously different in important ways, interest is in transfer.

Two types of transfer are often distinguished. *Near transfer* is to situations that are identical except for a few important differences. A person learns to draw a three-inch line and returns 2 weeks later to learn to draw a five-inch line. Any advantage in learning to draw a five-inch line could be attributed to near transfer from learning to draw a three-inch line. On the other hand, if a person in a list-learning experiment memorized a poem faster because of participation in the list-learning experiment, the transfer would be called *far transfer*. Transfer can be conceptualized as a continuum of situations progressively more different from the original learning experience. The more similar the original learning situation and the new situation, the more likely the transfer is to be called near transfer. The more difficult the original and new situations, the more likely the transfer is called *far transfer*.

Another useful distinction is between specific and nonspecific transfer. In *specific* transfer, the learner transfers the contents of learning to a new situation. Suppose a list-learning experiment taught the states and their capitals. If knowing state capitals was helpful in a later geography course, it would be a case of specific transfer. If list-learning helped in memorizing poetry, the specific content of the original learning experience could have no influence on the later learning of poetry. The act of learning a list in a laboratory teaches *nonspecific* things, like how to use strategies, how to break up practice, or how to maintain motivation. It is general skills or principles that transfer to the new situation in nonspecific transfer, sometimes called *general transfer*.

A more recent distinction between transfer situations drawn mainly by cognitive psychologists goes by several names. The main distinction is between the deep and surface structure similarities of a situation. An example is that all car dashboards give the same information, but that their dial configurations are different. *Deep structure* is the same but *surface structure* is different. On the other hand, an airplane dashboard contains dials similar to a car's, but the information presented by those dials is different. For car and plane dashboards, there is a similar surface structure but a different deep structure.

When transfer is discussed, greatest interest usually is in far, or general, transfer of deep structure and not in near transfer of surface structure. Transfer of general principles between markedly different situations is most important to those who explain individual differences in terms of transfer. It is far transfer of deep structure that most researchers would characterize as typical of highly intelligent behavior and an important adaptive mechanism of the human species. It is also far transfer of deep structure that is most difficult to get.

A HISTORY OF TRANSFER

Transfer has been one of the most actively studied phenomena in psychology. Regardless of orientation, philosophical perspective, or school of psychology, nearly everyone has something to say about transfer. Unfortunately, most of the history of transfer confirms Hegels remark that we seldom learn anything from history. Though there are many well-established experimental findings, they often have been ignored. It, therefore, seems advisable to review briefly the most important parts of the history of transfer.

Thorndike

E.L. Thorndike conducted a classic series of studies designed to assess the degree people transfer. These studies spanned a quarter of a century. One of the first conducted (Thorndike & Woodworth, 1901) in this series illustrates the general findings of this research.

Subjects estimated the area of rectangles between 10 and 100 sq cm. To help in estimation, subjects had three comparison squares of 1, 25, and 100 sq cm. After sufficient practice to produce improvement (1,000 to 2,000 trials) on the original series, subjects got two test series. The first test series consisted of rectangles between 20 and 90 sq cm not included in the original training series. The second test series consisted of shapes other than rectangles, like triangles and circles. On the second test series, errors after training were about 90% as large as errors before training. Thorndike and Woodworth concluded that there was practically no improvement on the general skill of judging the area of figures. Even the identical figures of series 1 showed less improvement than those explicitly trained.

A more convincing analysis compared successively larger squares in the original test series. Thorndike and Woodworth argued that, if subjects learned associations to specific stimuli, there would be no relationship between how well a subject did on one square and how well he or she did on the next larger square. If there was transfer, learning about one square should transfer to the next larger square. Thorndike and Woodworth found there was no relationship between how well subjects did on one square and how well they did on the next. This finding clearly supported a stimulus–response explanation of learning.

The best characterization of the outcome of this study and the whole series of subsequent studies is best given by Thorndike and Woodworth, themselves:

> The mind is…a machine for making particular reactions to particular situations. It works in great detail, adapting itself to the special data of which it has had experience….
>
> Improvement in any single mental function need not improve the ability in functions commonly called by the same name. It may injure it.
>
> Improvements in any single mental function rarely brings about equal improvement in any other function, no matter how similar, for the working of every mental function-group is conditioned by the nature of the data in each particular case. (pp. 249–250)

The principle, later proved in greater detail, is clear: Transfer is uncommon, but when it occurs at all it is between situations that are highly similar. Transfer occurs, when it occurs, because of common elements in the two situations. The

Discrete v continuous changes in ability over tasks. See Ferguson.

amount of transfer that occurs can be predicted from the proportion of common elements shared by two situations. Learning Latin helps in learning French. Both languages have specific elements in common, since many French words come directly from Latin.

Since the classic Thorndike and Woodworth (1901) experiment there have been literally hundreds, if not thousands, of experiments reaffirming the same point. Transfer is very difficult to obtain. When it is obtained, it is most often between highly similar situations. As a recent, but highly sophisticated variant of Thorndike and Woodworth's experiment, see Homa, Sterling, and Trepel (1981). They came to similar conclusions, particularly with respect to the effects of similarity and degree of training on transfer though their study had a different motivation.

Ferguson

The theory proposed by Ferguson accounts for intelligence using transfer. This theory would appear to be a contradiction to the argument that transfer is not important in intelligence. Because Ferguson defines transfer in a unique way, even if the theory is correct, it does not contradict what I have said about transfer and individual differences.

Ferguson considered learning to be a subclass of transfer. As previously discussed, each learning trial differs slightly from the previous one. If improvement occurs from trial to trial, there must be transfer between trials. Ferguson's theory was most concerned with changes that occur in learning that could be characterized as very near transfer. His position often is cited to support the importance of far transfer in individual differences in intelligence. Nothing could be farther from the truth.

As additional support for this point, Ferguson (1956) cited studies by Fleishman and Hemple (1954, 1955). In these studies, subjects learned (i.e., received many trials on) two tasks: a complex coordination task or a discrimination reaction time task. Subjects also took a comprehensive battery of ability tests. Fleishman found that at different points in learning, different ability tests correlated with performance on the learning tests. In Ferguson's (1956) own words:

> These studies show conclusively that substantial and systematic changes occur in the factor structure of the learning task as practice continues. The abilities involved at one stage of learning differ from the abilities involved at another stage. Thus conclusive experimental evidence exists to support the hypothesis of differential transfer. (p. 127)

(For a different view of these experiments, see Ackerman, 1986, 1987, 1988.)

Ferguson regarded transfer as continuous, producing changes in ability as learning proceeded. He thought discrete conceptions of transfer (the kind discussed in this chapter) were less useful for explaining individual differences than the continuous concept he advanced. Ferguson's theory only considers very close transfer between situations even more similar than Thorndike and Woodworth studied. As such it is probably better classified as a learning theory of individual differences, not as a transfer theory.

The general conclusion must be that Ferguson's theory, though interesting in its own right, has little relationship to the issues considered here. The frequent citation of this theory as support for the importance of transfer in individual differences is unjustified.

EVIDENCE ABOUT TRANSFER

There are several sources of evidence that might be considered to decide if transfer occurs and, if so, under what conditions. A first source of evidence is reviews conducted on the subject. A second source of information is the studies that have been conducted. These studies can be divided into two types: those that claim to find transfer, and those that don't. In the following sections examples of reviews, studies that find transfer, and studies that fail to find transfer, will be considered.

Reviews

There have been several recent reviews concerning transfer. These reviews have generally been exceptionally comprehensive. The opinion of these reviewers, based on all the literature, should be a primary consideration about the importance of the transfer as a cause of individual differences. Reviewers are in almost total agreement that little transfer occurs. Though space prohibits full presentation of evidence cited by these reviewers or even a complete discussion of all the reviews, a few examples will make the case.

Baldwin and Ford (1988) reviewed articles concerned with the transfer of training in the work place. American businesses have a major stake in fostering transfer of training, since they spend up to $100 billion each year to train workers. Yet the estimate is that not more than 10% of training transfers to the job. So business wastes $90 billion each year because of lack of transfer. The transfer discussed by the reviewer is not far transfer but rather near transfer. That is, much of the training reviewed was training a person for a specific job. Even when the person learned specific skills that would be used on the job, there was a failure to transfer the skills to the job.

Perhaps the wide range of literature reviewed by Singley and Anderson (1989) is more pertinent to the issue of individual differences than the job training literature. They reviewed both the theoretical and empirical literature from

Thorndike to the present. They acknowledge evidence for near transfer. But when it comes to general transfer, they conclude: "Besides this spate of negative evidence, there has been no positive evidence of general transfer besides a few highly questionable studies" (p. 25).

They also speculate on the reason general transfer (or far transfer of principles) gets so much continued attention despite so little empirical support. In their words:

> One reason why the notion of general transfer keeps rising from the grave is that it is such an attractive proposition for psychologists and educators alike. It is the one effect that, if discovered and engineered, could liberate students and teachers from the shackles of narrow, disciplinary education. Sustaining these longings is the fact that it is very difficult to prove that something does not exist. There is always another manipulation in the psychologist's tool box to try. (p. 25)

Studies Showing General Transfer

If there has been a failure to show far or general transfer, it is not because of lack of effort. (For the rest of this chapter, I will use the terms *far* and *general transfer* interchangeably. While there are differences in the two types of transfer, there are few differences in the conclusions to be drawn about them.) Studies attempting far transfer number in the hundreds if not thousands. And there are some classics frequently cited as evidence for the existence of far transfer in humans. Those studies are a good place to begin.

Judd (1908) did an early study claiming to show general transfer. Groups of boys threw darts at an underwater target. In one group, the experimenter told the boys about how water refracted light and that the principle of refraction would be useful in hitting the target. The control group boys practiced but got no instruction. The transfer test was hitting targets at different depths. Not surprisingly, the experimental group outperformed the control group on the so-called transfer tests. The results are not surprising, because the experimental manipulation was essentially to teach the experimental group a strategy and to tell them to use it. This hardly constitutes transfer. It does show that the strategy taught was successful at producing improved performance. It does show that subjects follow directions when told to use a strategy. But it does not show anything approaching spontaneous transfer.

An appropriate experiment similar to Judd's might be able to come to this conclusion but several changes in Judd's methodology would have to be made. (It is difficult to know exactly what Judd did, since the full report of this often-cited experiment is only a few paragraphs.) Instruction on refraction of light by water would have to be given in a situation where it was not possible for subjects to make the connection between the experiment and the instruction. The main idea of general transfer is that subjects can and do use a previously learned principle in a new situation. Teaching the principle in close association with testing transfer is not very different from telling subjects they should use the principle just taught. Telling subjects to use a principle is not transfer. It is following instructions.

Another problem with the Judd experiment (and many transfer experiments) is that the experimenter was not blind to subjects' conditions. Subjects were instructed and tested in groups. It appears that the experimenter gave instructions on refraction and tested the subjects for transfer. This is often the case in transfer experiments. If the experimenter is not blind to condition the data may be recorded with systematic bias. More importantly, the experimenter may subtly influence subjects' performance. No transfer experiment should be carried out without using a double blind procedure, particularly experiments assessing general transfer.

A study by Woodrow (1927) is another of the favorites of those who cite the importance of general transfer to intelligence and education. It is obvious that some who cite the study have never read it, because it contains obvious problems. Woodrow is not to blame, because he would not have seen the difficulty when he conducted the study, but modern investigators should have no problem finding the faults.

The purpose of the Woodrow study was to compare the improvement in memorization that would occur with practice in memorization as compared to gains produced by instruction in the general principles and strategies of memorization. Both the training group and the practice group participated for about 3 hours. Nearly half the time, the training group received instruction in principles of memorizing. During that time the experimenter *told* subjects— outright told—that certain strategies would be useful in memorizing certain kinds of material. They were not given practice in using these strategies on the exact kinds of material testing was to be on. So half of the training time was used telling subjects what strategies would be most effective on the test material. Woodrow never allowed subjects to practice the strategies on the material they were tested on, though he told subjects that the techniques they were learning would be useful on that material. For example, subjects were told certain techniques would be useful for memorizing Turkish vocabulary words on the posttest. Subjects practiced these techniques on nonsense-syllable-paired associates during training.

What were the practice subjects doing during this time? While training group subjects were being told the strategy to use on the upcoming posttest, the practice group memorized poetry and nonsense syllables—lots of nonsense syllables and lots of poetry. It is not surprising that, on some posttests, the control subjects got worse and performed more poorly than they had on the pretest. Interference theory was yet to be formulated, so Woodrow can be forgiven for not appreciating the effect of extended practice on the subsequent learning of similar material.

There are further problems with the study. First, all groups performed differently on the pretests, suggesting initial group differences. Second, the control group received no filler task to provide an attentional control. These difficulties are minor compared to the major problems of the study.

What can be concluded from Woodrow's study? What I conclude, as for the Judd study, is that, if you tell subjects about strategies and methods known to improve learning on specific kinds of material, tell them to use those strategies on that material and then follow this instruction with a test of that kind of material, subjects will use the strategy to improve their performance. This hardly constitutes proof of general transfer. It simply shows that subjects at the University of Minnesota in 1927 followed instructions. The implication of this study for education, then, is that a teacher should explicitly list the exact, precise situation to which transfer is desired to occur. As suggested later, that may be exactly correct, but it is not the conclusion proponents of general transfer imply when discussing this study.

Another newer study often cited as an example of general transfer is the study by Gick and Holyoak (1980). Subjects tried to solve the classic Dunker radiation problem. In this problem a tumor must be destroyed by radiation. A single ray would destroy the tumor and the surrounding tissue. Some way must be found to concentrate the X-ray at the location of the tumor without destroying the healthy tissue the ray must pass through. The solution is to give the patient smaller rays from several directions that converge at the cite of the tumor. Only at the place where the rays converge is the tissue destroyed. This problem is hard for even college students to solve.

The study was designed to see if an analogous solved problem would aid in the solution of the radiation problem. Before the radiation problem, subjects heard a story in which a castle is to be stormed by an army. For various reasons a force strong enough cannot be sent to the fortress. Fortunately, roads radiate out from the fortress. The leader of the invading force divides his army into smaller units, each advancing on the castle using a different access road.

There is an obvious similarity between this story and the radiation problem. College students must have trouble seeing this similarity. In the Gick and Holyoak study, they were explicitly told that the first story should serve as a hint in solving the second. Even then, some subjects failed to solve the second problem. When subjects are told that previous material may be useful in the solution of a new problem, it hardly seems reasonable to refer to the solution of the new problem as the result of transfer.

Subjects have not always been explicitly told to transfer. Sometimes instructions are more subtle. Novick (1990) gave subjects three problems. For all problems, subjects got a skeleton of a solution. For the control subjects, all representations were inappropriate for the problem. For the experimental subjects, the middle problem had a correct representation. The representation was a matrix arrangement that could be used to help solve the problem. The middle problem was about making pleasing combinations of five different pairs of pants and five different shirts. All subjects then solved a problem in which five different men had five different illnesses. Based on 10 clues for solving the problem, subjects were to work out the room number and illness of each man. The transfer problem and the second practice problem required different solution methods, but the use of a matrix would be useful (in different ways) in solving both problems. In the experimental group, 75% of subjects used a matrix to solve the problem, while only 21% of control subjects used a matrix in their solution.

Novick interprets the results as evidence for a more general kind of transfer, called *representative transfer*, because subjects transferred a way of representing the problem. The author neglects several factors that would make it surprising if the results had not been as they were. First, the fact that all the experimenter-supplied methods in the control condition were inappropriate might have discouraged the subjects from searching for 'tricks' to use. Second, only one of three experimenter-supplied methods was usable in the experimental condition. The contrast must have made the usable solution particularly salient. Maybe subjects would have tried a matrix even on a problem where it was entirely inappropriate. After all, it was the only method they had that worked during practice. It also appeared that using a matrix is an obvious method of solving this sort of problem. Supporting this point, 21% of control subjects used a matrix to solve the problem though they never saw a matrix in the practice problems. Finally, the high surface similarity between the five-blouse-and-slack problem and the five-patient-and-illness problem must have been a clue to subjects that the two problems had something in common. Unfortunately, no data are given about the number of control subjects who attempted to transfer the incorrect solutions they learned to the transfer problem.

As in most other studies of transfer showing general or representational transfer, examination of the experiment reveals details that make the results so context-sensitive they cannot be generalized beyond the experimental situation. Without showing this effect in other situations, it is unreasonable to conclude that representational transfer is a general phenomenon. The Novick study does not suggest, nor did the author imply, that people's problem-solving ability or intelligence could be improved if we could make them better at representational transfer.

Another recent study claims evidence for transfer in children. Brown and Kane (1988) taught children to transfer general principles from one situation to a different one. For example, in a training problem the child would learn to stack tires on top of each other. The stack of tires let a doll reach a shelf where other tires were to be stacked. The transfer problem required children to stack bales of hay so that a farmer doll could reach a tractor. There were three sets of problems where the general principles (stacking, pulling, or swinging) were the same. The surface structure for each story in the set was different.

The 'trick' used to get children to 'transfer' in this study was that all children got all six problems. If the child was unable to solve a problem, the experimenter demonstrated the solution and then gave the next problem. Children were always asked to repeat the solution to the problem. It is not surprising that children learn the 'rules of the game' over three problem sets. Learning the rules of the game is not what most would consider transfer. This experiment is more a demonstration of rule induction than transfer.

In any event, the results hardly justify the emotional conclusion of the authors that: "Preschool children are *not* extreme Thorndikians: they transfer on the basis of underlying structural similarity; they are not totally dependent on surface features to mediate transfers" (p. 518). This conclusion is particularly interesting because a study of similar design using different stimulus materials involving one of the authors (Campione & Brown, 1974) came to much different conclusions, namely, that: "The results are consistent with the hypothesis that the probability of obtaining transfer from one task to another depends upon the similarity of the task formats" (p. 409). While investigators should be allowed the freedom of changing their minds, it is unusual to see such similar studies interpreted in such diametrically opposite fashions. There is no general transfer, at least for the major conclusions of these two studies.

The amazing thing about all these studies is not that they don't produce transfer. The surprise is the extent of similarity it is possible to have between two problems without subjects realizing that the two situations are identical and require the same solution. Evidently the only way to get subjects to see the similarity is to tell them or to point it out in some not-so-subtle way. The experimental manipulations used in these studies remind me of the field hand who had an uncooperative mule who refused to budge despite his intense urging. The farmer who owned the mule saw the situation, walked over to the mule and struck it squarely between the eyes with a baseball bat. Taking the reins, the farmer gently said, "On," and the mule bolted forward. "The most important thing," the farmer said, "is to get the mule's attention." That seems the case with transfer studies that work. Those studies that don't explicitly tell the subject to transfer all use a trick of some sort to call the subject's attention to the fact that the two problems have the same solution and that the subjects should use the solution in following problems. The experimenter's manipulations have all the subtlety of the farmer's baseball bat. I have not yet found a transfer study where a baseball bat was used, but nearly everything else has been. I have not made a thorough search of the behavior modification literature, so there may even be studies where a baseball bat or its equivalent was used to produce transfer.

Studies That Fail to Show Transfer

Other recent studies that have used more refined definitions of *transfer* have had worse luck in producing transfer. As an example of a study with astounding similarity between problems where subjects fail to show large and reliable transfer effects, consider the study by Reed, Ernst, and Banerji (1974). This study attempted to obtain transfer between two similar problems. *Similar*, in this case, is an understatement. The first problem was the missionary–cannibals problem. Five missionaries traveling through the jungle come to a river with a boat at the landing. The boat holds only three people. On the other side of the river are five cannibals who want to cross the river in the opposite direction. It is evident the boat can be used to relay both missionaries and cannibals across the river, and that, on return trips, missionaries and cannibals must share the boat. The difficulty is that cannibals may never outnumber missionaries or the missionaries will be eaten.

The second problem is the jealous husbands–wives problem and is, in every respect, identical when jealous husbands and wives replace cannibals and missionaries. The solution, of course, is identical for both problems, and the problem space has been worked out in complete detail (Simon & Reed, 1976). When subjects first get the missionary–cannibal problem to solve, and then switch to the jealous husbands problem, there is no significant transfer. When the problems are in the opposite order, there is some transfer, but only when subjects get hints about the similarity of the problems. Despite enormous similarities that are even more salient in some of Reed's later experiments, subjects generally fail to transfer a learned solution to the isomorphic problem. Remember, the subjects were college students! It is astounding that there is no transfer between two such similar situations. If transfer doesn't occur in this study, it seems reasonable to conclude that it will be hard to produce.

Another study, by Reed, Dempster, and Ettinger (1985), shows the same effect in the real-world domain of algebra word problems. In several studies, subjects saw solutions to different kinds of algebra word problems. They then solved either equivalent or similar problems. Equivalent problems were identical except for different numbers, and nothing more. In the similar problems, the solution had to be modified slightly by the subject. Four experiments showed that students could solve equivalent problems only when they had the sample problem available during solution. Subjects infrequently solved the similar condition, even under the best of conditions. One other point: Subjects were all students in a college algebra class that had not yet studied word problems. The result of this study probably wouldn't surprise algebra teachers, but it surprised me. When transfer occurs, it requires heroic efforts to produce and even with draconian measures, the amount of transfer is small.

This is not an isolated study. There are many experiments that show the difficulty of producing transfer (e.g., Reed, 1987, for another by the same author). In each case, the situations are extremely similar, and yet college students fail to transfer learned solutions from one isomorph to another. Though it might be entertaining to go through the many cases where college students fail to notice the similarity between nearly identical problems, there is not space enough for it here. The previous examples should be sufficient to make that point

No-one has yet disproved Thorndike.

that what often is called transfer seldom is. Studies that show true, spontaneous transfer are rare if they exist at all.

The studies presented in the previous sections are just a small sampling of the studies that have attempted to produce transfer. Several general conclusions seem justified from the data reviewed. First, most studies fail to find transfer. Second, those studies claiming transfer can only be said to have found transfer by the most generous of criteria and would not meet the classical definition of transfer. In all of the studies I am familiar with that claim transfer, transfer is produced by 'tricks' of one kind or another. These 'tricks' most often involve just telling the subject to transfer by using hints or outright suggestions. In more subtle cases, the 'trick' includes manipulations that call the subjects attention, in obvious ways, to what the experimenter expects on the transfer problem. In short, from studies that claim to show transfer and that don't show transfer, there is no evidence to contradict Thorndike's general conclusions: Transfer is rare, and its likelihood of occurrence is directly related to the similarity between two situations.

TRANSFER AND EDUCATION

Two theories of education. There are two classic theories of education. The first, often called the *doctrine of formal discipline*, says that what should be taught are the general principles of learning and problem solving. These principles should be taught explicitly by instruction. But they should also be taught implicitly by selecting material for learning which most exercises the mind by subjecting it to formal discipline. For example, Latin and Greek are good subjects because they require the development of learning skills like memorization and they exercise the mind because of their difficulty.

As is no doubt obvious, this was the basic philosophy of a classical education. Students took courses, not so much for the content to be learned, but for the habits of mind these courses would develop. It was this theory of education that Thorndike set out to discredit in his early transfer studies. And it was this theory of education that Thorndike (1924) later discredited directly when he showed that learning Latin and geometry were no more useful in improving reasoning than other, more utilitarian courses like bookkeeping.

A modern variant of the doctrine of formal discipline accepts that neither specific nor general skills automatically transfer to a new situation. Instead, it is argued, teachers must 'teach for transfer.' Somehow, methods of instruction are to be developed which induce transfer to novel situations. It is hard to understand how a teaching methodology can be developed to promote transfer if it cannot be produced in a laboratory under controlled conditions.

The second theory of education is that if you want somebody to know something, you teach it to them. This is the philosophy of education that

Thorndike and many others since have adopted. This theory is repugnant to many cognitive psychologists and to some educators. To its opponents, the theory suggests that education is little more than the process of training parrots or producing zombie robots who regurgitate facts. The critics also argue that the main benefit of education is the degree learning transfers to new situations, that is, the degree the student can apply what has been learned to new, previously unexperienced situations in a creative way. But this argument denies the facts. To my knowledge, there is no convincing body of evidence showing college professors, to say nothing of high school graduates, regularly apply old learning to new, novel situations. We replay most of our behaviour exactly as we learn it.

I believe, as Thorndike and many others have believed, that we learn essentially what we are taught. Further, differences in effectiveness of education are largely because some are capable of learning more of what is being taught than others. This difference between people is due to biological or environmental differences. I believe the low esteem many cognitive psychologists have for the simple learning position has had a massive, intimidating effect on American education. It has made teachers feel guilty about teaching 'facts' and has prevented the use of rote learning even in appropriate situations.

A recent segment on "60 Minutes" illustrates the polarizing attitudes teachers have against 'simply teaching the facts.' A math teacher, Dr. Sikeston, wrote a series of math books based on the simple theory of education that students should be taught what they need to learn. He surveyed the math curriculum and listed the kinds of problems that students had to know. He then wrote a series of math books that presented these problems from easiest through most difficult and provided constant and regular drill on the earlier learned material. He claimed that his sequence of math books had produced substantial gains in math SAT scores for students who had used them.

The most interesting thing about this segment, ignoring whether these math books produced the kind of gains claimed, was the reaction of professional teachers. At one presentation, a member of the audience who was clearly hostile to the books asked if Dr. Sikeston's goal was to make students into robots who simply spit out math facts. At the other extreme was a teacher not being allowed to use the series in his school because the Texas Board of Education would not approve the books. The teacher was close to tears, because he felt that no other materials would be as effective with the minority students enrolled in his school. Obviously, the issue of which philosophy of education is best is a highly emotional one that polarizes practitioners.

It is not surprising that teachers show extreme attitudes. Cognitive psychologists, and other people who should know better, continue to advocate a philosophy of education that is totally lacking in empirical support. It seems the only way to enlist adherents is by emotional appeals and not empirical facts. Why should the practitioner be expected to come to sensible conclusions about educational philosophy when those who write the books are guided more by their prejudices than by existing data?

In summary, there is almost no evidence to support the educational philosophy of formal discipline or any of its variants. There is no good evidence that people produce significant amounts of transfer or that they can be taught to do so. There is, on the other hand, substantial evidence and an emerging *Zeitgeist* that favors the idea that what people learn are specific examples. Experts are experts because they have learned many more examples than novices. When the expert is studied, the behavior may look mystical and appear to be unexplainable without invoking complex concepts like transfer. However, current evidence suggests all that is necessary to be an expert is time, basic ability, and the opportunity to learn a large body of exemplars by experience.

When I began teaching, I thought it was important to make things as hard as possible for students so they would discover the principles themselves. I thought the discovery of principles was a fundamental skill that students needed to learn and transfer to new situations. Now I view education, even graduate education, as the learning of information. I try to make it as easy for students as possible. Where before I was ambiguous about what a good paper was, I now provide examples of the best papers from past classes. Before, I expected students to infer the general conclusion from specific examples. Now, I provide the general conclusion and support it with specific examples. In general, I subscribe to the principle that you should teach people exactly what you want them to learn in a situation as close as possible to the one in which the learning will be applied. I don't count on transfer and I don't try to promote it except by explicitly pointing out where taught skills may apply.

TRANSFER AND INTELLIGENCE

So far, the relationship between transfer and intelligence has been only implied. Near transfer is not the critical issue with respect to individual differences in cognitive ability. Near transfer occurs in a predictable way and differs across ability groups, as Thorndike and Ferguson both pointed out. There are two issues that need to be addressed with respect to the relationship between intelligence and transfer. The first, and perhaps most important issue, is the degree to which far (or general) transfer explains intelligence. The second issue is the degree to which any kind of transfer, either near or far, is central to an understanding of individual differences in mental ability. Each of these issues will be considered in order.

Does Transfer Account for Intelligence?

Many cognitive psychologists believe that a central deficit among those with low IQs or low school achievement is the inability to transfer. They argue that, if it were only possible to teach low IQ subjects to transfer what they learn to new

Explanation of intelligence? OR
To do with how which who can
learn?

18   DETTERMAN

situations, much of their intellectual deficit would be eliminated. Advocates of this position include practitioners (e.g., Feuerstein, 1980), researchers (Brown & Kane, 1988) and theoreticians (see Singley & Anderson, 1989, for a review of Piaget's research pertinent to this point).

There are several problems with this argument. The first is that there is no convincing evidence that far transfer occurs spontaneously. That point was made earlier. People do not spontaneously transfer even for situations that seem very similar. If there is a general conclusion to be drawn from the research done on transfer, it is that the lack of general transfer is pervasive and surprisingly consistent.

Second, if general transfer does not occur spontaneously, there is even less evidence that it can be taught to occur. In those studies claiming far or general transfer, the result can usually be explained by another mechanism. Sometimes the subject is, directly or indirectly, told what transfer is expected.

The conclusion that must be drawn from the many studies of general or far transfer attempted is that this type of transfer is a rare phenomenon. Most of this research has been done with college students who are at least in the upper half of the IQ distribution. It seems safe to say that transfer is not a phenomenon that will account for a large portion of the variance in intellectual functioning. Just the opposite conclusion seems best. People who know a lot about something are not experts because of their ability to transfer but because they know a lot about something. Chase and Simon (1973) estimated that chess experts have memorized as many as 100,000 chess facts. It seems more likely that the specific information people have learned is what makes them an expert or a novice. Acquiring the large numbers of facts needed to be an expert is based on, among other things, individual differences in basic cognitive ability. Transfer does not appear to be a very important part of this picture.

Medin and Ross (1989) carry this point a step further. Equating reasoning with intelligence, as many cognitive psychologists have in the past, they come to quite different conclusions than their cognitive predecessors. They make three major claims summarized, as follows: (a) reasoning is based on specific examples, not abstract principles; (b) induction (transfer) is not automatic but derives from the way examples are used; and (c) induction (transfer) is conservative. This last point is most important. Conservative transfer protects the learner from overgeneralization. Protection from overgeneralization is adaptive. Far transfers may take the learner out of the appropriate problem space, eliminating information essential for solving the problem (or making the induction). Medin and Ross are arguing that far transfer may be harmful, which is an open contradiction of what most in the field argue.

If general transfer cannot be shown in college students, it seems unlikely that it could play a major role in understanding intelligence. The opposite proposition, namely, that we learn specific facts and patterns of behavior, seems more likely from the evidence available. Understanding intelligence is unlikely to depend heavily on an understanding of transfer. Attempts to increase transfer are unlikely to make appreciable differences in a person's intelligence. Time would be better spent in understanding how specific domains of knowledge are learned, how they can be learned most efficiently, and what restrictions on learning are imposed by differences in basic abilities.

Transfer as an Epiphenomenon

Even if general transfer could be easily shown and amount of transfer was related to differences in IQ, there are still good reasons why transfer is not a cause of differences in IQ. The same reasoning applies to all higher order processes, often called *metaprocesses* (Detterman, 1980, 1982, 1984, 1986), such as transfer, rehearsal, executive processes, and so on. If transfer is found, it is likely there will be individual differences in transfer rate. Low-IQ subjects probably would show less transfer than high-IQ subjects, just as younger subjects show less transfer than older ones (Brown & Kane, 1988). This doesn't mean that these differences in transfer are capable of explaining differences in intelligence. That conclusion is much like claiming a Corvette goes faster than a Chevette because it has a louder engine. The loudness of the engine is a derivative characteristic of the power of the engine. While loudness may be associated with power, it doesn't explain it. If you removed the exhaust system from the Chevette, it would be louder and would go faster. That still doesn't mean that loudness explains speed. In the same way, if teaching transfer improves academic or even IQ test performance, it does not mean that transfer explains either IQ or academic achievement.

Probably transfer, like most complex cognitive processes, is a derivative of more basic processes. Although many have implied it, I know of no one who claims transfer is a basic, elementary, independent process.

Just because transfer can be explained by more elementary processes doesn't mean that it is unimportant or shouldn't be studied. It only means that transfer will not provide a fundamental explanation of individual differences in human ability. It is entirely possible that more complex, derivative processes may be more modifiable than the basic abilities that will account for intelligence.

There is some evidence to support this position from the Western Reserve Twin study (e.g., Thompson, Detterman, & Plomin, 1991). In this study, about 600 twins, about half fraternal and half identical, took tests of intelligence, academic achievement, and basic cognitive skills. Analyses of the relative contributions of heredity and environment suggested that basic cognitive abilities were less affected by environmental factors than were tests of academic achievement. This finding makes a good deal of sense. Basic abilities might be more fixed by biology than more complex, derivative skills affected by instruction. Limits on performance of complex skills are set by the basic

Epiphenomenon. Look at basic processes ← need to point out sim/dissim[?] tasks. Need to attend to ... dimensions relevant to ... new problem.

abilities used in those skills. Because the skills are complex, it may be possible to use other abilities to compensate for deficient abilities. Biologically determined basic abilities, then, would only set very broad limits on more complex skills. As an analogy, visual acuity may be biologically determined, but even severely visually impaired persons can perform many visual tasks as well as those with perfect sight, because they use other abilities like increased attention to compensate for the visual impairment.

If this analysis is correct, appropriate instruction is extremely important in determining that each person develops to their optimum ability. The goal of education would not be to develop higher order processes but to match a person's abilities to the method of instruction. There have only been a few examples of cases where that has been done (e.g., Conners & Detterman, 1987). The main obstacle is the lack of sound ways of defining basic skills.

POTENTIAL BASIS FOR TRANSFER

The transfer that does occur, mostly near transfer, requires some explanation in terms of more basic processes if transfer is epiphenomenal. There is an emerging consensus that an important step in producing transfer is to make sure subjects notice the similarity between the original and new situation. That is, an important part of transfer, when it occurs, is that subjects attend to the dimensions relevant to the solution of the new problem.

Zeaman and House (1963) made this point when they proposed an attention theory that explained differences in learning and transfer in intellectually normal and mentally retarded subjects. They tested college students and mentally retarded subjects on simple discrimination problems. Subjects learned that a circle was correct each time they saw the choice of a square and a circle. Part of learning the problem was ignoring irrelevant dimensions such as position, color, or texture that might be irregularly associated with the circle. For example, subjects had to learn to ignore that the circle was sometimes red and sometimes green. Zeaman and House discovered the difficulty mentally retarded people have in learning problems like this. It resulted from their inability to notice the correct dimension. Backward learning curves showed that, once mentally retarded subjects found the correct dimension, learning the problem proceeded as fast as for intellectually average subjects. The Zeaman and House attentional theory provides a sophisticated analysis of transfer effects based on the likelihood of noticing the dimensions relevant to transfer. The Zeaman and House position can be regarded as a thorough operationalization of Thorndike's principles of transfer where situational similarity can be exactly specified.

A better illustration of how differences in ability can affect transfer is supplied by the following classroom demonstration. Students first learn a simple two-choice discrimination problem such as the one described above. Once they

① See Zeaman & House ? Fundamental processes of memory. (Attention?. percepts & memory.

CASE AGAINST TRANSFER 21

have learned to make the correct response (choose the circle) on every trial, the experimenter switches to another problem without telling the subject. The correct dimension in the new problem is position. Color and shape are no longer relevant to solution. The correct choice is decided using double alternation such that correct responses are: left, left, right, right, left, left, right, right, and so on. Mentally retarded subjects solve this problem almost instantly, but college students almost never do. This is one of those very few, instructive instances where mentally retarded persons outperform college students. The reason for this difference is that position is a much more salient stimulus dimension for mentally retarded persons than for college students. Here is a case where transfer is negatively related to intelligence.

Attention is not a particularly well-defined construct. Before transfer is fully explained, what Zeaman and House call *attention* would have to be better understood. Explaining one unexplained, complex process by invoking another unexplained, complex process is not a satisfactory answer, as Zeaman and House realized. The main point is that basic processes responsible for detecting, representing, and remembering differences between stimuli probably will be the basic processes implicated in an explanation of transfer. Such processes are very likely to include fundamental operations of perception and memory. Individual differences in transfer will not be explained until there is a more complete explanation of the fundamental operations that compose it.

CONCLUSIONS

Santayana (1905–1906/1982) expressed the general belief that previous experience can transfer to new situations when he said, "Those who cannot remember the past are condemned to repeat it." But Hegel (1832/1982) may have been closer to the truth when he said, "What experience and history teach are this— that people and governments never have learned anything from history, or acted on principles deduced from it." Transfer has been studied since the turn of the century. Still, there is very little empirical evidence showing meaningful transfer to occur and much less evidence showing it under experimental control. There are two points to be made about this observation.

First, significant transfer is probably rare and accounts for very little human behavior. Studies that claim transfer often tell subjects to transfer or use a 'trick' to call the subject's attention to the similarity of the two problems. Such studies cannot be taken as evidence for transfer. We generally do what we have learned to do and no more. The lesson learned from studies of transfer is that, if you want people to learn something, teach it to them. Don't teach them something else and expect them to figure out what you really want them to do.

The second point relates to transfer and other cognitive abilities like strategies, reasoning, and those things often called metaprocesses. These processes are epiphenomenal, because individual differences in them are caused by differences in more basic processes. The study of these epiphenomenal processes has implications for improving instruction. Such epiphenomenal processes, however, have little role in basic explanations of individual differences in intelligence and cognition. Data from the Western Reserve Twin Project and other lines of evidence show that basic cognitive abilities are less affected by environmental sources than academic achievement. This suggests that a basic understanding of mental processes will not necessarily result in more effective instruction. Basic cognitive processes and epiphenomenal derivatives may be more resistant to change than the content of those processes. Knowledge of those processes will help in formulating educational interventions. These interventions will take individual patterns of ability into account in formulating instructional strategies for developing higher order processes.

REFERENCES

Ackerman, P.L. (1986). Individual differences in information processing: An investigation of intellectual abilities and task performance. *Intelligence, 10*, 101–139.

Ackerman, P.L. (1987). Individual differences in skill learning: An integration of psychometric and information processing perspectives. *Psychological Bulletin, 102*, 3–27.

Ackerman, P.L. (1988). Determinants of individual differences during skill acquisition: Cognitive abilities and information processing. *Journal of Experimental Psychology: General, 117*, 288–318.

Baldwin, T.T., & Ford, J.K. (1988). Transfer of training: A review and directions for future research. *Personnel Psychology, 41*, 63–105.

Brown, A.L., & Kane, L.R. (1988) Preschool children can learn to transfer: Learning to learn and learning from example. *Cognitive Psychology, 20*, 493–523.

Campione, J.C., & Brown, A.L. (1974). Transfer of training: Effects of successive pretraining of components in a dimension-abstracted oddity task. *Journal of Experimental Child Psychology, 18*, 308–411.

Chase, W.G., & Simon, H.A. (1973). The mind's eye in chess. In W.G. Chase (Ed.), *Visual information processing*. New York: Academic Press.

Conners, F.A., & Detterman, D.K. (1987). Information processing correlates of computer-assisted word learning in mentally retarded students. *American Journal of Mental Deficiency, 91*, 606–612.

Detterman, D.K. (1980). Understand cognitive components before postulating metacomponents. *Brain and Behavioral Sciences, 3*, 589.

Detterman, D.K. (1982). Does "g" exist. *Intelligence, 6*, 99–108.

Detterman, D.K. (1984). Understand cognitive components before postulating metacomponents, etc.: Part II. *Behavioral and Brain Science, 7*, 280–290.

Detterman, D.K. (1986). Human intelligence is a complex system of separate processes. In R.J. Sternberg & D.K. Detterman (Eds.), *What is intelligence? Contemporary viewpoints on its nature and definition* (pp. 57–61). Norwood, NJ: Ablex Publishing Corp.

Ferguson, G.A. (1954). On learning and human ability. *Canadian Journal of Psychology, 8*, 95–112.

Ferguson, G.A. (1956). On transfer and the abilities of man. *Canadian Journal of Psychology, 10*, 121–131.

Feuerstein, R. (1980). *Instructional enrichment: An intervention program for cognitive modifiability*. Baltimore, MD: University Park Press.

Fleishman, E.A., & Hemple, W.E., Jr. (1954). Changes in factor structure of a complex psychometric task as a function of practice. *Psychometrika, 19*, 239–252.

Fleishman, E.A., & Hemple, W.E., Jr. (1955). The relationship between abilities and improvement in practice in a visual discrimination reaction task. *Journal of Experimental Psychology, 49*, 301–312.

Gick, M.L., & Holyoak, K.J. (1980). Analogical problem solving. *Cognitive Psychology, 12*, 306–355.

Hegel, G.W.F. (1982). Philosophy of history, from introduction. In J. Bartlett (Ed.), *Bartlett's familiar quotes* (15th ed.). Boston: Little, Brown and Company. (Original work published 1832)

Homa, D., Sterling, S., & Trepel, L. (1981). Limitations of exemplar-based generalization and the abstraction of categorical information. *Journal of Experimental Psychology: Human Learning and Memory, 7*, 418–439.

Judd, C.H. (1908). The relation of special training to general intelligence. *Educational Review, 36*, 28–42.

Medin, D.L., & Ross, B.H. (1989). The specific character of abstract thought: Categorization, problem solving, and induction. In R.J. Sternberg (Ed.), *Advances in the psychology of human intelligence* (Vol. 1, pp. 189–223). Hillsdale, NJ: Erlbaum.

Novick, L.R. (1990). Representational transfer in problem solving. *Psychological Science, 1*, 128–132.

Reed, S.K. (1987). A structure-mapping model for word problems. *Journal of Experimental Psychology: Learning, Memory, and Cognition, 13*, 124–139.

Reed, S.K., Dempster, A., & Ettinger, M. (1985). Usefulness of analogous solutions for solving algebra word problems. *Journal of Experimental Psychology: Learning, Memory, and Cognition, 11*, 106–125.

Reed, S.K., Ernst, G.W., & Banerji, R. (1974). The role of analogy in transfer between similar problem states. *Cognitive Psychology, 6*, 436–450.

Santayana, G. (1982). The life of reason. Vol. 1. Reason in common sense. In J. Bartlett (Ed.), *Bartlett's familiar quotes* (15th ed.). Boston: Little, Brown and Company. (Original work published 1905–1906).

Simon, H.A., & Reed, S.K. (1976). Modelling strategy shifts in a problem solving task. *Cognitive Psychology, 8*, 86–97.

Singley, M.K., & Anderson, J.R. (1989). *The transfer of cognitive skill*. Cambridge, MA: Harvard University Press.

Thompson, L.A., Detterman, D.K., & Plomin, R. (1991). Associations between cognitive abilities and scholastic achievement: Genetic overlap but environmental differences. *Psychological Science, 2*, 158–165.

Thorndike, E.L. (1924). Mental discipline in high school studies. *Journal of Educational Psychology, 15,* 1–22.

Thorndike, E.L., & Woodworth, R.S. (1901). The influence of improvement in one mental function upon the efficiency of other functions. *Psychological Review, 8,* 247–261.

Woodrow, R.S. (1927). The effect of type of training upon transference. *Journal of Educational Psychology, 18,* 159–172.

Zeaman, D., & House, B.J. (1963). The role of attention in retardate discrimination learning. In N.R. Ellis (Ed.), *Handbook of mental deficiency.* New York: McGraw-Hill.

Chapter 2

Mechanisms of Transfer*

Robert J. Sternberg
Yale University

Peter A. Frensch
University of Missouri

A graduate student with an A in statistics asks for advice on how to analyze his data set. The data set requires only the simplest of analysis-of-variance for the data analysis.

A seventh-grader who writes admirably crafted and organized compositions in her English class writes papers in her science class that show almost no craft or organization.

An executive who specializes in corporate restructurings is hired away from Company A to do a restructuring in Company B for much better compensation. But the success that the executive experienced in Company A is not repeated in Company B, and the executive is cashiered after only a year in Company B.

A woman in a second marriage who "learned her lessons" in her first marriage responds to a request from her second husband in a way that she has learned to be particularly effective. Her foolproof response fails, and her husband explodes at her.

The above have in common the failure of learning in one setting to transfer to another setting. Such failures, we know, are common. Indeed, transfer of training often appears to be the exception rather than the rule, whether in school or outside of it. The difficulty people experience in achieving transfer naturally leads to the question: What are the mechanisms by which transfer occurs, and conversely, under what conditions is transfer more or less likely to occur? This is the question we address in the present chapter.

* Preparation of this chapter was supported by a contract from the Army Research Institute and from grants from the McDonnell and Spencer Foundations.

Our basic claim is simple, namely, that the degree of transfer obtained from one setting to another depends upon four mechanisms. We shall set out these mechanisms here, and then discuss each one separately in the remainder of the chapter:

1. *Encoding specificity*. This mechanism, set out as a principle by Tulving and Thomson (1973), states that whether or not an item is retrieved will depend upon the way in which the item was encoded. As extended here, the principle states that whether an item will be transferred will depend upon how the item was encoded.

2. *Organization*. This mechanism, discussed in the context of recall by Tulving (1966; see also Tulving & Thomson, 1973), specifies that whether or not retrieval will occur will depend on how information is organized in memory. As extended here, the notion is that organizations of information from old situations can either facilitate or impede transfer to new situations.

3. *Discrimination*. This mechanism, discussed in the context of recall and recognition by Anderson and Bower (1973) and Sternberg and Bower (1974), specifies that whether or not retrieval will occur will depend on whether information to be recalled is tagged as relevant for the given recall. As extended here, the notion is that discrimination affects transfer by tagging an item as either relevant or nonrelevant to a new situation in which that item might be applied.

4. *Set*. This mechanism, discussed by Luchins (1942) in the context of problem solving, specifies that whether someone sees a useful way of doing something depends in part upon the mental set with which he or she approaches the task. As extended here, the idea is that whether transfer occurs will depend in part upon whether the individual has a mental set to achieve transfer.

The four mechanisms fit into a framework for understanding learning and recall (see, e.g., Anderson & Bower, 1973). The first mechanism applies during encoding, the second during storage, and the third during retrieval, the three commonly accepted stages of learning and recall. The fourth mechanism applies during all three stages and deals with the state of mind one needs to obtain transfer: Transfer is enhanced when one actively seeks to transfer what one has learned.

In this chapter, we will consider each of these mechanisms for transfer in turn. Then we will consider how these mechanisms apply in a variety of kinds of situations in which transfer can occur. In particular, we will apply the mechanisms to understanding both experimental and everyday phenomena. After discussing in turn the mechanisms and their applications, we will consider the implications of these mechanisms for intelligence and for instruction.

FOUR MECHANISMS OF TRANSFER

Encoding Specificity

Suppose that you are presented with a list of paired associates to be learned. The words have a moderate prior association to each other, such as *ground–cold*. You are told that you will later be tested for recall on the second word of each pair, but that you should also learn the first word, as it may be a useful retrieval cue later on. After this phase of the experiment, you are presented with words and asked to generate associates of each word. One of the words might be *hot*, for which *cold* is, of course, an associate. After this generation phase, you are asked to look at the words you have just generated and to circle those that occurred during the acquisition phase. In this case, of course, *cold*, a word you generated as an associate of *hot*, was one of the words on the original list. People do surprisingly poorly in recognizing words from the prior list, with performances levels of only about one-quarter correct. Now suppose, however, that you are again given the original items from each pair, and are asked to recall the word that was associated with each original word. In this cued-recall task, subjects' performance will come close to two-thirds correct. Thus, in this paradigm, recall is actually better than recognition, an unusual result indeed. This paradigm was taken by Tulving and Thomson (1973; also Tulving & Wiseman, 1975) as showing the importance of the way in which a word is encoded for whether or not it is retrieved. The B terms in the A–B paired associates were encoded in a way that made the A terms better retrieval cues than the B terms themselves!

Encoding specificity is clearly relevant for transfer. The question here becomes one of whether information is encoded in a way so that, when it is later relevant for learning or performance in another situation, it is likely to be retrieved. For example, Bassok and Holyoak (1989) had subjects learn exactly the same principles in the context of both algebra and physics instruction. Later subjects in each subject-matter group were tested for transfer to the other kind of subject matter. Subjects in the algebra group showed excellent transfer to physics, but the reverse was not true at all. Why? On an encoding-specificity explanation, algebra is taught in a way that one is supposed to use the principles in other fields, such as physics. But physics is taught in a self-contained way, with physical content. The information is encoded in a way that is encapsulated with respect to other uses, including that in algebra.

In general, encoding specificity can be seen as explaining, to a large extent, why information learned in school can be so useless outside it. Students learn information, but not how to apply it. They may learn statistics, but not how to apply it to their lives, or even to real experiments. This is not to say that statistics cannot be applied (see Nisbett, Krantz, Jepson, & Kunda, 1983), but rather that it is often taught in a way so that what is encoded will not be retrieved when it is needed. Rather, the knowledge is essentially encapsulated and inaccessible (see Bransford, Nitsch, & Franks, 1977). Certainly, politicians seem only rarely to apply the lessons of history but instead make the same mistakes again and again. But this problem is not limited to politicians. Indeed, those of us who are psychologists know just how difficult it can be to apply our knowledge about psychology to our own lives.

Organization

Consider the following experimental paradigm, first used by Tulving (1966):

Subjects are presented with a list, A, of words to be learned in a free-recall paradigm. The subjects receive a number of trials on these words until they can recall all or almost all of them. Then subjects are presented with a new list of words to learn in a free-recall paradigm. The new list, which happens to be twice as long as the old one, may be completely nonoverlapping with the old list, BC, or it may be half-overlapping, AB. Traditional frequency theories of memory, according to which the strength of a trace will depend upon the frequency of its rehearsal (see Underwood, 1957), would predict that AB will be easier to learn than will be BC. However, we know that subjects spontaneously organize lists of words to be recalled, even if the words are apparently unrelated (Tulving, 1962). Thus, after several trials of free-recall learning of List A, subjects will have established an organization for A, and their free recall will show a strategy of output order that is not a function of order of presentation, which, in fact, changes on each successive trial. If subjects are now presented with a new list that partially overlaps the old one, and the order of word presentation on successive trials is again randomized, then it is reasonable to expect that the old organization of words may actually interfere with the new list, which requires incorporating new as well as old words. On this organizational view, the subjects who receive the AB list may actually have more difficulty in learning the new list than do the subjects who receive the BC list.

Experimental results in the "part-whole free-recall paradigm" in fact support the organizational view. After the initial few trials on the second list, where AB subjects do better simply because they recognize some of the new words as carry-overs from the old list, AB subjects do worse in free-recall learning than do CD subjects. Presumably, the lesser performance on the AB list reflects, at least in part, stereotypy of subjective organization that no longer works in the AB list. The phenomenon appears with roughly equal strength in a whole–part free-recall paradigm, where subjects first learn either AB or BC, and then learn A.

Although Tulving and others who did experiments of this kind did not use two lists of equal length, the effect would presumably occur in an AB to AC (versus AB to CD) list-learning situation as well. In fact, in this situation, a close parallel can be seen between the Tulving paradigm and the standard, paired-associates, A-B to A-C negative-transfer paradigm. In this paradigm (e.g., Greenberg & Underwood, 1950), learning a set of words, B, each as a paired associate to a word from Set A, results in negative transfer to the A-C pairings via *proactive inhibition*, a term whose meaning has never been fully explained. It is plausible that the organization construct applies for paired-associates as well as for free-recall learning, and that proactive inhibition may be due in part to the interference of the A-B organization with an A-C one.

Frensch (1990) performed a set of experiments relevant to the reorganization hypothesis. In one experiment, trials were divided into a learning phase and a transfer phase. In the learning phase, subjects practiced a simple multistep mental arithmetic procedure under different learning conditions. In the transfer phase, subjects were asked to learn a new version of the task they had practiced in the learning phase. The new version differed from the original task only in that one or more constituent steps had to be replaced with novel ones. Performances on the initial learning and transfer tasks were compared for two different groups of subjects: those who had formed higher level knowledge when they learned the original task, and those who had been prevented from forming higher level knowledge of the original task. The results demonstrated that, in accordance with the predictions, the transfer task was performed faster by subjects who had reorganized their knowledge of the original task than by subjects who had not reorganized their knowledge.

An experiment showing the relevance of the organization condition in game playing was done by Frensch and Sternberg (1989). In the experiment, bridge players of varying levels of skill played 12 simulated bridge games on a computer. Half of the games were played under normal conditions. In the other half, players were instructed to play slightly different versions of bridge. Version 1 introduced new nonsense names for honor-cards and suits, version 2 rearranged the order of honor-cards and suits, and version 3 modified the rule determining who began each round of play. Instead of the player who won the last trick going first, which is the common rule in bridge, the player with the lowest card in the last trick led into the next trick. The different versions were intended to tap different levels of subjects' information processing. Versions 1 and 2 were considered surface modifications; version 3 was expected to exert its effect on a deeper, more abstract and strategic level. The main result of interest here was that experts were more affected by the deep-structural change than by the two surface changes, whereas nonexperts were most affected by the surface changes. These results suggest the importance of the organization variable in transfer. The novices presumably organized information at a relatively surface-structural level (Chi, Glaser, & Farr, 1988), and so disruptions of surface structure had the more pronounced adverse effect on their play; the experts, in contrast, presumably organized information at a more deep-structural level, with the result that disruptions of deep structure had the more pronounced adverse effect on their play.

Organization matters, not only at the conceptual level, but at the motor level as well. For example, Lewis, McAllister, and Adams (1951) showed that the amount of practice on a motor task was negatively related to ability to learn a new, incompatible motor task. Their subjects used the Modified Washburn Apparatus, a device used for pilot training in World War II. This apparatus simulates an aircraft, containing a stick for two-dimensional manipulation and a rudder bar for one-dimensional foot operation. A set of display lights defined the amount the stick and rudder bar had to be moved. After they had spent 30 trials on making the prescribed movements, subjects had to learn a second task, in which movements were required that were antagonistic to the originally learned ones. After different degrees of practice on the second task, subjects were switched back to the original task. Lewis et al. found that the quality of performance on the original task had decreased and varied with the amount of practice on the interpolated task. Similar results were reported by Conrad and Hull (1968) for a task in which subjects had to key in eight-digit sequences on the original and modified telephone layouts.

Shiffrin and Schneider (1977, Experiment 1) reported a similar finding. In their study, subjects were trained for several thousand trials to detect visual targets among distractors in what they have labeled a consistent-mapping condition. When both the target and the distractor sets were reversed, detection accuracy fell far below that found at the very beginning of training. In fact, subjects needed about 2,400 trials of the reversal training to reach the level of performance equal to that originally obtained after 1,500 trials of learning.

Once an organization is automatic, it is extremely difficult to change, as shown in the Shiffrin-Schneider (1977) experiment as well as in experiments on the Stroop task. In the Stroop (1935) task, unattended dimensions of a stimulus interfere with the processing of attended dimensions, presumably because the processing of the unattended dimensions is automatically initiated by the presence of a certain stimulus situation. Once processing according to the old organization of information has started, it apparently cannot be readily stopped by conscious control (see Dyer, 1973; Kahneman & Chajczyk, 1983; MacLeod & Dunbar, 1988).

Discrimination

The negative-transfer results of the Tulving part–whole and whole–part free-recall paradigms appear not to be due entirely to organizational effects. Several findings suggest that a second factor is operative as well, namely, list discrimination. On this view, negative transfer is obtained because subjects have trouble discriminating which members of the A list carry over to the AB list. At first glance, this would seem absurd, since all members carry over. But in the early research of Tulving and others, subjects were not, in fact, informed that all words were carried over. Schwartz and Humphreys (1973) modified the paradigm so that subjects were given this information. Under this modification, positive rather than negative transfer was obtained. This result suggests that the negative transfer could not have been due totally to organizational effects, because subjects were not told about the overlap until after they had learned and, therefore, presumably organized the A list. Rather, the result suggests that subjects may have thought that only some of the words were carried over, and thus had difficulty in discriminating which ones these were.

This list-discrimination interpretation of the Schwartz-Humphreys results was suggested by Sternberg and Bower (1974), whose research was designed explicitly to test the list-discrimination hypothesis. They gave subjects the part–whole and whole–part free-recall paradigms (in separate experiments), but with a twist. In the second-list (AB or BC trials for part–whole learning, or A or B trials for whole–part learning), subjects were told to recall all tokens that they had heard from either list, and to write next to each token on which list it had appeared. If a word had appeared in both lists, then the subjects were to indicate as much. The results clearly supported the role of list discrimination in negative transfer. In the A to AB condition, some words were written down as only having occurred on the A list, even though any word on the A list also occurred on the AB list. In other words, subjects did, in fact, remember the word token, but not its list identity. Hence, in the typical paradigm, they would have suppressed its recall as irrelevant to the second list.

List discrimination is also potentially relevant to understanding proactive inhibition in A-B to A-C paired-associates learning. When, in the recall of C terms in the second list, one comes up with a token, one may not be certain whether it is actually the B term or the C term. Indeed, one may incorrectly label a B as a C or a C as a B. And if both are recalled, one may guess either B or C without being certain as to which is the correct, second-list pairing. Thus, the problem is not that learning failed, but rather that one is unable to discriminate on which list the recalled token appeared.

The discrimination interpretation is relevant when the materials to be learned are sentences rather than single words, and when the sentences are learned as part of a single list rather than as part of multiple lists. Anderson (1974) had subjects learn sets of sentences, such as "The doctor is in the bank" and "The fireman is in the park." Anderson varied the number of times each subject and each predicate were repeated in the 26 sentences with which he presented people. Thus, a given individual (such as a lawyer) might appear in multiple locations (such as a church and a park), or several individuals might appear in a single location. The paradigm is thus similar, although not identical to the A-B, A-C proactive inhibition paradigm. Anderson found interference in a reaction-time recognition paradigm, where subjects had to indicate whether or not they had seen a particular sentence. Reaction time increased with the number of times either a subject or predicate had been repeated in a new pairing. A discrimination interpretation of this result would suggest that the so-called *fan effect* is due to subjects' having more trouble discriminating correct pairings of persons with locations, the more pairings there are. Indeed, it is more difficult to imagine a given person in multiple places or multiple persons in a single place than to imagine a one-to-one pairing. On the discrimination interpretation, the amount of interference would decrease if the doctor were instead multiple doctors (such as Dr. Smith and Dr. Jones) in multiple instantiations of the same kind of place (such as the Fidelity Bank and the City Bank).

Discrimination, then, can apply to a variety of materials in a variety of experimental settings. For it to apply, there must be some confusion between types and tokens, where, say, one might have *doctor*, the type, as a token in two different lists, or *doctor*, the type, as a token in two different places.

Some of the most interesting examples of discrimination occur in everyday life. For example, the executive who is successful in one organization is lured to another organization to do the same thing. But he or she often does not reach the level of success in the new organization that was reached in the old organization. The problem may be one of AB to AC negative transfer. Only some of the techniques that worked in the old situation work in the new one; others don't. Moreover, there are new techniques to be learned (C) in the new organization that simply did not apply in the old. But the executive may have trouble figuring out which techniques that worked in the old organization work in the new one as well. The result is diminished performance.

The same applies in interpersonal relationships. We often feel that we learn from old relationships how to act in new ones. To some extent, of course, we do. But the same AB to AC negative transfer phenomenon may apply. Only some of what works in the first relationship (the A set) may work in the new relationship. At the same time, some of what works (the B set) will not carry over, whereas there are also new things to learn (the C set) that are uniquely relevant to the new relationship. The result, once again, may be negative transfer.

Set

Set refers to a certain way of seeing a task or situation that may carry over to other tasks or situations, whether or not it is appropriate. The classical demonstration of functional fixedness as caused by set was done by Luchins (1942). Luchins presented subjects with so-called *water-jug* problems. In these problems, subjects were asked how to get a certain amount of water using three different jugs, each holding a different amount of water. A large number of problems were presented, all of which could be solved by the same formula. For example, the problems might be soluble by filling up Jug B, then taking out of it the amount of water you could put into Jug A, and then twice taking out of it the amount of water you could put into Jug C. The formula, therefore, is $B - A - 2C$. The amounts of water that can go into A, B, and C can be variable, just so long as the final amount needed is variable. This formula will work if Jug A will hold 18 cups, Jug B 43 cups, and Jug C 10 cups, if the goal is to get 5 cups. Or the formula will work if Jug A will hold 9 cups, Jug B 42 cups, and Jug C 6 cups, in order to end up with 21 cups.

Suppose, now, that subjects have done a number of problems where the $B - A - 2C$ formula works, and they have more or less automatized the formula, whether or not they realize it. They are now presented with problems for which the old formula will work, but so will a much easier one, for example, $A - C$. Thus, subjects might be told that Jug A holds 23 cups, Jug B 49 cups, and Jug C 3 cups. Their goal is to get 20 cups. The old formula works, but so does the much simpler $A - C$ one. Subjects who have previously done set of problems with the $B - A - 2C$ formula are less likely to see the $A - C$ formula than are subjects who have not previously done the problems with the more complicated formula.

In the Luchins experiment and others like it, people transfer a technique for solving problems that has worked in the past. In this case, it works in the present as well, but there is also a much simpler way of doing the problems. Of course, the experiment can be set up so that the old technique no longer works. For example, Maier (1930) asked subjects to construct a hatrack in a room in which there were two poles and C-clamp. Subjects had a great deal of difficulty realizing that the problem could be solved by clamping the two poles together with the C-clamp and wedging them against the floor and the ceiling. The C-clamp then serves as the hook on which the hat can be hung. The problem is hard, in part, because we do not bring to the problem a set whereby hats are hung on C-clamps, C-clamps are used to wedge together poles to form a rack, and the floor and ceiling are used as wedges for poles. In fact, one could establish at least part of the set by calling to mind other devices such as pole lamps (see Sternberg & Davidson, 1983). But our prior set with respect to the items in the room does not match our prior set with respect to a hatrack. If anything, prior set will work against rather than for us.

Gick and Holyoak (1980, 1983) were interested in analogical transfer in problem solving, where mental set is also important. In one condition, they gave subjects the so-called Duncker (1945) radiation problem.

You are a doctor faced with a patient who has a malignant stomach tumor. The tumor is inoperable, but unless the tumor is destroyed, the patient will die. There does exist a kind of ray that could be used to destroy the tumor (X-rays). The good news is that if the rays all reach the tumor simultaneously at sufficiently high intensity, the tumor will be destroyed. The bad news is that, at this intensity, healthy tissue that the rays pass through will also be destroyed, and the patient will die anyway. At lower intensities, the rays will not destroy healthy tissue, but they will not destroy the tumor either. What type of procedure might be used to destroy the tumor with the rays while at the same time salvaging the healthy tissue?

Subjects typically come up with a variety of solutions, but the preferred solution is to suggest that weak rays be passed through the patient's body originating at a number of different points, such that they all converge at the point where the tumor is located in the stomach. The rays will thus be of sufficient intensity to destroy the tumor, but because only weak rays will pass through any of the healthy tissue, this tissue will be saved.

In some of the Gick and Holyoak experiments, subjects were presented with another problem prior to this one, the fortress problem. They were told of a general who wished to capture a fortress located in the center of a country. There were many roads radiating outward from the fortress. Unfortunately, all of the roads were mined so that although small groups of men could pass over the roads safely, large groups could not, because they would detonate the mines. The question was one of how a sufficient force could be directed against the fortress to destroy it without the force's being destroyed first by the mines.

The radiation and fortress problems are closely analogous, although not strictly isomorphic. One might plausibly expect that working first on the fortress problem would facilitate solution of the radiation problem. And indeed, it does, but only if subjects are primed to use the fortress problem to help them in solving the radiation problem. Subjects so primed do much better than control subjects who have never received the fortress problem. But if subjects are asked simply to learn the fortress problem and its solution as part of a "memory experiment," and then are asked to solve the radiation problem without being told of the relation between the two problems, the amount of transfer is rather dismal.

This kind of experiment is a good example of the importance of mental set in transfer. When subjects were in a memory experiment that was viewed as distinct from the problem-solving experiment, transfer did not occur. When, on the other hand, they were primed to view both situations as problem-solving ones that are interconnected, they showed excellent transfer.

THE ROLES OF TRANSFER IN INTELLIGENCE AND INSTRUCTION

Transfer has long been viewed as playing an important role in intelligence. Indeed, Ferguson (1956) defined *intelligence* in terms of transfer: The more intelligent person is the one who is better able to transfer information from one task or context to another. Several programs of research on intelligence have been built at least in part around the concept of transfer (see Campione, Brown, & Ferrara, 1982; Snow & Yalow, 1982). In the triarchic theory of human intelligence (Sternberg, 1985), transfer plays a part in intelligence through one of the knowledge-acquisition components—*selective comparison*, by which the relevance of old information for new purposes is recognized. Indeed, encoding specificity, organization, discrimination, and set establish some of the conditions under which selective comparison is more or less likely to occur.

Although people may differ in their base ability to transfer information, the analysis presented here suggests mechanisms by which instruction might be designed to make transfer more likely.

First, teachers need to take into account encoding specificity. They need to teach information in a way that will make it more flexibly retrievable later on. The best way to accomplish this goal is, first, explicitly to show students how they can apply the information they have learned in a variety of contexts, and then to require of students that they find applications themselves. It is an old saw that we need to "teach for transfer." Transfer does not occur because we want it to, but because we help students encode information in multiple contexts so that they are later more likely to retrieve that information when it might be relevant to them.

Second, teachers need to help students organize information in a way to facilitate transfer. A disorganized presentation of information not only impedes immediate learning but also impedes students' ability later on to transfer what information they have learned. Some of the more compelling demonstrations of the importance of being able to organize material were done by Bransford and Johnson (1972, 1973), who showed that understanding of a story was remarkably facilitated by subjects' being given a framework (in their case, a story title or picture caption) within which to organize information from the story. Script theory (Schank & Abelson, 1977) makes the same point. We should view it as our responsibility as teachers, rather than as the responsibility of students, to organize the information presented in a course. The organization should be both internally and externally connected (Mayer & Greeno, 1972): The various pieces to be learned should make sense in terms of each other, and in terms of other information the student has about the world. Such connections are often not drawn. Oddly enough, it is the exceptional rather than the typical teacher who starts a course or a lesson with a discussion of why and how what is to be learned is important to the students' lives. If the teacher does not know, the student cannot be expected to know either.

Third, we need to help students make discriminations that they will later need. When one learns a statistical package or word-processing system, how often is one informed of which features of the learning are general across a variety of packages or systems, and which are specific to the system being learned? How often do people discuss with each other which features of their own behavior are general across their interpersonal relationships, and which are specific to interactions with a particular other? An excellent example of how discrimination can be taught is in the way Spanish is taught, at least in some installations. Spanish vocabulary, grammar, and pronunciation differ somewhat from one country and region to another. In the Spanish instruction one of the coauthors has received, the book that was used specifically discussed which aspects of each were general, and which aspects were specific to particular areas (e.g., the difference in the pronunciation of the *c* and *z*, or the use versus nonuse of the personal second person plural *vosotros*, in Spain versus Latin America). Another good example of the teaching of discriminations is in many statistics courses, where students learn the assumptions underlying statistical tests so that they will know when the tests are applicable and when they are not.

Fourth, and perhaps most importantly, we need to establish a mental set for transfer. The way in which academic subjects are typically isolated from each other, and from any real-world use, does not encourage a mental set for transfer. Perhaps the single best thing we could do to turn around instruction would be to teach and then test knowledge for use rather than for its own sake. If students were directly shown how to use what they learn and then were tested in their ability to use rather than simply recall information, they would start to acquire the mental set needed for transfer. Present-day schooling does not encourage teaching for use, in part because of a vicious circle whereby teachers feel trapped into teaching for recall because of statewide and national tests, whereas the testers feel trapped into testing for recall because that is all that has been taught. We need to break the circle and encourage both teachers and testers to take responsibility for teaching in the way that will maximally benefit students—for transfer.

In the context of this point of view, the ongoing debate as to whether teaching for thinking should be separated from, or integrated into, the school curriculum becomes meaningless. Teaching should be for transfer, regardless of where it is done. A separate course can show students how to apply their thinking skills to life inside or outside the school, or can be a useless abstraction that students are unable to apply. An infused course can make connections between thinking skills and content, or it can teach thinking skills and content without ever really establishing the connection between the two. What matters is that we make connections, not that we argue over labels. And this chapter will have succeeded to the extent that those who have read it can go back to their own classrooms and use the four mechanisms of transfer we have discussed to enhance their own teaching and learning.

REFERENCES

Anderson, J.R. (1974). Retrieval of propositional information from long-term memory. *Cognitive Psychology, 5*, 451–474.
Anderson, J.R., & Bower, G.H. (1973). *Human associative memory*. New York: Wiley.

Bassok, M., & Holyoak, K.J. (1989). Inter-domain transfer between isomorphic topics in algebra and physics. *Journal of Experimental Psychology: Learning, Memory, and Cognition, 15*, 153–166.

Bransford, J.D., & Johnson, M.K. (1972). Contextual prerequisites for understanding: Some investigations of comprehension and recall. *Journal of Verbal Learning and Verbal Behavior, 11*, 717–726.

Bransford, J.D., & Johnson, M.K. (1973). Consideration of some problems of comprehension. In W.G. Chase (Ed.), *Visual information processing*. New York: Academic Press.

Bransford, J.D., Nitsch, K.E., & Franks, J.J. (1977). Schooling and the facilitation of knowing. In R.C. Anderson, R.J. Spiro, & W.E. Montague (Eds.), *Schooling and the acquisition of knowledge*. Hillsdale, NJ: Erlbaum.

Campione, J.C., Brown, A.L., & Ferrara, R. (1982). Mental retardation and intelligence. In R.J. Sternberg (Ed.), *Handbook of human intelligence* (pp. 392–490). New York: Cambridge University Press.

Chi, M.T.H., Glaser, R., & Farr, M. (Eds.). (1988). *The nature of expertise*. Hillsdale, NJ: Erlbaum.

Conrad, R., & Hull, A.J. (1968). The preferred layout for numerical data entry sets. *Ergonomics, 11*, 165–173.

Duncker, K. (1945). On problem-solving. *Psychological Monographs, 58* (5, Whole No. 270).

Dyer, F.N. (1973). The Stroop phenomenon and its use in the study of perceptual, cognitive, and response processes. *Memory and Cognition, 1*, 106–120.

Ferguson, G.A. (1956). On transfer and the abilities of man. *Canadian Journal of Psychology, 10*, 121–131.

Frensch, P.A. (1990). *Transfer of cognitive procedural skill as a function of degree of first-skill practice*. Unpublished doctoral dissertation, Department of Psychology, Yale University.

Frensch, P.A., & Sternberg, R.J. (1989). Expertise and intelligent thinking: When is it worse to know better? In R.J. Sternberg (Ed.), *Advances in the psychology of human intelligence* (Vol. 5, pp. 157–188). Hillsdale, NJ: Erlbaum.

Gick, M.L., & Holyoak, K.J. (1983). Analogical problem solving. *Cognitive Psychology, 12*, 306–355.

Gick, M.L., & Holyoak, K.J. (1983). Schema induction and analogical reasoning. *Cognitive Psychology, 15*, 1–38.

Greenberg, R., & Underwood, B.J. (1950). Retention as a function of stage of practice. *Journal of Experimental Psychology, 40*, 452–457.

Kahneman, D., & Chajczyk, D. (1983). Tests of the automaticity of reading: Dilution of Stroop effects by color-irrelevant stimuli. *Journal of Experimental Psychology: Human Perception and Performance, 9*, 497–509.

Lewis, D., McAllister, D.E., & Adams, J.A. (1951). Facilitation and interference in performance on the modified Washburn apparatus: I. The effects of varying the amount of original learning. *Journal of Experimental Psychology, 41*, 247–260.

Luchins, A.S. (1942). Mechanization in problem solving. *Psychological Monographs, 54* (6, Whole No. 248).

MacLeod, C.M., & Dunbar, K. (1988). Training and Stroop-like interference: Evidence for a continuum of automaticity. *Journal of Experimental Psychology: Learning, Memory, and Cognition, 14*, 126–135.

Maier, N.R.F. (1930). Reasoning in humans. *Journal of Comparative Psychology, 10*, 115–143.

Mayer, R., & Greeno, J.G. (1972). Structural differences between learning outcomes produced by different instructional methods. *Journal of Educational Psychology, 63*, 165–173.

Nisbett, R.E., Krantz, D.H., Jepson, D., & Kunda, Z. (1983). The use of statistical heuristics in everyday inductive reasoning. *Psychological Review, 90*, 339–363.

Schank, R., & Abelson, R. (1977). *Scripts, plans, goals, and understanding.* Hillsdale, NJ: Erlbaum.

Schwartz, R.M., & Humphreys, M.S. (1973). List differentiation in part/whole free recall. *American Journal of Psychology, 86*, 79–88.

Shiffrin, R.M., & Schneider, W. (1977). Controlled and automatic human information processing: II. Perceptual learning, automatic attending, and a general theory. *Psychological Review, 84*, 127–190.

Snow, R.E., & Yalow, E. (1982). Education and intelligence. In R.J. Sternberg (Ed.), *Handbook of human intelligence* (pp. 493–585). New York: Cambridge University Press.

Sternberg, R.J. (1985). *Beyond IQ: A triarchic theory of human intelligence.* New York: Cambridge University Press.

Sternberg, R.J., & Bower, G.H. (1974). Transfer in part-whole and whole-part free recall: A comparative evaluation of theories. *Journal of Verbal Learning and Verbal Behavior, 13*, 1–26.

Sternberg, R.J., & Davidson, J.E. (1983). Insight in the gifted. *Educational Psychologist, 18*, 51–57.

Stroop, J.R. (1935). Studies of interference in serial verbal reactions. *Journal of Experimental Psychology, 18*, 643–662.

Tulving, E. (1962). Subjective organization in free recall of "unrelated" words. *Psychological Review, 69*, 344–354.

Tulving, E. (1966). Subjective organization and effects of repetition in multi-trial free-recall learning. *Journal of Verbal Learning and Behavior, 5*, 193–197.

Tulving, E., & Thomson, D.M. (1973). Encoding specificity and retrieval processes in episodic memory. *Psychological Review, 80*, 352–373.

Tulving, E., & Wiseman, S. (1975). Relation between recognition and recognition failure of recallable words. *Bulletin of the Psychonomic Society, 6*, 79–82.

Underwood, B.J. (1957). Interference and forgetting. *Psychological Review, 64*, 49–60.

Chapter 3

A Schema-based Theory of Transfer*

Stephen K. Reed

San Diego State University

My first publication on transfer was titled *The Role of Analogy in Transfer Between Similar Problem States* (Reed, Ernst, & Banerji, 1974). We studied the transfer between two river-crossing problems, the missionary–cannibals problem and the jealous-husbands problem. The first problem requires moving three missionaries and three cannibals across a river under the constraint that cannibals can not outnumber missionaries in the boat or on either side of the river. The second problem requires moving three husbands and their wives across a river under the constraint that a wife can not be left in the presence of another man unless her husband is present.

A formal mapping exists between the two problems in which husbands correspond to missionaries and wives correspond to cannibals. However, an additional constraint exists in the jealous-husbands problem in that husbands are paired with wives. Moving two missionaries across the river corresponds to

* This research was supported by a National Science Foundation Grant 83-12763 and by Air Force Office of Scientific Research grants AFOSR 88-0008 and AFOSR 89-0107 to the author. Part of this chapter was written while I was a visiting scholar at the Center for Human Information Processing at the University of California, San Diego. Request for reprints should be sent to Stephen K. Reed, CRMSE, San Diego State University, San Diego, CA 92182.

moving two husbands across the river, but which two husbands are moved depends on which wives are on the other side.

It seemed to me that the two problems were good candidates for demonstrating transfer because of their similarities at both a surface (story content) and formal (search space) level. The results proved otherwise. Solving the jealous-husbands problem did not help subjects solve the missionary–cannibal problem, and solving the missionary–cannibals problem did not help subjects solve the jealous-husbands problem. Only when subjects were told the relation between the two problems did significant transfer occur and this occurred only from the jealous-husbands problem to the missionary–cannibals problem.

Approximately 10 years later I became interested in studying algebra word problems, and the use of analogous problems seemed to be a promising topic of investigation. Our research paradigm typically requires that students construct an equation to represent an algebra word problem. Because most college students have a lot of difficulty with this task, they are very dependent on examples. I have therefore been interested in how the relation between the example and the test problem influences their performance on the test problem.

A global distinction specifies this relation in terms of similarity of story content and similarity of solution procedure. This leads to a 2 × 2 classification that is shown in Table 3.1. An *equivalent* test problem has the same story content and solutions as the example. A *similar* test problem has the same story content but a different solution. Notice that it is necessary in the water-tank problem to subtract the quantity of water that is being used as the tank is filling. An *isomorphic* test problem has a different story content, but the same solution as the example. The problem in this case appears to be a motion problem, but is solved the same way as the example. And finally, an *unrelated* test problem differs on both dimensions.

Our initial study on this topic explored transfer to problems that were either equivalent or similar to the examples (Reed, Dempster, & Ettinger, 1985). Transfer was reasonably good to equivalent problems but was not very good to similar problems. Students were usually unable to adjust to changes between the example and test problem and would often try to use the same equation to solve the test problem without any modification.

Several years ago following a talk I gave at Psychonomics, Doug Detterman asked me whether researchers ever obtain positive transfer. Doug and I were colleagues at Case Western Reserve when I did my first transfer study, and he apparently detected some trends in my work and others' work on transfer. Transfer is difficult to obtain, and Doug is still skeptical, as illustrated by his chapter in this book. However, I think we are making slow progress in identifying what it takes to obtain positive transfer, and I will try to address this issue from my own perspective. I have continued to work with algebra word problems over the past 5 years, and this chapter gives me the opportunity to try to pull together some of my findings.

Research needs a unifying framework and I have found it convenient to think

Table 3.1.   A 2 x 2 Classification of the Relation Between the Example Problem and Test Problems (from Reed, 1987)

Example problem

A small pipe can fill an oil tank in 12 hours and a large one can fill it in 8 hours. How long will it take to fill the tank if both pipes are used at the same time?

Test problems
solution procedure

Story context	Same	Different
Same	Equivalent A small hose can fill a swimming pool in 6 hours and a large one can fill it in 3 hours. How long will it take to fill the pool if both hoses are used at the same time?	Similar A small pipe can fill a water tank in 20 hours and a large pipe can fill it is 15 hours. Water is used at a rate that would empty a full tank in 40 hours. How long will it take to fill the tank when both pipes are used at the same time, assuming that water is being used as the tank is filled?
Different	Isomorphic Tom can drive to Bill's house in 4 hours and Bill can drive to Tom's house in 3 hours. How long will it take them to meet if they both leave their houses at the same time and drive toward each other?	Unrelated An airplane can fly from city A to city B at an average speed of 250 mph in 3 hours less time than it takes to return from city B to city A at 200 mph. How many hours did it take to return?

about my work within the context of schema theory. The first section of this chapter therefore discusses the major assumptions of schema theory and shows how they are relevant to my research on algebra word problems. The second section discusses transfer to similar problems in which subjects must modify a solution to solve a problem that has the same story content. The third section discusses transfer to isomorphic problems in which subjects must overcome different story content to detect the identity of two solutions. Each of these two situations presents a different challenge, and I will discuss alternative approaches to increasing the amount of transfer for both of these cases.

SCHEMA THEORY

Schema

There are many introductions to schema theory but I particularly like a chapter by Perry Thorndyke (1984). Thorndyke claimed that, while schema theories are difficult to test and therefore underdeveloped as a descriptive theory, they provide principles for formulating a prescriptive theory. Prescriptive theories are particularly relevant for studying problem solving, because attempted solutions can be scored as either correct or incorrect, providing a measure of the effectiveness of instruction. Can we therefore use the principles of schema theory as an organizational framework for comparing alternative approaches to increasing transfer?

Before attempting to make some comparisons, I will define and list the properties of a schema, based on Thorndyke's paper. Thorndyke (1984, p. 167) defines a *schema* as a cluster of knowledge representing a particular generic procedure, object, percept, event, sequence of events, or social situation. This cluster provides a skeleton structure for a concept that can be *instantiated*, or filled out, with the detailed properties of the particular instance being represented. For example, a schema for the American Psychological Association annual meetings would contain the standard properties of a scientific conference such as its location, date, attenders, session types, and the length of presentations.

Thorndyke listed five characteristics of schema models that are generally shared by theorists who propose these models. The five characteristics are abstraction, instantiation, prediction, induction, and hierarchical organization.

A schema represents a prototypical *abstraction* of the concept it represents, listing those properties that define a typical instance. These properties provide the skeleton structure for the concept. The properties are represented as variables that can be filled out or *instantiated* by the particular instances that fit the schema. If the incoming information is incomplete, the schema may allow *predictions* about expected information and guide the interpretation of incoming information to match these expectations.

Schemata are formed by *induction* from experience with various instances of the general concept. This presumably occurs through a process of successive refinement in which expected properties become more clearly defined. And finally, schemata are *hierarchically organized* according to different levels of specificity. For example, expectations about the format of a particular convention are based on what typically occurs at professional conventions, in general. Before applying each of these characteristics to my own research, I want to briefly discuss the closely related concept of a *frame*.

Frames

The term *frame* has been used in the artificial intelligence literature in much the same way as the term *schema* has been used in the psychology literature. Minsky (1975) introduced the term *frame* to describe data structures for representing a stereotypical situation, after arguing that most theories in artificial intelligence were too local and unstructured to account for the effectiveness of thought. The advantage of formulating theories in terms of data structures is that they can be precisely described in programming languages such as LISP. The potential value of frames lies in organizing knowledge in a way that permits more effective processing through inheritance of values from more general levels in the hierarchy, from calculation through procedures that are attached to slots in the frame, and from the assignment of default (expected) values when none are provided (Thagard, 1984).

An early effort to develop a formal language that had these characteristics was the Knowledge Representation Language developed by Bobrow and Winograd (1977). The development was influenced by analogies to human information processing and was based on the following intuitions: (a) Knowledge should be organized around concepts with associated descriptions and procedures, (b) Descriptions must be able to represent partial and multiple viewpoints, and (c) Descriptions are compared to prototypes, which are usually the typical members of a class and exist at different levels of generality. The descriptions contain slots with attached procedures and are therefore consistent with how concepts are typically represented in frame theories.

An excellent example of a frame-based, problem-solving program is the FERMI system designed by Larkin, Reif, Carbonell, and Gugliotta (1988). FERMI is a computer-implemented expert reasoner that solves problems in the natural sciences by combining domain-specific knowledge with more general factual and strategic knowledge. Domain-specific knowledge consists of procedures for calculating specific values, such as learning a formula for calculating pressure drop. General principles, such as invariance and decomposition, are applied across several domains to calculate pressure drops for fluids, potential drops for electric circuits, and centers of mass for objects. Integrating the domain-specific knowledge with more general procedures makes it easier to apply old information in new ways, recognize general principles, and be consistent across problems.

The assumptions of schema and frame theories provide a framework for discussing the prerequisites for the successful transfer of knowledge. In the next section I suggest how knowledge about algebra word problems fits this framework.

Algebra Word Problems

Algebra word problems require that students convert a word problem into an algebraic equation in order to solve for an unknown variable. The following is a typical problem:

> *A car traveling at a speed of 30 mph left a certain place at 10:00 a.m. At 11:30 a.m., another car departed from the same place at 40 mph and traveled the same route. In how many hours will the second car overtake the first car?* (Problem 1)

Let's consider how the five characteristics of schema theory—abstraction, instantiation, prediction, induction, and hierarchical organization—are relevant for solving this problem.

1. Abstraction. Abstraction requires learning those properties of a problem that are needed to solve it. The above example is an overtake problem in which the distance traveled by one car equals the distance traveled by another car. However, the distances in these problems are seldom stated directly, but must be represented as the product of rate and time. The correct equation is

$$\text{Rate1} \times \text{Time1} = \text{Rate2} \times \text{Time2} \qquad (1)$$

The rate of travel multiplied by the time of travel for one vehicle equals the rate of travel multiplied by the time of travel for the second vehicle.

In order to construct a correct equation, students must learn that only the two rates and the two times are relevant for solving the problem. This knowledge is particularly important when there are irrelevant quantities in the problem, as in the following example (Krutetskii, 1976, p. 110):

> A train departed from city A to city B at a speed of 48 km per hour. Two hours later a second train followed it at 56 km per hour. At what distance from the starting point will the second train overtake the first, if the distance between the cities if 1,200 km, and there are twice as many cars on the first train as on the second? (Problem 2)

Krutetskii found that capable students were not impeded by unnecessary data, whereas incapable students were often confused when such data were introduced into the text of even the easiest problem. All quantities were perceived by the incapable students as being equally important. We would therefore hope that students who are shown a solution to Problem 1 would learn that the distance between the cities and the number of cars on the train were irrelevant values in Problem 2.

I am unaware of recent research that has investigated irrelevant information in algebra word problems, perhaps because the problems are so difficult even without irrelevant information. However, information that is relevant in one problem may be irrelevant in another problem, so we need to consider this issue in the study of transfer. Imagine that I changed the role between the similar test problem and the example in Table 1 so the test problem was now the example. In using the solution to the water-tank problem to solve the oil-tank problem, the student must learn that it is no longer necessary to subtract some quantity from the quantities that are added to the tank, that this part of the solution is now irrelevant. Successful transfer therefore depends on determining what part of the solution must be mapped from a source problem to a target problem (Gentner, 1983).

2. *Instantiation of Values.* The solution of the overtake problem (Problem 1) requires, not only that students identify the relevant quantities, but that they substitute the correct quantities in the 'slots' of the equation. An equation provides a frame-like structure, but many problems are difficult even when students are given the correct equation because they don't know how to enter the correct values (Ross, 1989; Reed & Ettinger, 1987).

For example, several steps are required to represent the time traveled by the earlier car in Problem 1. First, the problem solver must calculate the time difference between the two cars by finding the difference between 10:00 a.m. and 11:30 a.m. The procedure for finding this difference could be represented as a procedural attachment in Bobrow and Winograd's (1977) Knowledge Representation Language. Second, if the time traveled by the later car is represented by the variable t, then the time traveled by the earlier car is represented by the variable $t + 1.5$ hours. Students must know that they should add, rather than subtract, 1.5 hours. And finally, students must be careful to pair each of the times with the corresponding rate of travel. Students who had learned to carry out these operations in solving Problem 1 would hopefully be able to apply them in solving Problem 2.

3. *Predictions.* Schemas should make predictions about expected information and guide the interpretation of this information. I will distinguish between two kinds of expected information. One kind concerns the default values that go into the slots of a schema. For example, if most college courses are for three credits, then one might reasonably infer that a course is worth three credits in the absence of information. The expectation of a particular value is unreasonable for most word problems, however, because the quantities vary from problem to problem. As a contrast, a framebased system for diagnosing diseases can make use of expected values by determining which values of a patient's medical profile fall outside the normal range of values (Aikens, 1983).

A second kind of expectation requires knowledge of what information is required in order to solve a particular problem. In addition to studying students' ability to recognize irrelevant information, Krutetskii (1976) studied their ability to recognize when they had insufficient information. As was found for the identification of irrelevant data, only the most capable students were able to identify what information was missing from a problem.

We would probably have many irate students if we asked them to solve problems with missing information. But, as was the case for irrelevant information, an analogous problem may have missing information. This occurred when I asked students to use the solution of the oil-tank problem in Table 1 to construct a correct equation for the water-tank problem. I found that only 9 of 45 students were successful, and that the remainder typically did not know how to represent the water that was being used (Reed, 1987).

4. *Induction.* Induction is concerned with how schemata are formed from experience with instances of the concept. Hinsley, Hayes, and Simon (1977) proposed that, if schemata are important for solving algebra word problems, then problem categories should guide students' solutions. They tested this hypothesis by asking high school and college students to sort by 'problem type' 76 word problems taken from an algebra textbook. Students sorted the problems into 16–18 categories, and there was considerable agreement among the students regarding the identity of these categories (such as distance, interest, area, mixture, and work problems). The results also suggested that information about the problem categories, including relevant equations and diagrams, is useful for formulating solutions.

A limitation of this knowledge is that each category contains a variety of problems, each requiring a slightly different solution. Mayer (1981) refers to these variations as *templates* and developed a taxonomy of problem types from a collection of over 1,000 word problems taken from 10 textbooks. Thus the overtake problem in Mayer's taxonomy is only one of 13 templates composing motion problems, and these do not include river current problems. Other examples include one car traveling at different rates on a round trip, and two cars traveling toward each other to meet. Unfortunately, rather small changes in a problem can greatly reduce the effectiveness of an example (Reed et al., 1985; Reed & Ettinger, 1987). Thus one of the challenges for a prescriptive theory is to formulate how knowledge should be organized to allow students to effectively solve the variations of problems that exist in each of the categories identified by Hinsley et al. (1977).

5. Hierarchical Organization. Another challenge for a prescriptive theory is to specify how to organize knowledge at more general levels. Hinsley's subjects classified problems by using similarities in story content, and could often make their classifications after hearing only a few words. With increasing expertise, people are able to classify problems according to the similarity of solutions rather than the similarity of story content (Chi, Glaser, & Rees, 1982; Schoenfeld & Hermann, 1982; Silver, 1981).

The FERMI system, mentioned previously, is a good example of a system that exploits hierarchical organization through its knowledge of general principles and methods that apply to a large variety of domains. For example, one general method is decomposition, which decomposes a complex problem into simpler ones associated with its components. A combination function specifies how a desired quantity can be found from the quantities associated with the individual components. An advantage of a hierarchical organization is that general knowledge needs to be encoded only once and then can be used repeatedly on specific problems that share common solutions. I will return to this issue when I discuss isomorphic problems later in this chapter.

Summary. In conclusion, algebra word problems fit rather nicely into a schema interpretation. Students typically categorize problems and use equations associated with problem categories as a basis for solving the problems. The equations consist of concepts such as distance, rate, and time that represent the features of the different categories. These concepts are combined to form an equation and are replaced by instantiated values (numbers or variables) when the equation is applied to solve a particular problem.

The initially learned categories are based on story content and could be considered as basic categories in Rosch's taxonomy (Rosch, Mervis, Gray, Johnson, & Boyes-Braem, 1976). The subordinate categories would then be the templates in Mayer's (1981) taxonomy—the different variations in distance problems, mixture problems, etc. The superordinate categories would consist of isomorphic problems that share a common solution but have different story content. Acquiring expertise requires developing skills in both directions from the basic level. Students must learn how to modify an equation of a typical problem to create variations in order to solve similar problems within a category. They must also learn how to recognize isomorphic problems in order to apply the same general method across different categories.

In the following sections of the chapter I describe alternative approaches for promoting transfer within the general framework of schema theory. I first compare three methods for helping students solve similar problems. The first is analogy, which requires finding and applying the solution of a similar example. The second method is the use of a similar example and a set of procedures that specify how to modify the example to make it equivalent to the test problem. The third method is the use of multiple examples in which information has to be combined from at least two examples, each of which partially matches the test problem. I then compare three methods for helping students solve isomorphic problems. The first is analogy, in which students use the solution of an isomorphic problem. The second method is schema abstraction, in which the story content of two or more isomorphs is described at a more general level and the test problem is recognized as a member of the more abstract schema. The third method is direct instruction, in which the instructor explicitly informs students about isomorphic solutions.

TRANSFER TO SIMILAR PROBLEMS

Analogous Examples

Much of the current work on how people use previous experience to solve problems has focused on how they select and apply analogous solutions. The use of analogous solutions has been demonstrated across a variety of domains. For example, when learning to use a computer text editor or solve probability problems, students are often reminded of an earlier example (Ross, 1984). Learning to program recursive functions is also guided by analogy to worked-out examples, particularly during initial attempts (Pirolli & Anderson, 1985). Such findings have resulted in a greater emphasis on analogy as a basis for problem solving in general theories of skill acquisition (Anderson, 1987).

Transfer to similar problems is hindered by structural differences in the equations and students' tendency to duplicate the structure of the example (Reed et al. 1985, Reed, 1987). Although students find it very difficult to modify the structure of a solution, they are more successful in modifying a more inclusive solution than in modifying a less inclusive solution (Reed, Ackinclose, & Voss, 1990). In this study students had to decide, for each of six test problems, which of two examples they would prefer to use as an analogous problem. One example was less inclusive (such as Problem 3) and the other was more inclusive (such as Problem 5) than the test problem (Problem 4).

A group of people paid $238 to purchase tickets to a play. How many people were in the group if the tickets cost $14 each? (Problem 3)

A group of people paid $306 to purchase theater tickets. When 7 more people joined the group, the total cost was $425. How many people were in the original group if all tickets had the same price? (Problem 4)

A group of people paid $70 to watch a basketball game. When 8 more people joined the group the total cost was $120. How many people were in the original group if the larger group received a 20% discount? (Problem 5)

The less inclusive problem had missing information, and the more inclusive problem had excess information. Students were twice as successful when given a more inclusive solution than when given a less inclusive solution, but failed to show a preference for the more inclusive solutions when initially asked to choose between two analogies. Showing students the solutions before they made their choice didn't increase the selection of the more inclusive solution, and the amount of mathematical experience didn't influence selections. An implication for a prescriptive theory is students should be aware that it is better to have too much information than too little when selecting an analogous problem.

Examples plus Procedures

The difficulty with too little information is that people have to generate the missing information and incorporate it into the equation. A possible remedy for generating missing or altered quantities is to build instruction around procedures that can generate quantities that are in the test problem but not in the example. As discussed previously, procedures can be attached to slots in a schema for the purpose of generating values to fill the slot (Bobrow & Winograd, 1977; Larkin et al., 1988). For instance, in a work problem the two workers may work together either for the same number of hours or for a different number of hours. Students who learn how to solve the former problem need to know how to modify the solution when one worker labors for more hours than the other worker.

To assess the effectiveness of combining an example with a set of procedures, Reed and Bolstad (1991, Experiment 1) compared three different methods of instruction. In the Example condition students received a detailed solution to the following problem:

> *Ann can type a manuscript in 10 hours and Florence can type it in 5 hours. How long will it take them if they both work together?* (Problem 6)

In the Procedures condition students were given the correct equation along with a set of rules that specified how to enter values into the equation. The rules for representing time were:

1. Time refers to the amount of time each worker contributes to the task. If this value is stated in the problem, enter it into the equation. For example, if one person works for 5 hours, enter 5 hours into the equation for that worker.
2. Time is often the unknown variable in these problems. Be sure to represent the correct relative time among the workers if they do not work for the same time. If one worker works 3 hours more than the value (h) you are trying to find, enter $h + 3$ for that worker.

In the Example & Procedures condition students received both the example solution and the set of rules. After studying the instructional material for 5 minutes, all students attempted to construct equations for eight test problems that differed from zero to three transformations from the example. The transformation modified either *rate* (expressed relationally for the two workers), *time* (one worker labored longer), or *tasks* (part of the task had already been completed). Each of these is illustrated in the test problem that differed by 3 transformations from the example.

> *John can sort a stack of mail in 6 hours and Paul is twice as fast. They both sort 1/5 of the stack before their break. How long will it take John to sort the remainder if he and Paul work together, but Paul works 1 hour longer?* (Problem 7)

The four transformation levels and three instructional methods enabled us to evaluate the predictions of a model for each of these 12 conditions. Because both the example and procedures provide students with the basic equation for solving these problems, we assume that the probability of generating a correct equation is equal to the probability of correctly generating the values for the five quantities in the equation: the rate and time of work for each of the two workers and the number of tasks to complete. Students can generate these values by either matching the information provided in the example (m), following the rules provided in the procedures (r), or using their general knowledge about the problems (g). The parameters m, r, and g specify the probability of generating a correct value from each of these sources of knowledge.

Let's first consider the predictions for the instructional group which receives the example and the procedures. When the test problem is equivalent to the example, a student can generate all five values by using the matching operation. The probability of generating a correct equation is therefore m^5—the probability that the student correctly applies the matching operation to each of the values in the example. When the test problem differs by one transformation the probability of a correct equation is m^4. In this case the student can match four of the quantities but must use the procedures to generate the transformed value. Following the same logic, the probability of correctly generating an equation should be m^3r^2 for two transformations and m^2r^3 for three transformations. Assuming it is easier to match values in the example than follow procedures ($m>r$), the model predicts a decline in performance as the number of transformations increases.

When students have only the example, they must rely on their general knowledge to generate the transformed quantities. The probability of constructing a correct equation should therefore be m^5 for zero transformations, m^4g for one transformation, m^3g^2 for two transformations, and m^2g^3 for three transformations. The generalization gradient should be steeper for the Example group than for the Example & Procedure group if the rules increase the probability of correctly generating the transformed values ($r>g$).

When students have only the rules, there should not be a generalization gradient. In this case, the probability of constructing a correct equation should be r^5—the probability of correctly applying a rule to generate each of the five values.

Table 3.2 shows the observed and predicted values for each of the 12 instructional situations, based on parameter estimates of .96 for correctly matching information in the example, .65 for following a procedure, and .45 for using general knowledge. The model accounted for 94% of the variance in the data, as determined by the square of the multiple regression coefficient. The first column illustrates the steep gradient that occurs as the test problems become more dissimilar from the example. The fourth column illustrates that the rules were ineffective when presented alone and need to be clarified or supplemented with additional material. For instance, a set of procedures for teaching people how to operate a device can be facilitated with the addition of functional, structural, or diagrammatic information that enables better understanding and integration of the rules (Kieras & Bovair, 1984; Smith & Goodman, 1984; Viscuso & Spoehr, 1986).

The combined effect of the example and procedures was disappointing from an instructional perspective. The data in Table 3.2 show that the generalization gradient for the Example & Procedures group was not quite as steep as for the

Table 3.2. Observed and Predicted Values for the Reed & Bolstad Experiment (from Reed & Bolstad, 1991)

Transformations	Groups								
	Example			Procedures			Example & Procedures		
	Observed	Predicted	Model	Observed	Predicted	Model	Observed	Predicted	Model
0	82	81	m^5	19	12	r^5	82	81	m^5
1	36	37	m^4g	19	12	r^5	42	55	m^4r
2	18	17	m^3g^2	17	12	r^5	30	37	m^3r^2
3	0	7	m^2g^3	5	12	r^5	14	25	m^2r^3

Note. The predictions are based on parameter estimates of m = .96 (the probability of correctly matching the example), r = .65 (the probability of correctly applying a rule), and g = .45 (the probability of correctly applying general knowledge).

Example group, but was steeper than predicted by the model. Furthermore, the overall performance of these two groups was not significantly different, although both differed significantly from the Procedures group.

The results of this experiment demonstrated that a potentially effective way of organizing knowledge was unimpressive in application. Of course, our application may have been faulty and we attempted (unsuccessfully) to improve the procedures in a subsequent experiment. We also included an instructional condition in which students received a second example. This condition, which was more successful, is discussed in the next section.

Multiple Examples

A possible remedy for poor generalization among the variations of a problem is to present many examples to show the variations. Sweller and Cooper (1985) proposed that students need to be shown a wide range of worked examples in order to become proficient in solving problems. They based their conclusion on the finding that (a) students did better when studying worked examples of algebra manipulation problems than when attempting to solve the examples, and (b) the superiority of worked examples was specific to test problems identical in structure to the examples.

Learning to Instantiate Values. Reed and Bolstad (1991) compared the multiple-example method with the example-plus-procedures method on the variations of the work problem discussed in the previous section. Students in the two-example condition received solutions to both a simple version of the problem (Problem 6) and a complex version that was equivalent to Problem 7. Other groups received either a single example, a set of procedures, or an example and procedures. The percentage of correct equations on eight test problems for the different instructional conditions was 7% for the procedures, 32% for the complex example, 38% for the simple example, 45% for the complex example and procedures, 47% for the simple example and procedures, and 65% for the simple and complex examples. The group which received only the procedures performed significantly worse than all other groups and the group which received two examples performed significantly better than all other groups. Other differences were not significant.

The performance of the two-example group across the eight test problems suggested that the complexity of the values in the test problem was a more limiting factor on performance than the number of examples required to solve the test problem. A complex value occurs when either rate is expressed as a relation between workers, time is unequal across workers, or part of the task is completed. The percentage of correct equations was 90% when the test problem contained no complex values, 70% for one complex value, 66% for two complex values, and 55% for three complex values. A problem with zero complex values is equivalent to the simple example, and a problem with three complex values is equivalent to the complex example. The test problems between these two extremes required combining information from both examples.

The advantage of being able to combine information across two examples is that it eliminates the necessity of having to provide a training example for every possible test problem. The eight test problems in the Reed & Bolstad experiment represented the eight possible combinations created from three attributes (rate, time, tasks) with two values (simple, complex). In order to maximize transfer from two examples, it is necessary to establish the modularity of an attribute across changes in the other attributes. If students learn how to represent time when one worker labors more than the other, then they should ideally be able to transfer this knowledge to other problems when the other attributes (such as rate or tasks) change values. It was this assumption of modularity that allowed Reed and Bolstad to represent eight test problems by two examples.

Learning Subgoals. Catrambone and Holyoak (1990) have also argued that it is necessary to present a variety of training problems when students must learn different subgoals and methods for achieving those subgoals. They studied how variations in examples would affect students' ability to solve problems that dealt with the Poisson distribution. Examples of problems that require different goals and methods are the cookie problem:

Suppose you were making a batch of raisin cookies and you did not want more than one cookie out of 100 to be without a raisin. How many raisins will a cookie contain on the average in order to achieve this result? Use the Poisson distribution to calculate your answer. (Problem 8)

and the Detroit Tigers problem:

In a 162-game baseball season, the Detroit Tigers infield made a total of 107 errors. The table below gives the number of games in which x errors were made. Fit a Poisson distribution to x; that is, give the expected frequencies for the different values of x based on the Poisson model. (Problem 9)

Notice that the two problems use the Poisson distribution in different ways. In the cookie problem, the information $Prob(x) = .01$ can be used in the equation of the Poisson distribution to calculate the average number of raisins per cookie. In the Detroit Tigers problem, it is also necessary to calculate an average (average number of errors per game) but the method is simpler—divide the total errors by the total games. Furthermore, the goals are different in the two problems. Finding an average is only a subgoal in the Detroit Tigers problem, not the final goal as in the cookie problem.

Catrambone and Holyoak found that there was little transfer to problems that required modified subgoals and methods. For instance, students who had learned a procedure for solving the Detroit Tigers problem did very well on this problem, but poorly on the cookie problem. Students who learned a procedure for solving the cookie problem did very well on this problem but poorly on the

Detroit Tigers problem. Catrambone and Holyoak therefore recommended that students receive extensive practice on a variety of procedures, accompanied by explicit instruction on which subgoals and methods were required for each variation of a problem.

Summary

Algebra word problems have the potential advantage of being recognized as members of well-defined categories (Hinsley et al. 1977). The categories provide a starting point for formulating a solution to problems in the category. Solving a work problem, for example, usually requires representing the amount of work accomplished by a worker as a product of his or her rate of work and the amount of time he or she works. However, there can be many variations of problems within a category, requiring that students learn how to modify their solutions to fit these various templates (Mayer, 1981).

The potential advantage of classifying a problem as a mixture, motion, distance, work, or some other categorical problem is limited by students' inability to adjust to small changes in solutions. In fact, the evidence suggests that isomorphic solutions from a different category provide more useful information than similar solutions that belong to the same category (Reed, 1987). The limited usefulness of similar solutions can be improved by using solutions that are more inclusive than the test problem, but students do not seem to be sensitive to this dimension when choosing an analogous problem (Reed et al. 1990).

Another approach, based on procedural attachments, is to supplement a similar example with a set of procedures that specify how to enter values into the equation. Our attempt to improve transfer to similar problems by giving students an example and a set of procedures has thus far been less successful than giving students two examples that span the set of test problems (Reed & Bolstad, 1991). The success of the latter approach is consistent with the multiple-examples approach advocated by others (Catrambone & Holyoak, 1990; Sweller & Cooper, 1985) and demonstrates that students can selectively choose the appropriate quantities from each problem. Our finding that we needed only two examples to obtain good transfer to eight test problems is an encouraging verification of the minimal-sets approach discussed by Butterfield, Slocum, and Nelson (this volume).

TRANSFER TO ISOMORPHIC PROBLEMS

Analogous Examples

The ability to modify a solution to solve a similar problem is an important skill in becoming an efficient problem solver. Another important skill is to be able to recognize and apply a solution from an isomorphic problem. Because an isomorphic solution has the same structure as the test problem, the problem solver has to appropriately map the concepts in the solution onto the concepts in the test problem, rather than modify the solution.

Mapping Concepts. The claim that analogy involves a mapping of information is a general assumption that is shared by most theories of analogy, although factors that influence the mapping differ across theories (Hall, 1988; Holyoak & Thagard, 1989). One of the most influential theories of how people use analogous solutions is the structure-mapping theory proposed by Gentner (1983). The theory was primarily developed to account for mapping knowledge from a base domain onto a target domain that consisted of different objects, such as comparing an atom to a solar system. Because the objects differed, Gentner argued that it is the relations among the objects rather than the attributes of the objects that determined the mapping. Thus the relation between an electron revolving around the nucleus corresponds to the relation between a planet revolving around the sun.

Reed (1987) applied the general assumptions of the structure-mapping theory to predict the relative success of using analogous solutions to solve related test problems. Students received a solution to a mixture problem and to a work problem and had to construct equations to four variations of each example. The four variations consisted of two problems that were isomorphic and two problems that were similar to the example, as shown in Table 3.3 for the mixture problems. The example, one of the isomorphic problems, and one of the similar problems, are shown in Table 3.1 for the work problems.

The results of the study showed that students were significantly better in constructing equations for isomorphic test problems than for similar test problems, and were significantly better on the work isomorphs than on the mixture isomorphs. A subsequent experiment demonstrated that the amount of transfer was related to students' ability to identify corresponding quantities in the example and test problems, as would be expected from the structure-mapping model. Students were significantly better in generating the matching concepts for isomorphic problems than for similar problems and were significantly better on the work isomorphs than on the mixture isomorphs.

These findings are consistent with the ideas expressed in the structure-mapping theory of analogy (Gentner, 1983). Structure-mapping theory focuses on the formal structure of analogies and on how the concepts in one problem are mapped onto the concepts in another problem. The correspondences are an important determinant of transfer, and this approach has increased our understanding of transfer (see Gentner, 1989, and Ross, 1989, for contributions).

Understanding Examples. In our emphasis on evaluating how the mapping influences transfer, we have sometimes ignored how well students understand the example. The importance of understanding is illustrated in a study that Arthur Evans and I did on teaching students to improve their estimates regarding the concentration of a mixture. The task required estimating the concentration

Table 3.3. Isomorphic and Similar Mixture Problems (from Reed, 1987)

Example	Isomorphic Problems	Similar Problems
A nurse mixed a 6% boric acid solution with a 12% boric acid solution. How many pints of each are needed to make 4.5 pints of an 8% boric acid solution?	Mr. Smith receives 5% interest from his checking account and 14% interest from treasury bonds. How much money is in each account if he averages a 12% return on $4,500?	One alloy of copper is 20% pure copper and another is 12% pure copper. How much of each alloy must be melted together to obtain 60 pounds of alloy containing 10.4 pounds of copper?
$\text{Acid}_1 + \text{Acid}_2 = \text{Total acid}$ $P_1 \times A_1 + P_2 \times A_2 = P_3 \times A_3$ $.06 \times a + .12 \times (4.5 - a) = .08 \times 4.5$	$\text{Money}_1 + \text{Money}_2 = \text{Total money}$ $P_1 \times A_1 + P_2 \times A_2 = P_3 \times A_3$ $.05 \times a + .14 \times (\$4,500 - a) = .12 \times \$4,500$	$\text{Copper}_1 + \text{Copper}_2 = \text{Total copper}$ $P_1 \times A_1 + P_2 \times A_2 = \text{Total copper}$ $.20 \times a + .12 \times (60 - a) = 10.4$
	A grocer mixes peanuts worth $1.65 a pound and almonds worth $2.10 a pound. How many pounds of each are needed to make 30 pounds of a mixture worth $1.83 a pound?	An automobile radiator contains 16 quarts of a 20% solution of antifreeze. How much of the original solution must be drawn off and replaced with 80% antifreeze to make a solution of 25% antifreeze.
	$\text{Money}_1 + \text{Money}_2 = \text{Total money}$ $P_1 \times A_1 + P_2 \times A_2 = P_3 \times A_3$ $\$1.65 \times a + \$2.10 \times (30 - a) = \$1.83 \times 30$	$\text{Antif}^1 - \text{Antif}^2 + \text{Antif}_3 = \text{Total}$ $P_1 \times A_1 - P_2 \times A_2 + P_3 \times A_3 = P_4 \times A_4$ $.20 \times 16 - .20a + .80a = .25 \times 16$

when two components were mixed together, such as a 40% and a 70% boric-acid solution. Students gave a sequence of judgments as we systematically increased the proportion of the 70% concentration.

Our instruction included principles about functional relations (range, monotonicity, and linearity) that would help students give more accurate estimates. For instance, we told them that the concentration of a mixture must be between the concentration of the two components. We illustrated each principle with a specific example that was either equivalent (mixing acids of different concentration) or isomorphic (mixing water at different temperatures) to the test problems. Based on the ease of mapping between problems, we would expect that the mapping would be better for equivalent than for isomorphic problems (see Reed, 1989). But our instruction was significantly more effective when we used temperature rather than acid concentration to illustrate the principles. The difference is that mixing water at different temperatures is a familiar situation in which the principles were already fairly well understood before the instruction began.

Enhancing the understanding of the example may not only increase transfer but prevent a false feeling of security when transfer does occur. Successful transfer may occur because students are fairly good at matching patterns across problems without really understanding the examples. This could result in overgeneralization of a solution, causing negative transfer to problems where the solution does not apply (Novick, 1988).

The relative success in using isomorphic solutions is encouraging, but a limiting factor in applying isomorphic solutions is recognizing them (Gick & Holyoak, 1980). According to a theory proposed by Gick and Holyoak (1983), recognition of isomorphic problems is facilitated by schema abstraction in which corresponding concepts in the two solutions are recognized as specific instances of a more general concept. The next section discusses increasing transfer by representing problems at a more general level.

Schema Abstraction

Duncker's radiation problem. Gick and Holyoak's (1983) theory of schema abstraction was the outcome of a series of attempts to improve students' noticing an analogous solution to Duncker's radiation problem. The problem requires using radiation to destroy a tumor without harming the healthy tissue that surrounds it. A convergence solution involves dividing the rays so they will have a high intensity only when they converge on the tumor.

Before attempting to solve the radiation problem, some students read a story about a general who was able to capture a fortress by dividing his army along different roads so it could converge on the fortress. Because of mines on the roads, the army could not attack along a single road. The solution to the military problem was quite helpful when subjects were instructed to make use of the story when solving the radiation problem, but most subjects failed to notice the analogy between the two problems when not given a hint (Gick & Holyoak, 1980).

Noticing an analogy between isomorphic problems is limited by different concepts, such as army and fortress in the military problem and rays and tumor in the radiation problem. The similarity of the two solutions becomes apparent when the concepts are described at a more general level such as using force to overcome a central target. Gick and Holyoak (1983) found that their students were likely to form this more general schema if they read and compared two analogous stories before trying to solve the radiation problem. For example, some students read the military story and a story about forming a circle around an oil fire in order to use many small hoses to spray foam on the fire. Students who described the relation between these two stories were more likely to think of the convergence solution to the radiation problem than students who read only a single analogous story.

The benefit of creating a more general schema was demonstrated by Catrambone and Holyoak (1989), who used more-directed comparison instructions to explicitly require the creation of superordinate concepts. All subjects read the military and fire stories and wrote summaries of them. But some subjects received the following two statements:

1. The fortress is difficult to capture, because a large army of soldiers cannot attack it from one direction.
2. The fire is difficult to put out, because a large amount of water can not be thrown at it from one direction.

They were then instructed to write a third sentence in which the pairs of concepts *fortress* and *fire*, *army* and *water*, and *attack* and *thrown at* are replaced by a more general term. They were then shown the more general statement:

3. A target is difficult to overcome, because a large force cannot be aimed at it from one direction.

Subjects who received the more-directed comparison instructions and applied it to a third analogue were more successful in producing the convergence solution than students who received the less directed set of comparison instructions.

Word problems. Although these results are impressive, it is unclear whether they could be duplicated for complex problems such as algebra word problems. Research on students' ability to categorize problems according to the formal procedures required to solve them has shown that correct classification requires considerable expertise (Chi et al., 1982) or training (Schoenfeld & Hermann, 1982). Can detailed comparisons of isomorphic problems therefore result in the creation of abstract solution procedures for word problems?

Dellarosa (1985) was partially successful in using analogical comparisons to help students identify which word problems shared a common solution. Students were trained on problems that had three different story contents (vat, travel, or interest) and three different solution structures. She found that students who compared quantities and relations in one problem to quantities and relations in an isomorphic problem did significantly better in classifying problems according to the common solutions than did students who answered questions about individual problems. In a second experiment, Dellarosa found that students who did analogical comparisons also were more accurate in matching word problems to equations than were students who answered questions about individual problems. However, the analogical comparisons were not successful in helping students use the equations to solve problems.

Reed (1989) used three isomorphic mixture problems and three isomorphic distance problems to determine whether constructing an analogical mapping between two isomorphs would help students solve a third isomorph. In the mixture problems (the nurse, interest, and grocery problems in Table 3.3), two quantities are added together to make a combined quantity. These problems are solved the same way but belong to different categories in Mayer's (1981) taxonomy. In the distance problems, two distances are added together to equal the total distance, but the two objects are either traveling toward each other, traveling away from each other, or succeeding each other. These problems belong to the same category in Mayer's taxonomy, but represent different templates and are characterized by different spatial relations (converge, diverge, succession) between the two moving objects.

Subjects in my experiment attempted to construct equations for the series of three mixture problems and three distance problems that were counterbalanced for order of presentation. Providing an analogous solution helped students construct equations. The percentage of correct solutions increased from approximately 10% for the first problem in a series to 50% for the second problem, which was accompanied by the solution to the first problem. However, a detailed comparison of the first two problems through mapping concepts did not increase the solution rate for the third problem. Furthermore, success on the third problem was uninfluenced by whether students compared the first two problems or elaborated each individual problem. These findings failed to support a schema abstraction hypothesis, as did two follow-up experiments, which were designed to encourage schema abstraction.

Superordinate concepts. I have suggested several explanations of why abstraction did not occur, but I want to focus on the lack of superordinate concepts to describe a more general schema. As mentioned previously, superordinate concepts played an important role in the initial theoretical formulation of a convergence schema (Gick & Holyoak, 1983) and in subsequent instructional efforts to promote abstraction (Catrambone & Holyoak, 1989).

The creation of superordinate concepts has also been proposed by investigators working on artificial-intelligence approaches to analogical reasoning. Winston (1980) suggested that finding an analogy between two situations may require matching concepts at more general levels than those provided in the statement of the problem. However, he cautions that creating concepts that are too general will not sufficiently constrain the matches between two analogs. According to this hypothesis, abstraction requires creating concepts that are superordinate to the concepts in the isomorphic problems but are not so general that they do not sufficiently constrain the solution. A constraint on creating an abstract solution is that it may be difficult to find such concepts.

Because the concepts of distance, rate, and time do not differ in the distance problems, they do not have to be replaced by superordinates. Only the described action has to be generalized to replace the specific actions of *travel toward* in the convergence problem, *travel successively* in the succession problem, and *travel away* in the divergence problem. Although the superoridnate concept *travel* generalizes each of these actions, it is too general to constrain the spatial relation between the two objects that are traveling.

The lack of superordinate concepts is even more apparent in the mixture problems. Although there are some identical concepts in specific pairs of problems (such as money in the interest and grocer problems), none of the specific concepts can be generalized under a superordinate concept that applies to all three problems. Thus, volume is an important concept in the nurse problem, weight in the grocer problem, and interest rate in the interest problem.

Because it is difficult to create superordinate concepts for these problems it is necessary to consider alternative approaches for showing which problems have structural similarities. The options are to teach students at either a more specific level or at a more general level than superordinate concepts. I will first consider an exemplar approach in which isomorphs are learned as specific examples, without schema abstraction. I will then discuss a more general, content-free approach in which the problem solver attempts to construct equations without associating the equations with a particular story content.

Direct Instruction

Learning Exemplars. In a chapter about the specific character of abstract thought Medin and Ross (1989) propose that both laypersons and cognitive psychologists have overlooked the importance of specific examples because of a tendency to equate intelligence with abstract thought. According to their argument, reasoning often relies on specific examples rather than on more abstract knowledge. When abstraction does occur, it is conservative in the sense that it preserves more information associated with examples than is recognized in many theories of categorization and problem solving. But reliance on specific examples is not necessarily bad:

> At first thought, the idea of having knowledge tied to particular contexts and examples appears to be a limitation. We do not deny that there are situations where transfer of training is limited by context-bound knowledge. On the other hand, specificity has its virtues. In particular, we argue that specificity may make access to and application of relevant knowledge easier, may permit graceful updating of knowledge, may protect the cognitive system from incorrect or inappropriate inferences, and may provide just the sort of context sensitivity that much of our knowledge should, in fact, have. (Medin & Ross, 1989, pp. 190–191)

The Medin and Ross view does not imply that we must abandon attempts to represent knowledge at a general level, but it does imply that it is necessary to tightly link specific and abstract information in theories of problem solving. This conclusion is consistent with the guiding philosophy behind the construction of FERMI: Whereas expert system builders have focused on specificity and problem-solving researchers on generality, there have been few attempts to combine knowledge at different levels of generality (Larkin et al., 1988). FERMI represents such an attempt by connecting specific situations to general methods.

A general method, such as decomposition, applies to many different situations such as pressure drops for water pressure, potential drops in electric circuits, and centers of mass of objects. FERMI is able, through the assistance of a knowledgeable programmer, to relate the domain-specific knowledge associated with each of these situations to a general method, decomposition. Domain-specific quantities "inherit" the general procedures by directly linking each specific quantity (such as pressure drop) to a general method that can compute a value for that quantity.

Our problem is, how do we teach people to recognize that a general method applies to each of these situations? The vastly different content of these areas makes it unlikely that people will be able to combine them into a general category through schema abstraction. Even the analogical mapping between potential drops and pressure drops is not obvious (Gentner & Gentner, 1983), and the relation of both of these areas to centers of mass seems still more tenuous. Rather than hope the students will spontaneously recognize that a common method applies to each of these situations, we need to inform them directly of this relation. If there is no abstract schema that groups together the different problems that can make use of decomposition, then each of these problems would need to be separately learned.

The exemplar learning approach is illustrated by a recent study in my laboratory on the classification of motion problems according to whether the two distances in a problem should be equated, added, or subtracted (Reed & Sanchez, 1990). Each of these operations was represented by two different kinds of (isomorphic) problems, which are called *templates* in Rich Mayer's (1981) taxonomy. For instance, the round-trip and overtake templates are both problems in which two distances should be equated. In a round-trip problem people go on a round trip and travel the same route in both directions. In an overtake problem two people leave the same location at different times and one eventually overtakes the other. We found that there was absolutely no transfer between templates. Students who received training on one set of templates to represent the three operations did not show any improvement in classifying the other set of templates.

Learning Abstractions. An implication of this experiment is that we may have to teach students a wide variety of templates in order to assure that they can solve algebra word problems. This is perhaps an unfair conclusion, because we haven't attempted to teach them to represent problems at a more formal level. Ideally, we would like students to be able to solve problems across a wide range of story content and not be constrained by the story content of the examples.

This requires the ability to recognize formal relations in problems, as illustrated by the work on arithmetic story problems (Kintsch & Greeno, 1985; Riley, Greeno, & Heller, 1983). These investigations have used semantic relations to classify problems according to conceptual knowledge about increases, decreases, combinations, and comparisons involving sets of objects. These classifications include change, combine, and compare problems.

Change problems describe addition and subtraction as actions that cause increases or decreases in some quantity:

Joe had three marbles. Then Tom gave him five more marbles. How many marbles does Joe have now?

In *combine* problems there are two distinct quantities that do not change, and the problem solver is asked to consider them in combination:

Joe has three marbles. Tom has five marbles. How many marbles do they have together?

In *compare* problems there is a comparison between two quantities that do not change:

Joe has three marbles. Tom has five more marbles than Joe. How many marbles does Tom have?

These distinctions are useful, because problems that have the same arithmetic structure but different conceptual structure can differ substantially in their difficulty for children. Although all three of the above problems require simple addition, young children made many more errors on the compare problem than on the change and combine problems.

Algebra word problems and arithmetic story problems are alike in that both require that students learn conceptual knowledge about increases, decreases, combinations, and comparisons across sets of objects. They differ in that this conceptual knowledge is more complex for algebra word problems, and there is a richer taxonomy for algebra word problems based on story content (Hinsley et al., 1977; Mayer, 1981). Arithmetic story problems can have virtually any story content, and the story content by itself does not provide any clues about formal operations. For instance, various examples of compare problems include the following questions (Marshall, Pribe, & Smith, 1987): (a) How much longer does it take to cook roast beef than to cook chicken? (b) How much better did a gymnast do on the vault than on the balance beam? (c) How much higher is Mt. Ranier than Mt. Washington? and (d) How much less per hour does George make than Jeff?

One of the challenges for extending instruction on arithmetic story problems to instruction on algebra word problems is to determine to what extent it is necessary to rely on story content to help people solve algebra problems. Is it necessary to include many templates in the instruction, or can one combine general instruction on formal operations with a few well-chosen templates to obtain good transfer to other templates?

I don't believe we can answer this question yet. Researchers are still working to identify when transfer occurs and why it occurs, or fails to occur. Bassock and Holyoak's chapter (this volume) provides a good case history of this research for word problems involving either arithmetic or geometric progression. They have identified when transfer occurs but we still aren't certain why it occurs. More seems to be involved than simply the distinction between intensive and extensive quantities because all the problems contain intensive quantities if an intensive quantity is defined as a ratio of two concepts. Perhaps it is the size of the units, as they suggest, or perhaps there are other factors that will be identified in further research.

CONCLUDING COMMENTS

I want to conclude by briefly discussing the generality of the schema-theory approach presented in this chapter. I introduced schema theory by referring to Thorndyke's description of a schema as a cluster of knowledge that provides a skeleton structure for a concept that can be instantiated by the detailed properties of a particular instance. The skeleton structure in our research is an equation and instantiation requires replacing general concepts (such as distance, rate, time) with quantities in a particular problem. Solving similar problems in the same domain requires modifying the equation because a similar problem has either more or less relevant quantities than the example. Solving isomorphic problems requires finding corresponding concepts across different domains. This may require representing problems at a higher level of abstraction in order to recognize the isomorphism.

I don't want to imply that all transfer conveniently fits into a schema-theory framework. Constructing equations for word problems seems to provide a nice fit, but I am less enthusiastic about trying to fit my early research on the missionaries–cannibals problem into this approach. Ideas such as skeleton framework, instantiation of values, relevant versus irrelevant quantities, hierarchical levels that differ in generality, and procedural attachments have a more direct application in the word-problem domain than in the missionaries-cannibals domain.

A contrasting approach is a search-space framework in which subjects search for a solution (Newell & Simon, 1972). Gick (1986) has argued that a search is used when subjects do not have domain-specific knowledge for solving the problem and have to use general strategies such as means/end analysis. This is effective for small search spaces with a specific goal such as the missionaries/cannibals problem, but is not very helpful for algebra word problems where success is much more dependent on matching a test problem to domain-specific knowledge.

For very complex domains, expertise may depend on a combination of schema-based knowledge and general search strategies, as suggested by the study of electronic trouble shooting (Gott, Hall, Pokorny, Dibble, & Glaser, this volume). Results revealed that skilled performers used three general types of schematic knowledge: device models of the equipment, general models of the trouble-shooting approach, and well-organized procedural knowledge for adapting to different equipment. The search approach characterized individual differences in breadth-first versus depth-first search. Good trouble shooters typically use a breadth-first search in which they first evaluate the major components before going into depth on any particular component.

In conclusion, we need to continue to look for effective ways of organizing knowledge to help students improve their transfer. In many ways the FERMI model (Larkin et al., 1988) is an ideal method of organization. A frame-like skeleton structure provides an organizing framework for attached procedures that can calculate needed values. Problems that are solved by common methods are organized together so students can see the commonality across different domains. For complex domains such as statistics, physics, and algebra word problems, teachers, researchers, and textbook writers need to do more to make such an organizational framework apparent.

REFERENCES

Aikens, J.S. (1983). Prototypical knowledge for expert systems. *Artificial Intelligence, 20*, 163–210.

Anderson, J.R. (1987). Skill Acquisition: Compilation of weak-method problem solutions. *Psychological Review, 94*, 192–210.

Bobrow, D.G., & Winograd, T. (1977). An overview of KRL, a knowledge representation language. *Cognitive Science, 1*, 3–46.

Catrambone, R., & Holyoak, K.J. (1989). Overcoming contextual limitations on problem-solving transfer. *Journal of Experimental Psychology: Learning, Memory, and Cognition, 15*, 1147–1156.

Catrambone, R., & Holyoak, K.J. (1990). Learning subgoals and methods for solving probability problems. *Memory & Cognition, 18*, 593–603.

Chi, M.T.H., Glaser, R., & Rees, E. (1982). Expertise in problem solving. In R.J. Sternberg (Ed.), *Advances in the psychology of human intelligence* (Vol. 1, pp. 7–75). Hillsdale, NJ: Erlbaum.

Dellarosa, D. (1985). *Abstraction of problem-type schemata through problem comparison* (Tech Rep. No. 146). Boulder: University of Colorado, Institute of Cognitive Science.

Gentner, D. (1983). Structure-mapping: A theoretical framework for analogy. *Cognitive Science, 7*, 155–170.

Gentner, D. (1989). The mechanisms of analogical learning. In S. Vosniadou & A. Ortony (Eds.), *Similarity and analogical reasoning* (pp. 199–241). Cambridge, UK: Cambridge University Press.

Gentner, D., & Gentner, D.R. (1983). Flowing waters or teeming crowds: Mental models of electricity. In D. Gentner & A.L. Stevens (Eds.), *Mental models* (pp. 99–129). Hillsdale, NJ: Erlbaum.

Gick, M. (1986). Problem solving strategies. *Educational Psychologist, 21*, 99–120.

Gick, M, & Holyoak, K.J. (1980). Analogical problem solving. *Cognitive Psychology, 12*, 306–355.

Gick, M., & Holyoak, K.J. (1983). Schema induction and analogical transfer. *Cognitive Psychology, 15*, 1–38.

Hall, R. (1989). Computational approaches to analogical reasoning: A computational analysis. *Artificial Intelligence, 39*, 39–120.

Hinsley, D.A., Hayes, J.R., & Simon, H.A. (1977). From words to equations: Meaning and representation in algebra word problems. In P.A. Carpenter & M.A. Just (Eds.), *Cognitive processes in comprehension* (pp. 89–106). Hillsdale, NJ: Erlbaum.

Holyoak, K.J., & Thagard, P. (1989). Analogical mapping by constraint satisfaction. *Cognitive Science, 13*, 295–355.

Kieras, D.E., & Bovair, S. (1984). The role of a mental model in learning to operate a device. *Cognitive Science, 8*, 255–273.

Kintsch, W., & Greeno, J.G. (1985). Understanding and solving word arithmetic problems. *Psychological Review, 92*, 109–129.

Krutetskii, V.A. (1976). *The psychology of mathematical abilities in school children.* Chicago: The University of Chicago Press.

Larkin, J.H., Reif, F., Carbonell, J., & Gugliotta, A. (1988). FERMI: A flexible expert reasoner with multi-domain inferencing. *Cognitive Science, 12*, 101–138.

Marshall, S.P., Pribe, C.A., & Smith, J.D., *Schema knowledge structures for representing and understanding arithmetic story problems* (ONR Tech. Rep. No. 87-01). San Diego: San Diego State University.

Mayer, R.E. (1981). Frequency norms and structural analyses of algebra story problems into families, categories, and templates. *Instructional Science, 10*, 135–175.

Medin, D.L., & Ross, B.H. (1989). The specific character of abstract thought: Categorization, problem solving, and induction. In R.S. Sternberg (Ed.), *Advances in the psychology of human intelligence* (Vol. 5, pp. 189–223). Hillsdale, NJ: Erlbaum.

Minsky, M. (1975). A framework for representing knowledge. In P.W. Winston (Ed.), *The psychology of computer vision* (pp. 211-280). New York: McGraw-Hill.

Newell, A., & Simon, H.A. (1972). *Human problem solving.* Englewood Cliffs, NJ: Prentice-Hall.

Novick, L. (1988). Analogical transfer, problem similarity, and expertise. *Journal of Experimental Psychology: Learning, Memory, & Cognition, 14*, 510–520.

Pirolli, P.L., & Anderson, J.R. (1985). The role of learning from examples in the acquisition of recursive programming skills. *Canadian Journal of Psychology, 39*, 240–272.

Reed, S.K. (1987). A structure-mapping model for word problems. *Journal of Experimental Psychology: Learning, Memory, & Cognition, 13*, 124–139.

Reed, S.K. (1989). Constraints on the abstraction of solutions. *Journal of Educational Psychology, 81*, 532–540.

Reed, S.K. Ackinclose, C.C., & Voss, A.A. (1990). Selecting analogous solutions: Similarity versus inclusiveness. *Memory & Cognition, 18*, 83–98.

Reed, S.K., & Bolstad, C.A. (1991). Use of examples and procedures in problem solving. *Journal of Experimental Psychology: Learning, Memory, & Cognition, 17*, 753-766.

Reed, S.K., Dempster, A., & Ettinger, M. (1985). Usefulness of analogous solutions for solving algebra word problems. *Journal of Experimental Psychology: Learning, Memory, & Cognition, 11*, 106–125.

Reed, S.K., Ernst, G.W., & Banerji, R. (1974). The role of analogy in transfer between similar problem states. *Cognitive Psychology, 6*, 436–450.

Reed, S.K., & Ettinger, M. (1987). Usefulness of tables for solving word problems. *Cognition and Instruction, 4*, 43–59.

Reed, S.K., & Evans, A.C. (1987). Learning functional relations: A theoretical and instructional analysis. *Journal of Experimental Psychology: General, 116*, 106–118.

Reed, S.K., & Sanchez, F.J. (1990). *Generality of descriptions in categorizing algebra word problems.* Unpublished manuscript.

Riley, M.S., Greeno, J.G., & Heller, J.I. (1983). Development of children's problem-solving ability in arithmetic. In H.P. Ginsburg (Ed.), *The development of mathematical thinking* (pp. 153–192). New York: Academic.

Rosch, E., Mervis, C.B., Gray, W.D., Johnson, D.M., & Boyes-Braem, P. (1976). Basic objects in natural categories. *Cognitive Psychology, 7*, 573–605.

Ross, B.H. (1984). Remindings and their effects in learning a cognitive skill. *Cognitive Psychology, 16*, 371–416.

Ross, B.H. (1989). Remindings in learnings and instruction. In S. Vosniadou & A. Ortony (Eds.), *Similarity and analogical reasoning* (pp. 438–469). Cambridge, UK: Cambridge University Press.

Schoenfeld, A.H., & Hermann, D.J. (1982). Problem perception and knowledge structure in expert and novice mathematical problem solvers. *Journal of Experimental Psychology: Learning, Memory, & Cognition, 5*, 484–494.

Silver, E.A. (1981). Recall of mathematical problem information: Solving related problems. *Journal for Research in Mathematics Education, 12*, 54–64.

Smith, E.E., & Goodman, L. (1984). Understanding written instructions: The role of explanatory schema. *Cognition and Instruction, 1*, 359–396.

Sweller, J., & Cooper, G.A. (1985). The use of worked examples as a substitute for problem solving in learning algebra. *Cognition and Instruction, 2*, 59–89.

Thagard, P. (1984). Frames, knowledge, and inference. *Synthese, 61*, 233–259.

Thorndyke, P.W. (1984). Applications of schema theory in cognitive research. In J.R. Anderson & S.M. Kosslyn (Eds.), *Tutorials in learning and memory* (pp. 167–191). San Francisco: Freeman.

Viscuso, S.R., & Spoehr, K.T. (1986, November). *How does a mental model facilitate comprehension of instructions?* Paper presented at the 27th Annual Meeting of the Psychonomic Society, New Orleans.

Winston, P.H. (1980). Learning and reasoning by analogy. *Communications of the ACM, 23*, 689–703.

Chapter 4

Pragmatic Knowledge and Conceptual Structure: Determinants of Transfer Between Quantitative Domains*

Miriam Bassok   Keith J. Holyoak
University of Chicago University of California, Los Angeles

INTRODUCTION

Every problem situation we face differs from any that came before it—at least in simply occurring at a different time and/or place, and often in a host of other ways. Some of these differences are of course extremely important. A new problem may have features that render old solutions completely irrelevant, useless without major modification, or dangerously misleading. On the other hand, some differences are fairly unimportant, so that an old solution could provide a ready solution to the new problem. How do we decide that the

---

* Based on a paper presented at the symposium "Transfer on Trial," held at the Annual Meeting of the American Education Research Association, Boston, April 1990.

Preparation of this chapter was supported by NSF Grants BNS 86-15474 and BNS 86-15316. Requests for reprints may be sent either to Miriam Bassok, Department of Psychology, University of Chicago, 5848 S. University Ave., Chicago, IL 60637; or to Keith J. Holyoak, Department of Psychology, UCLA, Los Angeles, CA 90024.

differences between problems are or are not important? What allows us to decide that the past is or is not relevant to the present? How can instruction foster effective transfer?

In this chapter we will not undertake a full review of the factors known to influence transfer performance (see Brown, 1989; Gick & Holyoak, 1987; Singley & Anderson, 1989). Rather, we will focus on the impact of domain knowledge and the way it is taught on the problem solver's understanding of what aspects of the learned and the transfer problems are important, or "pragmatically relevant." After introducing some major factors known to affect transfer of knowledge, we will review a line of empirical work that we have performed to investigate transfer of solution procedures learned in various quantitative domains (Bassok, 1990; Bassok & Holyoak, 1985, 1989). Based upon the results of our own work and that of others, we will attempt to provide at least partial answers to our entering questions.

Similarity and Pragmatic Relevance

A typical experimental paradigm for investigating transfer involves problems that are amenable to the same or to a similar solution procedure—problems that share "pragmatically relevant" aspects that determine the appropriateness of their solutions. At the same time, however, these problems differ in "pragmatically irrelevant" features that have no impact on the requirements of their solutions.[1] Subjects are first presented with one or more training problems and asked to solve them (or to study presented solutions). Later, a new transfer problem is given, and the subjects are asked to attempt to solve it. The subjects may or may not be given some sort of hint that the information acquired during their initial training is potentially relevant to solving the transfer problem. If the subjects apply the learned method to the transfer problem (more often than do control subjects not exposed to the training), this is taken as evidence of transfer.

All too often in such experiments, when confronted with a transfer problem, subjects fail to notice and exploit potentially useful knowledge provided by the training examples (e.g., Gick & Holyoak, 1980). There are many reasons why transfer may fail, not least of which is that the problem solver may not have learned the training material particularly well in the first place (an obvious possibility that has nonetheless been ignored in some reports of transfer failure). Given that the initial learning has been established, transfer results are most often explained by the fact that retrieval from memory depends on semantic

---

[1] The distinction between what we are terming pragmatically relevant versus irrelevant features corresponds to what has sometimes been referred to as a distinction between *structural* and *surface* features (e.g., Gick & Holyoak, 1987; Holyoak, 1985; Holyoak & Koh, 1987; Ross, 1987). However, the term *structural* is also often used in the analogy literature to refer to relational aspects of mental representations (Gentner, 1983, 1989; Holyoak & Thagard, 1989). To avoid possible confusion, we will continue to use the term *structural* in the latter sense.

similarity (e.g., content), which is not necessarily correlated with the solution-relevant aspects. In particular, failure of transfer will occur when the differences in the pragmatically irrelevant aspects are much more salient than the similarities in the solution-relevant aspects.

A basic finding is that increasing any salient similarity between the training and the transfer material increases the probability that transfer will be attempted (Holyoak & Koh, 1987; Ross, 1984, 1987, 1989). Similarity of either the overall domain context or of specific concepts has a positive effect. Thus a statistics principle taught in the context of a medical problem is more likely to be subsequently applied to another medical problem than is a problem involving admission to graduate school (Ross, 1987); and a problem solved by use of a laser is more likely to yield transfer to a radiation problem involving an X-ray than is a problem solved by use of an ultrasound wave (Holyoak & Koh, 1987).

Several studies have differentiated people's ability to access relevant prior knowledge spontaneously from their ability to make use of such information once its relevance has been pointed out (Gentner & Landers, 1985; Holyoak & Koh, 1987; Ross, 1989). Superficial similarities in the content of the training and transfer situations appear to have a much more pronounced impact on access than on use of the prior information. For example, once a teacher points out its relevance, college subjects can apply a statistical principle taught in a graduate-admissions context to a medical problem about as well as if the initial training also involved a medical problem. Nonetheless, some of the pragmatically irrelevant aspects do affect application of previously learned solutions. For example, it is easier to apply the learned solution if the objects in the training and transfer problems fill similar roles in the two problems. It is thus easier to map a person to a person and a disease to a disease across two medical problems, rather than a person to a disease and a disease to a person (a *cross mapping*; Ross, 1987).

The impact of similarity on transfer can be understood if people use the default assumption (either explicitly or implicitly) that salient similarities and differences are correlated to the important, pragmatically relevant properties. According to Medin and Ortony (1989), "the link between surface similarity and deep properties...enables surface similarity to serve as a good heuristic for where to look for deeper properties" (p. 182). Both philosophers and psychologists have argued that human categorization (which is closely related to similarity) is oriented toward the service of predictive goals. As Holland, Holyoak, Nisbett, and Thagard (1986) put it, "The most obvious function of classification is to classify and organize instances. But in our view the classificatory function is in fact derivative of the more fundamental function of generating goal-relevant inferences" (p. 179). Thus the similarity structure forming the basis of categorization will in effect summarize causal regularities that determine when it is appropriate to expect that transfer from one situation to another is likely to succeed. Indeed, spontaneous access to previous problems is not based solely on similarities between obvious "surface" features; it is also sensitive to similarities in the less salient, yet solution-relevant, aspects of the training and transfer problems (Holyoak & Koh, 1987).

Reliance on similarities of salient aspects, which happen to be pragmatically irrelevant, may be increased by insufficient understanding of the learned material. It is often a nonobvious task to identify what aspects of the problem situation are solution-relevant, and a student may try to rely on solution-irrelevant aspects because they were relevant in other situations. For example, a physics student who knows from everyday experience that the shape of an object in free fall matters greatly in determining its velocity might believe that the shape of the block determined the solution of a motion problem in the "ideal" frictionless context assumed in the physics classroom. However, there is considerable evidence that people are capable of learning to classify situations based on underlying relations of pragmatic importance, while ignoring inconsistent surface cues. In the study of Chi, Feltovich, and Glaser (1981), physics experts categorized problems according to major principles that could guide their solutions (e.g., Newton's Second Law, conservation of energy), whereas novices classified problems on the basis of salient surface configurations (e.g., inclined planes, pulleys). In a similar vein, Novick (1988) found that greater expertise (in mathematics) was correlated with both more facile positive transfer between analogous but superficially dissimilar word problems, and with reduced negative transfer between apparently similar problems that in fact required different solution procedures. Work on human reasoning also indicates that, once people have acquired fairly abstract knowledge about important types of situations, they are able to transfer this knowledge to new cases with very different content than the cases encountered during their initial learning (Cheng & Holyoak, 1985, 1989).

Teaching Pragmatic Relevance

If learning concepts and categories based on pragmatically relevant features of situations is the key to promoting appropriate transfer, then the question naturally arises of how such knowledge can be taught. There are two basic approaches to promoting abstraction of important generalizations (although most instructional situations involve some combination of both).

First, a student might learn about the relevance of features by "bottom-up" induction from examples. By integrating information from multiple examples of a category, people can abstract the components shared by the examples. The features that remain relatively constant across examples are likely to be viewed as relevant, whereas those that vary from example to example are likely to be viewed as irrelevant. This basic learning procedure can be traced back to John Stuart Mill's "joint method of agreement and difference," and has been frequently used in machine-learning applications (e.g., Winston, 1975). The major predictions derived from models based on bottom-up learning are that generalization (and hence transfer) will increase with the number of examples provided, and also with examples that more accurately reflect the inherent variability of the category. Research on category learning provides basic support for these predictions, although with the important caveat that using more variable examples sometimes seems to impair (or at least not help) the early phase of learning (see Gick & Holyoak, 1987). For example, Gick and Holyoak (1983) found that studying two problem analogs rather than one appeared to foster induction of a *problem schema*, producing greater transfer to a novel case; however, decreasing the similarity of the two training examples (i.e., increasing their variability) produced no benefit.

To assist purely bottom-up generalization, the teacher has to carefully select and order the examples from which the student is to learn (Collins & Stevens, 1982; Elio & Anderson, 1984). The student is not required to engage in a deep analysis, and may succeed by tallying the distribution of features over the alternative categories being acquired. Bottom-up learning can take place in the absence of any prior knowledge of the domain (Zhu & Simon, 1987). The cost of this knowledge-independence, however, is that bottom-up learning often requires exposure to numerous examples and may lead to erroneous learning if irrelevant features are consistently present in the examples. Thus, if all the doctors one ever encounters wear a white coat, bottom-up learning by itself would lead to the expectation that wearing a white coat is essential to medical diagnosis.

The second approach to teaching pragmatic relevance makes use of "top-down" processes that depend on prior knowledge of the domain, coupled with active learning strategies that can allow the learner to make principled judgments about the importance of features to prediction or goal attainment. Theorists in the area of cognitive development have placed considerable emphasis on the role of children's naive "theories" in guiding the course of everyday concept acquisition (e.g., Carey, 1985; Chi, 1988; Keil, 1987). In machine learning, work on "explanation-based" learning exploits reasoning about the basis for a successful solution to produce generalizations from single examples of problems (Mitchell, Keller, & Kedar-Cabelli, 1986). In essence, if a feature is present in a problem situation but played no causal role in generating the solution, then it is considered irrelevant and therefore excluded from a generalization formed from the example. A study by Chi, Bassok, Lewis, Reimann, and Glaser (1989) demonstrated that, for students learning physics from worked-out examples, their ability to generate and complete explanations of why the examples were solved as illustrated was a major predictor of their subsequent problem-solving performance. Good students generated explanations that linked the example solution to physics principles that were previously introduced in the text. Such learning enabled them to isolate the relevant rules successfully and to apply them to novel problems.

We would expect that top-down processes in learning, to the extent they succeed in identifying nonobvious features of high pragmatic relevance, will foster more flexible transfer to novel but related problems. (See Medin, 1989, for a discussion of bottom-up and top-down approaches to category learning.) Often, however, the domain knowledge that should constrain the choice of aspects that are indeed relevant to the solution of the problems is fragmented and incomplete. In such cases the teacher (or the text) should provide direct instruction focusing the student's attention on the goal-relevant aspects. A number of studies have used techniques of this sort to foster transfer. Brown, Kane, and Echols (1986) taught children to analyze problems in terms of their goal structure, and thereby improved transfer of learned procedures to analogous but superficially different problems (see also Catrambone & Holyoak, 1989). Similarly, Schoenfeld (1979) was successful in teaching general heuristics for solving problems in mathematics, and Catrambone and Holyoak (1990) found that teaching a solution procedure in terms of clearly identified units (subgoals and methods) aided subsequent adaptation of the procedure in the context of novel examples.

Overview

In the remainder of this chapter we will review our empirical work that investigated transfer of solution procedures learned in the context of several ecologically valid quantitative domains. The general paradigm we have used is to teach subjects (high school or college students) a topic from either algebra, physics, or finance that includes procedures for the solution of domain-specific problems, and then to assess students' ability to apply what they have learned to analogous problems with very different content from the domain used in training. Our work differs from studies that examine transfer following training with one or more problem examples presented without a clear instructional context, in which case learners can interpret the training solutions only in terms of their general knowledge. In contrast, our research enables us to examine the effects of domain-specific constraints imposed upon the interpretation of learned procedures by the instructional process. In particular, by comparing transfer following instruction for similar procedures taught in different domains, we have begun to tease apart the roles of bottom-up and top-down processes for determining pragmatic relevance. As we will see, our results shed light on the interactions between the representation taken to be pragmatically central for the learned domain and the ease of both access and use of the learned solution methods.

TRANSFER BETWEEN ISOMORPHIC PROBLEMS IN DIFFERENT QUANTITATIVE DOMAINS

Isomorphic Subtopics of Algebra and Physics

Our project began with the observation that certain topics in algebra and physics have an extremely close formal relationship, are both taught at about the same time in high school, and yet are virtually never explicitly related to one another by teachers. This situation afforded us the opportunity to perform a natural experiment on transfer in the context of ecologically valid and content-rich quantitative domains. The basic method was straightforward: Students first learned equations to solve word problems in one domain (the source), and then later were tested on their ability to transfer the learned procedures to isomorphic problems from the other domain (the target).

Our initial experiments (Bassok & Holyoak, 1985, 1989) centered on two specific subtopics of high school algebra and physics curricula, namely, arithmetic progressions (algebra), and motion in a straight line with constant acceleration (physics). These two domains have several advantages for a study of transfer. Each has a rigorous formal structure, and each affords a wide range of examples dealing with a variety of everyday content domains. In addition, dealing with topics and problems from a typical high school curriculum conveys the benefit of possible direct implications for the educational system with regard to optimal structuring of the school curriculum.

Most important, the word problems within these two domains, although referring to very different contents, are structurally isomorphic. In general terms, an arithmetic-progression problem involves an expanding numerical sequence that begins from some initial term and changes in increments of constant magnitude (the common difference) up to some final term. The basic questions that can be asked about an arithmetic progression are the following: (a) How many *terms* are there? (b) What is the *value* of the *first term*? (c) What is the *value* of the *final term*? (d) What is the *common difference*? and (e) What is the *total sum* of these terms? The italicized words refer to major abstract categories involved in defining a schema for arithmetic-progression problems. Students are typically taught these terms, as well as equations sufficient to solve the kinds of problems that result from the above questions.

The content of the isomorphic physics problems refers to a body moving in a straight line, the velocity of which constantly increases or decreases with time (i.e., undergoes constant acceleration). Typical types of questions, corresponding to the algebra questions presented above, are the following: (a) How many *seconds* did the body travel? (b) What was the *velocity* at the beginning of the *first second*? (c) What was the *velocity* at the end of the *final second*? (d) What is the *constant acceleration*? (e) What was the *total distance* traveled

The isomorphism depends on mapping initial velocity onto the initial term in a sequence, discrete units of time onto the number of terms in the sequence, constant acceleration onto the common difference, and final velocity onto the final term. Total distance maps onto the sum of a different arithmetic sequence, in which each term is the distance traveled in the corresponding unit of time. Each of these topics is commonly taught in Grade 11 (at least in Pittsburgh, where our experiments were performed), but in different classes. Furthermore, despite the isomorphism that exists between the two types of problems, neither teachers nor textbooks typically mention that the topics are related (although some algebra textbooks may include one or two word problems referring to motion).

What would one predict about transfer between these two domains? Obviously, sheer pessimism about the potential for transfer superficially dissimilar problems would lead to the expectation that no transfer at all would be found. However, theory-based predictions require a careful analysis of exactly what is being taught in the two domains.

In the case of arithmetic progressions, the equations and associated terminology for variable assignment are very abstract and are intentionally taught so as to fit a wide range of contents given a certain set of necessary conditions. The key equations are $a_n = a_1 + (n - 1)d$, to calculate the nth term in a sequence (the arithmetic-sequence equation), and $S_n = (a_1 + a_n)n/2$, to calculate the sum of n terms (the arithmetic-series equation), where a_n is the nth term in the sequence, S_n is the sum of n terms, and d is the constant difference. The variables in the relevant equations are nonmnemonic, and the relations between the variables are illustrated abstractly using exercises without any specific content. The surface features that appear in typical word problems vary widely, including such differing story contents as deposits to a savings account, lengths of metal rods, or the number of seats in an auditorium. The problems include the types of semantic elements that students learn are generally irrelevant to the solution of algebra word problems (Kintsch & Greeno, 1985). Indeed, a simple rule for deciding that the equations might be applicable would be, "If a word problem is presented, and it mentions a constantly increasing quantity, then try arithmetic-progression equations." Such a content-free rule would allow even a novice to apply the equations to word problems with novel content.

The nature of what is learned from physics instruction is likely to be quite different. The formulas are taught as a means of solving a very distinct and specific group of problems—those dealing with a body moving in a straight line with constant acceleration. Here the key equations are $v_f = v_i + at$, to calculate the final velocity, and $S = (v_i + v_f)t2$ to calculate the total distance traveled, where v_i and vf are respectively the initial and final velocities, S is the total distance, a is the constant acceleration, and t is the duration of motion. The variables in the equations are given mnemonic names and notations related to physical concepts, such as a for acceleration or v for velocity. The critical structural relations, which students are taught to check, involve a moving body that travels in a straight line, the speed of which increases or decreases by a constant amount every successive unit of time over some time interval. A simple rule for identifying word problems of this type would be, "If a physics word problem is presented, and it involves time, and speed or distance, and constant acceleration, then try the constant-acceleration equations." The resulting representation will presumably be abstract to some degree, as the student should learn to ignore such superficial information as the nature of the moving body (e.g., a car, boat, or ball), and the purpose of the trip. Nonetheless, it is apparent that the semantic content is much more relevant in the case of physics than in the case of the corresponding algebra problems.

One illustration of the difference in content specificity is the fact that the parameters in arithmetic progressions have no units, and the number of terms is a pure count. In contrast, the parameters of constant-acceleration equations have specific units that bind the meaning of their values. For example, multiplying acceleration (m/s^2) by time (s) results in velocity (m/s), and multiplying velocity (m/s) by time (s) results in distance (m).

These differences between the pragmatically relevant semantic contents of problems in the two domains led us to predict an asymmetry in transfer: robust transfer from algebra to physics, but minimal transfer from physics to algebra. Indeed, based on our earlier discussion of factors that are believed to affect transfer, this prediction is overdetermined. Better transfer from algebra to physics than vice versa might result from any of several potentially important differences between the knowledge acquired in the two domains. In particular, since the word problems used in teaching arithmetic progressions are more diverse in content than are those used to teach physics, bottom-up induction should generate a more content-free schema in the case of algebra. Bottom-up induction is further supported by the top-down emphasis of direct instruction. Algebra instruction emphasizes the abstract nature of the appropriate arithmetic-progressions schema, whereas physics instruction emphasizes the importance of the physical concepts involved in the constant-acceleration schema. The top-down emphasis on generality versus specificity should be further enhanced by the general knowledge students bring to the learning situation. Thus students might approach these two domains with very different expectations, or "belief systems" (of the sort discussed by Schoenfeld, 1985). Prior experience with other types of mathematical word problems will encourage algebra students to treat the specific content of the arithmetic progression problems as pragmatically irrelevant. In contrast, physics is most probably perceived as a descriptive science. Accordingly, the learned equations would be interpreted as summaries or models of specific real-world relations.

Due to any or all of the previous factors, algebra students are likely to view constant-acceleration problems as a special case of arithmetic progressions. Thus transfer from algebra to physics will involve categorizing novel instances (constant-acceleration problems) as members of a known category (arithmetic-progression problems). In contrast, transfer from physics to problems dealing with nonphysics content will involve analogical reasoning between representations of approximately equal specificity, which is likely, of course, to be a much more demanding task.

Initial Results: Asymmetry of Transfer

Bassok and Holyoak (1985) performed an initial test of the prediction of asymmetrical transfer, in a study conducted within a natural school setting. The study involved 11th-grade high school students from an algebra class who had studied the topic of arithmetic progressions but who had not yet studied the physics topic of constant acceleration, and 11th-grade students from a physics class for whom the reverse was true. Table 4.1 presents examples of the kinds of word problems used in the tests. These involved both sequence and series

Table 4.1.   Matched Arithmetic-Progression (Algebra) and Constant-Acceleration (Physics) Test Problems: A Representative Set

Algebra	Physics

Sequence type
Given: a_1, d, n, find a_n

1. A boy was given an allowance of 50 cents a week beginning on his sixth birthday. On each birthday following this, the weekly allowance was increased 25 cents. What is the weekly allowance for the year beginning on his 15th birthday?	1. An express train traveling at 30 meters per second (30m/s) at the beginning of the 3rd second of its travel, uniformly accelerates increasing in speed 5 m/s each successive second. What is its final speed at the end of the 9th second?

Given a_1, a_n, n, find d

2. During a laboratory observation period it is found that the diameter of a tree increases the same amount each month. If the diameter was 8 mm at the beginning of the first month, and 56 mm at the end of the 24th month, by how much does the diameter increase each month?	2. What is the acceleration (= increase in speed each second) of a racing car if its speed increased uniformly from 44 meters per second (44 m/s) at the beginning of the first second, to 55 m/s at the end of the 11th second?

Series type
Given: a_1, a_n, n, find S_n

3. A mechanic has to cut 9 different length metal rods. The shortest rod has to be 6 ft. long and the longest rod has to be 10 ft. long, and each rod has to be longer than the one before by a constant amount. What is the total length of metal required to prepare these rods?	3. A jumbo jet starts from rest and accelerates uniformly during 8 seconds for takeoff. If it travels 25 meters during the first second and 375 meters during the 8th second, what distance does it travel in all?

Given: a_1, d, n, find S_n

4. Kate O'Hara has a job that pays $7,500 for the first six months, with a raise of $250 at the end of every six months thereafter. What was her total income after 12 years?	4. An object dropped from a hovering helicopter falls 4.9 meters during the first second of its descent, and during each subsequent second it falls 9.8 meters farther than it fell during the preceding second. If it took the object 10 seconds to reach the ground, how high above the ground was the helicopter hovering?

Tables 4.1, 4.2, and 4.3 reprinted from Bassok & Holyoak, 1989, Interdomain Transfer Between Isomorphic Topics in Algebra and Physics, *Journal of Experimental Psychology: Learning, Memory, and Cognition, 15*, 153–166. Copyright 1989 by American Psychologist Association. Reprinted by permission.

problems, and differed with respect to which variables were known and unknown. All subjects first solved transfer problems from the new target domain, followed by problems from the source domain. Performance on the source problems thus provided a baseline to assess the degree of transfer. In this and all the other experiments to be discussed, the primary measure of transfer was based on scoring of the method subjects used to solve the test problems. Many students are able to solve problems of the sort we used by general algebraic methods (e.g., repeated addition); thus, use of the more efficient solution method illustrated during training on the source domain, rather than simply solution accuracy, provides a more appropriate and sensitive measure of transfer.

As predicted, a striking transfer asymmetry was observed. Algebra students who had learned the arithmetic-progression method applied it equally often (72% of the time) to new algebra problems (with content similar to that of the problems used in training) and to novel physics problems. In contrast, physics students who had learned the constant-acceleration method applied it to *all* of the physics test problems but to *none* of the algebra transfer problems.

Given various methodological limitations of the initial study conducted in the school setting, we replicated the experiment with subjects who received instruction in the source domain in the lab (Bassok & Holyoak, 1989, Experiment 1). The subjects in the lab study were 12 9th-grade high-ability students from an accelerated program in science at a public high school. All subjects were tested individually. In an initial session lasting 1.5–3 hours, each subject completed a pretest on the source domain they were about to study and then was instructed in the source topic using training materials adapted from textbook treatments. Six subjects were taught arithmetic progressions, and six were taught constant-acceleration problems. A test was administered to ensure the material was mastered.

During a second session, conducted on the following day, subjects were first told they would be learning about a new domain. They were then asked to solve three transfer problems drawn from the novel target domain, under the guise of a pretest for the expected training. Next the subjects were asked to solve three matched problems from the source domain (a posttest), after which they were debriefed without further instruction. The entire session was tape-recorded for later analysis.

The results of the previous school-setting study were fully replicated in this lab experiment. After studying the relevant training materials, all the algebra students applied the learned arithmetic-progression method to the posttest algebra problems (to 17 of the total 18 problems). Similarly, all the physics students applied the learned constant-acceleration method to the posttest physics problems (to all 18 problems). Thus both groups acquired and used the learned method for the familiar source-domain problems. The two training groups differed radically, however, with respect to transfer. Whereas all algebra students applied the learned method in solving the physics problems (to 13 of the 18 possible cases), only one physics student applied the learned method to the unfamiliar algebra problems (to 2 out of 18 cases).

The oral protocols obtained from subjects working on the transfer problems provided more detailed evidence of qualitative differences in the manner in which transfer took place in the two directions. Table 4.2 presents three representative excerpts from the protocols of algebra-trained subjects solving physics problems on the transfer test. These subjects referred to the physics problems as a simple case of the familiar arithmetic-progression problems. They proceeded by retrieving the relevant equation, identifying the relevant variables, and inserting the values into the equation. The most striking feature of these transfer protocols is the absence of any indication that the subjects were dealing with unfamiliar problems. It seems that as we argued earlier, transfer from algebra to physics involves the application of a known problem schema to a new instance.

Table 4.2. Examples of Protocols: Transfer From Algebra to Physics

Algebra subject 1, solving physics problem 1:

I'm recalling the arithmetic progression
labeling the third second a_1, the fourth second a_2....
The equation was $a_n = a_1 + (n - 1)d$
and d equals 5
now n equals 7
a_7 is what we want to find out
is equal to a_1 which is 30, plus $(n - 1)$ which is 6,
times d which is 5, which is equal to 60.

Algebra subject 2, solving physics problem 1:

8 increases
$9 - 1 (n - 1)$
times the *common difference*, which is 5 m/s
and that should be equal to final speed.

Algebra subject 6, solving physics problem 3:

All right
a_1 equals 25, a_n equals 375,
and d equals the acceleration.
And now I have to do $S_n = (a_1 + a_n) n/2$.

Note. The problems appear in Table 4.1.

Given that only one subject showed any transfer from physics to algebra, the protocol evidence regarding the other direction of transfer was severely limited in scope. Nonetheless, the protocols of this subject, excerpted in Table 4.3, proved quite revealing. It is clear that the recognition of similarity proceeded in a much more laborious fashion than in algebra-to-physics transfer. The subject

Table 4.3.   Examples of Protocols: Transfer From Physics to Algebra

Physics subject 1, solving algebra problem 2:

Umm…well…I know there is a certain connection.
It's something *like acceleration*…
I mean it's really similar, because there is time and…

Maybe we can use a formula for acceleration, because
you have the beginning…it's *like the beginning speed,
the final speed,* and *the time.*

The *8 mm* as the beginning *speed*
and the *56 mm* as the end *speed*
and the 24 is umm…time.

Because it has the same kind of variables.

But maybe it isn't, we don't have a proof that it is.
I'll just try using that formula, maybe it will work.

It's like…for acceleration.
Cause we want to know *what the acceleration is*
Because they're asking us *how much it grew each month.*

Physics subject 1, solving algebra problem 3:

So, what we have to find again is the difference between each rod,
because they say it's a constant amount of difference.

Umm the difference between each rod…and it's constant.
OK, and that's again *like the acceleration.*

Because you have the *first amount*
and you have a *final amount*
and you have *something like the time.*

Note: The problems appear in Table 4.1.

initially noticed a possible analogy when working on the second of the three
transfer problems, which involved a sequence of diameters of a growing tree
(algebra problem #2 in Table 1). The first clue that seems to have triggered
reminding was based on the similarity between constant increase in the diameter
of a tree and constant acceleration, both of which involve a constant rate of
change over time. Once she had been reminded of the physics equation, the
subject tried to map the remaining variables into the relevant slots, mapping
initial diameter onto initial velocity, final diameter onto final velocity, and the
number of months onto the time slot. The analogical nature of the hypothesized
correspondences is suggested by such statements as "the beginning [diameter]
…it's *like* the beginning speed." It is apparent in the subsequent portion of the
protocol that the analogy was very tentative; however, she proceeded to work out
the suggested solution, which was in fact correct.

Table 4.3 also presents excerpts of the same subject's protocol as she solved the third problem, which involved finding the sum of the lengths of a series of rods. Once again the semantic link between a constant increase and acceleration provided the first reminding cue, again followed by an explicit development of the mapping. One important difference between this protocol and that for her first use of the analogy concerns the level of abstraction of the terms she used to refer to variables. For example, whereas in the first protocol she referred to the initial diameter as being "the beginning speed," in the subsequent problem she referred to the initial length as "the first amount," a more generalized and content-free concept. It thus appears that, in the context of working out the analogy for the first time, the subject induced more abstract concepts that began to approximate the arithmetic-progression schema that algebra-trained subjects were taught directly.

Is Diversity of Training Examples Crucial for Transfer?

Our early results thus confirmed our expectation of a strong asymmetry in ease of transfer between algebra and physics. However, as we pointed out earlier, there are several plausible explanations of this basic result. Our subsequent work was largely motivated by the goal of teasing apart some of these alternatives. We began by considering the factor that is most obvious from the point of view of bottom-up models of induction: differences in the diversity of training examples. Arithmetic progressions are typically illustrated by word problems drawn from a wide variety of content domains, whereas constant-acceleration problems are inherently restricted to moving bodies. The greater variability of content used to teach algebra would be expected to foster a more abstract, domain-independent schema, which would in turn aid subsequent transfer to problems with novel content, such as physics.

One obvious way to test whether diversity of examples is crucial to transfer is to teach algebra using examples with highly restricted content. If bottom-up induction is the key to successful generalization, providing training examples drawn from a single domain would sharply limit the abstraction of the schema acquired, and hence impair transfer. Accordingly, we compared transfer from algebra after teaching arithmetic progressions with examples drawn from one of three distinct contents: money, people, and motion (Bassok & Holyoak, 1989, Experiment 2). The money problems dealt with salaries, loans, and investments. For example:

> Juanita went to work as a teller in a bank at a salary of $12,400 per year, and received constant yearly increases coming up with a $16,000 salary during her seventh year of work. What was her yearly salary increase?

The people problems dealt with population growth, student enrollment, numbers of people in rows, and so on. For example:

> In 1975 a total of 22,630 people attended conventions at a convention center. If 2,000 more people attend conventions at the center each year, how many people will attend the center in 1990?

Finally, the motion problems were simply constant-acceleration problems of the sort we had used in physics instruction. We included these problems as instructional content for algebra in order to check the possibility that there is something inherently difficult about transferring procedures exemplified by physics content, regardless of whether the nominal topic is physics or algebra.

This experiment was conducted in the context of a college course in algebra at the University of Pittsburgh. The students in the class were drawn from a population of those who did not pass the university's algebra placement test. The 22 undergraduates who completed the study were thus considerably older, but less mathematically talented, than the 9th graders who served in the experiment described above. The experiment involved four consecutive class sessions, during which subjects completed a pretest, were instructed in arithmetic progressions with examples of worked-out and practice word problems drawn from one of the three content areas, and completed a posttest and transfer test. For students who were trained with money or people content, the transfer problems were from physics; for those trained with physics content, the transfer problems involved either money or people content.

Rather to our surprise, the results indicated that reduced diversity of examples did not greatly impair transfer. Transfer did not differ significantly across the three content areas used in algebra training (thus in particular, physics examples proved as good as those from any other content domain in teaching algebra). Collapsing across the three content areas, subjects applied the learned method to about 80% of the transfer problems. Although this transfer rate was significantly lower than the 97% application of the learned method obtained on the posttest with familiar content, it is nonetheless very high indeed—vastly higher than the near zero transfer rate from constant-acceleration problems to algebra problems with nonphysics content observed in the previous experiments. Thus is appears that bottom-up generalization from diverse examples—although not excluded as a contributor to transfer—is certainly not the major factor favoring transfer from algebra.

Does Domain-Specific Encoding Necessarily Preclude Transfer?

There remain, of course, a number of other factors that would favor the induction of a relatively abstract schema for arithmetic-progression problems, even when the examples are drawn from a single content area. High school and college students may come with strong beliefs about the inherent abstraction of algebra, and about the pragmatic irrelevance of the specific semantic content of the examples used to teach it. In the experiment above, arithmetic progressions were still introduced in terms of general equations with domain-independent variable names. One might well expect that if the material were taught with a more domain-specific derivation, in which the content domain is treated as highly significant, then transfer across domains would be more or less eliminated, as was the case with constant-acceleration training.

To examine whether training geared toward some specific domain (other than physics) would in fact cripple subsequent transfer, Bassok (1990, Experiment 1) designed a new set of materials nominally intended to train subjects to solve "banking" problems, which dealt with compounding interest on investments and loans. In order to maintain ecological validity, the mathematical structure used was not arithmetic but rather geometric progressions. The two central equations were $a_n = a_1 r^{n-1}$ (for sequence problems) and $S_n = a_1 (1 - r^n)/(1 - r)$ (for series problems), where r is the rate of change and the other variables are the same as those in the arithmetic-sequence equations. Although the equations for geometric progressions are somewhat more difficult than those for arithmetic progressions, the two topics are of similar conceptual difficulty, and with use of a calculator they are of similar computational difficulty.

Two sets of instructional materials, both based on banking, were developed. In the "applied-algebra" condition, students studied an algebra chapter on geometric progressions that was presented as a "mathematical insert" in the context of learning about banking. The algebraic material was couched in the usual general way, with the domain-independent equations given above, but the equations were only illustrated with examples from finance. In contrast, in the "banking" condition the equations were derived directly for banking concepts (e.g., annuities and compounding), using banking-specific notation (e.g., b for balance, i for interest rate). The banking condition was thus analogous to the physics-specific training employed in our earlier experiments.

Banking and matched nonbanking problems were constructed for use in a banking pretest and posttest and in a transfer test. Examples of matched problems are presented in Table 4.4. Each member of such matched problem pairs shared the same underlying problem structure, the same given and unknown variables, and similar numerical values.

The subjects in this experiment were 20 undergraduates who had not taken an algebra class for at least one year and whose major was not finance. Ten served in each of the two training conditions. Each subject participated individually in two sessions: an initial "pretest, study, posttest" session lasting 2–3 hours, and a "transfer" session lasting about 1 hour. During the transfer session, subjects initially attempted to solve all the transfer (i.e., nonbanking) problems without being informed that the problems were related to the banking material studied previously. (The transfer test was introduced as a pretest for training in algebra.) Those students who did not show spontaneous transfer were then asked to solve two of the transfer problems again, after being told that the banking material

Table 4.4.   Examples of Matched Geometric-Progressions Problems from Banking Pretest and from Algebra Nonbanking Transfer Test

Nonbanking	Banking
A: Sequence Type: Given: a_1, r, n, find a_n	
Because of its increasing popularity, each successive year a certain craft show attracts 1.3 times more people than during the previous year. If 1,000 people came to this craft show during its 1st year, how many people came during its 12th year?	A certain manufacturing company invested $10,000 in various government bonds. Each successive year the value of their investment increases 1.3 times its value from the previous year. How much will their investment be worth during the 12th year?
B. Series Type: Given a_1, r, n, find S_n	
A certain car has a leak in its exhaust system. Each successive time that the car's accelerator pedal is pressed, 0.6% more carbon monoxide is released into the air. If 0.2 ml of carbon monoxide were released with the 1st press of the pedal, how many ml will have been released into the air altogether during the first 10 presses of the pedal?	Mr. Daniel is repaying a loan he received from the bank. Each successive month he agreed to repay 6% more than during the previous month. If he paid $20 during the 1st month, what is the total amount of money that he will have repaid on the loan when he makes his 10th payment?

could be helpful. (Such a hint was not provided in any of our previous experiments.) Subjects talked out loud as they solved problems and their protocols were taperecorded for later analysis.

Both training conditions proved extremely effective, as the learned method of solution was used on 100% of the posttest problems (as compared to none of the pretest problems). The major question, however, was whether subjects would be able to recognize that the unfamiliar algebra word problems were amenable to the same type of solution as the familiar compound-interest problems. In fact, transfer of the learned method was considerably higher than we had expected, given the content-specificity of the training. In the applied algebra condition, 8 of the 10 students spontaneously noticed the relevance of their training, and these 8 applied the learned method to 81% of their transfer problems. The results for the banking condition were even more surprising. Five of these 10 students spontaneously transferred the learned method, applying it to 95% of their transfer problems. Transfer in both conditions was obviously incomplete, but far greater than obtained in previous studies using physics as the base domain.

Protocol analyses bolstered the conclusion that transfer from banking to general algebra was qualitatively, as well as quantitatively, distinctly different from transfer of physics to general algebra problems. Table 4.5 presents examples of excerpts from protocols obtained from subjects in the banking condition while they were solving the first algebra nonbanking problem for which spontaneous transfer occurred. Subjects proceeded by retrieving the relevant equation, identifying the variables, and instantiating them with the given values. This straightforward form of transfer clearly resembles that observed in protocols of transfer from algebra to physics (Table 4.2) much more than that observed in protocols of transfer from physics to algebra (Table 4.3). Furthermore, all of the seven subjects who did not show spontaneous transfer were nonetheless able to apply the learned method to the nonbanking problems once a hint was provided, and they did so in a manner similar to that observed in the cases of spontaneous transfer. Thus, even when content-specific training in finance blocked initial recognition of the relevance of the methods to the transfer problems, it did not cause difficulties in constructing an appropriate mapping.

It is important to emphasize that the fact that the domain-specific training did not severely block transfer cannot be ascribed to weakness of the "cover stories" used in training. When asked at the end of the experiment, "What are the major things you have learned?" all 10 students in the banking condition gave answers that focused on banking (e.g., "How to determine which banking systems are better, and what my total interest and balances would be at the end of each period"). Similarly, when asked, "Do you think the chapter will be useful to you?" the answers of all students in the banking condition referred to real-life

Table 4.5.   Examples of Protocols for Initial Transfers from Banking to Algebra Nonbanking Problems

Subject 1

I'm thinking this is very similar to what I learned yesterday...
it's just put in a different context.
Let's see if I can remember the equations...
1.3 to the 13th power...

Subject 2

This would be the same as yesterday...
and so if I can remember the formulas...
b_p equals b_1 times r to the p-1 so,
r to the 12th year equals...
1000 times r which is 1.3 to the 11th power.

Subject 3

OK, I'll use that formula...it is 1000 times 1.3 to the 11th.

Note: Solutions refer to the first algebra nonbanking problem in Table 4.4.

banking situations as appropriate contexts to apply the learned methods (e.g., "Yes, when I have a loan to pay or when I put money in the bank, this will help tremendously"). Thus, despite clear evidence that the subjects took the semantic content of the training very seriously, they were generally able to transfer the learned methods to novel domains.

Results complementary to those observed in the banking experiment of Bassok (1990) were obtained in an experiment by Bassok and Holyoak (1989, Experiment 3). In the latter experiment, subjects were first taught arithmetic progressions in the usual manner, and then tested on physics problems. However, for some subjects the physics problems were introduced as the pretest for physics training, after these subjects had first studied an introduction to major concepts related to motion (e.g., the difference between constant and accelerated motion). Subjects given this "motion" context showed reduced transfer from their algebra training to the physics transfer problems (although significant transfer was still observed). Thus it appears that a context that increases the apparent pragmatic importance of domain-specific concepts, either in the source or in the target domain, does impair spontaneous transfer. However, the impact of such content embedding seems insufficient to explain the near total failure of transfer from physics to general algebra problems we observed in our early experiments.

Does Transfer Depend on Matching Quantity Types?

The partial, yet substantial and straightforward, transfer from banking to nonbanking problems obtained by Bassok (1990) suggests that several of the possible explanations we raised for the overwhelming lack of transfer from physics instruction, as documented by Bassok and Holyoak (1989), are insufficient. In particular, methods for solving banking problems were not taught in a domain-general way; it is unlikely that subjects have prior beliefs that banking methods are domain-independent; the examples used in training were restricted to the single domain of finance; and the "banking schema" is in no obvious sense a category of which nonbanking problems are instances. Yet substantial transfer was nonetheless observed when banking rather than physics served as the source domain.

The apparent inadequacy of these alternative explanations led us to examine more closely the constraints imposed by the domain-specific physics knowledge on the appropriate conditions for solving constant-acceleration problems, and to compare these to the conditions imposed on the solution of arithmetic-progression problems. So far we have discussed similarity between problems using a very general distinction between their pragmatically relevant and irrelevant aspects. It is important to remember, however, that what makes certain aspects of a problem relevant for its solution depends to a large extent on the structural (or relational) configuration of that problem. Indeed, what makes two situations analogous is that a reasonably consistent mapping can be established between their respective configural structures. That is, it has to be possible to place the elements of the two situations into correspondence in such a way that the mapped elements consistently fill corresponding roles in the configural structures (Gentner, 1983; Holyoak & Thagard, 1989).

Our initial analysis of isomorphism between arithmetic-progression and constant-acceleration problems was in terms of the relation connecting an initial amount that increases by a constant value a certain number of times to a subsequent amount. For example, an arithmetic-progression problem situation might center on a person who weighs 100 pounds and gains 2 pounds every month for 5 months, at which time the person will weigh 110 pounds. The basic equation for solving such problems can be applied to any situation in which some quantity undergoes a constant change. For this purpose, it is perfectly reasonable to treat speed as such a constantly increasing quantity (e.g., if a car traveling at 50 mph constantly accelerates by 10 mph each minute for 3 minutes, it will reach a speed of 80 mph). These two examples have a consistent mapping, in which initial and final speeds map to initial and final weights, respectively, and constant acceleration maps to constant weight increase.

Note, however, that speed (m/s) is an *intensive* (rate) quantity that represents the ratio of distance (m) to time (s), whereas weight is an *extensive* quantity, not reducible to some underlying definition in terms of a rate relation holding between two different quantities. Accordingly, if we represent the concept of speed in terms of its intensive structure, it would not be isomorphic to the extensive quantity of weight. For the purpose of solving a constant-acceleration problem, speed can be treated as a unitary concept, making the structural inconsistency at the level of quantity type (intensive vs. extensive) irrelevant. Since constant increases in speed can be mapped to constant increases in weight, the two examples can in fact be viewed as isomorphic. But as soon as speed is psychologically represented in terms of its rate structure, the isomorphism will break down.

Examination of our physics training suggests that the "rateness" of speed is extremely important for understanding the conceptual structure of the domain, which focuses on the various relations between speed, time, distance, and acceleration. For example, multiplying speed (m/s) by time (s) results in distance (m), which is a distinctively different entity. It is therefore reasonable to assume that the "rateness" of speed will be included in the structural representation of the constant-acceleration problems. Such inclusion, in turn, makes the rational structure of constant-acceleration problems more complex than, and therefore nonisomorphic to, the structure of arithmetic-progression problems. In contrast, it is reasonable to expect that algebra training, focusing on procedures defined in terms of the relation of constant increase for any quantity, will lead students to treat speed as a unitary concept. In this case, as we have explained above, the constant-acceleration problems will be isomorphic to the arithmetic-progression problems.

It appears, then, that basic quantity types may provide an important element of the structure inherent in mathematical problems. Indeed, researchers in mathematics education have also argued that the degree of structural consistency between problems can depend not only on their overall mathematical structure (e.g., arithmetic-progressions), but also on the internal structure of the quantity concepts involved in the problems (Kaput, 1986; Schwartz, 1981, 1988). Kaput (1986) argues that variables denoting extensive quantities and those denoting intensive quantities may imply different interpretations of the mathematical operations they permit. In particular, intensive and extensive quantities are not additive in the same sense. Extensive quantities are strictly additive; for example, the total length of two rods is the sum of the two lengths. In contrast, adding intensive quantities is often meaningless. For example, if a car travelled for half an hour at 25 mph and then another half hour at 15 mph, we could not claim that its "total speed" was 40 mph.

Let us now return to the interpretation of our previous transfer results. In general, as we claimed at the beginning of this chapter, mathematical schemas learned as models of domain-specific relations will be somewhat more difficult to transfer to new domains, because the underlying structure must be abstracted from its content. Thus transfer is more difficult from banking than from algebra, and it is more difficult from physics than from algebra. Our present analysis suggests, in addition, that for complex concepts such as quantity types, prior learning affecting the level of conceptual representation deemed pragmatically important will thereby influence perceived structural correspondences, which we expect will in turn influence patterns of transfer.

In particular, the conceptual representation of a learned domain will determine whether discrepant quantity types will affect isomorphism at the level of the overall mathematical structure. Transfer from algebra to physics is easy, not only due to the abstractness of algebra, but also because the algebra training would lead students to conceive of speed as a unitary conceptual entity that can be easily instantiated in the learned rule. The extreme difficulty of transfer from physics can be explained by the fact that in addition to the domain-specific content, the core physical concept of speed is of a qualitatively different structural type than are the nonphysics concepts (e.g., potatoes or people) to which it would have to be mapped. This problem of incompatibility between quantities did not arise in the experiment of Bassok (1990) that examined transfer from banking to nonbanking problems, since both training (adding amounts of money) and transfer (e.g., adding numbers of people) involved concepts of the same quantity type (extensive).

This analysis makes the intriguing prediction that even transfer from physics should not be inordinately difficult if the nonphysics problems involve intensive variables that match the quantity type of the physics concepts. Which intensive quantities could match the intensive quantity of speed? Note that although the extensive/intensive distinction is a formal one, it may be necessary to distinguish quantity types on a more psychological basis. For example, both "meters per second" and "potatoes per day" are formally intensive; intuitively, however, they seem to differ in status. The intensive nature of speed is inherent to its very definition, and the two related dimensions, *meters* and *seconds*, appear to be combined to yield a single *conceptual entity* (Greeno, 1983). In contrast, *potatoes* and *days* do not seem to form a unitary entity; rather, it seems that one extensive quantity (potatoes) is counted by units of another extensive quantity (which could be either a time measure like *days*, or instead a space measure like *boxes*). Accordingly, Bassok (1990) argued that *pseudorate* quantities such as "potatoes per day" should be viewed as psychologically extensive, rather than intensive.

To test the possibility that transfer from physics to nonphysics problems with matching intensive quantities can be obtained, Bassok (1990, Experiment 2) trained 20 9th- and 10th-grade honors students on constant-acceleration problems, using the same training materials as in our previous work. The first "pretest, study, posttest" session lasted 1–2 hours, and the second "transfer" session (on the following day) lasted about an hour. Students were tested individually, and their problem-solving protocols were tape recorded.

Bassok constructed two sets of physics problems, which served as the pre- and posttests, and two sets of arithmetic-progression algebra problems of varied content that served as transfer tests. The algebra problems were intended to be either psychologically intensive (hence conceptually similar to speed) or psychologically extensive (hence dissimilar to speed). The intensive problems dealt with variables such as words/min and liters/sec; the extensive problems dealt with variables such as apples/day and dollars/month. For both types of transfer problems the constant change occurred as a function of time; thus time per se could not serve as a cue that would differentiate the two conditions. However, the intensive quantities in the algebra problems involved small units of time (seconds or minutes), as did the corresponding quantities in the physics problems, whereas the extensive quantities involved larger time units (days or months). Also, the intensive problems explicitly referred to the key variable as a rate (e.g., typing rate, precipitation rate), whereas extensive problems referred to the variable as an amount (e.g., salary, bushels). As in earlier studies, the structures of the problems were matched across all the sets. Table 4.6 provides examples of the matched physics, intensive algebra, and extensive algebra problems that were used. Ten subjects received each of the two algebra transfer sets, and talk-aloud protocols were tape-recorded for later analysis. As in the previous experiment of Bassok (1990) described above, subjects who did not exhibit spontaneous transfer were asked to solve two of the transfer problems again after receiving a hint to apply the methods they had learned in the prior training session.

The physics training proved very effective, as in our earlier studies. Students applied the learned method to 89% of the physics posttest problems, compared to none of the pretest problems. In addition, a separate control condition

Table 4.6. Examples of Matched Arithmetic Progression Problems from Physics Pretest and from Algebra "Intensive" and "Extensive" Transfer Tests

Physics	Algebra (intensive)	Algebra (extensive)
Sequence Type Given: a_1, a_n, n, find d		
1. What is the acceleration (increase in speed each second) of a train, if its speed increased uniformly from 15m/sec at the beginning of the first second, to 45 m/sec at the end of the 12th second?	Every typist goes through a 'warm-up' period during which his/her typing rate constantly increases until reaching a typical typing rate. Jane starts typing at a rate of 40 words per minute, and after 12 minutes reaches her typical typing rate of 58 words per minute. What is the constant increase in her typing rate during her 'warm-up' period?	Juanita went to work as a teller in a bank at a salary of $12,400 per year, and received constant yearly increases coming with a $16,000 salary during her 13th year of work. What was her yearly salary increase?
Series Type Given: a_1, a_n, n, find S_n		
An object dropped from a hovering helicopter takes 10 seconds to reach the ground. The initial speed of the object at the beginning of the first second is 0 m/sec, but due to gravity its speed uniformly increases 4.2 m/sec each successive second. How high above the ground was the helicopter hovering?	A certain solution forms a precipitate at the bottom of its container. The precipitate starts forming at a rate of 13.7 milligrams per second. As the precipitation proceeds, the concentration of the solution changes, and the precipitation rate constantly decreases by 1.2 milligrams per second every second. What is the total amount of precipitate that is formed during this period of 10 seconds?	A potato farmer gathers 35 bushels of potatoes on the first day of the harvest. The farmer estimates that on each successive day of the harvest, the amount gathered will be 4 bushels more than on the preceding day. If the harvest lasts 14 days, how many bushels altogether will the farmer collect during the 14 days of the harvest?

established that, without prior training, performance on the two sets of algebra transfer problems did not differ. The crucial results concern transfer to algebra from physics. For the extensive algebra problems, for which the key variable differed in quantity type from speed, the near-total transfer failure observed in our earlier experiments was replicated. Only one of the ten subjects spontaneously applied the physics method to an algebra problem; transfer was thus obtained on just one of the 40 possible cases. In contrast, partial but substantial transfer was observed for the intensive algebra problems, for which the key variable matched the quantity type of speed. Six of the 10 subjects noticed the relevance of their physics training and applied the learned method to at least one algebra problem; a total of 16 of the 40 possible cases were solved by the learned method.

Students's sensitivity to the nature of variables in the transfer problems was apparent in their solution protocols. Table 4.7 presents three excerpts from protocols obtained from subjects in the intensive condition when solving their first algebra problem. The recognition of similarity to constant-acceleration problems was immediate, and the mapping was easily constructed, much as in similar protocols for subjects transferring from banking to a nonbanking domain (see Table 4.5). Subjects either retrieved the relevant equation and instantiated it with the appropriate values, or constructed the equation directly for the given values. Note that, when prompted by the experimenter (see Subjects 1 and 3 in Table 4.7), subjects' explanations of similarity focused on the similarity between the problem's variable and speed (e.g., "It's just like her going faster"; "they are like the speeds"). Moreover, all subjects explicitly mentioned the intensive unit for the target variable (e.g., words per minute). These protocols thus indicate that similarity of the variables, in terms of quantity type, triggered the retrieval of the physics equations and facilitated their application to the algebra problems.

Mappings of physics knowledge to nonmatching extensive algebra problems was qualitatively different. Only one subject spontaneously showed transfer, on the final algebra transfer problem:

> "I took one of the formulas from the physics thing... It was the same thing... In the other one the final product was what you were looking for, and then they give you what you start with which was the 35, plus the number of bushels which would be the change per day times the time, which would be 14 days... so it worked out like the same thing."

Note that the student referred to similarity of the underlying structural relations, rather than to similarity of the quantities. The initial term was described, not as a concrete concept, but as the abstraction "what you start with," and the solution was based on the structural relation (i.e., arithmetic progression) connecting the "final product" with "what you start with" and with the "change per day times the time."

Table 4.7.   Examples of Protocols: Initial Transfer from Physics to Algebra "Intensive" Problems

Subject 1

This is pretty similar to the things we did with a straight line in physics. Maybe I can use something from that.
[Experimenter: How is it similar?]
Because *it's just like her going faster,* she's not moving in a straight line it's just how many words she types.
So it's just *like meters per second*...

Acceleration equals...
I'm using the acceleration formula
Her *acceleration* would be 8¹⁄₆ *words per minute*.

Subject 2

Subtract the *initial words per minute from the final words per minute* to get 18.
Divide that by the number of minutes to get 1.5...
So you get 1.5 *words per minute per minute.*

Subject 3

OK, this is similar to the last ones.
[Experimenter: How is it similar]
Well,...it has a time in it
and like...the *40 and 58 are the speeds*
well, not the speeds in this problem, but like in the physics problems...
they are *like the speeds*
So maybe use the same formula?
[Reads: What is the constant increase in the typing rate?]
Well, let's see...
58 − 40 = 18. So, 18 divided by 12 equals 1.5...
So, she increased 1.5 words per second.

Note: Solutions refer to the first algebra-intensive problem in Table 4.6.

Table 4.8 presents additional examples of transfer from physics to extensive algebra problems, obtained after the experimenter provided a hint to use the learned method. As in the case of spontaneous transfer, students abstracted the variable role (e.g., "whatever they start out with," and sometimes omitted reference to "speed," instead referring to the "beginning" and the "final." The third example in Table 4.8 demonstrates an effort to directly map variables. (Compare the first protocol in Table 4.3, obtained from the physics-trained subject from our earlier experiment who showed spontaneous transfer.) Note the momentary apparent mismapping between the "amount she made" and "distance," which unlike speed is an extensive amount. This student continued to develop explicit mappings between variables, and the successful mapping was constrained by the problems' analogous structures.

Table 4.8.   Examples of Protocols: Hinted Transfer from Physics to Algebra "Extensive" Problems

Subject 1

> Oh, so it's like yesterday
> like the speed or *whatever they start out with*
> [rereads the problem]
> the *final* would be 1,600
> and *what we start out with* is 12,400.

Subject 2

> Now I have to remember what I did from yesterday…
> beginning speed…ending speed…
> OK, I'll say this is the…
> [rereads the problem]
> so, beginning was $12,400…OK
> her final would be $1,600…and run,
> wait…times the time…13 years.

Subject 3

> Well, this would probably be related
> to the final speed…
> so, you would start off with the amount she made…
> no, this would be distance…
> you would add up the *beginning speed or the beginning salary*
> and the *end speed or the end salary*…
> then you divide it by 13.

Note: Solutions refer to the first algebra-extensive problem in Table 4.6.

In general, then, students did not spontaneously notice the underlying structural equivalence (i.e., the arithmetic-progressions structure) when there was a discrepancy between the quantity types of the key variables in the source and target problems. In order to map the learned relations, students generally had to abstract away from the specifically intensive characteristics of speed. Thus, for nonmatching variables, both spontaneous transfer and the ability to map were severely impaired. This difficulty did not result solely from domain-specific encodings, as transfer from physics to nonphysics problems with matching intensive variables was relatively straightforward.

CONSTRAINTS ON KNOWLEDGE TRANSFER: FUTURE DIRECTIONS

Our studies of transfer between different content domains that have the inherent structure of arithmetic or geometric progressions provide answers to some important questions, while raising intriguing new issues. For anyone who might care to put "transfer on trial" under suspicion that interdomain transfer is virtually nonexistent, these experiments return a resounding verdict of "not guilty." When subjects students were given training in abstract algebra, a clear majority were able to apply their knowledge to new domains—even when the training examples were drawn from but a single domain. When students were taught very specifically about banking, learning the relations between principal investment, interest rate, and number of compounding periods, 50% of the students then spontaneously recognized that the learned relations also hold for exponential increase in (for example) fish population. After learning about the physics of accelerated motion, 70% of students realized that constant decrease in the formation of a precipitate is like acceleration, and that the total amount of precipitate can be calculated using the distance equation learned in physics. Educators who may have feared that knowledge inevitably remains encapsulated in its training context should surely be heartened by these demonstrations of robust and highly flexible transfer.

Spontaneous transfer certainly did not occur for all students, and was reduced by domain-specific derivations of the mathematical procedures. Nonetheless, a very general hint that the previously learned material was relevant was sufficient to allow straightforward application of the learned procedures. Students were thus able to abstract structural relations from material initially acquired within an ecologically valid content domain. The domain content limited memory access to the source material, but had little or no negative impact on the post-access derivation of the appropriate mapping to the target domain. Our results thus extend similar findings in other work on analogical transfer (Gentner & Landers, 1985; Holyoak & Koh, 1987; Ross, 1987, 1989).

In contrast to the limited negative impact of changing content domains, both memory access and postaccess mapping were severely impaired when the quantity types of the key variables in the source and target problems did not match. Virtually no spontaneous transfer was obtained from constant-accelera-tion problems, with the intensive variable of speed, to nonphysics problems based on extensive variables, such as potatoes per day. When mapping was attempted (which occurred very rarely unless a hint was given), the process was laborious, often accompanied by abstraction of the mismatching variables to a level at which the difference in quantity type was eliminated. It appears that the quantity type determines central aspects of the structural representation used in mapping, leading to conflicts when structural constraints are applied in the mapping process. These results thus reinforce other evidence that structural mismatches, or structural correspondences that conflict with correspondences based on direct similarity of concepts, make mapping difficult (Holyoak & Koh, 1987; Ross, 1987, 1989; see Holyoak & Thagard, 1989).

This overall pattern seems closely related to people's ability to discriminate pragmatically relevant from irrelevant features of problem situations. Students with experience in learning mathematics appear to know that the typical content details contained in word problems that exemplify abstract equations are irrelevant, effectively screening them out from the resulting representations of solution procedures. The semantic content is more likely to be viewed as relevant, however, when the mathematical procedures are taught as algorithms specifically tailored to an ecologically valid knowledge domain, such as physics or banking. The semantic-content cues are then included in the encoded representation, and partially determine the range of retrieval cues that can subsequently access the representation. Nonetheless, if more structural cues provide access, or if a hint is provided, such domain-specific content generally does not greatly impair postaccess mapping, as people are able to make use of structural constraints to find correspondences between dissimilar concepts (Holyoak & Thagard, 1989).

The gravest difficulty is posed by conceptual differences based on mathematical quantity types, such as the contrast between intensive and extensive variables. Such distinctions are likely to be deemed pragmatically relevant for the excellent reason that, for some mathematical operations, they are in fact crucially important. The physics training elevated the perceived importance of these distinctions, whereas the algebra training made such distinctions seem irrelevant. Quantity type is not a simple semantic property that readily "drops out" of a mapping after structural constraints are applied; rather, it determines the structural representations given to key variables in the problems, so that a mismatch of quantity types directly corrupts the structural basis for mapping. Typically, a rerepresentation of the variables—the creation of new abstractions that eliminate the structural mismatch—is required in order for mapping to succeed.

As we have mentioned before, it is likely that the pattern of results we have observed will prove sensitive to the level of expertise of the problem solvers. In general, experts are presumably better able to assess the pragmatic relevance of features, and they will be better able to adjust their assessment to the requirements of particular problem structures (Novick, 1988). Thus we would expect the detrimental impact of domain-specific training content to be accentuated for students with lesser mathematical experience than those from the subject populations we have examined. Similarly, it is possible that the severe transfer impairment generated by mismatching quantity types will be reduced for more experienced mathematicians.

Although our results to date point to the crucial importance of conceptual structure in understanding mathematical transfer, we really have only a dim understanding of how these structural differences actually operate, or even how they are best characterized. We have emphasized the distinction between psychologically intensive versus extensive quantities, but the basis for this distinction is far from clear. As we pointed out, from a purely formal view even the psychologically extensive quantities used by Bassok (1990) are actually intensive. Yet she found, for example, that knowledge about speed was readily transferred to a problem involving price in dollars per minute, but not to one involving salary in dollars per year. What exactly is the difference? It is conceivable that the conceptual gap between speed and quantities such as "potatoes per day" is due to additional or alternative correlated dimensions, such as continuous versus discrete, or dynamic versus static. It is possible—indeed likely—that small variations in the phrasing of problems can greatly alter their psychological representations. For example, problems using explicit rate-like units (e.g., m/sec and $/min) may be more easily mapped than problems for which the quantities are not tagged by salient and similar units. Also, Bassok's (1990) study only demonstrated lack of transfer from intensive to extensive quantities, not vice versa. It is not clear whether the impact of a type mismatch will prove symmetrical. Indeed, one could interpret our original results in which abstract algebra was easily applied to physics, as a case of extensive-to-intensive transfer. It is possible that extensive quantities are perceived as simpler, or as the "default case" for general variables, whereas intensive quantities may be perceived as more complex or as the marked "special case." The most confident conclusion we can offer is simply that the complex interrelations among pragmatic knowledge, semantic content, and conceptual structure invite deeper exploration.

REFERENCES

Bassok, M. (1990). Transfer of domain-specific problem solving procedures. *Journal of Experimental Psychology: Learning, Memory, and Cognition, 16*, 522–533.

Bassok, M., & Holyoak, K.J. (1985, November). *Transfer between isomorphic topics in algebra and physics*. Paper presented at the 26th Annual Meeting of the Psychonomic Society, Boston.

Bassok, M., & Holyoak, K.J. (1989). Interdomain transfer between isomorphic topics in algebra and physics. *Journal of Experimental Psychology: Learning, Memory, and Cognition, 15*, 153–166.

Brown, A.L. (1989). Analogical learning and transfer. What develops? In S. Vosniadou & A. Ortony (Eds.), *Similarity and analogical reasoning* (pp. 369–412). Cambridge, UK: Cambridge University Press.

Brown, A.L., Kane, M.J., & Echols, C.H. (1986). Young children's mental models determine analogical transfer across problems with a common goal structure. *Cognitive Development, 1*, 103–121.

Carey, S. (1985). *Conceptual change in childhood*. Cambridge, MA: MIT Press.

Catrambone, R., & Holyoak, K.J. (1989). Overcoming contextual limitations on problem-solving transfer. *Journal of Experimental Psychology: Learning, Memory, and Cognition, 15*, 1147–1156.

Catrambone, R., & Holyoak, K.J. (1990). Learning subgoals and methods for solving probability problems. *Memory & Cognition, 18*, 593–603.

Cheng, P.W., & Holyoak, K.J. (1985). Pragmatic reasoning schemas. *Cognitive Psychology, 17*, 391–416.

Cheng, P.W., & Holyoak, K.J. (1989). On the natural selection of reasoning theories. *Cognition, 33,* 285–313.

Chi, M.T.H. (1988). Children's access and knowledge reorganization: An example from the concept of animism. In F. Weinert & M. Perlmutter (Eds.), *Memory development: Universal changes and individual differences* (pp. 169–194). Hillsdale, NJ: Erlbaum.

Chi, M.T.H., Bassok, M., Lewis, M.W., Reimann, P., & Glaser, R. (1989). Self-explanations: How students study and use examples in learning to solve problems. *Cognitive Science, 13,* 145–182.

Chi, M.T.H., Feltovich, P.J., & Glaser, R. (1981). Categorization and representation of physics problems by experts and novices. *Cognitive Science, 5,* 121–152.

Collins, A., & Stevens, A.L. (1982). Goals and strategies of inquiry teachers. In R. Glaser (Ed.), *Advances in instructional psychology II* (pp. 65–119). Hillsdale, NJ: Erlbaum.

Elio, R., & Anderson, J.R. (1984). The effects of information order and learning mode on schema abstraction. *Memory & Cognition, 12,* 20–30.

Gentner, D. (1983). Structure-mapping: A theoretical framework for analogy. *Cognitive Science, 7,* 155–170.

Gentner, D. (1989). The mechanisms of analogical reasoning. In S. Vosniadou & A. Ortony (Eds.), *Similarity and analogical reasoning* (pp. 199–241). Cambridge, UK: Cambridge University Press.

Gentner, D., & Landers, R. (1985). Analogical reminding: A good match is hard to find. In *Proceedings of the International Conference on Systems, Man, and Cybernetics.* Tucson, AZ.

Gick, M.L., & Holyoak, K.J. (1980). Analogical problem solving. *Cognitive Psychology, 12,* 306–355.

Gick, M.L., & Holyoak, K.J. (1983). Schema induction and analogical transfer. *Cognitive Psychology, 15,* 1–38.

Gick, M.L., & Holyoak, K.J. (1987). The cognitive basis of knowledge transfer. In S.M. Cormier & J.D. Hagman (Eds.), *Transfer of training: Contemporary research and applications* (pp. 9–46). New York: Academic Press.

Greeno, J.G. (1983). Conceptual entities. In D. Gentner & A.L. Stevens (Eds.), *Mental models* (pp. 227–252). Hillsdale, NJ: Erlbaum.

Holland, J.H., Holyoak, K.J., Nisbett, R.E., & Thagard, P.R. (1986). *Induction: Processes of inference, learning, and discovery.* Cambridge, MA: MIT Press.

Holyoak, K.J., & Koh, K. (1987). Surface and structural similarity in analogical transfer. *Memory & Cognition, 15,* 332–340.

Holyoak, K.J., & Thagard, P. (1989). Analogical mapping by constraint satisfaction. *Cognitive Science, 13,* 295–355.

Kaput, J.J. (1986). Quantity structure of algebra word problems: A preliminary analysis. In G. Lappan & R. Even (Eds.), *Proceedings of the 8th Annual Meeting of the PME-NA* (pp. 114–120). East Lansing, MI: PME-NA.

Keil, F.C. (1987). Conceptual development and category structure. In U. Neisser (Ed.), *Concepts and conceptual development: Ecological and intellectual factors in categorization* (pp. 175–200). Cambridge, UK: Cambridge University Press.

Kintsch, W., & Greeno, J.G. (1985). Understanding and solving word arithmetic problems. *Psychological Review, 92,* 109–129.

Medin, D.L. (1989). Concepts and conceptual structure. *American Psychologist, 44,* 1469–1481.

Medin, D.L., & Ortony, A. (1989). Psychological essentialism. In S. Vosniadou & A. Ortony (Eds.), *Similarity and analogical reasoning* (pp. 179-195). Cambridge: Cambridge University Press.

Mitchell, T.M., Keller, R.M., & Kedar-Cabelli, S.T. (1986). Explanation-based generalization: A unifying view. *Machine Learning, 1,* 48–80.

Novick, L.R. (1988). Analogical transfer, problem similarity, and expertise. *Journal of Experimental Psychology: Learning, Memory, and Cognition, 14,* 510–520.

Ross, B.H. (1984). Remindings and their effects in learning a cognitive skill. *Cognitive Psychology, 16,* 371–416.

Ross, B.H. (1987). This is like that: The use of earlier problems and the separation of similarity effects. *Journal of Experimental Psychology: Learning, Memory, and Cognition, 13,* 629–639.

Ross, B.H. (1989). Distinguishing types of superficial similarities: Different effects on the access and use of earlier problems. *Journal of Experimental Psychology: Learning, Memory, and Cognition, 15,* 456–468.

Schoenfeld, A.H. (1979). Explicit heuristics training as a variable in problem-solving performance. *Journal of Research in Mathematics Education, 10,* 173–187.

Schoenfeld, A.H. (1985). *Mathematical problem solving.* New York: Academic Press.

Schwartz, J.L. (1981). *The role of semantic understanding in solving multiplication and division word problems* (Final Report to NIE, Grant NIE-G-80-0144). Cambridge, MA: Massachusetts Institute of Technology.

Schwartz, J.L. (1988). Intensive quantity and referent transforming arithmetic operations. In J. Hiebert & M.J. Behr (Eds.), *Research agenda in mathematical education: Number concepts and operations in the middle grades* (Vol. 2). Reston, VA: National Council of Teachers of Mathematics; and Hillsdale, NJ: Erlbaum.

Singley, M.K., & Anderson, J.R. (1989). *The transfer of cognitive skill.* Cambridge, MA: Cambridge University Press.

Winston, P.H. (1975). Learning structural descriptions from examples. In P.H. Winston (Ed.), *The psychology of computer vision.* New York: McGraw-Hill.

Chapter 5

Transfer of Situated Learning

James G. Greeno   David R. Smith
Joyce L. Moore   University of California,
Stanford University   Santa Cruz

and the Institute for Research on Learning

> Conceptions are general because of their use and application, not because of
> their ingredients...the moment a meaning is gained, it is a working tool of further
> apprehensions, an instrument of understanding other things...Synthesis is not a
> matter of mechanical addition, but of application of something discovered in one
> case to bring other cases into line. (Dewey, 1910/1985, p. 281)

The question of transfer is often framed as asking whether some knowledge
learned in one situation will be utilized in another situation. If it is not, the
knowledge is said to be inert, or the person is said to have failed to apply
knowledge that he or she has.

This chapter presents a different view of transfer in the context of a general
view of cognition. In this alternative general view that is being developed (e.g.,
Brown, Collins, & Duguid, 1989; Greeno, 1989; Jordan, 1987; Laboratory of
Comparative Human Cognition, 1983; Lave, 1988; McCabe & Balzano, 1986;
Rogoff, 1990; Shaw & Alley, 1985; Shaw, Turvey, & Mace, 1982; Suchman,
1987), learning is considered to be essentially situated, an adaptation of a person
or group to features of the situation in which learning occurs. Knowledge—
perhaps better called *knowing*—is not an invariant property of an individual,
something that he or she has in any situation. Instead, knowing is a property that
is relative to situations, an ability to interact with things and other people in
various ways. An analogy with physics seems helpful. Physicists recognize that
motion is not a property of an object. The description of a moving object in

terms of speed, direction, and acceleration depends fundamentally on a frame of reference. It is not enough to say that the frame of reference influences motion—in fact, saying that is quite misleading. Rather, the property that we refer to as motion is a relation between an object and a frame of reference, and it makes no sense to try to characterize motion except with reference to a frame. Similarly, it may not suffice to say that cognition is influenced by contexts. In the view of situated cognition, we need to characterize knowing, reasoning, understanding, and so on as relations between cognitive agents and situations, and it is not meaningful to try to characterize what someone knows apart from situations in which the person engages in cognitive activity.[1]

In this relativistic view, knowing is ability to interact with things and other people in a situation, and learning is improvement in that ability—that is, getting better at participating in a situated activity. The question of transfer, then, is to understand how learning to participate in an activity in one situation can influence (positively or negatively) one's ability to participate in another activity in a different situation. The answer must lie in the nature of the situations, in the way that the person learns to interact in one situation, and in the kind of interaction in the second situation that would make the activity there successful.

When we adopt the view that cognition is situated, the issue of transfer is social in a fundamental way (cf. Laboratory of Comparative Human Cognition, 1983; Lave, 1988; Pea, 1989). Learning occurs as people engage in activities, and the meanings and significance of objects and information in the situation derive from their roles in the activities that people are engaged in. The goals of activity that are defined socially determine which features of situations are important and therefore play a major role in determining which features people will attend to in their interaction with objects and information in the situation. Conversations with others participating in the activity also influence attention as individuals come to attend to the same features in order to communicate and coordinate their actions (Stucky, in preparation). Perhaps most importantly, the activities of learning and performance can be defined socially in ways that encourage or discourage efforts to learn in order to transfer to a broader domain of situations, or, in a transfer situation, to try to relate the situation to the person's previous experience (Brown, 1989). In effect, social interactions influence people's understanding about what constitutes a domain of situations, so that activities that occur in different situations that belong to the domain can be expected to benefit from a common set of learning experiences.

---

[1] This view of cognition as being situated is a contemporary version of a views taken in many earlier discussions including those of Dewey and Bentley (1949) and interactional psychologists such as Riegel and Meacham (1978). We understand our role as continuing to develop the framing assumption of situated cognition as one side of a continuing conceptual and theoretical discussion that is inherent in the effort to formulate a satisfactory theory of mind.

Overview of the Chapter We present our discussion in six sections. In Section 1 we present a general view of transfer in terms of affordances and invariants of activity. We discuss three concepts: attunement to affordances, cognition of potential states of affairs, and affordances for reasoning.

In the next three sections, we discuss three sets of transfer studies. These examples illustrate transfer based on invariants involving the three aspects of cognitive activity discussed in Section 1.

In Section 2, we discuss experiments by Scholckow and Judd (Judd 1908) and Hendrickson and Schroeder (1941). In these studies, learning involved adjustment to a constraint in the situation, requiring transformation of a familiar activity. We propose a hypothesis in which initial learning can be accomplished in different ways that involve attending to different affordances in the situation. The test of transfer involves a transformation of the initial situation that leaves one of the initial affordances approximately invariant, but changes others. We hypothesize that transfer depended on which affordance or affordances were involved in the activity in initial learning, and how they were perceived in relation to other features of the situation.

In Section 3, we discuss experiments by Brown and Kane (1988) and Duncker (1935/1945) involving cognition of potential states of affairs, which we interpret as showing that this kind of prospective perception can be influenced by one's experience. Brown and Kane's experiment showed positive transfer, and Duncker's showed negative transfer, produced by conditions that we interpret as learning to perceive information that specifies potential states of affairs that either provide affordances for solving new problems or interfere with perceiving affordances for solutions.

In Section 4, we discuss studies by Wertheimer (1945/1959) and Sayeki, Ueno, and Nagasaka (in press), which illustrate two extensions of the concept of affordance: an affordance for conceptual reasoning, and an affordance for spatial transformations that preserves a quantity as an invariant.

In Section 5 we discuss our view of transfer in relation to other recent accounts based on concepts of information processing. Section 6 presents a brief theoretical reflection.

1. TRANSFER BASED ON AFFORDANCES AND INVARIANTS

In an activity, a person or a group interacts with objects and material in a situation. There can be a socially or personally determined goal of the activity, or the activity may simply be a process of interaction. The activity jointly depends on properties of things and materials in the situation and on characteristics of the person or group. Following Gibson (1979/1986) and Shaw et al. (1982), we call the support for particular activities created by relevant properties of the things and materials in the situation *affordances*. We use the term *abilities*[2] to refer to the characteristics of agents that enable them to engage in activities. Affordances and abilities are relative to each other: A situation can afford an activity for an agent who has appropriate abilities, and an agent can have an ability for an activity in a situation that has appropriate affordances. Performance of an activity also depends on the agent's motivation and perception of the affordance for the activity in the situation.

Transfer of a learned activity to a different situation involves a transformation of the situation and an invariant interaction of the agent within the situation. Figure 1 indicates the general idea that we use in our discussion here. An agent learns an activity in some situation, s1 The agent's interaction within the situation is indicated by the three-headed arrow a1 A transformation is applied to the situation, changing it to s2, and the question is whether the person knows how to act in s2, based on what he or she learned. The activity needed to interact within the new situation is a2. Transfer can occur if the structure of the activity is invariant across the transformation from s1 to s2 with respect to important features that make it successful, or if a needed transformation of the activity can be accomplished.

For an activity learned in one situation to transfer to another situation, as in the sketch of Figure 5.1, the second situation has to afford that activity and the agent has to perceive the affordance. In many cases, a situation affords several different kinds of interaction that all are regarded as successful performance. If the situation is changed, some of those interactions can still occur and others cannot, that is, the structure of some, but not all, versions of the initial activity are invariant across the transformation of the situation. If a learned activity is to transfer, then, it has to be learned in a form that is invariant across changes in the situation or that can be transformed as needed, and transfer depends as well on ability to perceive the affordances for the activity that are in the changed situation.

The activities that people learn are constructed and situated socially. To a great extent, the affordances that enable our activities are properties of artifacts that have been designed so those activities can be supported. The functions of these properties as affordances are shaped by social practices. People learn these practices, including the utilities of affordances, mainly by participating in them along with other people. The range of situations that provide affordances for an activity constitutes an important aspect of the socially constructed meanings of the properties of those situations, so that the potential for transfer between situations is shaped by the social practices in which people learn the activities.

---

[2] We prefer the term *abilities* rather than the coined term *effectivities* that Shaw et al. used, but we think that our meaning coincides with theirs.

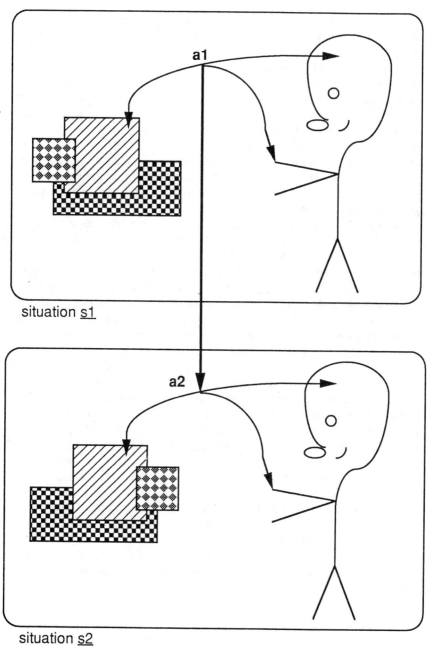

situation s1

situation s2

Figure 5.1   Transfer of a situated activity.

Transfer can occur from situations in which instruction deliberately shapes a student's activity, and in those cases the social interactions that constitute instruction play a crucial role. In order to result in transfer, instruction should influence the activity so that it includes attention to affordances that are invariant across changes in the situation and that will support successful interactions in situations that have been transformed. Instruction influences activity in many ways, of course, including the conversational use of symbols that represent important features of the situation and activity to guide students' attention. We view the role of representations, however, as instrumental in the service of acquiring abilities to interact successfully in situations, and acquiring these abilities can be quite a different matter from acquiring representations of the situations in which the interactions need to occur or representations of procedures that describe successful activities.

Gibson's theory of perception emphasizes processes of information pickup that he assumed do not depend on mediating mental representations, and his views are sometimes taken to be contrary to assumptions that mental representations ever play a role in cognition. We do not take this strong position (indeed, we do not think that Gibson did). We agree, rather, with Neisser's (1989) hypothesis that direct perception and recognition constitute two modes of perception. In direct perception information is *picked up* (Gibson's term) as the agent interacts in the environment. In recognition, features of an object are matched against stored patterns. For example, information for orientation and locomotion in space is mainly perceived directly, while information for identifying a specific object, such as your car in a parking lot, is recognized. The distinction corresponds to one in visual perception between ambient and foveal modes of processing (Liebowitz & Post, 1982). Of course, the information that is picked up directly has to correspond to distinctive states of the nervous system, and the term *representation* can be used for that correspondence (cf., e.g., Gallistel, 1990). We will use the term *symbolic representation* to distinguish representations in which physical or mental objects correspond to objects, events, properties, or relations in the domain that is represented.[3] For our purposes here, the main point is that affordances can be perceived without there being a symbolic representation of the properties that specify the affordances. In our view, the ways in which symbolic representations function in learning and cognition need to be analyzed for specific cases, and alternative hypotheses about the nature and roles of representations need to be considered and argued through.

---

[3] Symbols may be organized to form propositions, in which case the symbolic expressions have denotations and truth values. Symbols may also constitute physical or mental models that can simulate events that are represented. The general feature of symbolic representations, as we use the term here, is that the symbols are objects and that reasoning operations are applied to those objects to make inferences.

We need terminology that is more differentiated than Gibson's, and some helpful terms are provided by situation theory (e.g., Barwise, 1989; Devlin, 1988). In situation theory, a *state of affairs* is a relation that may or may not hold in a given situation. For example, in a situation that has a chair c and a person named Jay in it, the relation roughly stated as "c supports Jay" would hold if Jay is sitting, standing, or kneeling on the chair, or is in some other way supported by it; the relation does not hold if Jay is not being supported by the chair.

This allows us to define a *type* of situation. A representation of a situation type includes one or more parameters. For example, let χ be a parameter for a chair and let π be a parameter for a person. The "χ supports π" designates a situation type. Let S_{csp} stand for the type of situation in which some chair is supporting some person. A situation s is of type S_{csp} if there are a chair and a person in s, and the chair is supporting the person.

Situation types are related through *constraints*, and understanding situations depends on being *attuned* to constraints. For example, let S_{ssc} be the type of situation in which a chair is supported by something solid or a suitably dense liquid. (The relation of support can involve being suspended from a solid object.) We can be attuned to the constraint that any situation of type S_{csp} is also a situation of type S_{ssc}. Thus, if we see someone sitting in a chair, apparently floating in midair, we know that the appearance is wrong and that somehow that chair is supported, perhaps by wires.

Situations are extended in time, and we can apply this terminology to events as well as to static situations. For example, if an object moves through space along a given path, the location of the object will be on that trajectory, displaced from where it was before in the direction of the movement. Our attunement to constraints of movement in space enables us to interact with things and people in situations in which objects—including ourselves—move through space and thereby change their (our) locations, collide with other objects, and so on. We know that, if someone walks through a doorway from the hallway to the classroom, he or she will be in the classroom after passing through the doorway. If S_{pwd} is the type of situation in which a person is walking through a doorway into a classroom, and S_{pir} is the type of situation in which a person is in the classroom, then our knowledge of motion in space includes attunement to the constraint that any situation of type $S_{.pwd}$ is also a situation of type S_{pir}.[4]

We need to link the terminology of situation theory with the terminology of affordances and invariants. We do this with three concepts: (a) attunement to affordances, (b) cognition of potential states of affairs, and (c) affordances for reasoning, including reasoning with representations of concepts.

Attunement to affordances. Perception of affordances involves attunement to possibilities for activity in situations. As an example, consider the affordance

---

[4] Our informal notation here neglects many necessary details, including symbols to denote temporal sequences. See Devlin (1988) for more details.

that a doorway presents for walking through it, studied by Warren and Whang (1987). Suppose that S_{fjwd} is the type of situation with a doorway that affords walking through by Jay, and S_{jwd} is the type of situation in which Jay walks through the doorway; then we can say that S_{fjwd} affords S_{jwd}. As Shaw and Hazelett (1986) discussed, activities produce reciprocal modulations involving the world and the agent's cognition. Jay's abilities include the ability to walk through a doorway (comparable to the ability to grasp a cup, turn a handle, speak in a conversation, etc.) with his movements calibrated with the environment, so that the situation changes in a characteristic way while significant properties and relations are invariant. For example, walking through a doorway involves a change in the person's location, relative to a wall, but the person remains upright and supported by the floor or ground. Perceiving an affordance for an action involves picking up the information that specifies the structural invariants that support the action, which is included in a cognitive schema, in Bartlett's (1932) sense,[5] that organizes the person's participation in the action. We would say that Jay is attuned to the affordance of walking through a doorway if Jay's perceiving the relevant information about the doorway (that the width and height of the doorway are sufficient, relative to Jay's size) is part of an action schema in which Jay prospectively perceives the possibility of walking through the doorway, at least when Jay is motivated to walk through the doorway.

Motivation, in this case, means being engaged in an activity sequence in which getting to the space on the other side of the wall has significant functional value.[6] When an agent is in an appropriate motivational state, perceiving an affordance is tantamount to performing the activity that is afforded. For example, if getting into the classroom has a dominant functional value in Jay's current activity, then when Jay perceives the affordance of walking through the doorway into the classroom, he will walk through the doorway. In that case, the constraint relation between types of situations applies: if the situation is of type S_{fjwd}, then it also is of type S_{jwd}. On the other hand, Jay could perceive the affordance without walking through the doorway, at least immediately, for example, if he saw a friend and stopped for a conversation. He could also perceive the information that specifies the affordance without perceiving the affordance, for example, if he was painting the wall and needed to move his ladder.

Potential states of affairs. More generally, people can be cognizant of possible states of affairs that could hold in a situation but do not hold at present. Cognition of possibilities, like perception of affordances, depends on being attuned to constraints. The type of situation one is in could be transformed into

---

[5] "Schema' refers to an active organisation of past reactions, or of past experiences, which must always be supposed to be operating in any well adapted organic response" (Bartlett, 1932, p. 201).

[6] Gallistel (1980) discussed a concept of motivation in which the motivation for components of activity result from their fitting in more general activities that the organism is engaged in.

another type of situation, but whether that occurs depends on something else, which may be an action that the perceiver could perform or some other event. Inference of this possible change can occur through a process like the perception of an affordance, as Shaw and Hazelett (1986) noted. We hypothesize that schemata for events that have been perceived are similar to action schemata and support cognition of potential states of affairs in a similar way. Such event schemata enable inference of potential states of affairs through a process of perceiving information that specifies the possibility of a transformation in the environment, as perception of an affordance involves perceiving information that specifies the possibility of an action. The schema might support this kind of prospective cognition through enactment of mental simulations of the transformations that could cause the potential states of affairs to hold.

Affordances are a special case of potential states of affairs—the situation would support a certain activity. Jay might infer that he could walk through the door when he perceives the affordance, although his current activity involves finishing a conversation. Furthermore, there are cases in which one person can perceive an affordance for someone else's activity—if you see someone walking toward a doorway, you can perceive the affordance that is there for her or him. If you know that a doorway affords walking-through by Jay, you only know that Jay *could* walk through it—whether he does that is still an open question. Perceiving the affordance is based on perceptible information in the situation that specifies the affordance. Perceiving the affordance for Jay can be part of inferring the possibility of a potential state of affairs, Jay's being in the room on the other side of the door. Inferring that possibility, based on perceiving the affordance, depends on being attuned to the constraint that a situation of type S_{jwd} is also a situation of the type where Jay is (after the action) in the space on the other side of the doorway, that is, the state of affairs "Jay is in the classroom" will hold.

In other cases, a person can infer the possibility of a potential state of affairs that does not depend on a human action. If several books are stacked in an unstable pile, a person can infer (prospectively perceive) the possibility of the potential state of affairs that would hold if they fell over. The event of the books falling can be simulated, and the state of affairs that would result holds in that simulation. The potential state of affairs with books spilled can be inferred in the situation because it is the result of a transformation that can occur, and information that can be perceived specifies that possibility of that transformation.

Reasoning and concepts. Finally, we consider situations in which the actions a person can perform involve reasoning. We use the term *reasoning* to refer to some of the activities in which people put information into situations.

The information in a situation includes states of affairs that are *registered* (Smith, 1987) by a person, thereby being represented in the form of a propositional symbolic expression. Registered states of affairs are often communicated through language, thereby being included in a collection of information that is shared by participants in a conversation. We also intend the phrase *registered states of affairs* to include those states of affairs that a person represents propositionally with cognitive symbols, including the symbolic representations that result when objects or categories are recognized by matching stimulus features to patterns stored in memory (Neisser, 1989).

Many expressions of registered states of affairs represent information that a person perceives. These are states of affairs that already hold in the situation. In addition, potential states of affairs can be registered if they are perceived prospectively, when a person perceives the affordance structure of an action or other event in which the potential state of affairs will hold if an action or other event occurs.

The theoretical distinction between perceiving and reasoning is not sharp, and it could be drawn in several different places. One feature of reasoning seems to be the involvement of representations. In our discussion here, we apply the term *reasoning* when an inference includes an operation that transforms a representation. Representations include symbolic expressions that represent actual or potential states of affairs. Representations also include physical constructions such as diagrams, graphs, pictures, and models with properties that are interpreted as corresponding to properties of situations. Cognitive representations also include mental models that contain cognitive objects that correspond to objects, properties, or relations in situations, and that simulate actions or other events in situations. In our usage, then, the reference class of the term *reasoning* includes inferences that involve transformations of physical or mental propositional representations with processes that correspond to firing production rules, and it includes inferences involving transformations of representations in physical or mental models involving simulations of events. These inference processes may be entirely mental, with mental representations of propositions or with mental models, or they may be at least partially physical, with written representations of propositions as statements or formulas, or with diagrams or working physical models.

Note that to qualify as reasoning, we require that the objects that are manipulated function as representations. This excludes occurrences in which someone knows some rules for transforming notations in a language without knowing what the notations mean, as in Searle's (1980) parable of the Chinese room.

Our usage also excludes some occurrences in which symbolic representations are needed but are not transformed in the cognitive process. For example, a mailbox provides an affordance for posting a letter,[7] but that affordance is not specified in the visual information that is available when a person looks at a mailbox. The person has to recognize the object as a mailbox, which we

---

[7] The affordance of a mailbox is an occasional example in discussions of Gibson's theory (cf. Gibson, 1979/1986; Neisser, 1989).

hypothesize as registering a state of affairs and thereby having a symbolic representation that designates that the object is a mailbox. We do not suppose, however, that becoming cognizant of the affordance of posting a letter requires a transformation of the symbolic representation of the mailbox.[8] When a mailbox is recognized for what it is, the person can be cognizant of its affordance by knowing its role in the activity of posting letters. On this hypothesis, a mental representations of the mailbox is required, but no transformation of that representation is involved; hence, it does not qualify as an instance of *reasoning* in the sense that we use that term here.

Affordances for reasoning, on this account, are properties of representations in relation to a person's or group's abilities to use the representations to make inferences. Reasoning is an activity that transforms a representation, and the representation affords that transformational activity. Abilities for reasoning activities include knowing the operations to perform on the notational objects in the representation and understanding the semantic significance of the objects and operations.

Conceptual reasoning occurs when representations of concepts are included in the representations that are used in reasoning. A concept can be represented either explicitly, as an object, or implicitly, as a property or relation of objects. Generally, concepts correspond to properties or relations in a domain. When an object in a representation corresponds to a property or relation, that property or relation if *reified* (Smith, 1987) in the representation. In many of the examples that we discuss, those in Sections 4 and 5.4, the concepts are numbers, quantities, and numerical and quantitative variables. Knowing a set of concepts, including those of number and quantity, can be considered as analogous to knowing how to find and use things that are in an environment (Greeno, 1991). The concepts can be reified in a representation, represented by numerals and letters. Abilities to reason with these arithmetic or algebraic representations include knowing arithmetic or algebraic operations and how to use representations that are formed according to the conventions of arithmetic and algebraic notation. For someone with those abilities, arithmetic and algebraic representations present significant affordances for reasoning. We also discuss reasoning in Section 5.3 that we hypothesize as depending mainly on mental models in which a person can simulate an event that is described in a written or spoken text. In that case, according to our hypothesis, concepts such as permission to do something are represented implicitly as properties of the situations that are simulated, rather than being represented explicitly by symbols that reify them.

---

[8] Recognition may be accomplished through a process of activating a pattern of feature detectors, as in an EPAM (Feigenbaum, 1963) or connectionist (McClelland & Rumelhart, 1981) network. The feature detectors of such systems may be considered as symbols that denote the features of an object that causes it to be recognized as a mailbox; however, cognizance of the affordance of posting a letter does not involve transforming the representation of the features used in recognition.

2. SCHOLCKOW AND JUDD'S AND HENDRICKSON AND SCHROEDER'S REFRACTION EXPERIMENTS

EMPIRICAL FINDINGS

A classic example of transfer was conducted by Scholckow and Judd and was summarized by Judd (1908). Fifth- and sixth-grade boys were asked to throw a small dart to hit a target placed under 12 inches of water. Because of refraction of light, if the boy threw toward the apparent location of the target, the dart went beyond the actual location of the target under the water. One group of boys received an explanation of refraction of light. The other group "was left to work out experience without theoretical training" (Judd, 1908, p. 37). The two groups did about equally well in learning to hit the target. Then the level of the water was lowered to four inches.

> The difference between the two groups of boys now came out very strikingly. The boys without theory were very much confused. The practice gained with twelve inches of water did not help them with four inches. Their errors were large and persistent. On the other hand, the boys who had the theory, fitted themselves to four inches very rapidly. Their theory evidently helped them to see the reason why they must not apply the twelve-inch habit to four inches of water. Note that theory was not of value until it was backed by practice, but when practice and theory were both present the best adjustment was rapidly worked out. (Judd, 1908, p. 37)

The depth of water was shifted again to eight inches for both groups after they had mastered the four-inch condition, and the group without instruction about refraction "were again confused."

Hendrickson and Schroeder (1941) conducted a similar experiment to Scholckow and Judd's, and gave a more complete description of its methods and results. They had eighth-grade boys shoot an air gun at a standard rifle target submerged in water in a 20-gallon tub with a depth of 11 inches. The boy stood on an 18-inch platform eight feet from the center of the target. In the initial learning task the target was covered with six inches of water, producing an apparent horizontal displacement of about three inches. In the transfer task the target was covered with two inches of water, producing an apparent displacement of about one inch. A hit was counted if the shot was in the bull's-eye or the next ring, a circle of diameter 1.4 inches. In each task, the boy shot until he scored three consecutive hits, with the first of these counted as the trial on which the task was accomplished. Thirty boys participated in each of three groups: a control group and two instructed groups.

Each boy in the control group was shown where to stand, was told that the criterion was three consecutive hits, and was told that the number of shots to reach that criterion would be recorded.

Each boy in the instructed groups was given a written explanation of refraction, accompanied by Figure 5.2. The boy studied the explanation until he said he understood it; no questions were allowed.

The two instructed groups differed only in the inclusion of one sentence in the explanation for Group B that was omitted for Group A. The text that both instructed groups saw was as follows:

> Everything we see is visible because light comes from it to the eye.
> Objects under water, when seen from above, do not appear in their true positions. Thus, in the diagram, the rock at A seems to be at B.
>
> This deception is caused by the refraction, or bending, of the light beam ACD at the surface of the water. The light rays are bent because light moves faster in air than it does in water. The side of the beam marked E escapes from the water before the side marked F reaches the air. Therefore, side E gets ahead of side F and the ray of light is actually bent.
>
> We are not used to light rays being bent. Consequently, we suppose that the stone lies in a straight line from our eye, and we make the mistake of thinking that it is at point B. (Hendrickson & Schroeder, 1941, p. 209)

The additional sentence that was included in Group B's explanation was:

> It is easy to see from the diagram that the deeper the lake is, the farther the real rock A will be from the image rock B. (Hendrickson & Schroeder, 1941, p. 209)

Results are shown in Table 5.1. The instructional conditions apparently facilitated both initial learning and transfer. The differences in initial learning

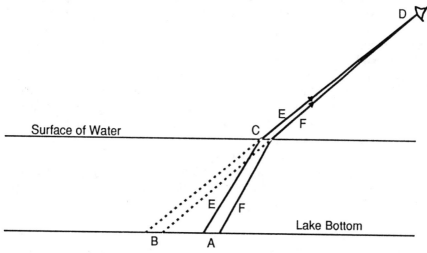

Figure 5.2   Diagram used by Hendrickson and Schroeder

Table 5.1   Mean Trials to Criterion for Shooting at an Underwater Target (from Hendrickson & Schroeder, 1941)

Group	Initial Learning (depth six inches)	Transfer (depth two inches)
Control	9.1	6.0
Instructed Group A	8.5	5.4
Instructed Group B	7.7	4.6

were not significant. With 95% confidence, the difference between Group B and the control was $-0.87 \leq \mu_{(C\text{-}B)} \leq 3.61$.[9] The best estimate is that Group B had about 15% facilitation due to the instruction that was given. Group A was apparently about midway in performance between Group B and the control group. The difference between Group A and the average of Group B and the control group was nearly zero, $-1.85 \leq \mu_{(A\text{-}(C+B)/2)} \leq 2.01$; therefore, there is no evidence that Group A was more or less similar to Group B than it was to the control group.

In the transfer task, the instruction given to Group B had a significant effect: $0.20 \leq \mu_{(C\text{-}B)} \leq 2.60$. The best estimate is that Group B's instruction resulted in about 23% positive facilitation. As in initial learning, Group A's performance in transfer was about midway between the control group and Group B, $-1.00 \leq \mu_{(A\text{-}(C+B)/2)} \leq 1.08$. If we consider the significant difference between Group B and the control group as the combination of two components: (a) the effect of the basic explanation given to both instructed groups, and (b) the effect of the additional information about the depth of the water, given to Group B, then there is no evidence that these two effects differed in magnitude.

Because the instructional conditions apparently affected the rate of initial learning, we need to consider whether the difference between groups in the transfer task should be interpreted as a result of differential transfer caused by the instruction. We believe that it should. At least two possibilities that would involve no differential transfer are inconsistent with the results. One possibility would involve no transfer at all—that is, learning to hit a target under six inches of water would have no effect on learning to hit the same target under two inches of water. That possibility seems very unlikely a priori, and is made more unlikely by the finding that all three groups required fewer trials in the transfer task than they did in the initial task.

Given that some transfer occurred, equal transfer across the groups would mean that the three groups all reached the same state of ability for the transfer task during their initial learning. That is, if the difference in instruction only produced a difference in initial learning, then the instruction would influence

---

[9] We have calculated confidence intervals based on the means and standard deviations that Hendrickson and Schroeder (1941) provided, using a pooled estimate of variance across the three conditions for the initial task and a separate pooled estimate for the transfer task.

the rate at which different groups reached the state of ability needed to get three consecutive hits, but their abilities at that point would not be different. In that case, however, the three groups should have been equal in the transfer task. The fact that the groups differed in the transfer task argues that what they learned during initial learning must have been different in some way that was relevant to their learning in the transfer task, not that they learned the same thing at different rates.

AN INTERPRETATION BASED ON AN INVARIANT AFFORDANCE OR A CONSTRAINT-BASED TRANSFORMATION

We offer an interpretation about the different amounts of transfer found by Hendrickson and Schroeder (1941) and Scholckow and Judd (Judd, 1908) as an illustration of the concepts of affordance and invariance that we think are central for the development of a theory of transfer.

The activity in this situation involved trying to hit a target by throwing a dart or by shooting an air gun. The goal was decided by the people who conducted the experiment—Scholckow, Judd, Hendrickson, and Schroeder—and apparently was agreed to by the boys who participated in the experiment. The activity of throwing something or shooting at a target is common among boys. The target affords being thrown or shot at, a dart affords being thrown or a gun affords being shot, and a free space between the boy and the target affords being thrown or shot through.

If the target had been on the floor in front of the boy, rather than under water, the activity probably would have been very familiar. Assuming previous experience in games such as throwing darts, pitching pennies, and tossing knives to stick in the ground, the fifth- and sixth-grade boys in Scholckow and Judd's experiment had already learned a complicated activity of throwing that includes perceiving the distance to the target, the height of the target relative to the boy's body, and the weight of the object being thrown. Similarly, the eighth-grade boys in Hendrickson and Schroeder's experiment probably knew an activity of shooting at targets. (We are not aware of an analysis of the affordances for throwing an object or shooting at a target, but such an analysis would probably not be conceptually difficult, following the pattern developed by Warren and his associates in analyses of stair climbing, Warren, 1984; running on an irregularly marked surface, Warren, Young, & Lee, 1986; and walking through an aperture, Warren & Whang, 1987.)

The familiar activity of throwing or shooting at a target through free space has to be modified when the target is under water. As the sketch in Figure 5.2 shows, light is bent by refraction, so a straight line from a student's eye through the point C on the surface hits a point farther away than the target at Point A. Actually, the situation is more complicated than Figure 5.2 indicates, because refraction affects the apparent depth as well as the apparent horizontal distance from the observer. Figure 5.3 shows side views of containers drawn to scale for the conditions used by Hendrickson and Schroeder (1941). We have calculated angles and locations based on a typical set of distances and heights. These calculations are illustrative; the actual values varied due to differing heights of the boys and variations such as leaning forward or backward as they aimed. Assume that a boy's eye level was 78 inches above the floor when he stood on the 18-inch platform. Consider a ray of light that passes from the center of the target, A, to the boy's eye, through point C on the surface of the water. Call the angle between the vertical and the light ray in water angle w, and call the angle between the vertical and the light ray in air angle a. The relation between angle a and angle w is $\sin(a)/\sin(w) = 4/3$, derived from Snell's Law and the refractive index of water. With six inches of water in the tub, angle a was 53.0 degrees, and angle w was 37.0 degrees. The apparent depth, from (apparent depth)/(true depth) = $\tan(w)/\tan(a)$, was 3.40 inches. The image of the target circle at location A, then, appeared at location B. The distortion consisted mainly of the bottom of the tub appearing less deep than its actual depth so that a shot aimed at the image B would miss the target by going beyond it. To hit the target, the boy had to aim along a line that would go straight to the actual location of target A. A straight line from the target at A to the boy's eye passed through Point G on the surface of the water, and a ray of light from that point corresponded to an image at F of an object actually located at E on the bottom of the tub. Therefore, if the boy aimed at point F, closer to him than B, his shot would hit the target at A.

The lower panel of Figure 5.3 shows the situation with two inches of water in the tub. The change in the level made very small differences in the angles: angle a was 52.3 degrees instead of 53.0 degrees, and angle w was 36.5 degrees instead of 37.0 degrees. The apparent depth was 1.14 inches. To hit the target under two inches of water, a horizontal correction was needed, again aiming at point F rather than at point B, but the amount of that correction was smaller with the two-inch depth than it was with the six-inch depth.

The two drawings in Figure 5.4 show the visual layouts as they would appear from a height of 78 inches and a horizontal distance of 96 inches from the center of the target. Hendrickson and Schroeder did not state the size of the targets they used or their location on the bottom of the tub. We have drawn targets of about 7.5 inches diameter, placed midway between the center of the tub and the far edge of the bottom. In this location, the targets would be easy to see from where the boys stood. Note that the different apparent depths of the water were visible features in the situation.

Our hypothesis about transfer assumes that there were multiple affordances in the situation for the activity of throwing or shooting. One possibility was simply to learn to aim at a point that was horizontally displaced from the image of the center of the target toward the boy. The affordance for this adjustment of the familiar activity was enhanced by the rings on the target. A boy could learn by

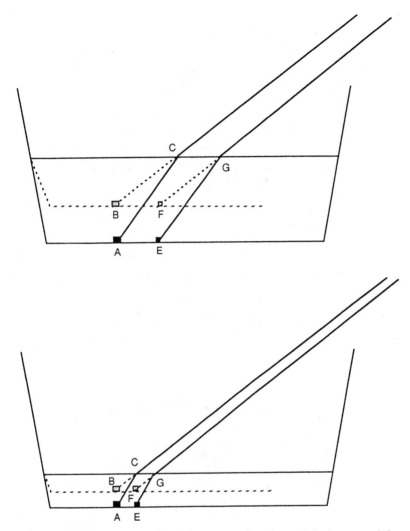

Figure 5.3   Side views of the tub, with apparent locations of the bottom of the tub, the center of the target (B), and a point to aim at to hit the center of the target (F), when viewed from the boy's position. Top panel: depth = 6 inches; bottom panel: depth = 2 inches.

trial and error to aim at a particular ring that was closer to him then the center of the target in order to hit the center.

If a boy aimed at a specific point displaced from the center of the target, and aimed at that same point after the depth was changed, his shots would then miss the center. In figure 5.3 with a 6-inch depth, the distance between B and F is·

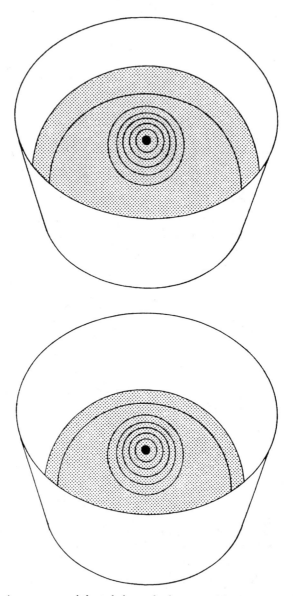

Figure 5.4.   Appearance of the tub from the boy's position. Top panel: depth = 6 inches; bottom panel: depth = 2 inches.

about 3.3 inches, while with a 2-inch depth the distance between B and F is about 1.1 inches, so aiming at the same point in the transfer situation would result in missing the center by about 2 inches.

Another adjustment in the initial learning situation would use an angular rotation between the apparent path of a pellet through the air and its apparent path after it entered the water. Figure 5.5 shows a side view of paths that a pellet would appear to have from the boy's point of view. (Recall that the boy's view is from a point above and to the right of the scene depicted in Figure 5.5). As a boy watched a pellet enter the water, its path would appear to bend upward. If the boy aimed at point B, the image of the target, then when the pellet entered the water at C, its path would appear to bend upward so that it would appear to hit the bottom of the tub at K, the image corresponding to point J on the actual bottom of the tub. To hit the center of the target at A, the boy needed to aim along another line that met the surface at point G. When the pellet entered the water at G its path would appear to bend upward and appear to hit the bottom at B, the image corresponding A. The boy could learn to aim along a line below the line that goes through C. The line to aim along to hit the center would go to the image at F, the image of a point on the bottom actually at E. The boy could attend to the angel between the straight line toward point F and the line that the pellet apparently followed after it entered the water, ∠FGB.

If a boy learned to correct his aim in the initial learning situation by visualizing the angle between the line of sight and the apparent path of the pellet under the water, then visualization of that same angle in the changed situation

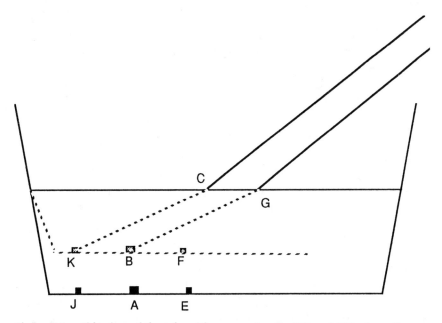

Figure 5.5.   Side view of the tub, with apparent paths (CK and GB) of a pellet after it enters the water at two different points on the surface.

would generate a line to aim along that would result in success. In Figure 5.3 with the 6-inch depth, $\angle$FGB is about 17.4 degrees, and with the 2-inch depth, $\angle$FGB is about 16.8 degrees.

A third possibility would involve focusing on the horizontal displacement of the point to aim at away from the center of the target, but relating that distance to the apparent depth of the water. Suppose that a boy adjusted his aim in the initial situation by focusing on a point closer to him than the center by a certain distance, d, the distance between B and F in the upper panel of Figure 5.3. When the situation was changed, the apparent depth of the water was decreased to about one-third of the previous apparent depth. The boy could make a proportional change in the distance between the center of the target and the point he aimed at. The change in the apparent depth was by a factor of 1/3, and if the boy changed the distance form d (with the 6-inch depth) to d/3 (with the 2-inch depth), then with the 2-inch depth he would aim at the image-point F, the point he needed to aim at to hit the center of the target.

Either the angular affordance or the relational-distance affordance would be sufficient to support successful transfer, but they could function in combination as well. Suppose that a boy aimed at point F in the initial situation, attending both to it horizontal distance from the center of the target and to the angular rotation of the apparent path of the pellet when it entered the water. When the depth of the water was changed, the boy could attend to the same image point on the bottom of the tub, and visualize the path that the pellet would take if he aimed at that point. Remembering the angle of rotation in the path from the initial situation, the boy could see that with the shallower water, the pellet would hit the bottom at a point closer to him than the center of the target. This could lead the boy to change the point he aimed at to be closer to the center of the target, perhaps by a factor that was approximately equal to the change in apparent depth.

The affordances of a distance between the apparent center of the target and another apparent point to aim at, an angular rotation of apparent path of a pellet, and the relation between the apparent distance between points and the apparent depth of water all provided ways for a boy to be cognitively connected with the situation in the activity of aiming a dart or an air rifle. Distances between points, angles between lines, and distances between plane surfaces all were features of the geometry of the situation, and either the distance or the angular rotation provided an affordance for modifying the action of throwing or shooting at the target that would support success in the initial learning situation. In other words, the action schema that a boy acquired initially could have incorporated either the distance or the angular rotation as a feature of the environment with which to calibrate aiming the dart or rifle. In our view, however, whether the activity transferred successfully when the water level changed depended on which affordance the action schema incorporated in initial learning, and how the boy applied the schema in transfer. If the activity was connected with the angular rotation, that affordance was invariant across the transformation of depth, and transfer therefore could occur simply by having the same activity in the transfer situation. If the activity was connected with the horizontal distance, that affordance was not invariant across the transformation of depth, and a change in the distance would have to be made. If the distance was seen in relation to the depth of water, successful transfer could occur if the boy was attuned to the constraint: [deeper water⇒greater distance], and therefore change the distance appropriately to accommodate to the new depth.

Our interpretation relates to Judd's (1908) in an interesting way. Judd believed that instruction in the theory of refraction "evidently helped [the students] to see the reason why they must not apply the twelve-inch habit to four inches of water." In our interpretation, whether the "twelve-inch habit" (or the "six-inch habit" in Hendrickson and Schroeder's, 1941, experiment) should be applied depended on what that habit was. If a boy's initial learning focussed on the apparent rotation of the path of the pellet, then applying the "twelve-inch habit" (or the "six-inch habit") is just what the boy should have done, because that activity would succeed in the transfer situation. In that case, knowing the theory of refraction would influence what the boy learned initially, rather than providing a reason to change the activity in the new situation. On the other hand, if a boy focussed on the distance from the center to the point he learned to aim at in the initial situation and related that distance to the depth, then the constraint [deeper water⇒greater distance] would play the role that Judd attributed to the theory; that is, attunement to the constraint would cause the boy to change the distance, thereby not applying the "twelve-inch habit" ("six-inch habit") in its original form, but with a significant modification.

How might we suppose that reading the brief text used for instruction could influence which of the affordances the boys incorporated into their action schemata in the learning situation? It seems reasonable to suppose that the discussion and the diagram of bending light rays might cause boys to attend to the apparent bending of the paths of pellets as they entered the water, which would increase the tendency to connect the activity of aiming with the affordance of an angular rotation. Further, the additional sentence given to Group B stated the constraint that deeper water causes a greater horizontal displacement, and reading and comprehending that sentence could have facilitated boys' being attuned to the constraint. Our analysis provides no basis for deciding which of the two affordances, or their combination, played the major role in supporting the transfer that occurred. A reasonable conjecture would be that both the angular rotation and the proportionality of horizontal distance to the apparent depth were effective. This is consistent with the pattern of Hendrickson and Schroeder's (1941) results, in which the instruction given to Group A apparently resulted in some positive transfer, but not as much as the instruction given to Group B.

In terms of constraints, both the learning and transfer situations had a path from the person to the target that afforded throwing a dart or shooting an air gun to hit the target. The action of aiming toward the apparent position of the target would not be successful, so the boys needed to learn a new constraint. We hypothesize that the constraint could be learned in several forms, each of which was a modification of the apparent direct path. One possible modification involved becoming attuned to a constraint: If you aim at a certain point, or at a point a certain distance closer than the apparent position of the target, you will hit the target. Another possible modification involved becoming attuned to a different constraint: If you aim so that a line that bends by a certain angle at the surface of the water goes through the apparent position of the target, you will hit the target. This constraint was invariant across the learning and transfer situations, so it would support transfer. The constraint in another possible modification involved a horizontal displacement, but with the amount of the displacement related to the apparent depth of the water. This second-order constraint would support transfer by requiring an adjustment of the quantity involved in the displacement constraint.

Concerning the role of mental representation, we speculate that, in aiming a dart or a gun at a target on the ground, a boy probably perceived and represented the target, but many other important features of the situation were perceived without being represented. We suppose that these would have included the distance between the boy and the target, the location of the target in relation to other nearby points, the line between the target and a point at which the dart was released or the pellet came out of the gun, the angle between that line and the ground, the weight of the dart or the pressure needed to pull the trigger, and many other features that could be relevant. Now imagine a skilled dart thrower or sharpshooter who saw (and represented) the target under water, aimed carefully, threw the dart or fired the gun, and saw that he had overshot the target by a considerable distance. This constituted a breakdown in the expected connection between the boy and the situation, and therefore an occasion to represent more features of the situation in an effort to correct the action. We hypothesize that the action schemata learned by the boys over several practice trials probably included constructions of mental representations with some features of the situation that they used to correct their aim.

A boy might have represented a line along the apparent bottom of the tub going through the apparent position of the target, and corrected his action by aiming at a point on that line nearer to him. This would involve a representation of the apparent location of the target in relation to some other locations in the situation that we suppose was not part of the boy's initial representation of the situation.

Another possibility is that the boy might have represented an angle equal to the amount that the apparent path of the pellet bent, and corrected his action by aiming so that the far side of that angle went through the target. In this case, the boy would have represented lines through the water and an angle between the lines that were not represented initially, In the transfer situation, if the boy represented the same angle as he remembered from his initial learning and chose a point to aim at based on that angle, he would succeed in hitting the target.

If a boy represented a line between the center of the target and the point he aimed at in his initial learning, and aimed at the same point in the transfer situation, he would undershoot the target. If he remembered the previous depth of the water, he could see that the water was less deep in the new situation, and could compare the new depth with a representation of the previous depth that he might visualize from memory. If he was in Group B, he might also have remembered a statement of the constraint included in the instruction, that "the deeper the lake is, the farther the real rock A will be from the image rock B," and decided to aim at a point nearer the center of the target. Some boys might have represented a numerical comparison between the new depth and the depth they remembered, saying to themselves something like, "About one-third," or "Less than half," and using the number they represented in determining how far away from the center of the target to aim.

The representations of lines and angles that we hypothesize are not contained in the mind in the usual psychological sense. They are, rather, a kind of spatial annotation of the perceived environment. For example, when you look at a doorway, you can visualize a line that goes diagonally from the upper left corner to the lower right corner, and you can visualize the angle that that line makes with a vertical line that bisects the doorway.[10] We expect that remembered representations also can be annotations of the physical environment, such as looking at the inside of the tub and visualizing a horizontal line that corresponds to the previous level of water that a boy remembered. Representations in the form of words, including the names of numbers, have a different relation to the physical objects in the situation than lines, angles, and so on that can be seen as inherent components of the situation. Verbal terms, such as *deeper* or *one-third*, can designate properties of the situation, and they provide symbols that can be used in reasoning apart from the physical situations that they refer to.

The cognitive outcome of initial learning that we hypothesize includes a process of representing some features of the situation in relation to an activity. This is different from a *schema* in the sense of that term currently in use by most theorists, in which a schema is a symbolic representation of a set of generic relations that is used to construct propositional representations in specific situations. The schemata that we hypothesize, following Bartlett (1932), are processes rather than data structures. A second important feature is that the representations that are constructed are representations of some features of the situation, such as lines, angles, and distances, rather than representations of the activity in the form of procedures. We assume that the boys learned to represent information in certain ways, and that the representations played a mediating role

---

[10] Simon (1978) gave a demonstration in which you imagine a rectangle, construct an imaginary vertical bisector, a diagonal from upper left to lower right of the rectangle, and a diagonal from the center of the base to the upper-right corner. He noted that most people can tell approximately where the two diagonal lines intersect. We suppose that visualizing lines in an imagined diagram is similar to, but harder than, visualizing lines in a spatial environment that is physically present.

that influenced the way in which they interacted with the objects and materials in the situation. The outcome of learning, however, was not itself a representation, either of the actions to be performed or of general propositions about the situation.

3. BROWN AND KANE'S'S AND DUNCKER'S STUDIES OF FUNCTIONAL TRANSFER

In this section we consider two experiments in which transfer occurred. brown and Kane (1988) demonstrated positive transfer by preschool children; Duncker (1935/1945) demonstrated negative transfer by adult participants. In both cases the solutions of problems depended on using some objects in the situation to perform an unusual function.

Empirical Findings

Brown and Kane (1988) presented three pairs of problems to 3, 4 and 5-year-old children. For each problem there was a three-dimensional set with toy people and objects so the child could enact the solution. One of the pairs of problems was the following:

> (A1)John, the garage mechanic, has a problem. He needs to take all of the tires that have been delivered to his garage and put them up on a shelf. But the shelf is too high and he doesn't have a ladder so he can't reach the shelf by himself. How can he solve his problem?

> (A2)Bill, the farmer, has a problem. He needs to put his bales of hay on top of his tractor so he can take them to the market. But Bill isn't tall enough to reach the top of the tractor by himself. How can he solve his problem? (Brown & Kane, 1988, p. 499)

The solution of both of these problems involves stacking objects to enable the person to reach the required height. In the garage problem, two tires are stacked; in the farm problem, two bales of hay are stacked. The other two pairs of problems involved (B1) pulling someone out of a hole with a spade, and (B2) pulling a boat ashore with a fishing rod; and (C1) swinging across a flooded stream with a willow branch, and (C2) swinging across a garden wall with clothes-drying lines. Each problem was presented, and if the child failed solve it, the experimenter showed the solution and asked the child to repeat the solution.

Some children worked in a No Reflection condition in which each problem was presented and solved or not, with no discussion of the solutions. A second group worked in a Reflection condition, in which each pair of problems was presented and the child was asked to say how the two problems were alike. (The

Reflection conditions differed somewhat among 3-year-olds, but Brown and Kane reported that the other Reflection conditions had the same effect as this Reflection condition.) There was also a Control condition in which children solved just one pair of problems after working on two irrelevant tasks, such as block design or seriation.

In all three age groups, children in the Reflection condition performed better than children in the Control condition on the final transfer problem, where there had been two previous opportunities to learn to transfer on the basis of solutions to the previous problems. For 3-year-old children, the Reflection condition was also better than the No Reflection condition, indicating that there was a significant effect of discussing the similarities between pairs of problems. The Reflection and No Reflection conditions did not differ for 4 and 5-year-olds; these children got the idea of transferring analogous solutions simply by experiencing the problems. Brown and Kane also reported data from the 3 and 4-years-old children in the Reflection condition on all three transfer problems. The 4-year-olds were significantly better than the 3-year-olds on the second problem, but not on the third, indicating that experiencing one pair of similar problems was sufficient for the 4-year-olds to learn to transfer, but that most of the 3-year-olds required two such experiences.

In contrast to Brown and Kane's illustration of positive transfer using objects for particular functions, a classic example of negative transfer was provided by Duncker's (1935/1945) experiment on functional fixedness. Duncker used five problems that required participants to construct some items out of various components that were provided, including some that were inessential. In the problem cited most often, the building materials included, among other things, three candles, some tacks, and three small boxes, about the size of ordinary matchboxes. The task was to mount the candles at eye height on a door "for visual experiments." The problem could be solved by tacking the boxes to the door, then mounting the candles in them. The problem was presented in two conditions: one with the boxes empty on the table, and the other with the boxes filled with various materials: the tacks, some candles, and some matches. The problem was more difficult if the box was being used as a container: three out of seven participants solved the problem in that case, compared to seven out of seven when the boxes were empty.

Another problem that Duncker devised involved a gimlet, a small boring tool with a handle at right angles to a shaft with a pointed, spiral cutting edge at the other end. The problem was to construct and arrangement for hanging three cords from a wooden support "for experiments in space perception." Two screw hooks were provided, and the participant had to find another means of supporting the third string. A solution was to screw the gimlet into the board as the third hanger. In one condition pilot holes for the screw hooks were already in the board; in the other condition the participant had to use the gimlet to bore pilot holes. The problem was harder in the condition in which the gimlet had to be used for its normal function of boring: 10 out of 14 participants solved the problem with the preparatory condition, compared to 10 out of 10 when the gimlet did not have to be used for boring.

In Duncker's experiment, participants worked on 41 problems in which the critical object was not used in an incompatible way, and all but one of these were solved. Participants worked on 49 problems in which the critical object was used in an incompatible way, and 30 of these were solved. Many subsequent experiments, especially with the box and candle problem, have confirmed that negative transfer occurs for a large number of individuals.

An Interpretation Based on Inference of Potential States of Affairs Influenced by Experience

In the experiments we discussed in Section 2, the agent's problem was how to perform an action to succeed in the transfer situation. It was obvious that the method to use to hit the target was to throw a dart or to shoot the air gun. The question was where to aim. In Brown and Kane's and Duncker's experiments, the question was what action to perform in order to achieve a functional goal.

As we stated in Section 1, we hypothesize that people can infer potential states of affairs based on schemata for actions and other events that are attuned to constraints involved in the affordance structures of situations. Some potential states of affairs are perceived prospectively in the context of ongoing events, such as a person seeing the trajectory of a moving object and ducking out of its way or moving to a location where he or she can catch it. Some potential states of affairs can be inferred by perceiving prospectively that something might happen, such as seeing the possibility that an unstable pile of books will fall over. Often, a potential state of affairs in inferred by prospectively perceiving the possibility of an action, such as seeing the possibility of being in a different location by walking along a visible path. Prospective perception of a potential state of affairs can be related to an affordance for one's own action or to an affordance for another agent's action.

Duncker's experiment required inference of potential states of affairs that could be achieved by constructing various kinds of physical structures. The states of affairs that were needed involved physical support, with one object in the situation such as a box or a gimlet functioning to support another object. Brown and Kane's experiment also required inference of potential states of affairs that could be achieved by constructing physical structures. The states of affairs were needed to provide affordances for actions such as climbing or swinging across a space. We hypothesize that in both experiments, the relevant inferences were probably made by prospectively perceiving the needed states of affairs in mental simulations that incorporated relevant constraints.

For transfer to occur, the problem solver needs to perceive an affordance of an event schema, and we interpret the transfer effects as changes in the likelihood that affordances were perceived, caused by the experimental variations. We hypothesize that both the positive transfer, in Brown and Kane's (1988) study, and the negative transfer, in Duncker's (1935/1945) study, resulted from tendencies for participants to perceive the same affordances in two situations. The different results occurred because, in Brown and Kane's experiment, the afforded activity was invariant across the transformation in providing a solution, while in Duncker's experiment, the afforded activity that provided a solution in the first situation interfered with perceiving a crucial affordance in the second situation.

Brown and Kane's problems involved using some object(s) in the situation to enable a kind of motion—climbing, pulling, or swinging. In our terminology, to solve a problem a child needed to perceive the affordance of the relevant object. In the first problem of each pair, an object with that affordance was used in solving the problem. For example, in the mechanic problem, the tires afforded stacking, and stacked tires afforded standing upon, and the solution of the problem depended on these affordances. The second problem presented a different scene with a different object that afforded the same kind of action as in the first problem. In the farmer problem, the child had to perceive that bales of hay afforded stacking in the same manner as tires, and once stacked, afforded standing upon.

Many preschool children did not transfer spontaneously, but most 4-year-olds did after experiencing one pair of problems, and most 3-year-olds did after experiencing two pair of problems and discussing their similarities. The children perceived affordances in one situation and, through experiencing and discussing other sets of problems, became attuned to the relevant affordances in a second situation. It was not simply that children perceived affordances in one situation and were therefore attuned to those affordances in another situation, but that these children learned to be attuned to those affordances through discussion (for 3-year-olds) and experience with a previous problem pair (4- and 5-year-olds). Transfer in this case involved learning to be attuned to the relevant affordances to solve a certain kind of problem. The social activity of discussion with an experimenter, or simply being presented with a pair of problems, influenced the transfer activity by directing attention to the invariant affordances in the two situations.

In Brown and Kane's experiment, positive transfer resulted from perceiving that a new situation was the same type as another situation that had just been experienced, where the similarity between situations involved affordances for similar potential activities. The problems were solved by creating affordances for activities such as climbing or swinging, and the affordances were created by activities such as stacking objects. The invariant structure of activity involved

(a) an affordance for building a structure, (b) an affordance provided by that structure for a (simulated) action, and (c) a function of that action for solving the problem. This structure remained invariant across a transformation of the situation in which the kinds of object involved were changed. Transfer consisted of perceiving the relevant affordances in the new situation. We hypothesize that this perception of affordances involved recognizing that the transfer situation was the same type as the initial learning situation, based on a potential state of affairs that could be inferred in both of the two situations. In the example of stacking the potential state of affairs was that a pile of objects could be constructed that would afford climbing.

It seems unlikely that learning in the experiment involved formation or significant changes of the children's schemata for the actions and events of stacking a climbing, swinging, or pulling. It seems more likely that the children learned to attend to affordances in the transfer situations involved in schemata for the actions that had succeeded previously, an example of a positive set for transfer (Brown, 1989). The experiment succeeded, on this view, because children came to view the transfer problems as potentially solvable with the same schemata as their respective initial problems. In effect, successive pairs of problems came to be treated as belonging to the same domain in the social setting that the experiment provided.

In Duncker's experiment, negative transfer occurred because there was a salient affordance for activity that was not invariant. For example, successful participants in the gimlet experiment were able to perceive prospectively a potential state of affairs in which the gimlet would support a hanging cord, in addition to perceiving the affordances that enable the gimlet's normal function of boring holes. Those participants who used the boring affordance initially were less likely to recognize the gimlet's potential role as a support. Similarly, in the candlestick problem, when the holding-objects function of a box was made salient the potential supporting function was less likely to be perceived prospectively. The standard interpretation, in our terms, is that the participants tended to perceive invariant functions of the objects, attending to the affordances for the actions they had just performed, rather than prospectively perceiving potential states of affairs that were unrelated to those affordances.

The use of the toys in Brown and Kane's study as models of possible situations involving real people deserves further discussion. We assume that the children incorporated constraints from both the toy situation and real experience into their activities with the dolls.

A toy situation has perceivable affordances of its own: for example, the toy tires afforded stacking, and the toy tractor afforded being pushed. In addition to these toy-world affordances, the children brought their own past experiences with the real world and some understanding of possible human activity to the situation. We assume that the children understood constraints that exist in potential human activity and used these in the solution of the problem, and that affordances in the toy situation and constraints from human activity functioned jointly in the children's problem solving to constrain their prospective perception of potential states of affairs. For example, lifting a doll up to the level of a toy shelf is an affordance of the toys in the model, but in a real situation that the model represents, that would correspond to a person being able to jump a few feet into the air lifting a heavy object such as a tire, and children apparently realized that the impossibility of such a maneuver by real people would rule out a "superjump" as a solution of the problem.

Models allow constraints to be imported from the modelled situation to the model situation, because the model can be interpreted as being the same type as the modelled situation with respect to some set of states of affairs. A model is useful for a particular reasoning task only if it supports interaction, either conceptual or physical, in the same way as the modelled situation. That is, there is some set of states of affairs that hold in both the model and modelled situation, and these states of affairs designate information that is perceived by the reasoner. We suppose that the models provided by Brown and Kane (1988) could be seen by children as being of the type in which some things can be stacked. In other words, the potential state of affairs, "Some things are stacked up" could be perceived prospectively as holding in the situation. Perceiving this potential state of affairs allowed children to solve the problem while complying with other constraints such as limitations on the ability of people to reach high places.

There are two further issues about the perception of affordances and potential states of affairs: The first concerns the information in situations that specifies affordances; the second concerns mental models. Studies by Warren and his associates (Warren, 1984; Warren & Whang, 1987; Warren et al., 1986) have identified the critical information in situations that specifies affordances for action such as climbing stairs or walking through an aperture. Similar experiments could be, but have not been, conducted to identify information that specifies affordances for use in supporting a person, a doll, a candle, or a piece of string. Even so, some reasonable conjectures can be made. For objects to afford stacking they should be reasonably solid with level surfaces, and for the stack to afford support the objects have to be sufficiently strong and large enough so that the structure is stable. One way for an object to afford support for a candle is for it to have a flat surface and be sufficiently strong to withstand the candle's weight. For an object, such as a tack, to afford fastening into a board (to attach a box), it should be small and pointed and have a surface that will provide friction.

Concerning mental representations, it seems unlikely to us that features such as the physical properties of the objects in Brown and Kane's and in Duncker's experiments correspond to symbols in cognitive representations when individuals perceive affordances. For example, when a child sees that toy tires and toy bales of hay can both be stacked, some relevant properties of the objects may be perceived directly as information that is "picked up" in Gibson's (1966) sense, rather than being recognized and matched to stored representations. It seems very likely that symbolic mental representations play an important role in transfer, but we suppose that these symbols correspond to potential states of affairs such as the possibility of making a stack of objects or the relation of support that would hold between a horizontal box and a candle. We assume that potential states of affairs, like affordances, are specified in the available information and can be perceived directly. They also can be registered—that is, a symbolic cognitive representation of the state of affairs can be constructed in the form of a proposition or an image, and such a representation can play a significant role in the person's reasoning.[11] Symbols in that representation, we hypothesize, would designate functional properties such as having a supporting structure, rather than physical features such as flatness and solidity. That is, perceiving that the situation is one in which things can be stacked would be recognized, in Neisser's (1989) sense, but the visual information that specifies that affordance would be perceived directly. Our account differs, then, from the one given by Weisberg and Suls (1973) for the candle problem, in which relevant features such as flatness are represented with tokens in information structures for pattern recognition.

Our account is consistent with statements made by children in Brown and Kane's experiment, for example:

E: You said my games are the same. How are they the same?

S5: They both have to put things on top.

E: Could your tell me a little more?
S5: In the farmer game we put these green things [yellow bales of hay] on top.

E: Umm.

S5: In the game we pile up wheels like before. Both games are for you to pile up things to reach. (Brown & Kane, 1988, p. 503)

Mentioning a property or relation in conversation provides strong evidence for its being represented by the speaker; therefore, we infer that the relation of being "on top,," being "pile[d] up," and the function "to reach" all were represented by this 3-years-old child during the discussion in which these remarks were

---

[11] Symbolic representations apparently can also occur and play a role in animal cognition. Köhler's (1929) famous observation of problem solving by a chimpanzee is a compelling example. A banana was outside Sultan's cage, too far to reach by hand or with a stick, and Sultan quit trying to reach the banana. Later, he was playing in the back of the cage with two sticks that were made to fit together, and he put them together. He got up suddenly, went to the front of the cage, and used the longer stick to reach the banana. In our framework, we would hypothesize that Sultan perceived the affordance of reaching with the stick, and perceived a potential state of affairs of the stick reaching the banana. The fact that this occurred while sultan was away from the front of the cage argues that this potential state of affairs was registered so that a symbolic representation was available as part of Sultan's cognitive situation and provided a basis for his evidently directed behavior.

made. The quotation lacks any mention of features such as flatness or solidity, and while the absence of something being mentioned does not guarantee that it was not represented by the child, it seems to us more plausible to assume that such features were perceived directly than that they were recognized and included in mental representations of the objects. In other words, we suppose that the children recognized the toy tires or bales as objects to put into a pile, and that they saw the flat surfaces and solidity of the objects, but they did not recognize the objects as being flat and solid.

4. WERTHEIMER'S AND SAYEKI, UENO, AND NAGASAKA'S PARALLELOGRAM STUDIES

In this section we discuss examples of reasoning about quantitative properties of geometric objects. These examples illustrate the idea that conceptual entities, as well as physical objects, have affordances, and that potential states of affairs can be related to conceptual, as well as physical, activity. At the same time, we hypothesize that the reasoning that occurred was situated activity, involving perception of affordances for transformations of figures represented in diagrams. We discuss two experiments that involve spatial transformations that preserve areas of geometric figures as an invariant. The first study is a classic example by Wertheimer (1945/1959, discussed in more detail by Luchins & Luchins, 1970) in which he contrasted instructional methods for finding the area of parallelograms. In a more recent study, Sayeki et al. (in press) used physical models to teach children invariant and variant properties of various transformations of geometric shapes.

Empirical Findings

Wertheimer taught some young children a method for finding the area of a rectangle by finding out how many unit squares fit into the rectangle. After the children had found the areas of several rectangles, Wertheimer presented a parallelogram, such as Figure 5.6, and asked the children to find its area.

Figure 5.6.   A parallelogram.

Wertheimer reported that several children succeeded in finding the area by transforming the parallelogram into a rectangle. His report of the solution by a 5½-year-old girl was as follows:

> She said, 'I certainly don't know how to do *that*.' Then, after a moment of silence; 'This is *no good here*,' pointing to the region at the left end; 'and *no good here*' pointing to the region at the right. 'It's troublesome, here and there.' Hesitantly she said: 'I could make it right here... but; Suddenly she cried out, 'May I have a pair of scissors? What is bad there is just what is needed here. It fits.' She took the scissors, cut the figure vertically, and placed the left end at the right. (Wertheimer, 1945/1959, pp. 47–48)

Wertheimer presented figures like those in Figure 5.7 to children after they found or were shown how to get the area of a parallelogram.

Some children solved the problems using what Wertheimer called *A-responses*, as in Figure 5.8.

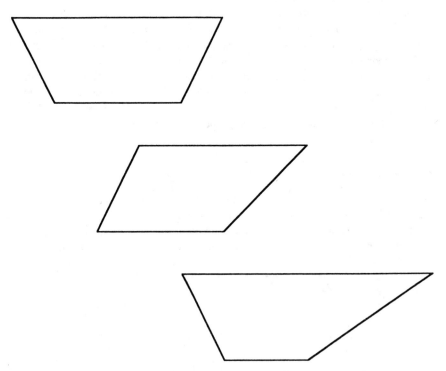

Figure 5.7.   Transfer figures following area of a parallelogram (Wertheimer, 1945/1959).

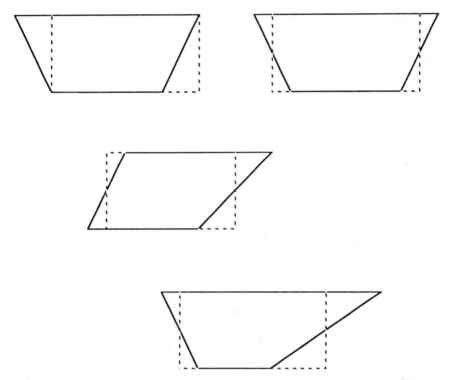

Figure 5.8.   A-responses to transfer figures (Wertheimer, 1945/1959).

Other children said that they had not learned "how to do those figures," or gave responses like those in Figure 5.9, which Wertheimer called *B-responses*, applying learned operations "blindly and unsuccessfully."

Wertheimer also conducted experiments in which he showed figures like those in Figure 5.10 after showing how to find the area of the parallelogram with auxiliary lines. The A-figures afford a transformation to a rectangle, while the *B-figures* do not. For some children, there was no distinction between the types of figures—they said they could not solve the problems or would

draw some auxiliary lines and give blind answers. But some consistently solve the A-problems and, sometimes after a brief period, reject the B-problems with: 'This one I can't do; I don't know what the area is'; or even, 'I don't know what the area of these little remainders is.' By contrast the area of the reminders is generally not mentioned in the A-cases; or the child may say, 'Of course I do not know the area of the little figures, but that does not matter as long as they are equal. (Wertheimer, 1945/1959, pp. 19–20)

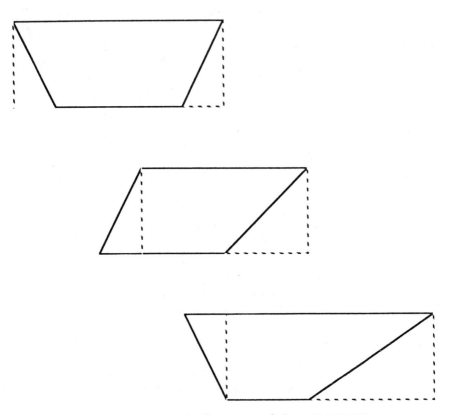

Figure 5.9   B-responses to transfer figures (Wertheimer, 1945/1959).

In a more recent study, Sayeki et al. (in press) contrasted the method of transforming parallelograms into rectangles, which is standard practice in Japanese schools, to the use of physical models. Fifth-grade students were given instruction in one of two conditions. The "Paper-cut" condition involved cutting paper parallelograms, such as those in Figure 5.11, to transform them into rectangles. The formula for finding the area of a parallelogram was then induced by the children. Students were also taught how to transform triangles and trapezoids into parallelograms, as illustrated in Figure 5.12, and then induced the formulas for finding the areas. Exceptions, such as obtuse-angled triangles and certain parallelograms, were taught as separate cases. Two examples are illustrated in Figure 5.13.

In the "Shapy" condition, students were presented with a deck of cards, illustrated in Figure 5.14. The edges of the cards that face forward form a rectangle. Various shapes of the same area can be made by transforming the deck; a parallelogram is also illustrated in Figure 5.14. As long as the number of

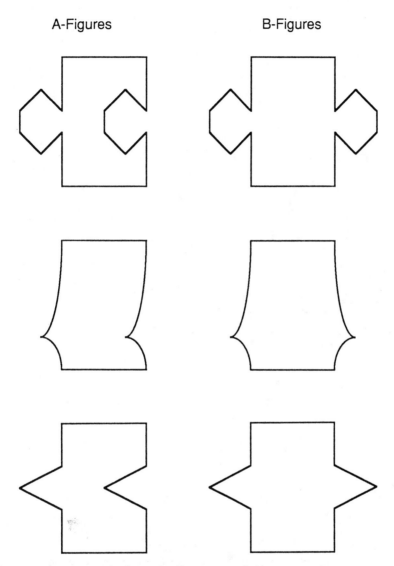

Figure 5.10.   Nonstandard transfer figures (Wertheimer, 1945/1959).

cards remains the same, the area is invariant across transformations. Students were allowed to transform a deck of cards, which they called Shapy, and were encouraged to consider whether the shapes had the same area, and why this was the case. Students were then asked to find variant and invariant features of the shape during transformation from a rectangle to a parallelogram.

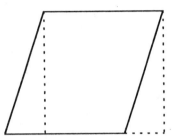

Figure 5.11.   The paper-cut model (Sayeki et al., in press).

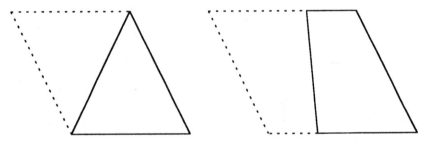

Figure 5.12.   Ways of producing parallelograms from triangles and trapezoids (Sayeki et al., in press).

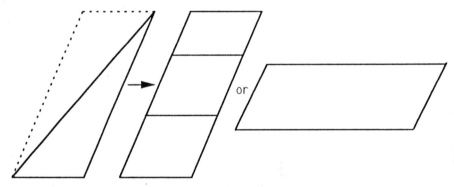

Figure 5.13.   Exceptional cases for the paper-cut model (Sayeki et al., in press).

Students were then given a flexible framework similar to a matchbox, illustrated in Figure 5.15, which was called Framer. The area surrounded by one side of Framer is twice that of one side of Shapy if both are standing straight; however, it fits exactly to Shapy if deformed to the point at which its height is the same as Shapy.

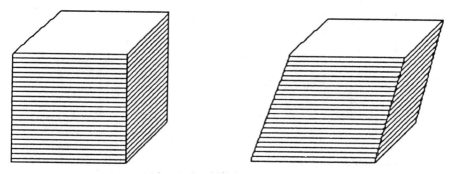

Figure 5.14   The "Shapy" model and a transformation (Sayeki et al., in press).

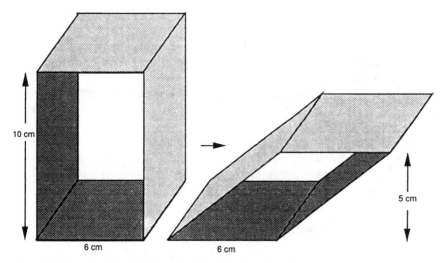

Figure 5.15.   The "Framer" model (Sayeki et al., in press).

Students were then asked to find as many different lines as possible that would divide the rectangle of one side of Shapy into two pieces with the same area. Figure 5.16 illustrates several of the shapes discovered by the students. Students then induced the formulas for finding the areas of triangles and a trapezoids, as in Figures 5.16b and 5.16d.

In the Shapy condition, most students were able to induce the formula for obtaining the area of a parallelogram based on their understanding of the variant and invariant features of the transformation of Shapy from a rectangle to a parallelogram. It was also not difficult for students to induce the formulas for obtaining the areas of triangles and trapezoids, once they had invented the

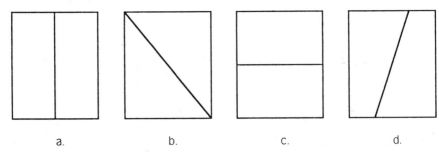

a.   b.   c.   d.

Figure 5.16.   Dividing Shapy into two shapes of the same area (Sayeki et al., in press).

methods shown in Figure 5.16 for dividing a rectangle into two shapes of the same area.

In the Paper-cut condition, few children discovered how to produce a rectangle from a parallelogram or how to find the area of a triangle or trapezoid. Since there were many exceptional cases, and finding the areas of parallelograms, triangles, and trapezoids was treated independently, the instruction took nine sessions for the control group and only five sessions for the experimental group.

A post test of 10 items relevant to finding the areas of parallelograms, triangles, and trapezoids was given to all students a week after instruction was completed. The Shapy group scored higher than the Paper-cut group on all 10 items, and significantly higher on three problems.

An Interpretation Based on Affordances For Reasoning

Our discussion of Wertheimer's (1945/1959) and Sayeki et al.'s (in press) results has three parts. First, we consider inferences of the numerical areas of rectangles. Then we consider transformations, including equivalence of parallelograms and other figures with rectangles and other transformations that preserve areas of parallelograms. Finally, we consider roles of algebraic formulas in understanding quantitative inferences about area.

Numerical Inferences of Area. Inference of the area of a rectangle from its length and width uses two constraints, one involving linear measures and the other involving numbers. Let S_{rlw} be a situation type with a rectangle r that has length l and width w, and let S_{ra} be a situation type with the same rectangle r that has area a. S_{rlw} is also a situation of type S_{ra}, but more specifically, the area a in S_{ra} is equal to $l \times w$ in S_{rlw}. Of course, use of this constraint depends on knowing what $l \times w$ is; that is, it depends on knowing a fact of multiplication in arithmetic. The inferences that are afforded by numerical values depend on the properties of numbers and mathematical operators, and involve cognitive activities. It seems reasonable to use the term *conceptual affordances* to refer to these mathematical properties.

A person who infers the area of a rectangle has not changed the rectangle, but has changed something about the information in the situation. Suppose that values of l and w are given in the problem. Thus, before the inference is made, the numerical quantities of the length and width are specified explicitly. The numerical quantity of the area is not specified explicitly, but the inference makes that specification explicit. The activity of reasoning, at least in this case, operates on and changes the state of information, rather than operating on and changing the state of physical objects in a situation, such as a dart and a target or a gimlet and some string. In terms that we introduced in Section 1, the activity adds new *registered* states of affairs that assert numerical values of quantitative properties. For someone who knows arithmetic and the constraint that relates lengths, widths, and areas of rectangles, the registered states of affairs that assert numerical values of the length and width of a rectangle afford an action of multiplying the numbers to infer the numerical value of the area.

Regarding mental representations, we suppose that, in order for someone to perform a mental operation on numbers, there must be symbolic representations of the numbers in the person's cognitive state. There are interesting questions about the representation of the operation. The result of an operation can be obtained, in principle, with or without its being represented as the result of the operation. There seems little question, however, that the result of the operation, the product of the numbers, would be represented symbolically as a number.

Geometric Transformations. The second part of our interpretation, which seems consistent with Wertheimer's, focuses on the students' understanding of geometric relations. Wertheimer's tutorial interactions with students began with discussions of the area of a rectangle, considered as the combination of unit squares. A parallelogram was then introduced, and children who got the concept apparently were able to compare the parallelogram with the rectangle and find differences that could be removed by cutting part of the parallelogram and moving it to the other end. Having learned to see the parallelogram as a figure that can be transformed into a rectangle, some students transferred that understanding to a large class of geometric figures.

We propose that the mental transformation of a parallelogram or other figure into a rectangle involves perception of an affordance for the transformation involving a potential state of affairs, analogous to the transformations involved in solving Brown and Kane's (1988) stacking problem or Duncker's (1935/1945) box-and-candle problem. In Wertheimer's case, there was a goal (set by the interviewer and apparently accepted by the children) to infer the area of a figure, comparable to a goal of reaching a high shelf or having a candle supported. The situation did not afford an action that would satisfy the goal directly, but it could afford an action that rearranged some parts of the situation so that there would be an affordance for an action to satisfy the goal. In the parallelogram problem, an action that would satisfy the goal was to infer the area by a numerical operation, and that was afforded by having a rectangle. In the stacking problem, the action was to simulate climbing to reach the shelf, and that action was afforded by having a pile of objects. And in the candlestick problem, the action was to fasten the candle onto a horizontal support, and that action was afforded by having a box that was attached to the wall.

The action of transforming a parallelogram into a rectangle has multiple affordances involving different action schemata, and in this way, the parallelogram problem is analogous to the problem of shooting at a submerged target. These problems are also similar in that they both involve perception of lines that are not physically present in the situation but that specify affordances for actions. A child could learn to identify a triangular shape at one end of a parallelogram and move it to the other end. The affordance for this is specified by parallel sides of a figure and a perpendicular line that connects a corner of the figure to the opposite side and thus forms a triangle at one end. This affordance was apparently learned by some children, who then produced what Wertheimer called B-responses, illustrated in Figure 5.9.

Another activity is more subtle, involving mental construction of a rectangle and congruence-matching of part of the parallelogram that is outside the rectangle with part of the rectangle that is not covered by the parallelogram. The affordance for this activity probably includes parallel sides that provide lines along which two sides of the rectangle can be constructed. The A-responses in Figure 5.8 can be produced by applying this congruence-matching activity to novel figures, assuming that the agent can perform rotations as well as translations to compare parts that extend beyond the rectangle with uncovered parts of the rectangle.

We conjecture, then, that transfer in Wertheimer's study depended on which affordance students attended to in solving the initial problem. We expect that transfer occurred when students learned to perceive the affordance for mentally constructing a rectangle and finding parts of the figure that extended beyond the rectangle that are congruent with parts of the rectangle that are not covered. This is a more complex activity than simply cutting off a triangle from one end of the parallelogram, which would solve the initial problem, but if the triangle-cutting activity was attempted in the transfer problems, it would not enable finding the area when the figures were changed to the transfer figures.

Learning with the Shapy model also involved a spatial transformation, but not one that involved detaching and replacing part of a figure. Instead, students learned with a physical model that illustrates a shear transformation that preserves area while changing shape. That area is invariant under a shear transformation may not be obvious, but it is not hard to construct a convincing argument that the total area covered by the edges of the same cards remains the same when the cards are merely realigned.

In Sayeki et al.'s (in press) study, students' attention was focused on features of the model that remained invariant when the shape was changed. The invariant relation of height, width, and area constitute a quantitative constraint. Specifically, if a situation is of type S_{phh}, containing a parallelogram with a specific base b and height h, then it also is of type S_{pa}, with a parallelogram with a specific area a, with $= b \times h$. This constraint among quantities provides an affordance for quantitative reasoning about a parallelogram without its having to be transformed into a rectangle. When a situation includes information that specifies the numerical values of the base and height of a parallelogram, that affords an inference about the numerical value of the parallelogram's area. Numerical values of a length of one side of a parallelogram, and of the perpendicular distance between that side and its opposite side, afford an inference of the numerical value of the area, using the action of multiplying the numbers. Sayeki et al.'s students may have learned to perceive that affordance more directly than Wertheimer's, through understanding area as an invariant property of all the figures related by a shear transformation, rather than as a property of rectangles which can be decomposed into unit squares. Use of Framer reinforced the meaning of the formula by showing that, in a quadrilateral system with different invariants (the lengths of its four sides) the area covaries with the height.

The mental representations involved in perceiving the affordance of transforming a figure are probably analogous to those involved in perceiving other affordances, such as constructing a pile of toy tires. The properties of the trapezoids in Figure 5.8 that make the transformations possible include parallel lines and symmetries around the midppoints of transverse lines. The property of a parallelogram that makes a shear transformation possible probably the pair of parallel lines on the opposite sides of the figure. It seems likely that children in Wertheimer's (1945/1959) and Sayeki et al's (in press) studies perceived these features, but they need not have had mental representations of them. It seems to us more plausible that the children represented features like those mentioned in Wertheimer's reports of conversations, properties of being "good" or "bad" with respect to the activity of relating the figures to the shape of a rectangle.

Formulas. In Sayeki et al.'s study, the invariant features of the width and height of the stack of cards were encoded in the formula for area, $a = b \times h$. A formula can provide a powerful representation because it can refer simultaneously to two constraints: a constraint in the domain of numbers and a constraint in a domain of quantities. In the present case, the quantitative domain is geometry: quantitative constraints are invariant relations among lengths, areas, and other geometric measures. The formula designates three geometric quantities that participate in a constraint, and it designates the type of numerical constraint that corresponds to the geometric constraint. It states in symbolic form the numerical operation used in the inference that is afforded by information about a parallelogram in a situation.

We propose a conjecture: one way in which a formula in a quantitative domain can be meaningful to a person is that he or she can interpret the symbolic expression both as referring to a numerical operation and to a constraint to which he or she is attuned in the quantitative domain. The process of becoming attuned to a constraint is undoubtedly important, and by no means well understood by us, but it seems reasonable to hypothesize that the instructional work with Shapy resulted, for many students, in becoming attuned to the quantitative constraint that links the bases, heights, and areas of parallelograms, in an action schema that included mental simulation of the shear transformation.

Wertheimer explicitly contrasted understanding the structural relation of shape and size with knowledge of the formula for the area of a parallelogram, $a = b \times h$, and rules for associating the variables b and h with the base and altitude of a figure. According to our conjecture, deficient understanding of the formula can result from a lack of semantic connection between the formula and a geometric constraint. Wertheimer provided an indirect connection. His instruction provided a way to become attuned to the quantitative constraint that links the lengths, widths, and areas of rectangles, and to a geometric constraint that links areas of parallelograms with areas of rectangles through a transformation. Sayeki et al. provided a more direct semantic connection to parallelograms. Their instruction provided a way to become attuned to the quantitative constraint that links lengths of bases, heights, and areas of parallelograms as an invariant relation across transformations of parallelograms.

Both Wertheimer's and Sayeki et al.'s instructional methods can provide students with a socially constructed concept of area as a quantitative geometric property. In both of these constructions, area is a focal concept. Wertheimer's instruction emphasized the concept of area of a rectangle related to its two linear dimensions. Sayeki's et al.'s emphasized the concept of area of a parallelogram related to its length and altitude. If Sayeki et al.'s paper-cutting method was less effective than Wertheimer's method, it might be because Sayeki et al. did not provide a focal concept of area in that instruction to organize the students' efforts to find a transformation with that quantity as an invariant.

Wertheimer tested transfer of his students' understanding by presenting trapezoids and other figures that afford transformations into rectangles. Sayeki et al. presented a way of generalizing their students' understanding to trapezoids and triangles. Their tests of understanding differed significantly. Wertheimer tested whether students could describe the transformation of a novel figure to a rectangle. Sayeki et al. tested whether students could induce a formula for the area of a novel geometric form. The operation of dividing a rectangle in half was introduced by the experimenters. The implications, involving constraints on areas of triangles and trapezoids, were apparently relations that many of the students were able to grasp.

5. RELATION TO OTHER THEORETICAL ACCOUNTS

In this section we discuss the relation of our view of transfer based on affordances with other current views that have been developed in the study of transfer. We begin with a discussion of the way in which our view is distinguished from several other current views of transfer. Then we consider two specific issues that have been analyzed using concepts of information processing and cognitive representation: transfer between problems presented verbally, and the role of formal symbolic representations in transfer. We consider interpretations of findings concerning these topics based on affordances and invariant structures of cognitive activity as alternatives to interpretations that have been given. Our interpretations include a hypothesis about mental models in which a person enacts simulations of situations that are described in texts and that provide reference for the terms of formulas.

Overview of Current Views

Figure 5.17 shows our understanding of the currently prevalent view of the transfer problem, as illustrated by Anderson and Thompson (1989), Bassok and Holyoak (this volume), Gentner (1983), Gick and Holyoak (1983), Greeno (1983), Holyoak (1984), Holyoak and Thagard (1989), Reed (this volume), and Singley and Anderson (1989). We contrast this with Figure 5.1, a sketch of our view.

In the view that we have sketched in Figure 5.17, in the initial learning situation, s1, a representation r1 is acquired, which mediates performance in that situation. When the situation is changed to s2, transfer will occur if r1 is adequate to support successful performance in s2 or if a different representation r2 of the transfer situation can be related to r1 in a way that enables initially learned actions to be carried out (perhaps with modifications) in s2. Various theories make different assumptions about processes of reasoning in the transfer situation, and these are coupled with differences in properties of the representations that are assumed to be required.

Figure 5.17 is a special case of Figure 5.1, involving a set of assumptions about the way agents and situations interact in activity. Where Figure 5.1 is not specific regarding roles of mental representations, Figure 5.17 reflects the assumption that mental representations play a key mediating role in cognitive activities, and that transfer depends primarily on a mapping between the agent's representations of the initial learning and the transfer situations.

The most straightforward assumption is that transfer occurs when r1 and r2 are the same—i.e., that transfer depends on an invariant representation. Gick and Holyoak (1983) arrived at this conclusion, and Greeno (1983) developed a simulation of learning and transfer based on the assumption that initial learning can include learning of a representation r1 in the form of an abstract symbolic schema that supports performance in both s1 and s2. The term *schema* in this sense refers to a data structure that can be activated when the features of a situation match the symbols in the schema, rather than an organized process, as

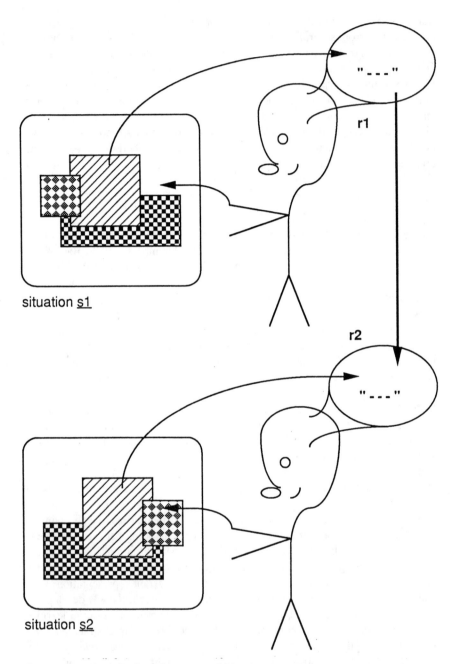

Figure 5.17.   Transfer based on a cognitive representation.

we used the term in earlier sections of the paper. We therefore use the term *symbolic schema* to refer to this hypothesis. According to this idea, generality is achieved by abstraction in the representation, that is, by symbols that designate properties and relations that are used to solve the problem and that can be recognized in both the initial and transfer situations. For transfer to occur, the learner has to have acquired a sufficiently general symbolic schema and has to be able to interpret the symbolic schema as a representation of the transfer situation. Holland, Holyoak, Nisbett, and Thagard (1986) referred to this interpretation as an encoding process, and argued that many failures of transfer occur because learning activities do not include sufficient experience in mapping features of varying examples onto the symbolic schema.

A version of the symbolic schema idea is used by Bassok and Holyoak (this volume) and Reed (this volume) for problems about numerical values of quantities that are solved using formulas. Formulas are abstract representations that can be used to specify arithmetic operations that result in the needed answer. Bassok and Holyoak, and Reed, consider transfer of solution methods that include use of the same formula for a transfer problem that was used in solving the problems presented in initial learning. In most versions of symbolic schema theory, such as Riley and Greeno's (1988) model of solving word problems in arithmetic, use of a solution method depends on recognizing a pattern of relations among the quantities that are described in the problem. In problems involving use of a formula, we suppose that the mental representation $r1$ would include a symbolic schema that represents the pattern of quantitative information in the initial learning problems, along with a representation of the formula or formulas that can be used to solve problems with that pattern of quantitative properties and relations. Transfer will occur if the pattern of quantities in the transfer problem is recognized according to the same schema that was used in initial learning. Transfer, therefore, requires a process of interpreting the learned symbolic schema in the transfer situation, for the same reason that schema interpretation is required according to hypotheses like Holland et al.'s (1986), where formulas are not used to represent solution methods.

Singley and Anderson (1989) also presented a straightforward version of Figure 5.17. Following earlier work on learning and transfer by Anderson (e.g., 1983) and others with the ACT* system, Singley and Anderson used the idea that production rules are the basic components of cognition. A production rule includes a representation of a condition, used to recognize a pattern of features in the situation, and a representation of an action, used to construct a pattern of

* Supported by the National Science Foundation, Grant BNS-8718918, and by the Institute for Research on Learning. We are grateful to Sue Allen for discussions of refraction, and to Noreen Greeno for help with graphic illustrations.

symbolic information when the rule is fired. A production rule can fire when the pattern represented by its condition is recognized. Singley and Anderson analyzed transfer by constructing production-rule models for tasks used in initial learning and in transfer. These models provide a hypothesis about $r1$ and $r2$; $r1$ is the set of rules hypothesized for the initial learning task(s), and $r2$ is the set of rules hypothesized for the transfer task. They assumed that the rules in their model of the initial learning tasks would be acquired when an individual learned to perform those tasks; that is, learners would acquire $r1$. Then when the transfer task was encountered, $r1$ would be part of the individual's knowledge. Positive transfer occurs to the extent that $r1$ and $r2$ overlap. An inference that transfer occurred involves comparing an individual who had the initial learning experience with someone who did not have that experience. The individual who had the initial learning would have acquired some of the production rules (those in the overlap of $r1$ and $r2$) that would not be part of the knowledge of an individual without the initial learning experience. Positive transfer would occur if those rules contributed to performance of the transfer task, because the individual without initial learning would have to learn those rules in the transfer situation. Negative transfer would occur if rules in $r1$ interfered with performance of the transfer task.

Holyoak and Thagard (1989) developed a model in which a pattern of properties and relations is recognized through activation of nodes in a connectionist network. This idea is like Singley and Anderson's (1989) in that it depends on $r1$ including representations of properties and relations in the initial situation that also are also included in $r2$, the representation of the transfer situation. In Holyoak and Thagard's model, a representation of a situation is a pattern of nodes that denote features of the situation. The pattern to which the network resolves depends on the weights of connections between nodes that excite or inhibit each other, and these weights are influenced by the initial learning activity. Transfer results, then, from tuning of connections in the initial learning in ways that contribute to representations in the transfer situation that facilitate solution of the transfer problem. As with Singley and Anderson's production rules, the elements of the system that are activated in the transfer situation contribute to the overall pattern of activity in transfer, either providing facilitation or interference.

Gentner (1983) and Holyoak (1984) assumed that there is a process of mapping between representations of situations that occurs in the transfer situation. According to this idea, $r1$ is a representation of the initial learning situation, including symbols that denote objects, properties, and relations. The person also has a representation $r2$ of objects, properties, and relations in the transfer situation and constructs a map between those two representations. The map is an identification of features in the two representations that correspond. Gentner assumed that relational features have higher priority than properties of individual objects. Holyoak (1984) distinguished mappings between symbols that are either structure preserving or structure violating, in that they either permit or prevent construction of problem-solving operators in the transfer problem that correspond to those in the initial problem. Once a map is constructed, other relations and procedures that are part of r1 can be imported to the transfer situation and therefore become available for enrichment of the person's representation and activity. The representation that results, r2, includes significant components of r1, and differs from r1 in the properties that are specific to the two situations. The tokens that represent features of r1 that are in r2 are abstract symbols in that they can be interpreted as representations of features in the two different situations. In contrast to Gick and Holyoak (1983) and Greeno (1983), Gentner (1983) and Holyoak (1984) assumed that the abstract representation r2 is constructed in the transfer situation, whereas Gick and Holyoak (1983) and Greeno (1983) assumed that the abstract representation is constructed in the initial learning situation and carried intact into the transfer situation. An intermediate position was taken by Anderson and Thompson (1989), who assumed that r1 is constructed according to a symbolic representation of a schema, including slots for specifications of a function and a form, and that r2 is constructed by tailoring the components of r1 by filling in or modifying its components as needed by symbolic operations.

Our View in Comparison

Regarding the standard view that we have depicted in Figure 17, the view that we present provides a generalization. In the accounts given by Anderson and Thompson (1989), Bassok and Holyoak (this volume), Gentner (1983), Gick and Holyoak (1983), Greeno (1983), Holyoak (1984), Holyoak and Thagard (1989), Reed (this volume), Singley and Anderson (1989), and other current theoretical discussions, the main questions for transfer are whether the learner acquires a suitable abstract representation during initial learning and whether he or she is able to apply or map that representation to solve the transfer problem. In the view that we have presented, symbolic cognitive representations can play an important role in transfer, but they are considered as instrumental parts of the activities that occur in the initial learning and transfer situations, rather than being fundamental and ubiquitous. Our view does not rule out cases in which someone learns to represent a situation in some specific abstract way in initial learning, and then is able to solve transfer problems by constructing that same abstract representation. We believe, however, that transfer that depends primarily on symbolic cognitive representations that are learned in one situation and applied in another is not the only kind of transfer there is; indeed, we believe that transfer mediated in that way by abstract, symbolic cognitive representations probably is atypical.

Our focus is on activities rather than on representations. Transfer, in this view depends on transformations of activity and is enabled by structural invariance in the interactions of agents in situations; these interactions can be described as action schemata, referring to the organizing principle of the activity rather than to symbolic cognitive representations. When situations are changed, the affordances they provide for activity change in some respects but not in others. Transfer of an activity can occur if the activity involves interaction with an affordance that is invariant, or, if the affordance changes, then transfer depends on there being a corresponding transformation in the activity. The invariance or transformation can be provided by an invariant or transformed symbolic cognitive representation, but it need not be.

The relation of our account of transfer in terms of affordances and invariants to concepts of symbolic schemata, structure mapping, and production rules involves the role of symbolic representations in transfer. According to a symbolic schema or production-rule theory, a symbolic representation of structure is stored in memory and then retrieved for use. In structure mapping a symbolic representation of structure is generated in the transfer situation, based partly on information about another situation that is retrieved. In the affordance-activity view, the structure that enables transfer is in the interactive activity of the person in the situation. The structures are general, and when transfer occurs it is because of general properties and relations of the person's interaction with features of a situation. A physical or cognitive symbolic representation may play a role in that activity, but symbolic representations are not necessary conditions for transfer.

We consider the roles of symbolic cognitive representations an empirical and theoretical question, to be analyzed in each case that is considered, rather than assuming that successful transfer always results from an invariant symbolic cognitive representation or a mapping between symbolic cognitive representations of the initial and transfer situations. We generally prefer an account that hypothesizes direct perception to an account that hypothesizes a mediating symbolic representation. Therefore, we adopt a hypothesis that includes symbolic cognitive representations when there is direct evidence for such a representation or when such a hypothesis seems to be required to provide a coherent explanation of performance. This approach contrasts with standard practice in cognitive science, in which the dependence of performance on symbolic representations is a framing assumption, and the question is what kind of representation provides the best explanation of data.

The hypotheses that we have presented in this chapter are examples. For the refraction experiments, we hypothesize that participants represented lines and angles in the spatial environment in which they learned to hit a submerged target, and may have represented numerical quantities in transforming their activity by determining a new distance from the center of the target to aim at.

For the experiments about functional transfer, we hypothesize that participants constructed symbolic representations of potential states of affairs that they perceived. These registered representations, as part of the cognitive situation, provided a basis for the person's determining an action to perform. Evidence that potential states of affairs were registered is in the recorded interviews that Brown and Kane (1988) reported, in which children referred to functional properties such as piles. Duncker (1935/1945) did not report thinking-aloud data from his functional fixedness experiment, but he reporteed thinking-aloud data of a participant in a problem-solving study involving the radiation problem, and that transcript includes many references to functional properties of the kind we hypothesize are included in registered potential states of affairs.

In Wertheimer's (1945/1959) parallelogram experiment, an example of evidence for a registered state of affairs was in the quotation he reported in which a child said, "What is bad there is just what is needed here. It fits." We take this as evidence that the child perceived and registered a relation of congruence between two parts of the figure.

Solving Problems Presented in Text

The examples with which we have developed our analysis of transfer involve problems that are solved by interacting directly with or reasoning directly about materials that are presented in the problem situation. This contrasts with much of the recent literature on transfer of reasoning (e.g., Bassok & Holyoak, this volume; Reed, this volume), which involves solution of problems presented as text. In the framework of symbolic schema theory, presentation of problems as text is unproblematic. The reader is assumed to construct a symbolic representation of the information in the text based on schemata stored in memory, and these symbolic schemata contain the basis for further inferences needed to solve problems. Then the ability to solve a problem depends on knowledge and processes that are characterized in a theory of language understanding, for which symbolic schema theory is well developed (e.g., Bower, Black, & Turner, 1979; Bransford & Johnson, 1973; Graesser & Nakamura, 1982). For example, in reading the following brief passage:

> Laurie went to a restaurant. She ordered the one vegetarian dish on the menu. She signaled for the waitress. She ate the food quickly and hurried back to her office. (Gerrig, 1988, p. 245)

adult readers in our society infer that Laurie paid for her meal, was probably on her lunch hour, and might be a vegetarian. Symbolic schema theories provide explanations for how these conjectures come about based on representations of commonplace activities in the form of scripts or memory-organizing packets that contain propositions about paying for meals, eating practices of different kinds of people, and durations of meals at different times of the day (e.g., Schank & Kass, 1988).

Our conjecture is that, in understanding texts, readers construct representations in the form of mental models that contain cognitive objects that behave in ways that simulate the physical objects, persons, and events that the texts describe. Rather than translating the text into another language, we propose that the text is used to construct a mental model that provides a surrogate for the situation that the text describes and in which the reader reasons as though he or she was in a situation like the one the model describes. This view of language understanding is consistent with ideas discussed by Fauconnier (1985) and Johnson-Laird (1983). Our version of the idea emphasizes inferences that can be made by operations on the mental models that simulate events that the models can simulate (Greeno, 1989, 1991), mental activity that Yates (1985) referred to as *enactment*. According to the idea that texts are understood through a process of mental modelling, understanding the passage about Laurie could involve constructing a mental model in which the reader is in Laurie's place at a restaurant and perceives states of affairs and affordances on her behalf. States of affairs that could hold in a situation of the kind described in the text also hold in the model. The model provides affordances and constraints for mental activities that have effects like those of corresponding activities that could occur in the simulated situation. Knowledge of a domain includes being able to include different kinds of objects and people in mental models that are constructed, so that different effects of simulative operations can be obtained. Inferences are made on the basis of simulations and the kinds of objects and people that are included in the model for the simulations to be consistent with information in the text. For example, a consequence of simulating the action of signaling for the waitress could be a simulation of the waitress coming to the table. If the enactment is continued, it would involve a simulation of some interaction between Laurie and the waitress, which could be Laurie's requesting and receiving her check. An enactment of leaving the restaurant would include a simulation of paying the bill.

The knowledge needed to reason in this way includes the ability to construct mental models with objects that have the properties needed to simulate events in the situations that are represented. We hypothesize that this ability includes processes for generating examples of concepts that are objects in the models. These conceptual objects combine, decompose, and interact with each other in ways that make simulative reasoning successful. Successful simulative reasoning, then, depends on abilities to generate appropriate conceptual objects and operate on them in ways that simulate events in the domain that is represented, rather than on propositional representations of rules. For this to work, mental models must incorporate constraints that make their behavior similar to the events that they represent. The idea of dynamic mental representations that are constrained in ways that match constraints of events in the world has been developed by Shepard (1984).

Mental models are abstract representations, in the sense that we use that term, because they can be constructed and used apart from the situations they represent. Mental models are denotational in that they have objects that correspond to objects or properties in situations that the models represent. They differ from symbolic representations that are descriptions or formulas, however, in that important properties of objects and events in situations are also properties of objects and events in the representation; Smith (1987) has used the term *absorption* to refer to this feature of representations. In a representation made up of sentences or formulas, operations on expressions in the representation change the expressions or produce new expressions. The resulting expressions can refer to new properties, but the properties of the expressions do not correspond significantly to the properties that the expressions refer to. In a model, operations on the representation change the state of the model in ways that correspond to changes that occur in the situation that the model represents, and the properties of the changed state or the transition between states are the same as properties of the situation that is represented.

We hypothesize that mental models mediate transfer between problems presented in the form of text. According to this idea, a story or problem presented in initial learning is represented with a mental model that simulates events or combinations of objects that are described. When a transfer problem is presented, a mental model of the problem situation is constructed, and the goal of the problem is represented as a potential state of affairs. The mental model constructed in initial learning may provide information about how to solve the transfer problem if objects or events in the two models have similar properties. Similar properties can include spatial relations, such as objects that move similarly in relation to each other, or functional roles, such as causal interactions or properties that avoid some consequence. The most important difference between this hypothesis of mental models and the more common hypothesis of abstract symbolic schemata is that properties needed for analogical problem solving may be properties of simulated events or objects, rather than being denoted by symbols.

We hypothesize that a person's ability to enact simulations in mental models depends on knowing that involves action schemata of the kind we have discussed elsewhere in this chapter. As we have pointed out, this sense of the term *schema*, which we take to be consistent with Bartlett's (1932) and Shaw and Hazelett's (1986) use of the term, is quite different from the propositional data structures that are generally hypothesized, which we have called *symbolic schemata*.

Readers of text can dynamically create models of situations and use these models rather than previously stored representations to understand the text. For example, consider the following two pairs of sentences from Garnham (1981):

The hostess bought a mink coat from the furrier,
The hostess bought a mink coat in the furrier's.

The hostess received a telegram from the furrier,
The hostess received a telegram in the furrier's.

The prepositional phrases in both pairs serve very different semantic functions, but the first pair of sentences is likely to be true in the same situation. Both of the sentences in the first pair can be understood by constructing a single mental model, while for the second pair of sentences, the model that corresponds to the first sentence does not support understanding of the second sentence easily, and vice versa. In fact, experimental participants tend to confuse the first pair more often than the second pair, and the sentences in the first pair do not seem distinct to the subjects (Garnham, 1981).

An application of symbolic schema theory to problem solving involves performance on Wason's selection task (1966). This task typically involves presenting participants with four two-sided cards from which participants must select those that need to be turned over to determine whether a particular rule has been followed. For example, one possible rule would be "If the card has an 'a' on one side, it must have an even number on the other side." The four cards presented with this rule might have as their visible sides an *a,b,6*, and *7*. Participants presented with this task typically select only the *a* card or the *a* and 6 cards, rather than the correct *a* and 7 card combination. These findings have been used to reject the view that participants reason via context-free abstract rules. Also, experiments with more meaningful rules like "If an envelope is sealed, then it has a 5d stamp on it" produce better performance on the selection task, which suggests that the context or theme of the selection rule can affect performance on the selection task (Johnson-Laird, Legrenzi, & Legrenzi, 1972). Some findings suggest that the effect of context may be based on experience. For example, performance is not enhanced for American participants who have not been exposed to this kind of postage stamp rule (Griggs & Cox, 1982).

Cheng and Holyoak (1985) proposed that performance on the selection task can be explained by pragmatic reasoning schemata. A *pragmatic reasoning schema* is a

> set of generalized context-sensitive rules which, unlike purely syntactic rules are defined in terms of classes of goals (such as taking desirable actions or making predictions about possible events) and relationships to these goals (such as cause and effect or precondition and allowable action). (Cheng & Holyoak, 1985, p. 395)

Cheng and Holyoak suggested that there are several types of pragmatic reasoning schemata, including permission, obligation, and causation schemata. The permission schema describes regulations for which taking particular actions requires the satisfaction of preconditions. Reasoning via the permission schema was offered as an alternative to solving selection problems by recalling particular experiences with the selection rule or counter examples.

Cheng and Holyoak described an experiment in which they gave participants from either Hong Kong or Michigan selection problems with and without permission-based rationales for the selection rules. One problem involved a postage rule that had been in effect in Hong Kong but not Michigan, and the other problem was novel to both groups of participants. Having a rationale improved performance in all cases except for the one in which the participants were familiar with the rule, where performance was excellent without the rationale. Cheng and Holyoak interpreted these results as supporting the pragmatic-schema account because having a rationale (in terms of permissions) facilitated performance on the selection task. The participants were shown, via the rationale, that their selection task was an instance of a permission situation.

In a second experiment, participants were provided with two selection problems. One of the problems was described in terms of actions A and preconditions P (i.e., permissions), but the other problem was Wason's selection problem. More participants picked the appropriate cards for the abstract permissions problem than for the relatively concrete Wason task. These findings were consistent with the pragmatic-schema account and suggested that it is the activation of the permission schema rather than concrete situations that facilitates performance.

We agree with the main substance of Cheng and Holyoak's (1985) account of reasoning in the Wason task. That is, we agree that successful reasoning is based on pragmatic reasoning schemata. We have a different idea, however, of what those schemata are and how they work. As an alternative to Cheng and Holyoak's interpretation in terms of symbolic schemata, we hypothesize that the participants use action schemata to construct simulative mental models in order to make the inferences that are required for the task. One effective process would be to construct versions of a model in which the proposition to be tested was and was not satisfied, and to register states of affairs that hold in the conditions where the proposition is false. For example, one rule used by Cheng and Holyoak involved permission to enter a country. The conditional proposition was that in order for someone to enter the country, a list of her or his inoculations had to include cholera. A mental model of the possibilities would include someone who was allowed to enter without the required entry for cholera. Two states of affairs hold: the card is marked *admitted*, and *cholera* is not on the list of inoculations. It is reasonable to expect, then, that participants would be more likely to include each of these as conditions for checking whether the other is satisfied, than would be the case when the problem was stated in terms of satisfying a less meaningful conditional proposition.

As an example involving transfer, consider a result obtained by Holyoak and Koh (1987), who found that application of analogous information to solve a transfer problem was improved when the information was in stories that had either structural or surface similarity with the problem. The problem was Duncker's radiation problem, and the stories were about repairing an expensive lightbulb. In a story with high surface and structural similarity to the transfer problem, the filament of the bulb is fused by laser beams that have to be distributed to avoid breaking the fragile glass bulb. In a story with lower surface and structural similarity, the filament has to be broken apart using ultrasound waves generated by several machines, because the intensity of a single machine is insufficient. A story with high surface and lower structural similarity used several laser beams of insufficient individual intensity, and a story with low surface and high structural similarity used ultrasound waves that had to be distributed to avoid breaking the fragile glass. The result of the factorial experiment was that both surface and structural similarity had significant main effects on the frequency of convergence solutions before a hint was given; and structural similarity, but not surface similarity, had a significant main effect on the total frequency of convergence solutions including solutions that participants provided following a hint in the form of a question whether the participant had tried to use the lightbulb story to help solve the radiation problem. The difference between the prehint and posthint findings resulted from a differential effect of the hint. With stories that had high structural and surface similarity to the transfer problem, the frequency of solutions following the hint was about equal to the frequency before the hint. In the other three conditions, solutions were considerably more frequent following the hint.

To interpret these findings, we hypothesize that, in understanding a story, the participant constructed a mental model including cognitive objects that represented a lightbulb, its filament, and laser beams or ultrasonic waves that passed through the glass bulb and either fused parts of the filament together or broke them apart. When the radiation problem was presented, we hypothesize that a mental model of the problem situation was also constructed, including cognitive objects that represented the tumor surrounded by healthy tissue, with a potential state of affairs in which X-rays destroyed the tumor. The different versions of the previous story should be useful in solving the problem to the extent that the enactments of fixing the lightbulb have properties that are similar to the mental model of the radiation problem, including the functional requirement of passing rays through healthy tissue harmlessly to destroy the tumor. The stories with laser beams or waves distributed to avoid breaking glass share with the transfer problem the functional requirement of protecting surrounding material, and the stories with laser beams rather than ultrasonic waves have objects that are more similar to the objects that represent X-rays in the transfer problem model. We agree with Holyoak and Koh's interpretation that the hint increased the likelihood of retrieving the solution of the first problem, and that this had an effect that interacted differentially with the two kinds of similarity. In our interpretation, retrieving the first solution involved reenacting a simulation of the lightbulb story. With high similarity of both the structural and surface features, participants may have reenacted simulations of the lightbulb story without the hint, which would have precluded there being any effect of the hint in that condition.

Because transfer between text problems depends on a representation of the initial situation, retrieval of that representation in the transfer situation is a major issue. Transfer experiments involve pairs of situations that differ in specific features but that have similar patterns of relational features. One theoretical possibility is that people reasoning via cross-situational analogies may be more likely to retrieve symbolic schemata or other abstractions than concrete examples because of difficulty retrieving relevant information from disparate situations. By standard similarity measures (Tversky, 1977) the features of a problem would be more similar to an abstract symbolic schema than to other specific problems that differ in specific features. The symbolic schema would have the similarities and almost none of the differences that a concrete analog would have to a problem. Particular experiences would be more difficult to retrieve, because it is unlikely that there will be direct semantic links between the problem at hand and examples in memory. Assuming that memory can be viewed as a network of semantically or episodically related elements, the only possible connections between the novel problem from one domain and stored analogs from another would be the relatively abstract elements implicit in the analog. These abstract elements are represented in symbolic schemata.

Given this expectation, it may seem surprising that, in experiments when individuals are shown a story or problem and asked to remember another story or problem that they have read or solved previously, they usually are much more likely to remember an item that shares superficial characteristics than one that is structurally similar. For example, Gentner and Landers (1985) presented participants with several "base" stories to read an memorize. Seven to 10 days later, participants were given new stories that differed from the base stories in systematic ways and were asked to recall analogous information. Gentner and Landers found that participants tended to retrieve the base story more often when the new story had characters with the same names and attributes as the base, despite differences in events and story structure. Similar results have been found in algebra word problem solving (Reed, Dempster, & Ettinger, 1985). Students tended to retrieve examples that were syntactically similar rather than conceptually similar to novel problems. Also, novices in domains tend to produce negative transfer by retrieving problems that are only superficially similar to the target problem (Novick, 1988).

These results suggest that surface feature information of examples has a strong role in the retrieval of analogous information. It could be that memorial representations contain symbols for both superficial and structural features, but that superficial features provide better cues for retrieval. It is also possible, however, that the structural features are often not present in symbolic representations stored in memory. This would be consistent with the idea that texts are used to construct simulative mental models, with symbols stored in memory denoting superficial features such as the kinds of objects in the model, but structural features such as how the objects interact may not be represented until the model is constructed and used to enact simulations of events.

In experimental tasks, although surface features influence the retrieval of stored information, there is evidence that structural similarity can help as well. Subjects tended to retrieve base stories better when simple relations (e.g., shoot(x,y)) as well as object attributes were shared with target stories than when merely object attributes were shared (Gentner & Rattermann, 1987). Surface information has also been shown to affect how people apply analogous information. Ross (1987) showed that the details of examples of statistical principles could affect applications of the principle. When both the story line and object descriptions were similar to those in the training examples, 74% correctly applied the principle compared to 36% when the story line was similar but the object descriptions were dissimilar. More recently, Ross (1989) has attempted to distinguish between surface features that affect access and those that affect use of information. Perhaps a surface that is more complex than Osgood's (1949) with distinctions between types of surface and structural features is necessary to account for more of the data. Examining the conditions under which transfer occurs has revealed that both surface and structural similarity influence the access and application of analogous information. In the symbolic schema-based view of transfer, an account would take some form in which the different effects of surface and structural similarity in retrieving and using analogous information would be explained in terms of roles played by different symbolic representations. In the mental model-based view of transfer, an account would take a form in which retrieval of information would depend on cues that result in the cognitive activities of constructing mental modes reenacting simulations in a way that make properties of their behavior available for application in new situations.

The hypothesis that structural features are implicit in the simulated behavior of mental models, rather than explicit in symbolic representations, is also consistent with the large effects of hints of facilitating analogical use of stories or previously solved problems. For example, in Gick and Holyoak's (1980, 1983) studies in which participants read and memorized a story and then were asked to solved an analogous problem, participants rarely used the idea from the story unless a hint was given. When no hint was given, only 30% of the participants produced the analogous solution used in the original story, but when given a hint that the story might be helpful, 50% of the participants produced a correct analogous solution. Spencer and Weisberg (1986) also showed that hints aid transfer, finding that, when participants were given two stories, only 5% of the participants used an analogous solution without a hint as compared to 57% of those who received a hint. According to the idea that analogical solutions are mediated by enactments in mental models, a hint could result in the individual's reconstructing and running a mental model that represents the events described in the story, and recognize the structural similarity of the story to the present problem in that process of enactment.[12]

---

[12] We find it odd to discount performance that occurs after a hint as not counting as transfer, as Detterman (this volume) seems to. Performance that occurs after a hint still requires ability to apply information from the story to solve the problem, and suggestion of a method would not be effective unless the individual could use the method effectively.

Gick and Holyoak (1983) found significant spontaneous transfer when they presented participants with two stories that were analogous to a transfer problem and asked them to describe the similarities between the stories. More recently, research has shown that comparing stories on several dimensions enables participants to transfer across contexts after delays of a week (Catrambone & Holyoak, 1989). Kamouri, Kamouri, and Smith (1986) argued similarly that induced abstractions that improve transfer are the basis of advantages of exploratory learning over more traditional methods. They also suggested that unstructured environments promote analogical thinking by evoking a process of comparing old and new information while exploring the problem space. According to the hypothesis of mental models, use of multiple examples and discussion could have two effects. One effect would be to call attention to the shared structural features of enactments in mental models, including registration of those features in symbolic representations. Such representations could occur and facilitate transfer as a supplement to the basic representational mode of mental models, rather than as a full-fledged abstract schema. The other effect would be to encourage a set to consider relations between the problem presented in transfer and other previously presented problems or stories, which seems consistent with Kamouri *et al.*s conjecture about exploratory learning as well as with Brown and Kane's (1988) findings, discussed in Section 3.

A considerable amount of research will be needed to develop and test the hypotheses of simulative reasoning in mental models that we have presented here in a preliminary way. One research question is to compare the effects of different situation models of examples on analogical transfer, and one of us (Smith) is currently conducting research on this question.

Formal Representations

In the view that we are presenting, abstract formal representations can play an important role in reasoning. We focus primarily on representations that are found in the world, as written or drawn symbolic expressions, and on cognitive representations of physical representations that simulate operations on those physical representations. An abstract representation, such as a formula, a diagram, or a verbal description, can help agents direct their attention to those features of a situation that are known to be invariant, and can therefore make more likely the kind of learning that will transfer as well as the occurrence of transfer in new situations when an appropriate abstract representation is provided. These representations can be parts of situations, either by their being there or by their being put into a situation by a person, and they then are available to be used by the individual in whatever way he or she can. Representations in the situation can be an important resource, and can be crucial mediators in the social settings in which learning occurs. In our view, abstract physical representations can play an important mediating role in reasoning, either as resources that are given or that the reasoner constructs for herself or himself. The role of representations that the reasoner constructs can be particularly significant, as Hall (1990) has shown. These representations, however, are material resources in the situation, as Hall emphasized, and their importance is not inconsistent with our view that a theory of transfer does not have to assume that symbolic cognitive representations always mediate the transfer that occurs.

Formulas and other abstract representations in formal symbolic systems can play a particularly valuable role in communicating and reasoning. Knowledge of a formula, however, does not guarantee a general capability of understanding or reasoning. Like other physical contents of situations, formulas can afford a variety of actions.

As formulas are usually taught in school mathematics, they provide recipes for calculation. If numbers are given, a calculation can be performed according to the formula and an answer is thereby obtained. The manipulations of equations in algebra permit a single formula to provide an appropriate recipe for several different versions of a problem. For example, the area of a parallelogram is found with the equation $a = b \times h$, where b is the base, h is the height, and a is the area. If the height is unknown and values are given for b and a, the equation can be solved for h and then calculations carried out. According to this standard view of formulas, a problem solver has to be able to construct a mapping of information from the problem or other situation to the variables of the formula. The meaning of a formula, in this view, is the set of calculations that it supports.

Another way of viewing the role of formulas focuses on a different aspect of their meaning. In Section 4.2 we gave a conjecture that a formula can have a dual meaning, referring simultaneously to numerical calculations and to a constraint in a quantitative domain. The constraint is an invariant relation among quantitative properties. Our discussion in Section 4.2 involved situations that include physical objects that the formulas refer to. In this section we extend our earlier remarks in two ways. First, we consider references of formulas to quantities that are represented in mental models. Then, we discuss a way in which formulas may be helpful in learning for transfer.

In Section 5.2 we discussed mental models as representations of situations that texts describe, which include mental objects that terms in the texts can refer to. Our hypothesis here is that mental models can play a similar role for formulas. That is, a way of understanding a formula involves constructing a mental model that includes objects that terms in the formula refer to.

In the context of a specific problem, a mental model can provide a simulation that includes approximate quantitative correspondence to the information given in the problem. Consider the following problem:

> There are two four-sided figures. One is a square; its sides are six inches long. The other figure is a parallelogram; its sides are also all six inches long, and its height is one inch. What are the areas of the two figures?

The problem can be solved easily using formulas, $A = s^2$ and $A = b \times h$. The formulas specify calculations: $6 \times 6 = 36$ and $6 \times 1 = 6$. If a mental (or physical) model is constructed, the terms in the formulas, s, b, and h, also refer to properties of two geometric forms, one of which is square, and the other of which has a sharp angle at one bottom corner and at the opposite top corner, is much shorter than the square, and its total lateral extent is almost twice that of the square. The different answers, 36 and 6, correspond to the fact, apparent in the model, that the area of the square is much greater than the area of the parallelogram. We suppose that construction of such a mental model for this problem would be facilitated by the kind of instruction that Sayeki et al. (in press) gave with the Shapy and Framer physical models, which we discussed in Section 4.1.

We offered the hypothesis in Section 5.3 that a problem-solving method will transfer easily between verbally presented problems if the problems are represented with the same mental model or with mental models that are generated by the same process schema. Here we use this idea to discuss transfer between problems that can be solved using the same formula.

The idea of transfer based on mental models can be used to interpret findings by Bassok (1990) and by Bassok and Holyoak (1989), reviewed by Bassok and Holyoak (this volume). They identified a variable that they call *quantitative type* that influences the amount of transfer that occurs between problems. In one experiment, Bassok (in press) taught students to solve problems in elementary physics involving constant acceleration, with variables of velocity, acceleration, time, and distance using the formulas $a \times v_f = v_j + at$ and $S = (v_j + v_j)t/2$. She then gave transfer problems with two kinds of quantitative variables: intensive quantities such as words typed per minute or rate of precipitation of a solution, or quantities she considered to be psychologically extensive, such as annual salary or bushels of potatoes harvested in day. Quite a few of the participants (6 of 10 students, on 16 of 40 problems) apparently transferred their physics knowledge to problems with intensive quantities, but only one student, on one problem, transferred physics knowledge to problems with psychologically extensive quantities.

We hypothesize that the success of transfer with the same quantity type could occur because students are able to use a single mental model to represent the quantitative relations in both problems. A mental model for problems involving intensive quantities might simulate continuous processes with rates that change continuously over time. Problems involving psychologically extensive quantities might require a model in which the increasing variable has a single value for each interval. In learning to solve physics problems, we would expect that many students acquired a schema for constructing mental models of processes in which the rate variable changes continuously in time. The transfer problems with intensive variables could be represented with mental models that they could construct with that same schema. The transfer problems with psychologically extensive variables, however, were not easily represented with that schema, and, therefore, transfer almost never occurred to those problems.

 .ve need a hypothesis to account for an asymmetry in transfer that Bassok and Holyoak (1989) obtained between physics problems about motion with constant acceleration and algebra problems that could be solved with formulas for arithmetic series, $a_n = a_i + (n-1)d$ and $S_n = (a_i + a_n)n/2$. Students who had learned to solve problems with the algebra equations frequently used those formulas when they were given problems about motion with constant acceleration, but almost none of the students who had learned to solve physics problems with formulas involving constant acceleration used those physics formulas in solving problems of the series type. The lack of transfer from physics to algebra is consistent with the finding we discussed just previously, which we interpret as indicating that the schema for constructing mental models about problems involving continuously changing rates does not provide an adequate means of representing problems in which values of a variable quantity are associated with discrete intervals of time. The finding of significant transfer from algebra to physics, however, requires an explanation. We hypothesize that the schema for constructing models with discrete changes in a rate parameter can be used successfully to construct mental models for representing problems about motion. Although the problems describe processes with velocities that change continuously in time, students can associate values of velocity with discreet intervals of time and obtain correct answers using the formulas for arithmetic series. This hypothesis attributes the asymmetry to greater flexibility in representing information about one kind of quantitative process than another. Information about a continuously changing process can be represented easily, either with a mental model with a variable quantity that changes continuously over time, or with a mental model with variable quantity that has values associated with discrete intervals or moments in time. Information about a quantity that has a value for each discrete interval apparently is hard to represent with a mental model of a variable quantity that changes continuously.

 We now consider a way in which formulas can play a useful role in learning about physical systems that can facilitate understanding and transfer, using Sayeki et al's (in press) experiment as an example.

 The symbols in a formula denote variables and mathematical operations. When the formula is interpreted as a description of a physical system, the symbols correspond to quantitative properties of the system and ways in which those quantities interact. The formula $a = b \times h$ can be used to focus attention on some basic features of these quantities' interaction. $b \times h$ focuses on the multiplicative interaction of the base and height of a figure in determining the area. While the models in Sayeki et al.'s (in press) study focused on the variant and invariant properties of a transformation, the formula involved in finding the area of a parallelogram focuses on how those properties interact to determine the area.

 We hypothesize that use of a formula and other symbolic representations can contribute to transfer if they influence the learner to perceive information in the learning situation that constitutes affordances that are present in both the learning situation and the situation of transfer. Learning to perceive these affordances in a situation can occur as a kind of "backward" process in which performance of an activity results in more attention to the properties and relations of the situation that support the activity. The question about transfer is whether learning to perceive the affordances in one context will increase the likelihood of their being perceived in another context.

We hypothesize that formulas and other symbolic representations can facilitate that perceptual learning by influencing students to perceive properties of the learning situation in a particular way—specifically, as affordances for reasoning about quantities. The properties and relations have multiple aspects. For many school tasks, the aspects that are transferable are quantitative. We hypothesize that learning for transfer would involve learning to perceive the relations in the event of transforming shapes as relations among quantities.

This hypothesis can be stated quite precisely in theoretical terms, although its empirical test would be more difficult to specify. It is possible to perceive the transformation of one shape into another, but to reason about the quantitative aspects of the transformation in a way that is conceptually distinct from the physical transformation. Each of the components of the event has a quantitative property. Reasoning can proceed by noticing the quantitative properties separately, associating them with numbers, and then applying a mathematical operation to the numbers to make an inference. Another possibility, however, is to perceive the event as an interaction among quantities. In this version, quantitative properties with numerical values are perceived as features that interact, and the events are relations among those quantities and their numerical values.

Use of mathematical representations in learning with Shapy and Framer does not guarantee that students would perceive transformations as relations between quantities. In fact, they could have the opposite effect of encouraging reasoning about numbers separately from their roles as properties of quantitative events. We conjecture, however, that, in an appropriate use, formulas could facilitate learning to perceive quantitative events in an integrated, transferable way.

We expect that this appropriate use would focus on relations between mathematical representations and events in the situation. Special emphasis would be given to correspondence between relations in the mathematical expressions and relational features of the events. For example, the relation of multiplication in a formula corresponds to the quantitative relation between base and height in finding an area. Focusing on these relations, we believe, would make it more likely that students would learn to perceive the relational properties of Shapy and Framer quantitatively, and the formulas provide physical systems with properties that denote the quantitative relations, and therefore can be discussed and understood specifically.

If our conjecture is correct, then a use of formulas and other symbolic representations, such as graphs, to call attention to quantitative relations would be an effective way of teaching that would result in stronger transfer to another situation with the same structure.

6. A GENERAL PERSPECTIVE

We conclude with a brief general sketch of psychological theories of transfer and a remark on relations of our view to general views in the psychology of learning and transfer. We relate our view to four general epistemological frameworks for theories of mind: three that Case (1987) calls empiricist, rationalist, and sociohistorical, and a fourth framework of ecological psychology. Each of these has a characteristic stance regarding the nature of transfer.

Empiricist and rationalist theories assume that transfer occurs because of structures that are represented in the mind. In an empiricist theory, including all those we discussed in Section 5.1, mental structures are built from elements that are not strongly constrained. Cognitive structures are acquired, but their structural features are emergent. Minds are assumed to be labile, at least initially, so that the features of the world that are experienced are reflected in the mental structures that are acquired. The classical empiricist analysis of transfer was by Thorndike and Woodworth (1921), who presented a view of transfer based on "identical elements" as an alternative to an idea that mental faculties or powers are strengthened by exercise. It was noticed, for example by Woodworth (1938), that the concept of *element*, in its technical sense of a sensory quality or reflex, is too limiting, and that the intention of the claim is to insist on an analysis of the constituents of concrete behavior and cognitive activity that are shared across situations. Woodworth proposed that the idea might better be called the theory of identical components. Empiricist theories of transfer, including analyses based on stimulus-response associations (e.g., Kendler & Kendler, 1959; Osgood, 1949), as well as those we discussed in Section 5.1, can be seen as efforts to understand what the components of cognitive activity and situations are, to account for the transfer and the lack of transfer that occur. The formalisms of symbolic computation are suited well for expressing empiricist hypotheses. Programming languages provide virtually unrestricted means for constructing symbolic expressions to represent whatever structures a theorist hypothesizes, and therefore provide appropriate media for representing the kind of unconstrained cognition and learning that empiricist theorists typically consider.

Rationalist theories, notably those contributed by Piaget and by gestalt psychologists such as Katona (1940), as well as Duncker (1935/1945) and Wertheimer (1945/1959), whom we discussed previously, have followed the Kantian intuition in assuming that cognitive structures are constrained by general properties of the mind. Important features of cognition result from structural constraints, such as the gestalt laws of grouping, that the mind imposes on experience, a process that Piaget called *assimilation*. Rationalist assumptions, in this sense, are included in theories of language that assume, following Chomsky (1965), that the learning of language depends on basic abilities to organize linguistic information that do not have to be learned. Assumptions that children's learning depends on significant constraints that help them organize information in many domains are being explored actively in developmental psychology (e.g., Gelman, 1990).

Empiricist and rationalist accounts of transfer share the crucial assumption that transfer depends on the cognitive structure that the learner has acquired in initial learning and can apply in the transfer situation. They differ in their general approach to how those representations are acquired in initial learning. An empiricist theorist generally looks for elements (or components) that overlap between the two situations, while a rationalist theorist generally looks for shared structure that a learner could carry over from initial learning to the transfer situation,

Sociohistorical theorists, such as the Laboratory for Comparative Human Cognition (1983), Lave (1988), and Pea (1989), following Leont'ev (1981), Vygotsky (1962), and others, focus attention on structure that is constructed in social activities. Transfer, in this view, depends primarily on a person's having learned to participate in an activity in a socially constructed domain of situations that includes the situation where transfer can occur. Transfer depends on structure in the situation that is primarily socially defined, and that has been included in the person's previous social experience.

Ecological theorists such as Shaw et al. (1982) and the contributors to McCabe and Balzano's (1986) volume, following Gibson (1966, 1979/1986) also focus their attention on structures outside of the mind, but they are have been concerned mainly with structures in the physical environment. The ecological theorists' conception of action as an interaction with the environment, often involving direct perception rather than being mediated by mental representations, is a key aspect of the view that we have developed.[13]

In the view that we have developed in this chapter, analyses of transfer focus on structures of activity, considered as interactions of agents in the situations of initial learning and transfer. In this way, our view shares the orientation of sociohistorical and ecological discussions in attending primarily to constraints on activity that result from the structures of situations, rather than to mental

---

[13] Anderson's (1990) recent monograph presented analyses based on assumptions about structures of information in the environment and derived implications about structures of representations in the cognitive system, assuming that mental activity would be optimized. Anderson's approach is interesting, but differs fundamentally from ours and those of others who are trying to develop a view of situated cognition. We formulate cognitive processes as interactions between agents and situations, including other agents, and try to analyze the properties of those interactions. In Anderson's recent analysis, the relations between situations and mental processes are deductive.

representations of structure. In most of our discussions in this chapter social factors have been in the background, and the main focus of attention is on whether individuals carry learned activities from the initial learning situation to the transfer situation. Our analyses here, therefore, are related more directly to the contributions of ecological psychologists than to the discussions of cognition in its social and cultural contexts.

Our more general view, however, is that the understanding of cognition that we need should take account of its being situated in both the physical and the social aspects of its environment. Our discussions in this chapter, while focusing mainly on the interactions of individuals with physical aspects of the situation, have included some attention to aspects of the social situation in which the meanings of tasks are constructed and attention is focused on some physical aspects of the situation rather than others. We are hopeful that, in future research, these two lines of theoretical work, involving consideration of social and the physical ecology of cognition, can become more fully integrated.

REFERENCES

Anderson, J.R. (1983). *The architecture of cognition.* Cambridge, MA: Harvard University Press.

Anderson, J. R. (1990). *The adaptive character of thought.* Hillsdale, NJ: Erlbaum.

Anderson, J. R., & Thompson, R. (1989). Use of analogy in a production system architecture. In S. Vosniadou & A. Ortony (Eds.), *Similarity and analogical reasoning* (pp. 267–297). New York: Cambridge University Press.

Bartlett, F. C. (1932). *Remembering: A study in experimental and social psychology.* New York: MacMillan.

Barwise, J. (1989). *The situation in logic.* Palo Alto, CA: Center for the Study of Language and Information, Stanford University.

Bassok, M. (1990). Transfer of domain-specific problem solving procedures. *Journal of Experimental Psychology: Learning, Memory, and Cognition, 16,* 522–533.

Bassok, M., & Holyoak, K. J. (1989). Interdomain transfer between isomorphic topics in algebra and physics. *Journal of Experimental Psychology: Learning, Memory, and Cognition, 15,* 153–166.

Bower, G., Black, J. B., & Turner, T. J. (1979). Scripts in memory for text. *Cognitive Psychology, 11,* 177–220.

Bransford, J. D., & Johnson, M. K. (1973). Considerations of some problems of comprehension. In W. G. Chase (Ed.), *Visual information processing.* New York: Academic Press.

Brown, A. L. (1989). Analogical transfer: What develops? In S. Vosniadou & A. Ortony (Eds.), *Similarity and analogical reasoning* (pp. 369–412). New York: Cambridge University Press.

Brown, A. L. & Kane, M. J. (1988). Preschool children can learn to transfer: Learning to learn and learning from examples. *Cognitive Psychology, 20,* 493–523.

Brown, J.S., Collins, A., & Duguid, P. (1989). Situated cognition and the culture of learning. *Educational Researcher, 18*, 32–42. (Also available as Report No. IRL88–0008, Institute for Research on Learning, Palo Alto, CA.)

Catrambone, R., & Holyoak, K. J. (1989). Overcoming contextual limitations on problem-solving transfer. *Journal of Experimental Psychology: Learning, Memory, and Cognition, 15*, 1147–1156.

Cheng, P.W., & Holyoak, K. J. (1985). Pragmatic reasoning schemas. *Cognitive Psychology, 17*, 391–416.

Chomsky, N. (1965). *Aspects of a theory of syntax*. Cambridge, MA: MIT Press.

Devlin, K. (1988). *Logic and information. Volume I: Situation theory* (draft). Palo Alto, CA: Center for the Study of Language and Information, Stanford University.

Dewey, J. (1985). How we think. In J. A. Boydston (Ed.), *The middle works of John Dewey. Volume 6, How we think and selected essay, 1910–1911* (pp. 177–356). Carbondale, IL: Southern Illinois University Press. (original work published 1910)

Dewey, J., & Bentley, A. F. (1949). *Knowing and the known*. Boston, MA: Beacon Press.

Duncker, K. (1945). On problem solving. *Psychological Monographs, 58* (Whole No. 270). (Original German work published 1935).

Fauconnier, G. (1985). *Mental spaces: Aspects of meaning construction in natural language*. Cambridge, MA: MIT Press/Bradford Books.

Feigenbaum, E. A. (1963). The simulation of verbal learning behavior. In E. A. Feigenbaum & J. Feldman (Eds.), *Computers and thought*. New York: McGraw-Hill.

Gallistel, C. R. (1980). *The organization of action: A new synthesis*. Hillsdale, NJ: Erlbaum.

Gallistel, C R. (1990). *The organization of learning*. Cambridge, MA: MIT Press/Bradford.

Garnham, A. (1981). Mental models as representations of text. *Memory and Cognition, 9*, 560–565.

Gelman, R. (Ed.). (1990). *Cognitive Science 14*(1) (Special issue on structural constraints on cognitive development).

Gentner, D. (1983). Structure-mapping: a theoretical framework for analogy. *Cognitive Science, 7*, 155–170.

Gentner, D., & Landers, R. (1985). *Analogical reminding: A good match is hard to find*. Paper presented at the International conference of Systems, Man & Cybernetics, Tucson, Arizona.

Gentner, D., & Rattermann, M. J. (1987). Analogy and similarity determinates of accessibility and inferential soundness. *Proceedings of the 9th annual conference of the Coquitive Science Society*. Hillsdale, NJ: Elbaum.

Gerrig, R. J. (1988). Text comprehension. In R. J. Sternberg & E. E. Smith (Eds.), *The psychology of human thought* (pp. 242–266). New York: Cambridge University Press.

Gibson, J. J. (1966). *The senses considered as perceptual systems*. Boston, MA: Houghton-Mifflin.

Gibson, J. J. (1986). *The ecological approach to visual perception*. Hillsdale, NJ: Erlbaum. (Original work published 1979)

Gick, M., & Holyoak, K. J. (1980). Analogical problem solving. *Cognitive Psychology, 12*, 306–355.

Gick, M., & Holyoak, K. J. (1983). Schema induction and analogical transfer. *Cognitive Psychology, 15*, 1,–38.

Graesser, A. C., & Nakamura, G. V. (1982). The impact of a schema on comprehension and memory. In G. H. Bower (Ed.), *The psychology of learning and motivation* (Vol. 16, pp. 59–109). New York: Academic Press.

Greeno, J. G. (1983). Forms of understanding in mathematical problem solving. In S. G. Paris, G. M. Olson, & H. W. Stevenson (Eds.), *Learning and motivation in the classroom* (pp. 83–111). Hillsdale, NJ: Erlbaum.

Greeno, J. G. (1989). Situations, mental models, and generative knowledge. In D. Klahr & K. Kotovsky (Eds.), *Complex information processing: The impact of Herbert A. Simon* (pp. 285–318). Hillsdale, NJ: Erlbaum. (Also available as Report No. IRL88-005, Institute for Research on Learning, Palo Alto, CA)

Greeno, J. G. (1991). Number sense as situated knowing in a conceptual domain. *Journal for Research in Mathematics Education, 22*, 170–218.

Griggs, R. A., & Cox, J. R. (1982). The elusive thematic-materials effect in Wason's selection task. *British Journal of Psychology, 73*, 407–420.

Hall, R. P. (1990). *Making mathematics on paper: Constructing representations of stories about related linear functions.* Doctoral dissertation, University of California, Irvine.

Hendrickson, G., & Schroeder, W. H. (1941). Transfer of training in learning to hit a submerged target. *Journal of Educational Psychology, 32*, 205–213.

Holland, J. H., Holyoak, K. J., Nisbett, R. E., & Thagard, P. R. (1986). *Induction: Process of inference, learning, and discovery.* Cambridge, MA: MIT Press.

Holyoak, K. J. (1984). Analogical thinking and human intelligence. In R. J. Sternberg (Ed.), *Advances in the psychology of human intelligence* (Vol. 2). Hillsdale, NJ: Erlbaum.

Holyoak, K. J., & Koh, K. (1987). Surface and structural similarity in analogical transfer. *Memory & Cognition, 4*, 332–340.

Holyoak, K. J., & Thagard, P. (1989). Analogical mapping by constraint satisfaction. *Cognitive Science,13*, 295–356.

Johnson-Laird, P. N. (1983). *Mental models: Towards a cognitive science of language, inference, and consciousness.* Cambridge, MA: Harvard University Press.

Johnson-Laird, P. N., Legrenzi, P., & Legrenzi, M. (1972). Reasoning and a sense of reality. *British Journal of Psychology,63*, 395–400.

Jordan, B. (1987). *Modes of teaching and learning: Questions raised by the training of traditional birth attendants* (Rep. IRL87–0004). Palo Alto, CA: Institute for Research on Learning.

Judd, C. H. (1908). The relation of special training to general intelligence. *Educational Review, 36*, 28–42.

Kamouri, A., Kamouri, J., & Smith, K. H. (1986). Training by exploration: Facilitating the transfer of procedural knowledge through analogical reasoning. *International Journal of Man-Machine Studies, 24*, 171–192.

Katona, G. (1940 *Organizing and memorizing.* New York: Columbia University Press.

Kendler, H. H., & Kendler, T. S. (1959). Reversal and nonreversal shifts in kindergarten children. *Journal of Experimental Psychology, 58*, 56–60.

Kohler, W. (1929). *The mentality of apes.* New York: Harcourt Brace.

Laboratory of Comparative Human Cognition (1983). Culture and cognitive development. In W. Kessen (Ed.), *Handbook of child psychology, volume I: History, theory, and methods* (pp. 295–356). New York: John Wiley & Sons.

Lave, J. (1988). *Cognition in practice: Mind, mathematics and culture in everyday life.* Cambridge, UK: Cambridge University Press.

Leont'ev, A. N. (1981). The problem of activity in psychology. In J. V. Wertsch (Ed.), *The concept of activity in Soviet psychology.* White Plains, NY: Sharpe.

Liebowitz, H. W., & Post, R. B. (1982). The two modes of processing concept and some implications. In J. Beck (Ed.), *Organization and representation in perception.* Hillsdale, NJ: Erlbaum.

Luchins, A. S., & Luchins, E. H. (1970). *Wertheimer's seminars revisited: Problem solving and thinking* (Vol. I). Albany, NY: Faculty-Student Association, State University of New York at Albany.

McCabe, V., & Balzano, G. J. (Eds.). (1986). *Event cognition: An ecological perspective* Hillsdale, NJ: Erlbaum.

McClelland, J. L., & Rumelhart, D. E. (1981). An interactive activation model of context effects in letter perception: Part 1. An account of basic findings. *Psychological Review, 88,* 375–407.

Neisser, U. (1989, August). *Direct perception and recognition as distinct perceptual systems.* Paper presented at the Cognitive Science Society meeting, Ann Arbor, MI.

Novick, L. R. (1988) Analogical transfer, problem similarity, and expertise. *Journal of Experimental Psychology: Learning, Memory, and Cognition, 3, 510–520.*

Osgood, C. E. (1949). The similarity paradox in human learning: A resolution. *Psychological Review, 56,* 132–143.

Pea, R. D. (1989). Socializing the knowledge transfer problem. *International Journal of Education Research, 11,* 639–663 (Also available as Report No. IRL89–0009, Institute for Research on Learning, Palo Alto, CA.)

Reed, S. K., Dempster, A., & Ettinger, M. (1985). Usefulness of analogous solutions for solving algebra word problems. *Journal of Experimental Psychology: Learning, Memory, and Cognition, 11,* 106–125.

Riegel, K. F., & Meacham, J. A. (1978). Dialectics, transaction, and Piaget's theory. In L. A. Pervin & M. Lewis (Eds.), *Perspectives in interactional psychology* (pp. 23–48). New York: Plenum Press.

Riley, M. S., & Greeno, J. G. (1988). Developmental analysis of understanding language about quantities and of solving problems. *Cognition and Instruction, 5,* 49–101.

Rogoff, B. (1990). *Apprenticeship in thinking.* New York: Oxford University Press.

Ross, B. H. (1987). This is like that: The use of earlier problems and the separation of similarity effects. *Journal of Experimental Psychology: Learning, Memory, & Cognition, 4,* 629–639.

Ross, B. H. (1989). Distinguishing types of superficial similarities: different effects on the access and use of earlier problems. *Journal of Experimental Psychology: Learning, Memory and Cognition,* 15, 456–468.

Sayeki, Y., Ueno, N., & Nagasaka, T. (in press). Mediation as a generative model for obtaining an area. *International Journal of Educational Research.*

Schank, R., & Kass, A. (1988). Knowledge representation in people and machines. In U. Eco, M. Santambrogio, & P. Violi (Eds.), *Meaning and mental representations*(pp. 181–200). Bloomington, IN: Indiana University Press.

Searle, J. R. (1980). Minds, brains, and programs. *The Behavioral and Brain Sciences, 3*, 417–457.

Shaw, R., & Alley, T. R. (1985). How to draw learning curves: Their use and justification. In T. D. Johnston & A. T. Pietrewicz (Eds.), *Issues in the ecological study of learning* (pp. 275–304). Hillsdale, NJ: Erlbaum.

Shaw, R., & Hazelett, W. M. (1986). Schemas in cognition. In V. McCabe & G. J. Balzano (Eds.), *Event cognition: An ecological perspective* (pp. 45–54). Hillsdale, NJ: Erlbaum.

Shaw, R., Turvey, M. T., & Mace, W. (1982). Ecological psychology: The consequence of a commitment to realism. In W. B. Weimer & D. S. Palermo (Eds.), *Cognition and the symbolic processes (Vol. 2, pp. 159–226). Hillsdale, NJ: Erlbaum.*

Shepard, R. N. (1984). Ecological constraints on internal representation: Resonant kinematics of perceiving, imagining, thinking and dreaming. *Psychological Review, 91*, 417–447.

Simon, H. A. (1978). On the forms of mental representation. In C. W. Savage (Ed.), *Perception and cognition: Issues in the foundation of psychology* (pp. 3–17). Minneapolis, MN: University of Minnesota Press.

Singley, M. K., & Anderson, J. R. (1989). *The transfer of cognitive skill.* Cambridge, MA: Harvard University Press.

Smith, B. C. (1987). *The correspondence continuum* (report CSLI-87–71). Palo Alto, CA: Center for the Study of Language and Information Stanford University.

Spencer, R. M., & Weisberg, R. W. (1986). Context-dependent effects on analogical transfer, *Memory & Cognition, 14*, 442–449.

Stucky, S. (in preparation). Situated language use and efficient cognition.

Suchman, L. (1987). *Plans and situated actions.* Cambridge, UK: Cambridge University Press.

Thorndike, E. L., & Woodworth, R. S. (1901). The influence of improvement in one mental function upon the efficiency of other functions. *Psychological Review, 8*, 246–261.

Tversky, A. (1977). Features of similarity. *Psychological Review, 84*, 327–352.

Vygotsky, L. S. (1962). *Thought and language.* Cambridge, MA: MIT Press.

Warren, W. H., Jr. (1984). Perceiving affordances: Visual guidance of stair climbing. *Journal of Experimental Psychology: Human Perception and Performance, 10*, 683–703.

Warren, W. H., Jr., & Whang, S. (1987). Visual guidance of walking through apertures: Body-scaled information for affordances. *Journal of Experimental Psychology: Human Perception and Performance, 13*, 371–383.

Warren, W. H., Jr., Young, D. S., & Lee, D. N. (1986). Visual control of step length during running over irregular terrain. *Journal of Experimental Psychology: Human Perception and Performance, 12*, 259–266.

Wason, P. C. (1966). Reasoning. In B. M. Foss (Ed.), *New horizons in psychology.* Harmondsworn, UK: Penguin.

Weisberg, R., & Suls, J. M. (1973). An information-processing model of Duncker's candle problem. *Cognitive Psychology, 4*, 255–276.

Wertheimer, M. (1959). *Productive thinking* (enlarged ed.). New York: Harper & Row. (Original work published 1945)

Woodworth, R. S. (1938). *Experimental psychology*. New York: Henry Holt.

Yates, J. (1985). The content of awareness is a model of the world. *Psychological Review, 92*, 249–284.

Chapter 6

Transfer, Abstractness, and Intelligence*

Stephen J. Ceci and Ana Ruiz

Cornell University

In this chapter we shall discuss the role of psychometric intelligence (IQ) in transfer. As will be seen, an exploration of this relationship necessitates that we say something about the moderating role of abstractness, because both intelligence and transfer are alleged by many to require the abstraction of a hidden structure (i.e., the eduction of underlying principles). Consistent with this claim, Das (1987) remarked

> I have suggested that far transfer...depends on the eduction of a principle. More intelligent children are apt to observe that apparently different tasks may require the same processing; less intelligent children are less likely to notice this. Therefore, the extent of transfer must depend on intelligence to some degree. The relation between IQ and transfer is supported by more than one author in this book. I have a hunch that there is an IQ threshold (70-75) below which the eduction of an underlying process does not occur.

* Preparation of this chapter was supported by grants from the National Institutes of Health, DHHS #5RO1HD22839 and KO4HD00801 to the first author. Requests for reprints can be sent to either author at: HDFS, Cornell University, Ithaca, NY 14853.

Das's claims about the role of IQ in transfer are interesting and important, but they bear scrutiny. They presuppose that IQ scores reflect the degree to which individuals can be abstract enough to educe underlying structure—a characteristic of an intellligent person. We shall have more to say about this supposition in the Discussion. First, we turn to the history of research on these issues.

A BRIEF HISTORY OF TRANSFER

Although scholarly treatises on the topic of transfer have been around since the time of Aristotle's *DeAnima,* the scientific debate over it did not take shape until the beginning of the 20th century when two camps of researchers argued about its prevalence and causal mechanisms. In this section we will briefly describe some research on three interrelated concepts, *transfer, abstractness,* and *intelligence,* and argue that to the extent transfer occurs at all, it is fairly circumscribed and domain specific, not reflective of greater general intelligence or abstractness.

The idea that great advances in knowledge and technology have resulted from individuals' ability to transfer solutions across diverse domains is, if not a fiction, a rare event that is not characteristic of the vast majority of advances. While high school algebra teachers might understandably hope that their students will be able to calculate their bowling averages, scientific demonstrations of the ability to transfer knowledge across domains is far from commonplace. Elsewhere, one of us has chronicled examples of the limits of transfer, even among individuals with high measured psychometric intelligence (Ceci, 1990), and we shall not rehash that literature here except to note that several of the contributors to this volume have provided some of the most compelling evidence for the limited role of transfer, at least under naturally occurring conditions. Indeed, even among select groups of high school and college students who have received training in solving structurally isomorphic arithmetical progression problems in algebra versus constant acceleration problems in physics, transfer from physics to algebra can be an extremely illusive phenomenon (e.g., Bassok & Holyoak, 1989). The explanation for such content-sensitivity of transfer has usually involved the notion that the underlying representation for high-transfer topics (e.g., algebra) is more abstract than the representation for low-transfer topics like physics, and as a result of this greater abstractness students can conceive of the underlying elements as common to a unitary conceptual entity that can be accessed by some learned rule (Bassok & Holyoak, this volume).

In this chapter we shall take a different tact and argue that what makes some knowledge easier to transfer than other types is not the abstractness of its conceptual structure but rather the combination of an invitation to transfer that is contained in the original learning, coupled with an elaborated knowledge representation that is sufficiently well developed that most problems are *re-presentations* of parts of it. Viewed in this manner, transfer is essentially a function of doing what one is told can or should be done with the contents of their representations, rather than being more or less able to instantiate the underlying structure of a problem. This view seems similar to the one put forward independently by Detterman (this volume). We shall have more to say about this later, but first we review some historical notions of transfer.

Transferring Training. Around the turn of this century, the "theory of formal disciplines" was quite popular (see Ceci & Ruiz, 1992; Detterman, this volume; Payne & Wenger, in press). This theory held that training in one discipline enabled one to think more effectively in other disciplines. For example, specific training in Latin and chess were regarded as exercises that fostered the development of logical reasoning in general. Therefore, learning how to reason in one context was thought to transfer to reasoning in other contexts. This view continued to attract proponents throughout the century and current expressions of it can be found in the work of cognitive scientists who tout the benefits of learning computer programming languages. In a review of this literature, Salomon and Perkins (1987) stated:

> The most widespread...argument in favor of teaching programming concerns its possible impact on generalizable cognitive skills. For example, Feurzeig, Horwitz, and Nickerson (1981) argued that programming provides an opportunity to develop rigorous thinking, learn the use of heuristics, nourish self consciousness about the process of problem solving, and in general achieve significant cognitive advances. Similarly, Linn (1985) analyzed the cognitive requirements of different levels of programming, expecting them to be potential cultivators of the processes involved in general problem solving. Papert (1980) urged that programming experience in *Logo* could equip the learner with powerful ideas about learning in general. (Salomon & Perkins, 1987, pp. 149–150)

Not everyone, however, shared the belief held by the proponents of formal disciplines that transfer is common. Thorndike (1906) challenged the view that transfer was ubiquitous by arguing instead that learning in one context only transferred to another context to the extent that the number of "identical elements" in two contexts overlapped. His model was a neural one, suggesting that the neural pathways that were excited by each element could be important because the overlap in these excited elements was responsible for transfer, when it does occur. As Detterman describes in his chapter, Thorndike's evidence came primarily from subjects' performance on simple perceptual discrimination tasks on which they had received prior training on one form and were than asked to solve a related but physically dissimilar form (Thorndike & Woodworth, 1901).

Thus, Thorndike's view of the limited nature of transfer was in opposition to those who favored a broader view of transfer that went beyond stimulus–response, or feature overlap, theory (cf. Judd, 1908). In support of his theory, Judd had fifth and sixth graders throw darts at a target submerged under 12 inches of water until they improved at hitting it. Half of them were also taught laws of refraction. After a comparable amount of time spent trying to hit the target, Judd then submerged it beneath only 4 inches of water. Now the group which had been taught the laws of refraction outperformed the group which had received only practice. This suggested to Judd that the former group had subjectively come to a shared meaning of the two tasks, and that this was why they had transferred expertise from one to the other and it is also why the latter group had not.

In the 50 years following this debate between Thorndike and Judd, numerous psychologists have described (mostly failed) attempts at transfer, though, as will be seen, there have been some notable recent exceptions. Because transfer, when it does occur, is attributed to the abstractness of the initial learning (Ceci, 1990), it is interesting to inquire into the notion of *abstractness*. What exactly does it mean to be abstract?

The role of Abstraction in Transfer. The ability to engage in abstract thinking has been heralded as one of the hallmarks of intelligence since the very beginnings of the testing movement and continues to this day to be seen as the centerpiece by researchers and laypersons alike (e.g., Cattell, 1971; Sternberg Conway, Ketron, & Bernstein, 1981; Terman, 1921). In fact, Jensen (1980), commenting on the difficulty of defining intelligence verbally, stated, "If we must define it in words, it is probably best thought of as a capacity for abstract reasoning and problem solving" (p. 19). Moreover, in the child development literature, the ability to abstract has been viewed as the pinnacle of intellectual development by numerous researchers and theorists (e.g., Case, 1985; Piaget, 1976; Vygotsky, 1962). In short, it has been suggested that one can be knowledgeable but not intelligent if one is not abstract enough to be able to transfer knowledge, whereas one cannot be intelligent without also being abstract enough to transfer across domains. High-IQ individuals are thought to be more abstract than low-IQ persons (Jensen, 1980), and as a result they are supposedly more likely to transfer solutions learned in one domain to another (Itzkoff, 1989).

Whenever someone with a low IQ functions on what appears to be an abstract level, an argument is frequently made that such complexity can only occur for such persons within a highly elaborated domain of knowledge. Thus, when a low-IQ person exhibits complex behavior, it is thought to lack abstractness. By abstractness is meant that these persons do not detect and/or rely on principles or rules that underlie problems they are attempting to solve, because if they did, they would be better able to transfer from the solution at hand to similar cases in other domains. That they do not transfer implies that they do not solve problems by abstracting underlying rules or principles. According to this line of reasoning, instances of complex behavior among individuals who possess low-IQs are the result of their fixation on the contents of a single highly elaborated domain of knowledge (e.g., chess, work, sports, gambling, love). Fixation on a single domain allows one to accrue elaborate information in that domain which is often sufficient to solve even very complex problems in that domain. Accordingly, low-IQ individuals do not solve complex problems from the vantage point of having abstracted an underlying rule or principle, but from the vantage point of having learned a great deal of highly specific material that is yoked to highly specific solutions. A case in point is the street bookie in Brazil, an individual who often can quote prices for various complex combinations of lottery animals with great accuracy despite little or no formal education (Schliemann & Acioly, 1989). These men are unable to transfer their knowledge of probabilities to isomorphic problems that involve different materials, however, leading researchers to conclude that schooling conveys greater flexibility for transfer.

Transfer refers to a recognition that various terms and entities of one set can be mapped onto those of another set. What is considered as far transfer for one researcher may be considered near transfer by another. "How far is far transfer? . . . what is considered *far* by an experimental psychologist who is trying to teach mentally retarded subjects a rehearsal strategy for rote learning a list of items may be *near,* almost inconsequentially near, for the social activist who is preparing them to live in a productive life! (Das, 1987, p. vii). Transfer research is a complicated field, and there are numerous variations for mapping elements from one set onto those of another set, as well as numerous variations in constraints that can be imposed on these mappings (see Gholson, Eymard, Long, Morgan, & Leeming, 1988). For example, consider what is termed a "partially mapped homomorphic transfer" problem. A boat to carry three male and two females across a river can carry at most two people at a time (and always must carry at least one person). But no wife may ever be in the presence of any male, unless her husband is also present. Only one of the pairs is married, that is, the other female is not a wife. So there are no constraints on her consorting with any of the three males. These five individuals can safely cross the river in seven moves, but there are over 60 different seven-move schedules that can be mapped!

Transfer between two tasks may occur within the very same domain, for instance, from an appreciation of the scheduling sequence that is required to solve the classic "missionaries and cannibals" problem, wherein a single missionary cannot be left alone with two or more cannibals, to an appreciation of the routes that may be traversed to solve an isomorphic problem involving "jealous husbands and wives."

Transfer can also take place across two completely different domains, as in the algebra to physics example provided by Bassok and Holyoak (this volume). Although a mapping can be guided by the abstraction of a general rule, it need not be, and it often appears to those who do this kind of research that it is not. Brown and Kane (1989), for example, report the case of a child who learns to transfer without even being presented the problem, simply because he had come to expect that the solution to all problems of this type required the same procedures, thus allowing him to answer before the question was even posed! Moreover, Gholson et al. (1988) have shown that transfer from the problem of the three jealous husbands to the isomorphic problem of the three missionaries is superior than vice versa, whereas transfer from a problem dealing with two missionaries to an isomorphic one dealing with two jealous husbands is better than the reverse! Clearly, the specifics of the stimuli have a large bearing on whether transfer occurs. This has been known for at least 20 years, since Birch and Bortner (1970) got children to transfer from a task using wooden dolls when they appeared unable to do so when geometric shapes had been employed (also see Cole, 1976, for a similar demonstration). So transfer can occur even when a subject does not appreciate an underlying rule, and this explains the less than pervasive nature of transfer when it does occur. Even if one can transfer without being abstract, one cannot, some have alleged, be abstract and yet fail to transfer, except under very unusual and artificial circumstances. Detterman has provided a challenge to this line of argumentation by asserting that those studies that have provided evidence of transfer have "rigged" the outcome by simply informing subjects of the isomorphism and/or instructing them to carry out similar operations in two domains.

Throughout this century, researchers from such diverse fields as psychology, philosophy, and neurology have provided definitions of *abstractness*, but these definitions have been very different (e.g. Beaumont, 1983; Jaques, 1978; Pikas, 1966). The first comprehensive empirical treatment was provided by Goldstein and Scheerer in their 1941 monograph entitled *Abstract and Concrete Behavior: An Experimental Study with Special Tests*. Based on observations of returning brain-injured veterans from World War I, these researchers began to assemble a picture of abstractness that was quite global. They termed it the *abstract attitude*, to convey their belief that abstractness was something more than just cognitive; it pervaded the entire personality of the organism—hence the term *attitude*. Veterans with frontal lobe damage who had difficulty with tasks that were thought to require abstract thinking (e.g., assembling a cube out of four smaller ones) convinced Goldstein and Scheerer that the frontal lobe was the seat of their deficit. This touched off a half century of debate and the ultimate refutation of their neurological explanation when it was shown that patients with posterior lobe damage had similar difficulties on the Goldstein-Scheerer battery (Beaumont, 1983).

Despite the problems with their neurological model, Goldstein and Scheerer's description of abstraction continues to be influential. The abstract individual, according to them, is one who can shift perspectives flexibly, plan ahead, hold in mind various actions simultaneously, and analyze separate parts in relation to a whole. The concrete person, on the other hand, is someone who is unreflective, rigid, and *yoked to an immediate perceptual experience*. This last point gets at the heart of the distinction: Concrete individuals' performance are confined to their immediate perception of experience, whereas abstract individuals can go beneath the surface of perceptual appearances and infer an underlying rule. Goldstein and Scheerer (1941) regarded this as an essential distinction of the two modes of behavior (p. 22).

Our own view holds that being abstract means having lots of knowledge relevant to solving a specific class of problems. This view is bound to displease many of our cognitively oriented colleagues. But it does accord with recent thinking about neural networks, in which researchers attempt to model thinking after the human brain, emphasizing the basic unit of information processing, the neuron, and its ability to connect with millions of neighboring neurons to form pathways of activation and/or inhibition that come to represent thinking. In recent versions of connectionist theory (e.g. Rumelhart, 1991), it is precisely an expert's ample knowledge within a domain that allows his or her knowledge representation in that domain to be re-presented in the problem at hand. In other words, the within-domain knowledge is so ample and elaborately structured that it is hard to present an expert with a problem that is not already represented therein or that cannot easily be construction through processes such as analogy and comparison.

In the remainder of this chapter we shall briefly review some recent work by cognitive psychologists on the topic of transfer, with a view toward answering the following question: Do measures of so-called *general intelligence,* the best known of which is the IQ score, predict the ease, accuracy, and depth (i.e., the distance) with which one can transfer when original learning is comparable (see Campione & Brown, 1987; Nye, Burns, Delclos, & Bransford, 1987, for findings that illustrate that group differences exist in far transfer, though not near transfer)? To address this question, we will describe a case study of two men who differ markedly in their IQ scores, while they attempt to solve what for them is a novel problem—but one that is isomorphic with a problem they have already solved in another domain.

Recent Research on Cognitive Transfer. Ann Brown and her colleagues (Brown, in press; Brown & Kane, 1988; Brown, Kane & Echols, 1986) have reported a number of demonstrations of preschoolers' transfer under conditions where they have sufficient experience in the task domain and when the two tasks are similar. For example, in one series of tasks, children who learned that a certain material (e.g., grains of corn) can be transported across a river by using a straw, also transferred the same solution to transporting other materials across other barriers with a straw.

Bassok and Holyoak (1989) have shown that there is considerable difficulty involved in training college students to transfer certain statistical rules (like the Poisson distribution principle), even when a great deal of support and practice is provided, and indeed, even when the transfer is "local," that is, within the same domain (albeit one that is probably not elaborately structured for these participants). Their work calls into question the presumption that transfer is a ubiquitous process that is freely invoked by those with high IQs. On the other hand, Nisbett, Fong, Lehman, and Cheng (1988) have found limited evidence that other kinds of statistical reasoning can be taught to university students, and that some of them are able to transfer this knowledge to new domains immediately following training. After 2 weeks, however, much of the transfer appears lost. So, given the difficulty of achieving transfer *within* some domains, it should come as no surprise to find that transfer across knowledge domains, although it can occur, frequently does not. This has prompted one observer to comment that:

> The question for which we do have some empirical answers has to do with how generalizable cognitive training is from one subject area to another. As of now, the answer is not very much. (Schooler, 1989, p. 11)

According to the Law of Large Numbers *(LLN)* (Nisbett et al., 1988), transfer should proceed in accordance with the rule that holds the large samples are necessary to generalize about groups that are more variable on a given attribute than groups that are less variable (Nisbett et al., 1988). Adults seem to appreciate this rule in some contexts quite well—appreciating, for example, that a small sampling of a slot machine's behavior or a rookie's batting performance is inadequate for generalizing about their performance over the long haul. Yet, in other contexts, adults are quite unlikely to appreciate this rule (e.g., realizing that empathy or altruism expressed by someone they just met at a party is a poor basis for generalizing about the manifestation of such traits over the long haul of a social relationship).

Others have reported similar failures among college-aged subjects to transfer. Leshowitz (1989) gave a broad cross-section of college students "everyday" problems that contained principles taught in introductory social science courses (e.g., the need for control groups). Yet, of the hundreds of students tested, hardly any demonstrated even a semblance of methodological thinking about these problems, despite the considerable number of science and math courses they had taken.

Thus, notwithstanding the pervasive and often-stated assumption that transfer is ubiquitous, the empirical picture is far less clear. The research has prompted Rogoff (1981) to ask critically, after reviewing the cross-cultural literature on transfer and generality.

> What conclusions about generality can be drawn from successful performance on a syllogism problem? That the individual (a) will do well on the next syllogism? (b) will do well on other kinds of logic problems? (c) will be logical in many situations? or (d) is smart? (p. 127)

Regardless of whether transfer occurs frequently or only rarely, it is clear that there are large individual differences when it does occur: Some participants successfully transfer, while others do not. Presently, little is known about the characteristics of those who fail or succeed to transfer, save the presumption that the latter have higher levels of general intelligence (Itzkoff, 1989). We turn to this assumption next.

The Issue of Generality. One of the stickiest issues facing contemporary cognitive psychology is that of *generality.* We assert that is "sticky" because it appears to be assumed, rather than proven, that intelligent individuals are by definition those who are capable of acting intelligently in general—capable of transferring knowledge and insights across domains. It is not too great of a simplification to say that Jensen's "Type 2 intelligence"—that is, the ability to draw inferences, transform symbolic input, and to correlate information from one domain with that from another (Jensen, 1980), Spearman's "g" (Spearman, 1904), Sternberg's "executive" (Sternberg, 1985), and Itzkoff's "cortical glue" (Itzkoff, 1989), are all variations on this same theme of "intelligence as transfer or generality." Consider this: In psychometric research, the often large and reliable first principal component that is extracted from a matrix of intertask correlations among cognitive measures is interpreted as the magnitude of an individual's *general* ability to solve problems (see Ceci, 1990, for review of this position); the large first principal component is taken to mean that a person has a specified amount of mental power to transfer solutions across a very wide range of problems.

> An enormous amount of evidence argues that with a high "g" an individual is enabled to enter a civilized society along a number of professional, vocational pathways—medicine, law, scholarship, arts, and business. Persons with high "g" can retrain themselves to do many different tasks in one lifetime and often at a highly creative level. (Itzkoff, 1989, p. 85)

The Role of General Intelligence in Transfer. Despite the reasonableness of the above view, there is surprisingly little data to support it. And the supporting data come from comparisons of normal and retarded or borderline retarded subjects who are not shown to be comparable on original learning at the outset, and who are given relatively brief periods of instruction prior to transfer (Campione & Brown, 1987; Nye et al., 1987). What is needed is a situation where individuals who differ in their level of general intelligence are shown to be comparable solving a problem in one domain and then are given an extensive periods of exposure to an isomorphic problem from a different domain. The present case study was undertaken to determine whether an individual's IQ was related to his or her ability to succeed at a complex transfer task, one requiring multiple interaction effects and an appreciation of nonlinearity. Our aim was not simply to assess the role of IQ in a transfer task the way one might assess the role of field independence, impulsiveness, or any other individual difference measure, but to ask whether IQ, which is assumed by many to index the abstractness and generality of cognitive processing, is in fact related to one's ability to solve a complex task that is homomorphic with another task they have already learned to solve in a different domain. Our goal is to provide some empirical evidence for the view that IQ is related to complexity and generality of thought, by virtue of its correlation with transfer across complex tasks. While the hazards of generalizing from a case study are well known, we felt that the following data would provide preliminary evidence about a thorny issue that is difficult to tackle experimentally with large samples.

Background Research. In our previous research, we studied a group of men who attended harness races practically every day of their adult lives, in order to gain an understanding of the basis for their expertise at predicting posttime odds (Ceci & Liker, 1986a).[1] Based on their knowledge of racing facts and their ability to correctly predict posttime odds, we distinguished them as either experts or nonexperts.

---

[1] Expertise was based on precision at predicting posttime odds rather than on more "intuitive" measures such as the number of race winners picked or the amount of money won. This was done for two reasons. First, it is not possible to gather reliable data on the actual amount of money won or lost. Individuals may over- or underestimate their winnings for a variety of reasons (e.g., fear that the interviewer will report them to the IRS, as all payoffs that exceed 300 to 1 are supposed to be cashed at a special IRS window; or they may not wish word to circulate that they had won a large pay-off, for fear that others will want to borrow from them; or they may overestimate their winnings in order to impress the interviewer with their prowess). So, for these and other reasons, the use of "earnings" as a criterion was not feasible. Concerning the use of "number of winners" as a criterion of expertise, there are other problems having to do with the nature of parimutuel wagering. In brief, short of correctly picking winners in over 95% of races (a feat that no one has yet come even close to!), the sheer number of winners that one picks is unimportant. What really matters in parimutuel wagering is to avoid overvalued horses and select undervalued one, that is, ones that the betting public has not bet commensurate with their "true" odds. Even if one were to pick 50% winners (not difficult to do, as the favorite alone wins 38% of races at the tracks studied), one could still lose money. Yet, one *could* actually win money if one picked only 5% winners, provided they were sufficiently undervalued by the public. While there are many different models of probability that can be applied to racing data, take a simple model of independence between two horses in the same race, to illustrate why accuracy assessing true odds is what racing is all about. Suppose that the #1 horse is the heavy favorite, say 1 to 5 (20¢ on a dollar, or $2.40 return on a $2.00 wager). But suppose the expert assesses this horse's chances of winning to be more like 5 to 2 ($7.00 return for a $2.00 wager). Now suppose that another horse in that race, the #8 horse, is being bet at 10 to 1 ($22.00 return on a $2.00 wager), even though the expert assesses this horse's "true" odds closer to 4 to 1 ($10.00 return on a $2.00 wager). According to some models, the #1 horse will win 10 out of every 17 direct match-ups with the #8 horse (i.e., at 5:2 true odds, he will win 10 out of 35 races while the #8 horse, with true odds of 4:1, will win only 7 out of 35). Yet, at 1:5 posttime odds, the #1 horse is a poor wager, even though in any given race he has a better chance to win than the #8 horse (10 to 7). A gambler will definitely lose money betting horses like #1 (e.g., in the example given here, one would lose $46 every 35 match-ups, assuming a constant $2.00 wager at 1:5 post time odds with a horse whose "true" odds were 5:2). Yet, the individual who accurately assessed the mismatch between the #8's horse's posttime odds and his "true" odds, could win a lot of money even though he selected fewer winners than his counterpart. Thus, the measure of expertise that was used was odds estimation, not winners or earnings.

Although both experts and nonexperts were far more knowledgeable than were amateurs about horse racing and were far better at predicting posttime odds than were amateurs, they differed greatly among themselves. The group called experts was excellent at estimating the odds on each horse be at post time (they could do this several hours before post time, by studying variables contained in the racing program), while the nonexperts were far less accurate. We asked the men in these groups to handicap real races as well as hypothetical races we designed. The hypothetical races were included to separate variables that were often too correlated in actual races to determine their contribution to an expert's decision. In the hypothetical races, these variables were allowed to covary systematically.

We demonstrated that expert handicappers employed a complex, multiplicative model involving multiple interaction effects. By regressing 25 racetrack variables on experts' assessments of odds, we were able to show that simple additive models failed to account for the complexity of their decisions. Experts not only took into consideration more variables when handicapping a race, but they did not simply "add up" this information. Rather, they developed implicit algorithms that gave more or less weight to different types of information. And each type of information changed the way they thought about the other types.

The correlation between an expert's IQ score and the b weight for a seven-way interactive term (which is a surrogate for their cognitive complexity and was shown to be highly correlated with their success at predicting odds) was .07. This means that, even though the greater use of complex, interactive thinking was causally related to success at predicting odds, there was no relation between such complex thinking and IQ. Thus, assessment of the experts' intelligence on a standard IQ test was irrelevant in predicting the complexity of their thinking at the racetrack (Ceci & Liker, 1986a, 1988). Within either group (experts or nonexperts), IQ was unrelated to handicapping complexity. Between groups, however, there was an invariant finding: Experts with low IQs always used more complex, interactive models than did nonexperts with high IQs, and their success was due in large part to the use of these complex interactive models. IQ was useless in predicting both how complexly these experts reasoned and the number of variables they considered interactively in their judgments. (Interestingly, the success of experts at making these computations depends, in part, on their skill at doing mental arithmetic and, in particular, at subtractions that cross fifths boundaries. Yet this skill was unrelated to their scores on the mental Arithmetic scale of the IQ test, too.)

It could be argued that IQ is still a valid predictor of intellectual functioning, despite the failure to find it correlated with complexity in the racetrack task. After all, the participants in the racetrack study attended the races nearly every day of their adult lives, and perhaps those with high IQs developed the complex understanding needed to estimate odds long before those with low IQs. By subjecting two of these individuals to a new task that was novel for both of them, but that depended on a similar algorithm to the one they used at the racetrack, we could assess whether the man with a high IQ would be quicker at reinventing the complex algorithm to succeed at this new task. To our knowledge, there are no data on such a question, and our present effort represents a rather crude first pass.

METHOD

Participants. Two men participated in this study. One man was a 46-year-old self-employed business man with a master's degree in mathematics education and an IQ of 121. The other man was a retired, 74-year-old dock worker with an IQ of 81 and a fifth-grade education. Both men had participated in an earlier study of expertise in racetrack handicapping (subjects 20 and 29, respectively, in the Ceci & Liker, 1986a, study). And both had been rated as experts in that study, demonstrating comparable use of a complex multiple interaction term in their decisions (see Table 6 of Ceci & Liker, 1986a).

Neither participant reported having had prior experience in the stock market before participating in this exercise: Neither man had invested in stocks in the past or claimed to have known anything about the variables that influence actual market forces, or to have played stock market games like *Millionaire*. To make sure that these two individuals had no substantive knowledge or beliefs about the stock market that might differentiate than at the start of this study, we asked them 24 multiple choice questions that were designed by a market consultant to the project to assess basic-level understanding of stock market mechanisms (see Appendix A for a sample of these). On this quiz neither man achieved an above-chance score answering questions about basic stock market mechanisms. While it is still possible that these men might have differed on some more subtle knowledge-based measure, it appears that neither was sufficiently knowledge-able to have had an advantage or disadvantage because of background experience.

Procedure. Both men were presented 600 trials of a stock market game that required them to estimate which of two stocks would have the best future earning-to-price ratio, or P/E ratio (a stock's price divided by its earnings per share). One of the two stocks was always listed at the market average, and the other was a stock that was to be evaluated against the average, by estimating the probability that it would yield a higher P/E ratio than the average. To present comparative information for stocks, a commercial program that was developed by *Value Line* for use by stock analysts was modified. It incorporates 38 variables, but for this task only 18 were covaried in order to provide com-parability with the racetrack tasks that these men were accustomed to. A single page described two stocks (one being the composite market average and the other being a novel stock) along 18 variables. The subject was charged with deciding the probability that the novel stock would return a higher P/E ratio than the market average. Table 6.1 depicts a sample page with two stocks. All stocks were identified only as numbers, to avoid any expectancies associated with certain ticker names (e.g., IBM).

The participants were informed that the information presented was fictitious, and the task was a game to see whether they could determine the rule that predicted P/E ratios. They were informed that the information to be presented had been prepared in such a manner that the P/E ratio could be inferred, but that it was not obvious how this was done and it was their job to try to figure out the rule. Some of the information to be presented was sufficient to predict which stocks would have the most favorable future price/earnings ratio (P-E ratio), but not all information presented would be useful. Finally, even among those categories of information that were useful in determining P/E ratio, not all were of equal importance to determining the P/E ratio. Each of the 18 variables listed in Table 6.1 were explained to the participants, and examples were provided until they indicated that they understood what the variables stood for. In addition, a glossary of the meaning of all 18 variables was available throughout the study.

The rule to establish whether a particular stock's P/E ratio would rise or fall above the market average was precisely the same one used by these men to establish posttime odds at the racetrack. In short, it was a seven-factor equation, with multiple interaction effects.

Table 6.1. P/E ratio comparison of market average (#72) with another stock (#132).

Variables	#72	#132
1. Timeliness Rank	1	3
*2. Beta	1.65	1.35
3. Book value/share	38.33	44.51
4. 3-mo. % price change	4.5	-2.42
5. Safety Rank	2.0	1.0
6. Price Stability	60	85
7. Financial Strength	A+	A++
*8. Market Value/Sales (Smill)	14734.3/8685	74267/59041
*9. 5-Yr Dividend Growth	3.2	4.5
10. Current Yield (%)	0.0	2.8
*11. Current P/E Ratio	15.4	14.9
*12. Current EPS	6.01	8.72
13. Recent Price	110.400	123.325
14. 12-mo. High/Low	110.255/59.370	175.655/122.800
*15. Price-Book Value	2.31	2.47
*16. Debt as % of capital	5	9
17. % Retained to Com Eq	9.7	10.4
18. % Return Net Worth	9.9	19.2

Note: Asterisk (*) indicates that variable was part of interaction term.

In the course of presenting the 600 trials, these seven variables were consistently relevant to the P/E ratio prediction task. This was done implicitly, through the use of an algorithm that was written to generate the stock market date, but that was not explained to the participants until after the 600 trials had been completed. The task for the participants was to infer the nature of the algorithm, and the seven factor interactive term that determined the P/E ratios. These seven variables (denoted by asterisks in Table 6.1) were weighted by the algorithm to provided deterministic outcomes; only these variables could serve as the basis for making *consistently* accurate P/E ratio predictions. Thus, as in harness race handicapping, occasionally irrelevant independent variables might be associated with changes in the dependent variable (P/E ratio), but over the long haul only the seven variables interacted to consistently determine P/E ratios. Again, the men were not informed until after the 600 trials of the isomorphism between the manner in which these seven stock market variables could be weighted and multiplicatively combined to determine P/E ratios and the seven variables in harness racing that determined posttime odds. That is, they were not expressly informed of the similarity between the rule governing P/E ratios and the one that they routinely employed at the racetrack. The goal of presenting these trials was to see if these two individuals would realize, on the basis of the 600 feedback trials, that: (a) only 7 of the 18 independent variables that were presented were deterministic of P/E ratios, (b) simple main effects and lower-level interactive models were inadequate for determining P/E ratios, and (c) they would be able to construct more complex models akin to those they had already demonstrated in another domain (harness racing).

Although the variables used in this transfer task represent actual stock market variables that stock analysts consider important, the task was quite different from actual stock market analysis. Not only was the format for presenting the stocks different (two-stock comparisons that required a forced choice among them), but a number of variables that analysts consider important were excluded in order to keep the number at 18. Thus, no product development, political, or historical data were provided for any stock, nor general economic data that could bear on decisions. Finally, the task was quite unlike the one facing serious investors, who must take into account the joint performance of entire portfolios that were assembled to balance risk, market sensitivity, diversification, and so on. Our goal was simply to see whether an algorithm that had been used in one domain might emerge in another in which it was instrumental.

The object of each trial was for the participants to sift through the simulated data on the 18 independent variables, and predict whether the stock on that page represented a superior future P/E ratio to the market average. The participants performed this task independently and made their decision by marking a sheet of paper given to them. At a given session (approximately 1 hour), participants were presented, on average, 10 pages of two-stock comparisons, with a range between 4 and 12 trials. The number of trials they were given depended on their schedules and interest level that day. These trials were usually administered prior to or following the races in a clubhouse restaurant. The 600 trials were spread out over an 18-month period. Although participants were invited to take as much time as they wished to make their selections, 97% of these one-page trials took between 5 minutes and 10 minutes. It was stressed that the stocks in this game were fictitious and not to be found in any newspaper, and that behavior could not be improved by reading financial reports or by any type of studying.

Following every P/E prediction from a two-stock comparison, the participant was given feedback in the form of the future P-E ratios for each of the two stocks on that page. This is similar to harness racing where, following an expert's estimation of probable odds for horses in a race, he or she observes the actual odds. A tally was kept each day so that participants could keep track of their overall performance (i.e., the percentage of time they correctly predicted whether the novel stock would return a better P/E ratio than the market average P/E ratio). Although they were not informed about the other participant's performance by the experimenters, they often informed each other of their overall prediction rates, through they were asked not to divulge the strategies or variables they used.

Although this task was structurally similar to the one these participants confronted on a daily basis at the racetrack, there were several important differences. First, and foremost, there was no actual financial risk or gain involved in this task, unlike the racetrack task. Second, participants were not provided the same level of extensive experience on this task that they had with the racetrack handicapping task. And within this less extensive period of experience, they were presented the actual trials much less frequently than they experienced them at the racetrack. That is, in contrast to their 20 years' experience at the track, these men were provided only about 18 months' experience at this market task. However, to handicap the comparable number of races ($n = 600$) would take approximately 12 weeks (10 races/day $\times$ 5 racing days/week), whereas these 600 stock market trials were spaced over 18 months. Finally, the level of motivation, although seemingly high, could not be equated with that involved in harness racing for these men. The latter enterprise was a fundamental aspect of their adult lives, one that had not waned over more than 20 years of daily involvement.

Figure 6.1 depicts the participants' accuracy at predicting stock rises in this fictional simulation as a function of the number of trials they observed. As can be seen, even after 600 trials, these two participants were far from adept, though they were both able to predict P/E ratios considerably better than chance, which is 50% in this two-choice task. At the end of 600 trials, both participants had acquired part of the complex seven-way interactive model that drove the simulation, to roughly similar degrees.

To analyze the implicit algorithm the men developed to guide their P/E ratio decisions, a modelling procedure based on Ceci and Liker (1986a,b) was

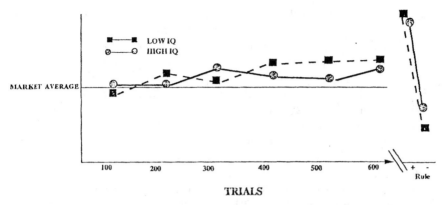

Figure 6.1.   Probability of predicting whether a stock will exceed the market average. "Rule" refers to provision of information that the task was analogous to the racetrack task (+), and subsequently altering the correct racetract weightings (−) without warning.

employed. This is a modification of the general linear procedure, so that parameters can be estimated without fully crossing all levels of each variable with those of the others.[2] The analytic approach was to assess whether the nonadditive combination of variables (the seven-way interaction term) had a unique net effect on the participants' decisions about P/E ratios, net the simple additive effects of the individual vairables. Therefore, this interactive term was added after all of the variables were first entered into the model in order to determine whether this interaction term resulted in a reduction of the sums of squares error independently of the variables' additive effects.

The higher IQ participant used what amounted to a combination of main effects and lower order interactive effects. For example, during his final 200 trials, he combined the value of a stock's *Beta* (an index of sensitivity to overall fluctuations in the markets)[3] with its riskiness (judged against the standard of

---

[2] Separate regression analyses were run for each subject in a linear model in which vectors represented the characteristics of each stock on the variables as well as on a composite seven-way interactive term. This latter term was constructed to produce P/E ratios in a manner similar to the way race horses' posttime odds were derived. The dependent variable in these analyses was the log of the odds of the P/E ratio probabilities (see Ceci & Liker, 1986a, for details). A standard stochastic error term was included. The basic model assumes that vectors combine additively and b-coefficients represent the relative importance of each in predicting P/E ratios. Of course, the computer program that generated the P/E ratios was nonadditive, since the purpose of the study was to determine whether experts who deploy this same nonadditive algorithm in another context (racing) would rediscover its relevance in a novel context.

[3] *Beta* was derived from a least squares regression between the percentage of change in the long-term market average and the percentage of change in the short-term price of that stock, adjusted for the tendency to regress to the mean.

the market itself, with stocks being either above or below the market average in their riskiness) and often multiplied this value by two other values that he derived. During earlier trials, he had used other implicit models of equivalent complexity, though these resulted in somewhat inferior performance.

The lower IQ participant employed appears to be a series of three-way interactive models. The best predictive value of these models was observed during his final 230 trials. Here he took into consideration the 5-year dividend growth of a stock, the market liquidity for that same stock (which in turn was derived by multiplying the price of the stock by the number of its outstanding shares), and is *Beta*. While these three-way interactions were superior to lower order ones, they still were far from satisfactory.

Thus, following 600 trials neither racetrack expert succeeded in rediscovering the same seven-way interactive model that governed their racetrack predictions, even though both were able to perform above chance in predicting whether a stock's P/E ratio would exceed the market average. Their implicit algorithms had become stable at the time of the final trial, and it is unlikely that they would have continued to change with increased experience.

Following the 600th trial, we explained to the men that the same model they employed at the racetrack could be used to predict P/E ratios in this task, and allowed them 25 additional trials to see if they could apply in this context. As can be seen in figure 6.1, when given this information, both men quickly figured out what the seven relevant variables were and how much relative weight to assign to each of them. They reached "ceiling" levels of accuracy within the next 25 trials.

Finally, after they had reached ceiling, we altered the relative weights assigned to these seven variables to make sure the men had been using the same algorithm they used at the racetrack. In other words, if they were using the same algorithm, then altering the weights is expected to reduce their estimation accuracy to chance. This is essentially what happened, though due to a fortuitous association of some of the altered weights on trials 625 to 650, the performance dropped below chance when the alterations were made.

CONCLUSIONS

What answers do these findings suggest to the questions raised in the *Introduction?* Before addressing this question, an important caveat is in order. It is evident that the study needs extension. As already noted, perhaps these men would show even greater prediction on the stock market task if they were subjected to personal monetary risks. These two men may have required thousands of trials to develop the equivalent mental algorithm that they used at the racetrack, and therefore the 600 trials that were provided here might have been insufficient for attainment of the full seven-way interactive model, even though both of these men had stabilized after 400 trials and showed no signs of continuing to "tune" their models during the final 200 trials.

In an earlier progress report of these men's stock market predictions following the first 400 trials, we wondered whether they would immediately perceive the correct algorithm if they were informed of the isomorphism with the racing task:

> One might wonder what would happen if the men were informed of the isomorphism. We have no doubt what the answer would be . . . It is almost certainly the case that had we informed the men of the relevance of the racetrack algorithm for the stock market task, they would have solved the latter within two hundred trials (i.e., the time needed to sort out the seven variables that interacted and assign the correct relative weights). However, it is worth bearing in mind that the goal of this study was not to see how many trials would be necessary to develop a new mental model or to see whether these men could adapt an old model to a new context if they had been instructed to do so, but rather to see if a comparable level of cognitive complexity would spontaneously be reinvented to provide a solution in a new problem domain. That is, we wanted to see whether the cognitive complexity that was associated with expertise at the racetrack was domain-specific, or whether it was *general*. (Ceci & Ruiz, 1992, p. 24)

It appears that neither participant gained any sudden insight into the appropriateness of his already-developed racetrack model, but sought to develop a new model. Given the task demands and the novelty of the domain, this is perhaps a wise strategy. The alternative would be for these men to go through life trying to fit a model they developed for a highly specific situation (racing) to situations that were in need of entirely different models. More than one military commentator has noted that generals lose battles by fighting the last war.

Concerning the main topic of interest, namely, the extent to which transfer is related to IQ, the present study is suggestive, though not definitive.

These results suggest that cognitive complexity is not as general as some have supposed. Perhaps if we had given these two men additional trials, the participant with a higher IQ may have developed a more complex model than the lower IQ person. However, this is sheer speculation, because nothing in the data after the first 600 trials differentiated these two men—not their P/E ratio prediction accuracy, not their model complexity.

Historically, IQ has been viewed as an index of general learning ability, a view that still has its supporters (see Lidz, 1987). For example, several participants at the *Journal of Educational Psychology's* 1921 symposium on the nature and measurement of intelligence held the view that learning ability was the sine qua non of intelligence. Dearborn (1921) noted that "theoretically, it would follow that measurement of the actual progress of learning would furnish the best test of intelligence" (p. 211), and Buckingham (1921) argued that intelligence ought to be regarded "as ability to learn, and as measured by the extent to which learning has taken place or may take place" (p. 273). According to this perspective, the higher IQ subject in this study ought to have outperformed the lower IQ one, but this is not what happened. It might be that the task was simply too difficult for any transfer to occur, and that, if an easier task were used, the high IQ man would excel. However, there is good evidence that both men in this study performed better than chance, and that both of them developed mental models of price/earnings prediction that entailed interactive thinking. Yet there is no evidence that the high IQ man's model was more complex than the low IQ man's model. If IQ is a measure of cognitive complexity, then why was it that the high-IQ man did not generate a more complex than the low IQ man's model. If IQ is a measure of cognitive complexity, then why was it that high-IQ man did not generate a more complex than the low-IQ man? Why did the high-IQ man not develop his terminal level of complexity on fewer trials than the low-IQ man? These are important questions that cannot be answered on the basis of the present data, but ones that will require the use of new tasks that are better calibrated to yield optimal levels of complexity by the end of data collection, so that one need not guess about what might have happened if additional trials had been provided.

A view is emerging in developmental psychology that depicts the IQ score as a measure of a single type of cognizing, rather than as a measure of some generalized aptitude for complex thinking that it has been claimed to be (Ceci, 1990). IQ seems to reflect academic–verbal performance that is highly related to the possession of a codified set of background knowledge (primarily verbal knowledge gained through schooling and vital to performance on IQ tests, employment screening tests, and SATs). IQ and other alleged indicants of general ability are good predictors of a wide range of real-world endeavors (school, work, social satisfaction), but it appears that "prediction" and "explanation" are fundamentally disjunctive processes. In the future, psychologists might spend more energy focusing on the causal paths between IQ and real-world accomplishments, in an effort to explain the bases for these predictions. The anticipation, based on the present findings and on other studies (Ceci & Liker, 1986a; Dörner & Kreuzig, 1983; Gardner, 1983; Schneider, Körkel, & Weinert, 1989), is that it will not be through the generalized ability to engage in complex thinking that IQ tests have their predictive power. Even low-IQ individuals may have the ability to engage in complex, multicausal reasoning, when care is taken to control for background knowledge and motivation (e.g., Schneider et al., 1989). This claim carries with it the following "moral": Causal impressions are apt to be misleading when it comes to judging an expert. Even an expert with a low IQ may be a good expert, and more complex than a nonexpert who posseses a high IQ. Perhaps this is why IQ scores are less predictive of supervisor ratings than they are of discrete work products (Stitch, 1975), and why IQ adds little or nothing to the prediction of future earnings when social class and education are taken into consideration (Henderson & Ceci, in press). In other words, employers and others who interact with individuals who have IQ scores below 100 may have realized that their capabilities go well beyond their scores; that they are capable of complexity and depth if they are provided with the requisite background knowledge. Whether this research will show that low-IQ individuals require longer periods of training to acquire such background knowledge is a matter we cannot answer at this time, though the present findings indicate that the answer may not be as obvious as some expect.

It is a sad reality that many individuals exist who have large repositories of knowledge, but who have no ability to integrate it to derive complex insights (Sternberg, 1985). Not everyone who experiences the same environment that Mozart experienced will become as insightful into musical structures as he did. Sheer facts, in the absence of an organizational plan that permits the simultaneous integration and differentiation of the facts, will not help develop expertise. This is because the expertise of the form we have studied is predicated on more than a passive factual retrieval system. Research is converging on the view that the critical factor in the development of expertise is the manner in which facts are integrated and differentiated in one's knowledge base (Chi & Ceci, 1987; Streufert & Nogami, 1989). Exposure to relevant information is therefore necessary but insufficient for expertise to develop. Experts are motivated to revise their mental models until they achieve a maximum fit with the external world.

REFERENCES

Bassok, M., & Holyoak, K.J. (1989). Interdomain transfer between isomorphic topics in algebra and physics. *Journal of Experimental Psychology: Learning, Memory, and Cognition, 15*, 153–166.

Beaumont, J. G. (1983). *Introduction to neuropsychology.* New York: Guilford Press.

Bortner, M., & Birch, H. G. (1970). Cognitive capacity and cognitive competence review. *American Journal of Mental Deficiency, 74*, 735–752.

Brown, A. L. (in press). Analogical learning and transfer: What develops? In S. Vosniadou & A. Ortony (Eds.), *Similarities and analogical reasoning.*

Brown, A. L., & Kane, M. J. (1988). Preschool children can learn to transfer: Learning to learn and learning from example. *Cognitive Psychology, 20*, 493–523.

Brown, A. L., Kane, M. J., & Echols, C. H. (1986). Young children's mental models determine analogical transfer across problems with a common goal structure. *Cognitive Development 1*, 103–121.

Buckingham, B. R. (1921). Intelligence and its measurement: A symposium. *Journal of Educational Psychology, 12*, 271–275.

Campione, J., & Brown, A. L. (1987). Linking dynamic assessment with school achievement. In C. S. Lidz (Ed.), *Dynamic assessment* (pp. 82–115). New York: Guilford Press.

Case, R. (1985). *Intellectual development from birth to adulthood.* Orlando, FL: Academic Press.

Ceci, S. J. (1990). *On intelligence . . . more or less: A bioecological treatise on intellectual development.* Englewood Cliffs, NJ: Prentice-Hall. (Century Series in Psychology)

Ceci, S. J., & Liker, J. (1986a). A day at the races: A study of IQ, expertise, and cognitive complexity. *Journal of Experimental Psychology: General, 115,* 255–266.

Ceci, S. J., & Liker, J. (1986b). Academic and non-academic intelligence: An experimental separation. In R. J. Sternberg & R. Wagner (Eds.), *Practical intelligence: Origins of competence in the everyday world.* New York: Cambridge University Press.

Ceci, S. J., & Liker, J. (1988). Stalking the IQ–expertise relationship: When the critics go fishing. *Journal of Experimental Psychology: General, 117,* 96–100.

Ceci, S. J., & Ruiz, A. (1992) The role of general ability in cognitive complexity. In R. Hoffman (Ed.), *Intelligent systems theory.* (pp. 218-232). New York: Springer-Verlag.

Chi, M. T. H., & Ceci, S. J. (1987). Content knowledge: Its restructuring with memory development. In H. W. Reese & L. Lipsett (Eds.), *Advances in Child Development and Behavior, 20,* 91–146.

Cole, M. (1976). A probe trial procedure for the study of children's discrimination learning and transfer. *Journal of Experimental Child Psychology, 22,* 499–510.

Das, J. P. (1987). Foreword. In C. S. Lidz (Ed.), *Dynamic assessment.* New York: Guilford Press.

Dearborn, W. F. (1921). Intelligence and its measurement: A symposium. *Journal of Educational Psychology, 12,* 210–212.

Dörner, D., & Kreuzig, H. (1983). Problemlosefahigkeit und intelligenz [Problem-solving ability and intelligence]. *Psychologische Rundhaus, 34,* 185–192.

Gardner, H. (1983). *Frames of mind: The theory of multiple intelligences.* New York: Cambridge University Press.

Gholson, B., Eyemard, L., Long, D., & Leeming, F. (1988). Problem solving, recall, isomorphic transfer, and nonisomorphic transfer among third grade and fourth grade children. *Cognitive Development, 3,* 37–53.

Henderson, C. R., & Ceci, S. J. (in press). *Is it better to be born rich or smart? A bioecological analysis of the independent effects of IQ and social status in determining life-course outcomes.* Cambridge, MA: MIT Press.

Itzkoff, S. W. (1989). *The making of the civilized mind.* New York: Longman.

Jaques, E. (1978). *Levels of abstraction in logic and human action.* London: Heinman Press.

Jensen, A. R. (1980). *Bias in mental testing.* New York: Free Press.

Judd, C. H. (1908). The relation of special training to general intelligence. *Educational Review, 36,* 28–42.

Leshowitz, B. (1989). Its time we did something about scientific illiteracy. *American Psychologist, 44,* 1159-1160.

Lidz, C. S. (1987). Historical perspectives. In C. S. Lidz (Ed.), *Dynamic assessment* (pp. 3–33). New York: Guilford Press.

Nisbett, R., & Ross, L. (1980). *Human Inference: Strategies and shortcoming of social judgment.* Englewood Cliffs, NJ: Prentice-Hall.

Nisbett, R., Fong, G., Lehman, D., & Cheng, P. (1988). *Teaching reasoning.* Unpublished manuscript, University of Michigan, Ann Arbor.

Nye, N. J., Burns, M. S., Delclos, V. R., & Bransford, J. D. (1987). A comprehensive approach to assessing intellectually handicapped children. In C. S. Lidz (Ed.), *Dynamic assessment* (pp. 327–359). New York: Guilford Press.

Payne, D. & Wenger, M. J. (in press). Improving memory through practice. In D. Hermann, H. Weingartner, A. Searleman, & C. McEnvoy (Eds.), *Memory improvement: implications for memory theory*. New York: Springer-Verlag.

Piaget, J. (1976). *The psychology of intelligence*. Totowa, NJ: Littlefield, Adams.

Pikas, A. (1966). *Abstraction and concept formation*, Cambridge, MA: Harvard University Press.

Reed, S. K., Dempster, A., & Ettinger, M. (1985). Usefulness of analogous solutions for solving algebra word problems. *Journal of Experimental Psychology: Learning, Memory, & Cognition, 11*, 106–125.

Rogoff, B. (1981). Schooling and the development of cognitive skills. In H. Triandis & A. Heron (Eds.), *Handbook of cross-cultural psychology* (Vol. 4, pp. 233–294). Rockleigh, NJ: Allyn and Bacon.

Rumelhart, D. (1991, January 24). *Neural networks*. Paper presented at the Annual OERI Conference. Washington, DC.

Salomon, G., & Perkins, D. N. (1987). Transfer of cognitive skills from programming: When and how? *Journal of Educational Computing Research, 3*, 149–169.

Salomon, G., & Perkins, D. N. (1989). Rocky roads to transfer: Rethinking mechanisms of a neglected phenomenon. *Educational Psychologist, 24*, 113–142.

Schliemann, A., & Acioly, N. (1989). Mathematical knowledge developed at work: The contribution of schooling. *Cognition and Instruction, 6*, 185–221.

Schneider, W., Körkel, J., & Weinert, F. (1989). Expert knowledge and general abilities and text processing. In W. Schneider & F. Weinert (Eds.), *Interactions among aptitudes, strategies, and knowledge in cognitive performance* (pp. 114–136). New York: Springer-Verlag.

Schooler, C. (1989). Social structural effects and experimental situations: Mutual lessons of cognitive and social science. In K. W. Schaie & C. Schooler (Eds.), *Social structure and aging: Psychological processes*. Hillsdale, NJ: Erlbaum.

Spearman, C. (1904). General intelligence objectively determined and measured. *American Journal of Psychology, 15*, 206–221.

Sternberg, R. J. (1985). *Beyond IQ: A triarchic framework for intelligence*. New York: Cambridge University Press.

Sternberg, R. J., Conway, B., Ketron, J., & Bernstein, M. (1981). People's conceptions of intelligence. *Journal of Personality and Social Psychology, 41*, 37–55.

Stitch, T. (1975 June). A program of Army functional job reading training (HUMRRO Final Report FR–WO (CA)–75–7), Alexandria, VA: Human Resources Research Organization.

Streufert, S. & Nogami, G. (1989). Cognitive style and complexity: Implications for I/O psychology. In C. Cooper & I. Robertson (Eds.), *International review of industrial and organizational psychology* (pp. 93–143). New York: Wiley.

Thorndike, E. L. (1906). *Principles of teaching: Based on psychology*. New York: Seiler.

Thorndike, E. L., & Woodworth, R. (1901). The influence of improvement in one's mental function upon the efficiency of other functions. *Psychological Review, 3*, 247–384, 553.

Vygotsky, L. (1962). *Thought and language*. Cambridge, MA: MIT Press.

APPENDIX A

(Sample questions given to the participants to establish their lack of expertise in the stock market)

1. The phrase "50½—51,200 by 100" is:
    a) a range
    b) a special bid
    c) a size and quotation
    d) a "fill and kill" order

2. When stocks are left in a "street name" by a cash account customer, the "beneficial owner" is:
    a) the brokerage firm
    b) the Depository Trust Company
    c) a nominee
    d) the customer

3. A corporation has 1,000,000,000 shares authorized. 50,000,000 shares were issued and 1,000,000 are in the treasury. How many shares are outstanding?
    a) 1,000,000
    b) 49,000,000
    c) 50,000,000
    d) 100,000,000

4. The job of monitoring proper payment for an acceptable delivery of securities is the responsibility of:
    a) the margin dept.
    b) the cashier's dept.
    c) the purchase and sales dept.
    d) the research dept.

5. Which of the following services is not performed by a mutual fund custodian?
    a) providing investment advice
    b) paying out dividends and distributions
    c) safeguarding the fund's money and securities
    d) maintaining records for the fund

6. Prices on most OTC stocks may be found by looking....
    a) the composite tape
    b) in the pink sheets
    c) in the Blue List
    d) in the yellow sheets

7. Bonds are normally quoted in:
   a) dollars and cents
   b) percentage par value
   c) decimal fractions
   d) dollars and eights of dollars

8. Assuming the same issue and maturity dates, the highest yield would be earned by investing in which product?
   a) US Government bond
   b) Municipal Bond
   c) B-rated corporate bond
   d) AAA-rated corporate bond

9. Bonds usually pay interest:
   a) monthly
   d) every 90 days
   c) every six months
   d) annually (only)

10. An investor purchases 100 shares of ABC Corp's common stock (par value $1 per share) for $5,000. If ABC Corp. goes bankrupt, the investor could not lose more than:
   a) $100
   b) $4,000
   c) $5,000
   d) Impossible to determine as the investor's personal property may be attached

Chapter 7

Cognitive and Behavioral Analyses of Teaching and Transfer: Are They Different?

Earl C. Butterfield, Timothy A. Slocum,
and Gregory D. Nelson

University of Washington

Learning refers to the change in a subject's behavior or behavior potential to a given situation brought about by the subject's repeated experiences in [that] situation...(Bower & Hilgard, 1981, p. 11)

transfer of learning occurs whenever prior-learned knowledges and skills affect the way in which new knowledge and skills are learned and performed. (Cormier & Hagman, 1987, p. 1)

no empirical or theoretical chasm separates transfer from...learning. (Gick & Holyoak, 1987, p. 10)

Thorndike and Woodworth (1901a, b, c) suggested that transfer cannot be distinguished from learning. Some subsequent workers elevated this suggestion to a conclusion (e.g., Gick & Holyoak, 1987; Detterman, 1990; Thorndike, 1914). Nevertheless, most workers have assumed that transfer is distinct from learning, and that the two require separate theoretical treatment (cf. Osgood, 1949; Ellis, 1965; Cormier & Hagman, 1987; Salomon & Perkins, 1989). Most have sought to distinguish learning from transfer by looking for differences between teaching and testing experiences. If teaching and testing situations are "the same," most psychologists and educators have said that the effects of the earlier on the later experience are due to learning. If a "different" prior experience influences later behavior, most psychologists and educators have said transfer has been shown.

A problem for the usual distinction between learning and transfer is that judgments of "same" and "different" depend on the level of analysis used to compare experiences. It is always possible to adopt a level of analysis according to which two given situations can be described as the same, and it is always possible to find a level of analysis at which two given situations can be described as different. Consider a typical concept formation lesson. During a teaching session, positive examples are given (e.g., pictures of an elm and a cedar) to define the features of a concept (tree), and negative examples are given (e.g., azalea and telephone pole) to distinguish the concept from other concepts. During testing, new positive (e.g., walnut and fir) and negative (e.g., camillia and cactus) examples are given, and a learner is required to label them as trees or not. At the lower level of example names (elm and walnut, azalea and camellia), teaching and testing examples are different: Transfer has been tested. At the higher level of category names (trees and non-trees), teaching and testing examples are the same: Learning has been tested.

The conventional distinction has never been workable, and it will remain unworkable until there are principled ways to select one's level of analysis for judging whether two situations are the same or different. Until then, there will be unresolvable disagreements as to when transfer has been observed or even when it has been tested (Detterman, 1989). We need a more workable way to conceive of what we mean by transfer than one that depends on trying to judge whether two situations are the same or different.

THREE FUNDAMENTAL QUESTIONS

the consequences of learning can be measured for a continuum of subsequent tasks. (Gick & Holyoak, 1987, p. 10)

We must recognize two classes of stimuli: one is a class correlated with a reinforcement contingency; the other is the class in the presence of which responding occurs. Our interest is not in either class alone but in the correspondence between them. (Catania, 1984, p. 130)

the fundamental issue concerns the acquisition of a particular use of knowledge and the range of circumstances over which that use will extend. (Singley & Anderson, 1989, p. 29)

As the quotes above imply, the fundamental issue is not whether particular changes in behavior illustrate learning or transfer. The fundamental issue is the range of circumstances in which particular learning is used. The fact for which educators and psychologists seek an explanation when they try to distinguish transfer from learning is that—when they examine learning at a single level of analysis—some teaching produces reliably improved performance across a broader range of circumstances than other teaching. It is this issue of the generality of learning that we address in this chapter.

Because we see no principled difference between learning and transfer, we will not use the term "transfer" except in quotations. Because we do see relationships between instruction and subsequent performance, we will speak instead of *instructional situations* and *target domains*, of *teaching examples* and *test items*. According to this way of speaking, students are taught with instructional examples in order to promote performance in a target domain. Performance in a target domain is assessed with test items. Perfectly effective teaching results in perfect performance on all test items from a target domain. More general learning applies to more or broader domains.

Why some teaching results in more general learning is the question at issue, and it reduces logically to three more tractable questions:

Question 1: What is the unit or form of learning?
Question 2: How does one teach so as to know the content of learned units?
Question 3: How can one know the range of use of what has been taught?

This chapter offers answers to these three questions. The answers are necessarily partial, especially for the second and third questions, but they are nevertheless illuminating.

In the first section of this chapter, we fully describe two well-developed answers to Question 1—What is the unit of learning? In brief, a behavioral answer is that *discriminated operants* are learned (e.g., Catania, 1984; Skinner, 1968). A cognitive answer is that *productions* are learned (e.g., Singley & Anderson, 1989). We describe the elements of discriminated operants and productions, and we map elements of productions onto elements of operants, matching (a) production context descriptions to operant discriminative stimuli, (b) production goals to operant reinforcers, and (c) production actions to operant responses. In addition, we match (d) production goal setting to operant establishing operations, and we argue that (e) production systems are analogous to chains of operants, and that (f) the cognitive argument that different productions may apply to any given testing situation is analogous to the behavioral argument that the same situation may set the occasion for competing operants. We show that experimental and educational teaching and testing situations—ranging from simple stimulus generalization through complex analogical reasoning—are characterized in functionally identical terms by radical behaviorists and production system cognitivists. We conclude that productions and discriminated operants are functionally and structurally identical.

In the second section of this chapter, we argue that Question 2—How does one teach so as to know the content of learned units?—also has been answered analogously in cognitive and behavioral treatments of instruction. We point out similarities between what cognitivists and behaviorist see as effective ways to teach so that particular contextual elements are salient for learners, namely, teaching (a) simple concepts, (b) concepts known as generative frames, and (c) minimal sets of recombinative context-action relations using (a) carefully selected and sequenced examples and (b) nonexamples and (c) verbally expressed rules. We also point out similarities between behavioral and cognitive ways of teaching goals and subgoals, their ways of teaching complex chains of invariantly and of flexibly ordered units, and their approaches to reducing competition among learned units.

In the third section of the chapter, we argue that Question 3—How can one know the range of use of what was taught?—has also been answered analogously by behavioral and cognitive investigators. The answer is to analyze or decompose teaching situations and target domains in ways that constrain teaching. We consider how the specificity of context descriptions, grain size of responses, and organization of learned units embodied in a decomposition constrain instruction and thereby determine the generality of what is learned.

In the fourth and final section of the chapter we suggest an agenda highlighted by similarities in behavioral and cognitive approaches for future research on teaching for general use of learning.

AN INVITATION TO OUR READERS

It is not too far off the mark to say that it took about ten years for the ideas contained in Skinner's 1966 paper to develop, independently in cognitive psychology. Now that they have developed they are guiding principles of the field. (Hunt, 1988, p. 252)

We prepared to write this chapter by comparing what are generally viewed as incompatible answers to the foregoing three questions. We compared answers given by radical behaviorists and by production-system cognitive theorists. For one of the authors, the behavioral perspective was more familiar and served as his guide to the cognitive perspective; for the other two, the cognitive perspective was more familiar, bringing meaning and structure to the behavioral perspective. The mix of perspectives helped counteract the constant temptation to set up the less familiar viewpoint as a straw man for one's own, more familiar position.

Because behavioral and cognitive investigators have emphasized incompatible differences between their approaches, we had to compare their answers as best we could. We compared the answers by analogy. In terms of Gentner's (1989) formulation, our analogical reasoning occurred in four stages: (a) *access* to two domains of knowledge that might be related (i.e., behavioral and cognitive analyses of learning and teaching), (b) *mapping* of parallel elements between the two domains, (c) analogical *inference* regarding the structure and content of one of the two domains, and (d) *evaluation* of mapping to the other domain and comparability of the inferences in the domains. In other words, we identified elements in operant and production analyses of learning that appeared to map onto one another, and we evaluated the similarities in their theoretical functions and in their relations to other elements in their respective domains. Whenever we say in this chapter that operant and production analyses are analogous, we mean that they posit parallel elements that are identical in their theoretical functions and in the structure of their relations to other elements, which are also identical in theoretical function. By *analogous,* we mean "functionally and structurally identical," not "somehow similar." This chapter is the fruit of the evaluation stage of our collaborative exploration of the analogy.

We were astonished that our evaluations forced us to conclude that radical behavioral and cognitive workers have given analogous answers to our three questions. We resisted this conclusion for many months, and we expect our readers to resist it, too. We expect readers to doubt, as we did, that behavioral theory can encompass the mental events in cognitive theory. We expect readers to resist our implication that behavioral analyses of concept learning are rich enough to encompass what cognitive analysts mean by concepts. We expect readers to resist our implication that cognitive treatments of motivation are comparable to behavioral treatments of reinforcement and establishing operations. Therefore, we hasten to say that our central claim is only that production system and operant answers are the same to the three questions posed above, not that the two approaches are wholly identical.

As all behaviorists and cognitivists know, behavioral and cognitive theories are different (cf. Lachman, Lachman, & Butterfield, 1979; Schnaitter, 1986; Skinner, 1977). Thus, behaviorists interpret both overt and covert behavior as resulting from prior reinforcement, and cognitivists explain overt behavior in terms of concurrent covert events. Cognitivists more often leave unsaid the learning determinants of current performance, explaining it in terms of underlying productions. Nevertheless, they acknowledge that learning influences performance. Behaviorists feature learning histories in their interpretation of current performance, but they acknowledge covert events nevertheless.

At several points in the first three sections of the chapter, we discuss possible differences between cognitive and behavioral approaches. In the end, we will have considered many ways in which behavioral and cognitive approaches have been said to differ. Some of these ways are real; some are not. We argue that, as real as some of the differences are, they fade to naught when studying learning from an instructional perspective. We explain why the interpretive differences between them in no way invalidate our conclusion that operant and production theorists have answered our three questions analogously.

Even though behavior analysts and cognitive theorists do disagree on some issues, and even though they have worked separately, with very little cross-referencing, they have taken very similar steps toward understanding how to teach for excellent performance in particular target domains. This can be interpreted positively as important replication, or negatively as needless duplication. Either way, future progress would be more rapid if cognitive and behavioral camps drew more on each other's work.

Regardless of your present views about how many real differences there are between behavioral and cognitive theory, we invite you to suspend for the moment any disbelief you may experience about similarities that we will highlight. We invite you to hear us out, to consider fully our reasons for believing—like Hunt (1988)—that the similarities shared by cognitive and behavioral theories are also real. We invite you to consider that their shared similarities provide a basis for important advances in understanding and producing learning that has desired ranges of use.

QUESTION 1:
WHAT ARE THE UNITS OF LEARNING?

Before describing analogous relations between production system and operant answers to our three fundamental questions, we describe the units of learning from each perspective.

Discriminated Operants as Units

A *discriminated operant* is a class of responses made more probable by the presence of a discriminative stimulus and the current effectiveness of an historically associated reinforcer. Responses can be overt or covert. They can act directly on the external environment, change the learner's contact with external stimuli, or create internal stimuli. Discriminative stimuli can be internal or external to a learner. Either way, they become discriminative by having been present when a class of responses was reinforced. As a result of such history, the presence of a discriminative stimulus makes a class of responses more likely, but only when the consequences that made it discriminative are again reinforcing. Establishing operations are stimuli (e.g., instructions from a parent or a sheet of unanswered math problems) or events (e.g., lack of food or finishing an early part of a complex cognitive routine) that determine what consequence is currently reinforcing.

Our version of Michael's (1982) example of discriminated operants is shown in the left column of Table 7.1. Suppose that a journeyman electrician has been

Table 7.1.   Operant and production analyses of dismantling an appliance

Operants (O) and Establishing Operations (EO)	Productions (P)
EO1 Instructions to dismantle appliance	**P1** IF a goal is to follow instructions and instruction is to dismantle broken appliance THEN set a goal to dismantle appliance
O1 CURRENT REINFORCER: Dismantled appliance DISCRIMINATIVE STIMULUS: Appliance with cover RESPONSE: Unsnap cover and look inside	**P2** IF a goal is to dismantle an appliance and the appliance has a cover THEN unsnap the cover and look inside
EO2 Seeing slotted screw securing a part in appliance	**P3** IF a goal is to dismantle an appliance and a screw is securing a part THEN set a goal to get a screwdriver
O2 CURRENT REINFORCER: Screwdriver DISCRIMINATIVE STIMULUS: Assistant RESPONSE: Ask assistant for screw driver	**P4** IF a goal is to get a screwdriver and an assistant is nearby THEN ask assistant for a screwdriver
O3 CURRENT REINFORCER: Dismantled appliance DISCRIMINATIVE STIMULUS: Slotted screw and screwdriver RESPONSE: Insert screwdriver in slot of screw and turn clockwise.	**P5** IF a goal is to dismantle an appliance and a screw is securing a part and you have screwdriver THEN insert screwdriver in slot of screw and turn counterclockwise

told to dismantle a broken appliance. After unsnapping a face plate, he sees an assembly that is held on by a slotted screw. He asks his assistant for a screwdriver and continues dismantling the appliance. This scenario can be described (see Table 7.1) as having two establishing operations (EO1–EO2) and three operants (O1–O3).

The three operants in Table 7.1 are linked by establishing operations and discriminative stimuli to form a chain. Instructions to dismantle an appliance (EO1) make a dismantled appliance a current reinforcer, increasing the likelihood of past responses (e.g., cover removal) that have led to dismantled appliances. The response in O1 of removing the cover reveals a screw, which serves as an establishing operation (EO2) that makes screwdrivers reinforcing. In O2, the current reinforcer (screwdriver) and discriminative stimulus (assistant) set the occasion for requesting a screwdriver. The screwdriver is a discriminative stimulus for removing the screw (O3). There is no third establishing operation, because EO1 (instructions) makes the consequences of opening the appliance (O1) and removing the screw (O3) currently reinforcing. In other words, O1 and O3 have the same current reinforcer. Together, these three discriminated operants and associated establishing operations form a chain[1] linked by responses and events that change discriminative stimuli and current reinforcers.

Production as Units

A *production* is an If-Then, Condition-Action rule. When its conditions are satisfied, its action occurs. The condition side of the rule contains goals and contextual descriptions. The action side of the rule contains physical or mental activities, including the setting of goals that enter the condition side of other productions. The action side of a production can contain other productions.

Return to the scenario of an electrician dismantling an appliance. In the right column of Table 7.1, the scenario is described as having five productions (P1–P5). The instruction to dismantle an appliance creates a goal to dismantle (P1) that is a condition for P2. The action of P2 reveals a screw to be removed. P3 makes securing a screwdriver a goal, which is a condition for P4. P4 secures a screwdriver that is a condition for P5. P2, P3, and P5 share a goal, even though its source was the instructions that initiated P1. Together, P1–P5 form a system of productions linked by actions and events that change contexts and goals.

The productions in Table 7.1 are written at comparable levels of generally, but they could have been written to have more or less generality. So could operants O1–O3 and establishing operations EO1—EO2. As written, P2 applies to any screwdriver. It could have been written more generally to apply to any tool (i.e., IF a goal is to get [a tool]), leaving it to other productions to translate [a tool] into a screwdriver. Or, P2 could have been written more specifically for a particular kind of screwdriver (Phillips head) of a particular size and color (small and red). The system P1 + P2 + P3 + P4 + P5 could even have been written as a single, more general production:

IF a goal is to follow instructions
    and you have been instructed to dismantle a broken appliance

THEN dismantle the appliance.

---

[1] We use the term *chain* without implying that the sequence it represents ever occurred before. The sequence it represents is simply the result of one unit setting the occasion for the next. Throughout the chapter we use the operant term *chain* and the production term *system* to convey this meaning.

The generality of the terms in a production or an operant controls its range of applicability. Deciding how generally to describe the conditions and actions for a particular skill is a critical part of task decomposition and is considered in connection with Question 3.

Four Analogous Aspects of Discriminated Operants and Productions

Teaching and target situations may be similar with respect to any of the parts of units of learning, for example, productions and operants. Productions have four parts, namely (a) context and (b) goal statements on the condition (IF) side, and (c) actions and (d) goal setting on the action (THEN) side. Discriminated operants have three parts, namely, (a) discriminative stimuli, (b) current reinforcers, and (c) responses. In addition, there are (d) establishing operations. In the next four subsections, we draw parallels between these aspects of production and operant analyses of learning.

Discriminative Stimuli and Context Statements.

the greater the perceived similarity of the two situations, the more likely it is that transfer will be attempted. (Gick & Holyoak, 1987, p. 16)

An identity between two problem situations that plays no causal role in determining...solutions to one or the other [is] a surface similarity....In contrast, identities that influence goal attainment [are] structural similarities. [Distinguishing] between surface and structural similarities hinges on their relevance...to attainment of a successful solution. (Holyoak, 1985, p. 81)

Behavior analysts call the conditions that set the occasion for a target response its *discriminative stimulus*. Note that the singular term *stimulus* can refer to combinations of stimuli (O3 in Table 7.1) as well as to an individual stimulus (O1 and O2). Cognitive theorists speak of represented conditions, and they call the represented conditions that lead to a target action the *context statement* of a production (i.e., the nongoal portion of IF statements), which may also refer to individual stimuli (P1–P4) or to combinations of stimuli (P5). Cognitivists say that practice and feedback make some stimuli perceptually salient—likely to be represented—and that represented stimuli determine whether a target action occurs. Behaviorists say that stimuli become discriminative as a result of reinforced practice.

Whether a learner makes a particular learned response in a test situation depends in part on the similarity of the test's stimulus features to the features that controlled the target response during learning. In behavior terminology, if a target situation contains discriminative stimuli for a learned responses then the learned response becomes more likely. In cognitive terms, if a target situation's represented features match the contextual conditions of a learned production, then the production's action becomes more likely.

Both cognitive and behavioral theorists describe the conditions under which a learner makes the right response for the wrong reasons. In behavioral terminology, a discriminative stimulus is said to differ from stimuli that are correlated with reinforcement (Catania, 1984; Michael, 1982). In cognitive terminology, some surface features are said to be salient and some structural features not salient (Gentner, 1989; Gick & Holyoak, 1987; Novick, 1988). Surface features contain no information critical for correct responding, whereas structural features do contain information critical for correct responding. Despite their terminological differences, these are the same description.

Real vs. Represented Objects and Contexts.

The antecedent conditions in [production system] computer simulation are assumed to be represented symbolically in short-term memory; that is, the effective environment is not the environment as it really exists but as it is represented mentally. In contrast, in behavior analysis the effective environment is objective. (Reese, 1989, p. 17)

problem solvers are always responding to something. What they are responding to, though, are not physical characteristics of an external problem. They are responding to their internal representations of that problem. The words "internal representation" are . . . jargon of cognitive science rather than operant conditioning. The idea, however, is clearly stated in Skinner's (1966) paper, when he speaks of "discriminative stimuli." (E. Hunt, 1988, p. 250)

Many writers have argued that a fundamental difference between behavioral and cognitive analyses concerns whether individuals respond to the objective world or to their subjective representation of that world. The language of the two systems supports this argument. Behaviorists speak of stimuli, while cognitivists speak of representations, but they use their different words to convey the same ideas (E. Hunt, 1988, p. 250).

Although behaviorists begin by positing objective stimuli, they do not argue that objects and events effect every individual in the same way. Instead, they believe that the effect of the objective environment depends on one's learning history. Environments have objective characteristics, but the effects of those characteristics depend on factors that are unique to the individual (i.e., subjective). The subjective factors—the effects of history—that cognitivists place in representations are placed by operant analysts in discriminative stimuli, conditioned establishing operations, and conditioned reinforcement.

Think about what is necessary for the following production to have psychological reality:

IF you have a hammer
    and a nail is protruding,

THEN hammer the nail.

Unless you know what a person considers to be a hammer, such a production is useless as a psychological account of his or her thinking and behavior. In production analyses, the required knowing is a matter of representation. In behavioral analyses, it is a matter of stimulus control. Given a claw hammer, these are relatively simply matters: A person would hit the nail. But what about a ball peen hammer, sledge hammer, large wrench, or rock? Whether a person would hit a nail with one of these objects depends—in cognitive analyses—upon what a person represents as hammers and—in operant analyses—on what stimuli control hammering. Both behavioral and cognitive analyses assume that the importance of an object or event depends not on its physical characteristics, but on the learner's history with similar objects or events. So the question of what objects are discriminative for hammering is analogous to the question of what objects are represented as hammers.

Conclusion. Discriminative stimuli are analogous to salient stimuli, which are described in contextual (nongoal) descriptions on the IF sides of productions.

Goals and Current Reinforcers.

a wide range of evidence indicates that similarity of goals and processing between training and transfer tasks is extremely important in enabling facile transfer. (Gick & Holyoak, 1987, p. 34)

Operant and production theorists agree that performance on test items depends on motivation as well as on similarity of the items to teaching examples. Production theorists speak of motivation as *goals*, and they include them on the condition side of productions along with descriptions of salient contextual stimuli (P1–P5 in Table 7.1). Instead of goals, behavior analysts speak of current reinforcers (O1–O3). A reinforcer is the behavioral version of a goal, because saying that some one has a goal is like saying that they will do things that have obtained that reinforcer in the past (cf. Michael, 1982; Skinner, 1957). Environmental events are sources of both goals and current reinforcers (see discussion below of goal setting and establishing operations).

A goal on the IF side of a production is an assertion that a particular consequence is currently reinforcing. A cognitivist would say that people won't act appropriately in a given context unless they have adopted the goals which the action would further. A behaviorist would say that people won't respond in the presence of a discriminative stimulus unless the consequences that have resulted from that response in the past are currently reinforcing. In terms of the electrician scenario, P3 asserts that the electrician will ask for a screwdriver if screwdriver acquisition is currently a goal. O2 asserts that the electrician will ask for a screwdriver if screwdrivers are currently reinforcing.

Conclusion. Goals are analogous to reinforcers.

Actions and Responses. Comparing the THEN statements of P2, P4, and P5 with the Responses in O1–O3 shows that all actions that do not set goals are analogous to responses. (We consider the actions of P1 and P4, which do set goals, in the next section.) What cannot be seen in this comparison is that the actions and responses need not be overt. Operant analyses apply to covert stimuli and responses as well as to overt ones. Suppose we ask a child to multiply 23 by 14. The child may write the problem on paper, write the intermediate products of 92 (4×23) and 230 (10×23), then write the sum of the products, 322 ($92 + 230$). Behavior analysts would refer to the overt chain of written discriminative stimuli and responses to explain the multiplication. Requiring that the child perform the multiplication without pencil and paper would not change the behavioral explanation. Making intermediate stimuli and responses covert is assumed not to change their discriminative function in a chain (this example is based on Catania, 1984; cf. Skinner, 1957).

Mental Processes and Covert Behavior.

In computer simulation, most if not all of the simple behaviors are mental. In behavior analysis, most simple behaviors are overt, although some are covert. (Reese, 1989, p. 15)

There are responses, like attending, remembering, imagining, and thinking, that are not easily observed directly...it would be inappropriate to define behavior solely in terms of movement. (Catania, 1984, p. 350)

Behavioral and cognitive analyses do differ in the frequency with which they refer to mental events. Cognitive analyses include more references to mental events than behavioral analyses. Nevertheless, both kinds of analyses apply to both kinds of events. Both cognitive and behavioral analyses are designed to account for behavior, and both cognitive and behavioral theorists recognize that behavior has important covert concomitants.

Binary vs. Probabilistic Action

Although the existence of productions has a discrete, all-or-none quality....[they] continue to accumulate strength after their initial formation. Increased strength of productions means more rapid and reliable performance. (Singley & Anderson, 1989, p. 51)

The definition of a discriminated operant—"a class of responses made more probable"—shows that behaviorists view behavior probabilistically. Productions are cast as IF-THEN rules, suggesting that cognitivists view action as binary. Whether these facts reflect a basic difference between behavioral and cognitive theorists depends upon whether production theorists posit mechanisms that yield probabilistic expectations for action from binary productions.

In order to provide a probabilistic prediction of the effects of the amount of practice on performance, Singley and Anderson (1989, p. 51) posit increases in the strength of productions due to practice. More practice yields more strength, which translates into a higher probability of correct performance. On this ground alone it is certain that production analyses are not basically different from operant analyses with respect to the question of whether action is probabilistic.[2]

Conclusion. Responses are analogous to actions that do not change or set goals.

Establishing Operations and Goal Setting.

An establishing operation, then, is any change in the environment which alters the effectiveness of some object or event as reinforcement and simultaneously alters the momentary frequency of the behavior that has been followed by that reinforcement. (Michael, 1982, pp. 150–151)

Setting a new goal in a production system is equivalent to changing what is currently reinforcing. A cognitivist says goal setting has occurred. A behaviorist says that an establishing operation has acted. The setting of subgoals to dismantle an appliance (P1) and to get a screwdriver (P3) are equivalent to the two establishing operations in Table 7.1.

Establishing operations are distinct from discriminated operants (EO1 and EO2 in Table 7.1), whereas goal setting occurs in productions (P1 and P3). In the cognitive view, goal setting is an action (Singley & Anderson, 1989), but in the operant view it is an effect of a stimulus (Michael, 1982). That stimulus may appear as the result of an environmental event (e.g., instructions to dismantle in EO 1) or as a result of a learner's response (e.g., looking at the screw in EO 2), and in either case it determines what is currently a reinforcer (i.e., a goal). Whether goal setting occurs outside or inside a unit of learning is only a notational matter, because the functions of establishing operations are exactly the same as those of goal setting, just as the functions of current reinforcers are the same as those of goals.

---

[2] Working memory limits, uncertainties about learners' representations, and the strengths of competing productions are less intrinsic sources of the probabilistic nature of production accounts of behavior.

Conclusion. Goal settings on the THEN sides of productions are analogous to establishing operations.

Is there more to motivation than goals? It is commonly said by behaviorists that cognitive theorists slight motivation by reducing it to goal statements. Because behaviorists speak often of establishing operations and reinforcement, it is less common for cognitive theorists to accuse them of slighting motivation. The facts that goals are analogous to reinforcers and goal setting is analogous to establishing operations indicate that production theorists are no more neglectful of motivation than behaviorists.

Behaviorists' frequent reliance on tangible rewards, such as food, and depriving establishing operations, such as reduction of caloric intake, make it common for cognitive theorists to say that they neglect more abstract and typically human motivation. This assertion ignores the fact that the behaviorist concept of reinforcement is based exclusively on the function of consequences, not at all on their form. Any consequence, no matter how abstract, can be a reinforcer, and any situation, no matter how academic, can be an establishing operation, given the proper learning history (e.g., Konarski, Crowell, & Duggan, 1985). Not even the most radical behaviorist assumes that motivation stems only from depriving establishing operations and reward only from eating. Production analyses are in no way inconsistent with behavioral views of motivation.

Productions and Operants as Rules

rules (even self-stated rules) control behavior, by definition. Just as in a chain of behavior, however, one response may be said to "control" another, but only in the context of actual causes that establish both responses and the relation between them. (Hayes, 1986, p. 361)

Suppose someone has been told the rules of chess. Then theoretically, that person has the knowledge to play a perfect game....Of course, to expect this amount of transfer is ridiculous.... What a person has to learn is how to deploy his knowledge in specific game situations. (Singley & Anderson, 1989, p. 29)

Having considered analogous relations between elements of behavioral and cognitive units of learning, we turn to the nature of the units themselves. Productions, schemata, grammars, and other cognitive concepts can be viewed as rules. So viewed, it may seem that cognitive theory claims that all behavior is rule-governed. Behavior analysts argue that much important human behavior is *not* rule-governed. Does this reflect a fundamental difference between behavioral and cognitive theorists? To answer this question, it is necessary to distinguish two meanings of the word *rule* as it is used in psychology (Reese, 1989).

One meaning of *rule* is a statement that controls behavior. This meaning recognizes that a learner who understands a statement can often conform to its prescription. There is no disagreement between cognitivist and behaviorist researchers that some behavior is rule governed in this sense.

A second psychological meaning of *rule* is a regularity in behavior. This sense of the word acknowledges that much behavior can be described and predicted from rules formulated by observers such as psychologists. This sense does not imply that the rules had any governing role in the learning or execution of the behavior described. It implies only that behavior is rule describable. There is no disagreement between cognitive and behavioral thinkers that all behavior is rule-describable.[3] Both would be out of business otherwise. Productions and discriminated operants are correctly considered rules formulated by psychologists to describe behavior patterns.

The case of learning to speak is relevant here, because many still believe that Chomsky's (1959) critique of Skinner's (1957) *Verbal Behavior* established that language is rule governed and therefore cannot be explained in operant terms. In fact, Chomsky's critique established that language is rule-describable. Children's speech is organized. The rules of grammar describe that organization well, but they do not govern language acquisition: No careful observer of children believes that they learn to speak by following grammatical rules. Children acquire language from experience in communities of speakers who seldom enunciate rules that could govern language acquisition. Language is rule describable, but it is not rule governed. Chomsky's critique is irrelevant to whether language can be explained in operant terms (Lachman et al., 1979).

Rule-governed behavior is the product of a verbally stated rule, rather than instruction by example. From the cognitive perspective, *declarative knowledge* is knowledge *that* certain relationships exist or certain actions are appropriate, whereas *procedural knowledge* is knowledge of *how to* respond to a situation. Repeating a rule you were told demonstrates declarative knowledge. Acting in a way implied or described by a rule you were told reflects declarative-to-procedural learning.[4] Behaviorists' use of the term *rule-governed behavior* is analogous to cognitivists' use of *declarative-to-procedural learning*. The quote from Hayes (above) capsulizes the behavioral approach to the use of rules and is similar to Singley and Anderson's (above) recognition that declarative-to-procedural learning needs to be explained rather than assumed. For work toward this goal from the production system perspective see Singley and Anderson (1989, chap. 7). For work from the situated cognition perspective see Suchman (1987) and Dreyfus and Dreyfus (1986). For work from behavioral perspectives see the volume edited by Hayes (1989). For a comparison of approaches to these issues see Slocum (1990).

---

[3] Rule-governed behavior is, of course, a subset of rule-describable behavior.

[4] This is normally called declarative-to-procedural "transfer." We avoid use the word "transfer" to emphasize that it cannot be distinguished from learning.

Conclusion. The process of learning to follow rules, of learning to formulate rules to guide one's own behavior, and the relations between rule-governed and rule-describable behavior in the acquisition of skilled repertoires are active research areas in both cognitive and behavioral psychology.

Interactions among Units

The analogy between operants and productions goes beyond the similarity of the parts of units and of the units themselves to interactions among units. Next we consider two interactions: (a) linking units to describe more complex behaviors, and (b) determining dominance among several units primed by a given setting.

Units Can be Linked. Both cognitive and behavioral theorists argue that complex behavior consists of sequences of simpler units. Behaviorists call them *chains* of operants, and cognitivists call them *systems* of productions. In the foregoing sections "Discriminated Operants as Units" and "Productions as Units," we showed that productions and operants are alike in that they can be linked together to create sequences of units called chains or systems. We showed too that goal setting and establishing operations play comparable roles in the linking, as do responses that produce discriminative stimuli and actions that produce context statements for subsequent operants and productions, respectively.

Conclusion. Production systems are analogous to operant chains.

Alternative Productions and Competing Operants. Comparable interactions among units can be seen too in cognitive and behavioral treatments of the fact that any situation allows many actions. Adherents of both approaches recognize that the existence of alternative reactions to any situation is a chief source of ambiguity about what learning will be used in a testing situation. Cognitive theorists recognize that the conditions of more than one production may be fulfilled by a given situation. To decide which production will fire, they assess the strength of competing productions. The production with the most similarity and the greatest associative strength with the test's contextual conditions and goals has the highest overall strength. It fires (Anderson, 1983; Siegler, 1989). Behavior analysts compare the strength of competing operants. The overall strength of a discriminated operant depends upon the present value of its past reinforcers, the schedule on which it has been reinforced, the strength of discriminative stimuli, and the effort required to make the response. The response from the competing operant with the greatest overall strength is made. The strength of competing operants serves the same function for behaviorists that the strength of alternative productions serves for cognitivists.

In acknowledging the existence of competing actions, cognitive theorists speak about the difficulty of knowing which of several productions best match current conditions. Behavior analysts speak about the difficulty of knowing which stimuli in current situations have been made discriminative by past reinforcement. These ways of speaking are functionally equivalent, because current representations are constrained by prior experience.

Conclusion. Behavioral accounts of competing operants are analogous to cognitive accounts of competing productions.

Mapping Operants onto Productions

Table 7.2 summarizes our analogical mapping of operants and productions. The upper portion of Table 7.2 shows equivalences between parts of productions and parts of discriminated operants and establishing operations. The lowerportion shows equivalences between two kinds of interactions among units. The right column of Table 7.2 summarizes the common functions of analogous units and analogous interactions of operants and productions. We believe our mapping justifies the claim that discriminated operants and productions are analogous

Our analogy extends to the similarity of elements of cognitive and behavioral units of learning, the similarity of two interactions among units, the similar use of procedures to make overt events covert, and sharing of the idea that current performance depends upon past learning. This is similarity enough to allow much mutually beneficial collaboration on problems of teaching and learning.

Presentational versus Representational Interpretations.

A presentationalist position is the view that phenomena...constitute a level of reality that needs to be addressed and understood in its own right, at its own level.

Table 7.2. Analogical mapping of productions and discriminated operants

Parts of Units		Shared Function
Production	**Discriminated Operant**	**Shared Function**
IF context	Discriminative stimulus	Increase likelihood of action/response
IF goal	Effective reinforcer	Increase likelihood of action/response
THEN goal	Establishing operation	Link units
THEN action	Response	Solve problem or change subsequent conditions
Interactions of Units		
Alternative Production	Competing Response	Account for variability among actions with same context and goals
Production System	Operant Chain	Account for complex behaviors

> *A representationalist position, by contrast, holds that immediately given phenomena are representative of events or processes taking place at some level, . . . and it is at this deeper level that the truly important realities of nature are found. . . . the issue of presentationalism versus representationalism [behaviorism vs. cognitivism] more directly concerns the* <u>interpretation</u> *of what is presented, or the* <u>understanding</u> *of its meaning, or its* <u>explanation</u>. (Schnaitter, 1986, p. 300)

Our analogy does not extend to explanations. As all behaviorists and cognitivists know, behavioral and cognitive interpretations and explanations are different. Thus, Schnaitter (1986, p. 300) argued that behavioral theorists (i.e., presentationalists) address reality at its own level, but cognitive theorists (i.e., representationalists) seek explanations at a deeper level. We think this is *the* basic difference between the two. It manifests itself ubiquitously in the language of the two groups of theorists. We are certain from the months we have spent analyzing the analogical relations between operant and production theory that the languages used by the two camps are formidable barriers to mutual understanding. We believe that many of their language differences stem from the difference between representationalist and presentationalist views.

As presentationalists, behavior analysts define an *operant* as "a response *made more probable*" to avoid implications of causation from a deeper level of analysis. To avoid mentalism, they speak of *internal stimuli* instead of thoughts. They define *establishing operations* as "environmental events, operations, or stimulus conditions" instead of as goal setting, because making them external leaves them at the level of events to be explained instead of casting explanations at a lower level. The entire body of behavioral terminology is cast in uncompromising presentationalist terms.

Cognitive psychology, on the other hand, has been said to be "predicated on the belief that it is legitimate—in fact, necessary—to posit a separate level of analysis which can be called the 'level of representation'" (Gardner, 1985, p. 38). As representationalists, cognitivists place the important determinants of behavior at a deeper level than the behavior itself. Productions are seen as mental structures that cause behavior, not as descriptions of behavior. Learning results in changed representation, not simply changed behavior patterns. All "observable psychological phenomena are taken to be the outcome, product, or manifestation of information-processing mechanisms and processes that underlie them" (Schnaitter, 1986, p. 301).

Certainly the most salient difference between cognitive and behavioral analyses is the centrality of mentalism to cognitive psychology and its exclusion from behavior analysis. Mentalism is inherent in the representationalist orientation of cognitive psychology and it is excluded by behaviorists' presentational stance. A second source of the mind vs. behavior difference is the differential overtness and complexity of performances targeted for investigation by cognitive and behavioral researchers. Although behavior analysts recognize the importance of covert behavior and such behavior poses no theoretical problems for them, cognitive psychologists have far more often analyzed behaviors that have important covert aspects. Complex performance such as LISP programming, a cognitive staple, would be a surprising target of behavioral analysis.

The analysis of complex tasks involves the description of a great many component parts. Specification and organization of these components is an issue of *structural* analysis. Cognitive psychologists have paid primary attention to structural issues. The language of mentalism lends itself well to the description of structure. In contrast, behavior analysts have given most of their attention to questions of *function* of behavior. This is best accomplished with relatively simple tasks carried out under differing environmental conditions. Functional relations are well described in the language of stimuli, responses and consequences. Structure and function, however, are intimately connected. Functions are embodied in some structure, and structures arise and are selected for their function. These relations are implicitly recognized by each school. (The preceding part of this paragraph is due to Catania, 1984.) For cognitive psychologists, a valid account of behavior must include the effects of a learner's history. Singley and Anderson note: "the fundamental issue concerns the [prior] acquisition of a particular use of knowledge and the range of [future] circumstances over which that use will extend" (1989, p. 29) Behavior analysts acknowledge structure with the concept of the operant. The operant "provides the basis for discussing the structure of behavior" (Catania, 1984, p. 107).

The differences between cognitive and behavioral analyses associated with presentationalism vs. representationalism do not invalidate our analogy, nor do they justify workers from one perspective ignoring the work of those from the other perspective. In spite of the differences in terminology, the two approaches attempt to analyze the same thing. Whether explanations are cast at the level of the phenomena observed or at a different level, they are claims about behavior. If a cognitivist shows that under certain conditions a student does not represent a book as a thing to hammer with, then a behavior analyst can conclude that the book is not in the class of stimuli that are discriminative for hammering. Similarly, if a behavior analyst demonstrates that a student is engaging in a particular covert behavior, a production theorist can infer a corresponding production.

Our point is that even the most basic definitions of behavioral and cognitive workers are couched in languages that the other finds opaque. Nevertheless, we believe that their linguistic conventions are mutually understandable, because their meanings are analogous. We hope this chapter will contribute to the successful translation of each language into the other, because such translation makes it possible to see that there are many more real similarities—and far fewer differences—between behavioral and cognitive analyses than generally is imagined. It makes it possible to entertain the possibility of a joint approach to instruction.

The Tapestry of Learning

Next, we illustrate the broad range of teaching and testing arrangements describable as operants and productions. Table 7.3 presents 13 teaching-testing conditions selected to range from quite simple to quite complex. The first column summarizes the results of prior teaching for each of the 13 examples without going into particulars of how certain stimuli came to be discriminative or what currently effective reinforcer make the described action likely. Discussion of the details of these important issues is deferred to the next section, where we discuss Question 2-How does one teach so as to know the content of learned units? Column 2 describes test context and goals, and column 3 describes correct actions for each test from a target domain.

We use Table 7.3 to illustrate the difficulty of deciding in any principled way which situations measure learning and which measure "transfer." Each row in the table adds an element (noted in column 4) not covered by the foregoing rows, thereby moving from very concrete and simple to very abstract and complex. Our discussion highlights relationships between the 13 teaching-testing situations. We invite readers to look for a principled dividing line between learning and "transfer" as they proceed through the table. We have been unable to find one.

We also use Table 7.3 to extend the generality of our argument that discriminated operants are analogous to productions. The columns are headed with both operant and production labels to show that they apply equally well to all 13 examples. In the text, we describe the examples alternately in operant and production terms, to show in another way that cognitive and behavioral analyses of learning apply equal well.

A final use of Table 7.3 is to introduce examples of teaching-testing arrangements to which we refer throughout the rest of this chapter. Table 7.3 is a knowledge base that we will use as we answer Questions 2 and 3.

Table 7.3 begins with a nonhuman example of stimulus generalization (row 1). In the presence of objects of several different hues of red, we reinforce a pigeon's pecks of a key, while at the same time we extinguish pecking in the presence of nonred stimuli (column 1). Later, when the pigeon is shown an object with a red hue never encountered before (column 2), it pecks at a higher rate than if shown a new nonred hue (column 3). A behaviorist would say that the pigeon came under the stimulus control of a range of hues. A cognitivist would say that the pigeon's production specified conditions that were broad enough to include the tested range of hues. Either could say that the pigeon has learned the concept *red*. It is a simple concept, hinging only on frequency of visible light, but it is a concept nevertheless. Even this simple case shows that one cannot teach a concept by presenting only positive examples: If that had been tried in the experiments represented by row 1, pecking every hue presented would have been followed by

Table 7.3.   Production and discriminated operant characterizations of 13 teaching-testing situations.

Previously Learned Productions (Operants)	Test Context (Discriminative Stimuli) and Goals (Currently Effective Reinforcers)	Present Action (Response)	Novel Element
1. will peck for red and not for nonred	• novel hue of red • other colors	• pecks key • [other response]	control by a single attribute of the object
2. will peck for picture of tree and not for picture of nontree	• novel picture of tree • pictures of other objects	• pecks key • [other response]	control by multiple attributes of the object
3. will use arithmetic progression algorithm correctly when presented with an appropriate story problem	• arithmetic progression story problem • other arithmetic story problems	• executes arithmetic progression algorithm • uses other solution strategies	complex response chain; novel context
4. • will retrieve specified token from correct container • when handed particular token, will insert into device to make it work	• containers and device present, asked to make device work	goes to appropriate container, removes token, and puts token into device	novel chaining of intact, familiar units, with first unit creating the context for the second
5. • will make lemonade when given juice can and all necessary utensils • will ask for spoon when needed to stir coffee, tea, etc	• experimenter presents everything needed except spoon • student's overt behavior blocked by inability to stir lemonade	asks for spoon	addition of novel response to chain, with subject's overt behavior setting up establishing operation
6. • will read in presence of text • will look up (in a dictionary) unknown words from a list containing known and unknown words	• experimenter presents text to be read • student's covert reading of text interrupted by encounter with unknown word *glerm*	• looks up "glerm" in dictionary	product of subject's *covert* behavior serves as an establishing operation for adding one chain to another

Table 7.3. (Continued)

Previously Learned Productions (Operants)	Test Context (Discriminative Stimuli) and Goals (Currently Effective Reinforcers)	Present Action (Response)	Novel Element
7. • generative frame "This is a _____" • generative frame "Is this a _____?"	• is presented with object and told "This is a glerm" • is presented with same object mixed with other objects and asked "Is this a glerm?"	says "yes"	frame allows responses to a variety of situations, including other frames
8. • generative frame "Could I please have a _____?" • names *spoon*	lack of spoon	asks for spoon	generative frame used to respond to never-before encountered situation (asking for a spoon) due to frame plus ability to name spoon
9. told: "a closed figure with three sides is a triangle"	• three-sided figure • other figures	• says "triangle" • says "not a triangle"	verbally mediated learning
10. • knows a dollar is equivalent to four quarters • knows a quarter is equivalent to five nickels	• a magazine that costs one dollar • change purse with no dollars or quarters, but lots of nickels	offers 20 nickels for the magazine	equivalence relation as a generative frame—action learned in presence of one discriminative stimulus performed in presence of equivalent stimuli
11. • will choose particular token from mixed container of tokens • when handed particular token, will insert into device • generative frame from combining separately learned skills	• presence of container of mixed tokens • presence of device	selects appropriate token, then puts token into device	generative frame for combinatorial chaining of intact units

Table 7.3.   (Continued)

Previously Learned Productions (Operants)	Test Context (Discriminative Stimuli) and Goals (Currently Effective Reinforcers)	Present Action (Response)	Novel Element
12. can explain how an army can invade a city center without being detected (by splitting forces and entering from different directions)	problem of how to administer enough radiation to kill a tumor without killing the surrounding healthy tissue	applies the split forces strategy (administer many small doses from different directions)	analogical reasoning, with mapping of novel task to known contexts used to generate actions in present context
13. learns arithmetic progression algorithm in math class	• arithmetic progression story problem in physics class • other physics story problems	• uses arithmetic progression algorithm • uses other strategies	"self-initiated" application of efficient and effortful strategy at appropriate times

reinforcement. We would be reinforcing indiscriminate pecking of the key. A discriminative stimulus can be defined only in the context of negative examples. Although this may seem obvious, much research has been done to confirm the idea in more complex situations than are depicted in row 1 (e.g., Carlson & Schneider, 1989).

Although row 1 may seem to illustrate learning, it could be argued that it measures "transfer," because the tested hue of red was not used during teaching. Perhaps it was never encountered by the pigeon. Nevertheless, the pigeon responds to novel red stimuli the way it responds to familiar red stimuli. Stimulus novelty is immaterial to the pigeon: It has simply been taught something whose range of use extends beyond the teaching examples. Researchers in artificial intelligence who attempt to program machines to respond to novel stimuli as if they were familiar recognize how important a skill this is.

Row 2 shows that the technique illustrated in row 1 can be used to teach multidimensional, naturally occurring concepts, such as *tree, water,* or *cat,* even to pigeons (Hernstein, Loveland, & Cable, 1976). Such concepts differ from unidimensional stimulus generalization (row 1) in that a set of multiple features are the concept's defining attributes, and there is no definite set of features present in all positive examples and absent from all negative examples. From early infancy, humans use shared features to treat novel objects as familiar (Fagan & Singer, 1983). The teaching procedures of rows 1 and 2 allow pigeons to acquire such abstract concepts as *novel picture* (MacPhail & Reilly, 1989).

Although we have so far illustrated learning using only examples that require a simple response, more complex actions or series of actions can also be taught as concepts. For instance, if a student already knows how to execute an algorithm for solving arithmetic progression problems (row 3), then insuring its use on appropriate story problems is a matter of teaching the concept "story problems that require arithmetic progression." In the presence of examples of this concept, the student will use the algorithm; in its absence, the student won't. Such concepts can be taught simply by juxtaposing positive and negative examples. In behavioral terms, we would be establishing control by a particular set of discriminative stimuli, a process not that different from teaching a pigeon to distinguish between a *tree* and a *bush*. In cognitive terms, we would be teaching a production with a condition statement that specifies those situations in which the algorithm is appropriate.

Suppose, now, we teach a child to operate a gumball machine (row 4) by having him take a nickel we hand him, insert it in the slot, and turn the handle. In addition, suppose we separately teach the child that, if we ask for a nickel, he can get one for us from a purse on the table, but if we ask for a penny, he should look in a box (column 1). What happens when we present the child with the gumball machine, the box of pennies, and the purse of nickels? The child will go directly to the purse for a nickel, put it in the gumball machine, turn the handle, and get the gumball (column 3). In the cognitive literature this is called combinatorial transfer (Crisafi & Brown, 1986). The first unit's response, getting the nickel, provides the lacking condition for the second unit to fire. What motivates getting the nickel during testing? During teaching, the instructor made getting a nickel a goal by requesting one. During testing, the presence of the gumball machine makes getting a nickel attractive. In behavioral terms, the machine acted as an establishing operation to make nickels reinforcing (i.e., goals).

Sequential combining of intact behaviors, such as securing and then using a nickel to get gum, is called *automatic chaining* in the behavioral literature. Epstein (1987) taught pigeons to peck a target banana, to push a box to a target, and to climb on a box, and extinguished flying in the cage. The pigeon was then presented with a suspended banana and a box. With little random behavior, the pigeon pushed the box under the banana, climbed on the box, and pecked the banana, a response that could be called insightful as well as an example of automatic chaining.

A somewhat different chaining of units is represented in row 5, which assumes students with severe mental retardation were taught a chain of units for making lemonade: (a) open a can of lemonade, (b) pour it into a pitcher, (c) add water, and (d) stir with a spoon. Students were taught to make lemonade in the presence of a can of juice, a pitcher, and a spoon. They were also taught to ask for a spoon when one is needed for purposes other than lemonade making (column 1). What happens when such a student is asked to make lemonade, but no spoon is provided (column 2)? Lemonade making would proceed until the lack of a spoon became a problem (unstirred lemonade), at which point the student would request a spoon (column 3).

The critical feature of row 5 is that the student's actions make a spoon valuable, whereupon the student makes a response that had not previously been part of the chain. According to a behavioral analysis, the student created an establishing operation (unstirred lemonade), which made a spoon reinforcing, which increased the likelihood of asking for a spoon. Once the spoon was in hand, the conditions were met for the next response in the normal chain. According to a cognitive analysis, the student has a spoon-asking production that states "If the goal is to get a spoon, then ask for a spoon." As the student proceeded with the lemonade-making production, she was faced with unstirred lemonade, whereupon the student set a goal of getting a spoon, which caused the spoon-asking production to fire, which caused the conditions to be satisfied for the next procedure in lemonade making.

Powerful functions are served by units that modify separately taught chains when the context is right and a learner's behavior acts as an establishing operation. Such units monitor or alter conditions for the next behavior in a chain. Cognitivists refer to this category of units as metacognitive, superordinate, and executive routines. To behaviorists, such units are discriminated operants under the control of students' previous behavior. We will say more on this topic later.

Comparing rows 4 and 5 to row 6 of Table 7.3 shows that chains of covert (i.e., cognitive) actions are not conceptually different from chains of overt actions. Rows 4 and 5 involve student-generated establishing operations (i.e., goal setting). In row 4, goal setting linked two units to form a chain. In row 5, an establishing operation motivated the execution of a unit learned separately from an ongoing chain. In both cases, the actions of the units in the chain were overt. In row 6, when a student looks up an unknown word embedded in a text, we can infer an unseen sequence of behaviors (reading known words) until the reading of *glerm* (column 2) produces a feeling of not knowing (the covert stimulus) that establishes the word's definition as a goal. The student could just as easily have read the passage aloud, thereby making the covert behavior more observable. Neither behaviorists nor cognitivists consider covert chains to be fundamentally different from overt ones. However, both recognize two practical differences. One is that identifying links in covert chains requires more inference than identifying links in overt chains, and the other is that teaching covert chains often requires that they be made overt so we can observe their actions.

Each row of Table 7.3 exemplifies a unit or sequence of units that generate responses in novel circumstances. Greater behavioral or cognitive novelty results from units that describe general relations between elements of other units (row 7). All normal English-speaking children learn from repeated experiences that being told about an object "This is a [noun]" allows correct responses later to questions such as "What is this?" and "Is this a [noun]?" as well as to the command "Give me the [noun]" This kind of unit is called a *frame*. The essential characteristic of a frame is *generativity:* Once formed, a frame allows a learner to interpret novel stimuli and generate novel responses from single instances (e.g., learn the name of an object on first encountering it). In essence, a generative frame is an intentionally incomplete unit, a production within which some of the conditions contain empty slots to be filled with new examples.

Many children with mental retardation learn to name objects but do not spontaneously ask for them when they need them. To solve this problem, a frame can be taught to establish a relation between naming and asking, as in row 8, which is an elaboration of row 6, the difference being that a student is taught to name an object and then to request the object. After enough objects, a student abstracts the relation between names and requesting, and thereafter asks spontaneously for any thing she can name (Hall & Sundberg, 1987).

Concepts are often taught to humans verbally rather than by example (row 9). Frequently a rule is given, then it is illustrated with a series of examples and nonexamples. Rules describe relations among units. Students must know the rule-described relations to benefit from rule-based instruction. For instance, a rule such as "a closed figure with three sides is a triangle" assumes that the student has already learned the units "closed figure", "three," and "sides" in addition to the frame "X is a Y." When these assumptions are valid, verbal instruction can be much more efficient than pure teaching by example. The goal of the instruction in row 9 is similar to the goals in the first two rows of the table. The difference is that the rule-based instruction of row 9 assumes complex relations among previously learned units.

Suppose that an educated adult who is unfamiliar with our currency has been taught that a dollar is worth four quarters and that a quarter is worth five nickels (row 10). When told at the newsstand that a particular magazine costs one dollar, he would have no difficulty interpreting this to mean that four sets of five nickels would be equally acceptable; with a little mental arithmetic he would know that he could have the magazine for 20 nickels. This relation between one stimulus and another is called "stimulus equivalence." Hayes (1989) argues that stimulus equivalence is but another example of a frame based on reinforcement of responding symmetrically to two stimuli: "In this view, equivalence is...dis-criminative behavior under the control of a particularly complex aspect of the social/verbal environment" (p. 357). In cognitive terms, productions can have IF-side conditions that describe relations among stimuli.

In row 11, we describe a modified version of the example in row 4, in which a child linked the separately learned units of getting coins and operating a gumball machine. Young children who do not spontaneously link such units will learn a general frame for combining separately learned units if they are given several analogous examples (Crisafi & Brown, 1986). Note that the only difference between row 4 and row 11 is the greater likelihood in row 11 that a student will combine separately learned skills without prompting. Teaching a generalized response frame increases the likelihood.

Haring (1985) has provided a particularly clear example of teaching general frames. Having been taught how to play with one boat, one airplane, and one car, Haring's students did not generalize the taught playing to other boats, planes, or cars. However, after teaching one kind of playing with a whole series of boats and another kind with a whole series of planes, yet a third kind of play appropriate to cars occurred without further teaching. This is an example of learning an abstract relationship between a behavior appropriate to one example and behavior appropriate to other examples from the same class: "If you have been taught to do something with one member of a class, it is appropriate to do it with other members of the class." This is highly general learning that can be described as a production cast at a high level of abstraction.

We turn next to analogical reasoning (row 12). In Duncker's classic problem-solving task, students are asked to suppose that a patient has a cancerous tumor, and the only possible treatment is to use X-rays to destroy the tumor; however, the dosage of X-rays necessary to kill the tumor would also kill the healthy tissue in its path. The student is asked how the necessary dosage of X-rays can be directed at the tumor without killing healthy tissue. Few students solve the tumor problem put this way (Gick & Holyoak, 1980, 1983). Few students solve it even if they have been previously exposed to the solution of a related problem: An invading army needed to capture the center of a city, but a force large enough to do the job would be detected before it could reach its objective. The solution? Split the invading force into many small units, and have them converge on the city center from different directions. Many learners do solve the tumor problem, *if* it is hinted that the previously told story may be useful (Gick & Holyoak, 1983), or *if* particular emphasis is given to the structural features of the soldier problem when it is taught (Brown, Kane, & Echols, 1986; Catrambone & Holyoak, 1989), or *if* they are presented with more than one analogous problem before being asked to solve the target problem (Crisafi & Brown, 1986; Gick & Holyoak, 1983). Use of an analogous story which shares more surface features with the target story also increases use of the analogy (Gentner & Toupin, 1986).

The issue raised in row 12 is whether shared properties of two problems are sufficient to prompt solution of the second problem in a way similar to a solution taught for the first problem. Gentner's (1988) breakdown of analogical reasoning into the stages— (a) accessing, (b) mapping, (c) drawing inferences, and (d) evaluating—suggests that a student given only a single earlier analog has had little opportunity to separate surface features of the problems from their underlying structural features, so irrelevant surface similarities control access. From the behavioral perspective, the desired response has not yet come under the control of discriminative stimuli. From either perspective, the student is not likely to use a similar solution for a second problem, but given more examples, students can form a frame (or script, or schema) or a set of discriminative stimuli that make an appropriate response more likely for subsequent problems. Viewing choice of solution to later problems as a matter of analogical reasoning, we can say that more examples allow structural features and goals to affect access to a learned solution and to guide appropriate mapping onto later problems (Carbonell, 1986; Holyoak, 1985). Researchers in machine learning are trying to simulate analogical reasoning as a way of making machines think and learn more like humans (Holyoak & Thagard, 1989; Larkin, Reif, Carbonell, & Gugliotta, 1988; for review, see Hall, 1989).

In the final row of Table 7.3, we have a typical school situation. A strategy for handling certain problems is learned in a math class. Later, in a physics class, a problem is presented to which the math strategy could be applied. Alternatively, a strategy learned first in a physics class is appropriate later in a math class. The question is, do students use the instructed strategy in the later class without specific direction to do so? Bassok and Holyoak (1989) found that students apply learning from math instructions to physics problems from the domain of the math instruction, but they less often use learning from physics to math problems from the same domain. The example in row 13 is not different in kind from the one in row 3: Both require application of a previously learned strategy.

We include row 13 because it is representative of what many educators think of as "transfer", namely, self-initiated choice of an appropriate behavior in an applied setting, in lieu of other less efficient but more familiar competing behaviors. It is important to note that *self-initiated* is a problematic description. The chosen strategy is self-initiated only in the sense that the setting (room, subject matter, experimenter) is not similar to the one in which the behavior was learned, nor are any instructions given regarding how to go about solving the problem. Both noticing that the arithmetic progression strategy applies to the physics story problem and application of the strategy are controlled by combinations of stimuli and establishing operations, as in row 3. By demoting "self-initiated behavior" to row 3's discriminative stimuli and establishing operations, we gain an appreciation for the types of instruction that produce learning whose range of use could be cited as evidence of "transfer" (see Bassok & Holyoak, 1990).

Conclusion. *Transfer* cannot be distinguished from learning. Teaching and learning are a tapestry that does not lend itself to such labels as *near transfer* and *far transfer*. Each row of Table 7.3 contains elements of what is conventionally referred to as learning and of what is conventionally referred to as *transfer*.

What Does It Mean That Many Important Behaviors Have Not Been

Described as Operants or Productions? Table 7.3 shows that discriminated operants and productions apply to a wide range of teaching/testing situations. Of course, Table 7.3 does not describe all kinds of behavior. It includes only examples of some behaviors that have been analyzed theoretically and experimentally. Resourceful scientists and experienced researchers will readily identify interesting performances that are not illustrated in Table 7.3. For example, some might say that neither productions nor operants apply to flexible behavior[5], behavior that depends on rich knowledge bases, or arational behavior, which raises an important question. Is pointing out domains that have not been analyzed in terms of a theory enough to impugn the theory?

Identifying behaviors that have not been completely analyzed in operant or production terms impugns those theories only if it is shown that those behaviors (a) are describable by another theoretical system, and (b) that system is not reducible to production and operant terms. Lacking these two steps, asserting that operant and production systems do not apply to some behavior only says that the behavior may be worth analyzing.

It can be valuable as a guide to research to point to incompletely analyzed behaviors. Some of the most captivating examples of inadequately analyzed behavior have been pointed to by advocates of the view that cognition is situated (Dreyfus & Dreyfus, 1986; Greeno, 1989; Suchman, 1987). The canonical example is navigation by Trukese islanders, who sail to distant destinations by steering in ad hoc response to momentary conditions of wind, waves, stars, clouds, etc., without apparent reference to a planned course or route that is distinct from the actions of steering. European navigation, on the other hand, is governed by a set of rules and techniques for planning a route and monitoring one's adherence to it.

The fact that one and the same activity—navigating at sea—is apparently treated as a rational, structured domain by Europeans and as an arational, unstructured domain by Trukese (Dreyfus & Dreyfus, 1986) indicates that effective behavior, even in a complex domain, can be acquired either by following rules (the European way of learning navigation) or by direct experience with exigencies (the Trukese way). Can operant and production system analyses account for both ways of learning, or is a new theory needed?

Operant theorists distinguish between contingency-based behavior and rule-governed behavior (Catania, Shimoff, & Mathews, 1989; Skinner, 1968, 1977). The parallel distinction in production theory is between procedural learning and declarative-to-procedural learning (Singley & Anderson, 1989). We see this as the same distinction drawn by situated cognition theorists between arational and

---

[5] We treated flexibility as a matter of generativity, which we did describe in both operant and production terms. See pp.   —   .

rational behavior (Dreyfus & Dreyfus, 1986). Moreover, both operant and production theorists have offered detailed explanations of the acquisition and execution of both kinds of behavior, and their explanations are alike. Thus, the description given by Catania and his colleagues of behavior that is jointly rule-governed and contingency-based is remarkably close to the description of Dreyfus and Dreyfus about how to become an expert.[6]

The argument that we need a theory of situated cognition is valuable, because it highlights the desirability of further analysis of interesting behavioral domains. Indeed, those who have argued the need for a theory of situated cognition have provided a prototype of how to find insufficiently analyzed domains. The way is to look for behaviors that depend on extensive experience and, having found some, exclude from consideration those for which experts describe their behavior in terms of rules and for which rule-governed behavior yields better performance than that shown by the experts. This guarantees that neither behavioral nor cognitive theory *has accounted* for the remaining behaviors, but it says nothing about whether such theories *can account* for the behavior.

Conclusion. Determining whether one theory can account for a behavior and another cannot is discovered by precise theoretical comparisons of the theories, attempts to apply each to the behavior in question, and empirical tests of differential predictions of the theories. In the absence of theoretical comparisons and empirical tests, correct assertions such as those about flexibility, rich knowledge bases, and arational behavior reduce to pointing out that some domains of behavior have not been analyzed *yet* in any theoretical terms.

Do Operant and Production Analyses Have Undesirable Formal Properties?

It has been argued that operant and production systems have undesirable formal properties. Thus, Pressley (personal communication, February 1990) spoke for many when he said that both systems are too rigid, that is, describe all behavior, no matter how complex, with a few basic terms—discriminative stimuli or conditions, responses or actions, reinforcers or goals, and so on. It is true that they do, but saying so is not a serious criticism unless it can be shown that some other theory (a) allows more flexibility by specifying a larger number of basic terms, (b) is not reducible to operant or production terms, and (c) applies to behaviors that production or operant analyses do not.

Conclusion. It would be a substantial contribution to show these three things, but to the best of our knowledge they have not been shown.

---

[6] Slocum (1990) contains a detailed comparison of the similarities between the arguments by Catania and by Dreyfus and Drefus. it also shows that the teaching procedures recommended by proponents of the theory of situated cognition are identical to teaching procedures recommended by operant and production theorists.

QUESTION 2:
HOW DOES ONE TEACH SO AS TO KNOW WHAT IS
LEARNED?

Teaching for generalization begins with an analysis of the structure of the subject matter for stimulus response patterns having great generality of application, and then selecting teaching approaches that establish patterns that capitalize on these regularities. (Alessi, 1987, p. 26)

In order to know the range of applicability of learning, we must know not only the unit of learning (Question 1), but also what is learned (Question 2). We must know the *content* of acquired productions and discriminated operants. We must know students' representations of the teaching context, their goals on entering the context, their subgoals as they work on learning problems, students' actions, how our teaching has organized their learned productions into systems, and competing productions students might use despite our teaching. Behavior analysts and cognitive researchers have given comparable answers to the question of how to teach so as to know what students learn. They have devised similar teaching techniques.

Our next purpose is to summarize teaching principles that allow confident inferences about what students learn. We consider in order (a) how to teach so that particular stimuli become salient and control particular actions, (b) teaching goals and subgoals, (c) teaching chains, and (d) teaching to reduce competition among operants or productions.

Teaching Contextual Salience or Stimulus Control

When working in their specialty areas, experts see novel situations as occasions for particular skilled responses and as distinct from superficially similar situations that call for other responses. In other words, experts attend to critical features instead of surface features of problems from their areas of expertise. They have acquired various concepts of the form "situations in which action X is appropriate." Teaching such concepts is the most effective way to influence the range of use of learning. Behaviorists call it *establishing stimulus control.* Cognitivists call it *making structural features salient.* Whatever the teaching is called, exceedingly subtle and remarkably complex situations can be made to elicit particular actions.

Teaching Concepts with Examples. Here we treat teaching concepts by example. Then we turn to the functions of supplementing exemplification with the teaching of rules.

Teaching a concept requires selection of instructional examples that logically convey to students one and only one interpretation of when an action is appropriate. In cognitive terms, this means selecting examples that constrain students' representations to the structural or critical features of problem situations. It is tempting to conclude that this approach applies only to well-structured problems, but it applies to any problem that can be illustrated. Any problem whose solution can be learned can be illustrated.

General Case Instruction (Albin & Horner, 1988; Engelmann & Carnine, 1982) is an efficient technology for influencing students' representations. It is a system of rules about selecting and sequencing (a) positive examples to define the range of a concept, and (b) negative examples to specify its limits. General Case Instruction assumes that learners will generalize or *interpolate* from positive examples used during instruction to all examples whose discriminative features fall between those of the positive examples given, and that students will discriminate or *extrapolate* from negative examples to exclude discriminative stimuli that diverge more radically from the positive examples than the negative examples given (Engelmann & Carnine, 1982). These assumptions motivate the selection of positive examples whose critical features extend to the limits of a concept's boundaries and which share surface features with negative examples. General Case Instruction holds that concepts can be taught unambiguously by following five principles of exemplification:

1) THE WORDING PRINCIPLE. To make a sequence of examples as clear as possible, use the same wording on juxtaposed examples.

2) THE SETUP PRINCIPLE. To minimize the number of examples needed to demonstrate a concept, juxtapose examples that share the greatest possible number of features.

3) THE DIFFERENCE PRINCIPLE. To show differences between examples, juxtapose examples that are minimally different and indicate that the examples have different labels. (discrimination)

4) THE SAMENESS PRINCIPLE. To show sameness across examples, juxtapose examples that are greatly different and treat the examples in the same way. (generalization)

5) THE TESTING PRINCIPLE. To test the learner, juxtapose examples that bear no predictable relationship to each other. (Engelmann & Carnine, 1982, p. 43)

Implicit in the five foregoing principles is the idea that efficient concept teaching requires special sequencing of instructional examples. Table 7.4 illustrates a typical General Case Instruction sequence and the wording, setup, difference, sameness, and testing principles. Table 7.4 is a beginning sequence for the concept *suspended*. The sequence begins with two negative examples that rule out many possible interpretations of *suspended*. The juxtaposition of examples 2 and 3 show the difference principle. These examples are similar in many respects; however, one is a positive example and one is a negative.

Table 7.4. A general case teaching sequence for the concept "suspended" (from Engelmann & Carnine, 1982, p. 81)

Example	Example Type	Teacher Says
1.	Negative	The block is not suspended.
2.	Negative	The block is not suspended.
3.	Positive	The block is suspended.
4.	Positive	The block is suspended.
5.	Positive	The block is suspended.
6.	Negative	Is the block is suspended?
7.	Positive	Is the block is suspended?
8.	Positive	Is the block is suspended?
9.	Negative	Is the block is suspended?
10.	Positive	Is the block is suspended?
11.	Negative	Is the block is suspended?
12.	Positive	Is the block is suspended?

Juxtaposition of examples 3 and 4, and examples 4 and 5, demonstrate the sameness principle. Each pair shows greatly different positive examples. Example 5 is juxtaposed with 6, showing the difference principle again. The wording and setup principles are embodied in the similar physical features of the examples. The testing principle is exemplified in items 6 through 12.

The lesson in Table 7.4 is exceedingly simple, to the point that some would say that nothing new is offered to the student from the beginning to the end of the sequence. However, when students err, they have over- or undergeneralized, and a teacher can readily infer what additional instructional examples to present. Further, strong conclusions can be drawn about what students know after such teaching sequences.

The principles of General Case Instruction have been shown to be valid and efficient, even when combined into large-scale programs designed to teach many concepts and their associated actions (for reviews, see Engelmann & Carnine, 1982, chaps 29, 30), and they are echoed in the formulations of other behavioral and cognitive theorists. Thus, after reviewing evidence from the cognitive literature on selecting instructional examples, Gick and Holyoak (1987, pp. 24-26) made the following observations, which, in brackets, we relate to General Case Instruction:

Optimal generalization will depend not only on the number of examples provided, but also on their representativeness with respect to . . . the inherent variability of the category instances [Recognition of the need for examples that convey one and only one interpretation and the assumption of interpolation].

. . . exposure to relatively variable training instances [The sameness principle]. facilitates classification of novel instances [assumption of interpolation]

... Exposure to instances that vary in surface features will allow people to form generalized rules that are not restricted to overly specialized contexts, thus facilitating transfer [The difference principle].

Variability of instances will not facilitate transfer, however, if the variation involves changes in structural features—those relevant to category membership or to applicability of a solution method [Assumption of extrapolation and recognition of the need for examples that convey one and only one interpretation of a concept].

... exposure to relatively similar items may help establish generalized rules [The setup principle];

... more variable instances can be used to elaborate the rule set [The sameness principle].

Although Gick and Holyoak are less specific than Engelmann and Carnine about how to select and sequence instructional examples, they emphasize the same considerations in similar terms.

Teaching Generative Frames. All concepts are generative, allowing a person to make accurate responses to novel stimuli. This includes very simple concepts. For example, a person seeing a species of tree he or she has never seen before nevertheless could identify it as a tree. It also includes more complex concepts, such as the generative frame "When you know what to do with one example of a concept, you can do it with other examples."

An experiment by Haring (1985) shows how to teach generative frames by example. Haring's students were children with moderate and severe mental handicaps who had not learned to play with toys. He divided toys into conceptual classes such as airplanes, tanks, and animals. Beginning with one example from each conceptual class, he taught appropriate play (e.g., moving airplanes nonvertically through the air, moving tanks on the ground in straight lines and through sharp turns, etc.). This teaching did not generalize to other toys within each class. Then, he taught other examples from an arbitrarily selected category until the children generalized to untaught examples in that category. After doing this for several categories, he observed that children played as taught with all examples of categories. Learning this kind of frame has been called *learning to learn* ((cf. Crisafi & Brown, 1986).

When generative frames are taught by the same principles as other concepts, strong inferences can be drawn about the contexts in which learning will be used, and contexts of use are especially far-flung for frames (cf. Alessi, 1987). For instance, in row 7 of Table 7.3 we saw that teaching children to relate the frame "This is a [noun]" to other frames, such as "Bring me the [noun]," "Which one is the [noun]?" and "A [noun] is an example of a [another noun]" allows children to generate many untaught responses. Similarly, teaching relationships among a set of facts such as $2 + 5 = 7, 5 + 2 = 7, 7 - 2 = 5$, and $7 - 5 = 2$ allows more efficient instruction of the entire set of basic arithmetic facts, because it teaches a transformation of mathematical expressions. Thus, if examples used during teaching imply logically one and only one interpretation of a generative frame, and if examples are sequenced as described by both behavioral and cognitive thinkers, then strong inferences can be drawn about what students learn and strong conclusions follow about the contexts in which they will use their learning. Otherwise, only tentative inferences and weak conclusions are possible (Engelmann & Carnine, 1982; Stokes & Baer, 1977).

Many experiments can be viewed as tests of whether students use frames that are not taught explicitly. For example, Butterfield and Nelson (1991) taught many examples of how to solve two problem types (e.g., balance scale and shadow projection) that required integrating information from two dimensions, and they looked for use of the frame on a third type (e.g., inclined planes). They found that many of their subjects applied the instructed knowledge and procedures to the third problem type, suggesting that many invoked the untaught frame: "Stimulus dimensions A and B are analogous to stimulus dimensions C and D."

Can analogical reasoning be viewed as use of generative frames? Gentner's (1989; Gentner & Toupin, 1986) structure-mapping theory of analogy suggests that it can. In her theory, generative frames about higher order relations are the basis for judging the structural similarity of potentially analogous situations. A fair paraphrase of her account is that analogical reasoning is guided by the frame "When relations among critical features and their functions in one universe match up with relations among critical features and their functions in another universe, a good analogy has been found." In Haring's (1985) experiment on play and Butterfield and Nelson's on integrating dimensions, students' success depended on what Gentner would call *structure mapping*. The foregoing frame is also a fair paraphrase of Schank and Abelson's (1977) discussion of how people use *scripts* to interpret current settings and of some of Piaget's (1952) arguments about uses of *schemata*. Moreover, this entire chapter is an elaboration of that analogy. Our deliberate application of this frame (see Table 7.1) to the universe of behavior analytic and production concepts is what has convinced us that discriminated operants are analogs of productions, that operant and cognitive teaching principles are the same, and that task decomposition is a shared tool of behavioral and cognitive analysts.

Viewing analogical reasoning as use of a generative frame, and recalling that frames are concepts, highlights similarities between teaching very simple concepts ("Make the sides of an equation equal") and teaching analogies. For example, teaching simple concepts requires a minimum of several examples, and studies that attempt to promote analogical reasoning by providing only a single example usually fail (e.g., Gick & Holyoak, 1980; Reed, Ernst, & Banerji, 1974). The likely reason is that a single example provides no basis for learning a frame.[7] That is, the use of only one example provides no basis for generalization, and it precludes teaching for generalization by preventing implementation of the setup, sameness, and difference principles (Engelmann & Carnine, 1982). Studies that have included more than one example have found the use of frames on new analogous instances (Butterfield & Nelson, 1991; Catrambone & Holyoak, 1989; Crisafi & Brown, 1986; Gick & Holyoak, 1983).

Teaching Minimal sets.

The minimal stimulus-response set is called the <u>generative</u> set, and the goal repertoire which can be produced by various combinations of stimulus-response elements is called the <u>universal</u> set. The important issue for designing efficient instructional programs is that each of these minimal repertoires contain a finite set of stimulus-response elements that can be brought under abstract stimulus control and then combined and recombined (by the learner) to meet response requirements in an indefinitely large [target domain] . . . [Some] subject areas can be arranged in roughly parallel strands so that stimulus-response patterns from one strand can be transformed into another by a relatively simple operation. (Alessi, 1987, p. 18)

Concepts are single learned units, for example, operants or productions. Although frames describe relations between units, they can be taught as if they were units. We turn now to teaching frames, which secures stimulus or contextual control over test items from a large target domain.

Skinner (1957) introduced the term *minimal repertoire* to describe small units of verbal behavior that can be assembled into a large number of composite behaviors. For instance, when reading phonetically, a fluent student quickly assembles and blends new combinations of letter–sound correspondences. Each letter–sound is a small unit in a minimal repertoire or generative set, and these units can be combined to pronounce any word. The target domain for phonics instruction is all phonetically regular words.[8]

Italian, Spanish, Hebrew, and Finnish are almost entirely regular phonetically: Each acceptable sound in their pronunciation is associated with a different letter or combination of letters. But teaching letter–sound correspondences alone does not produce accurate reading of all words in even these languages, because reading depends as well on blending the correspondence

---

[7] Teaching a single example does elicit later analogical reasoning, if the training is augmented by verbal instruction that focuses on the structural features and goal structure of the example (Klahr & Carver, 1988). Verbal instruction is covered below, under the heading Teaching by Rule.

[8] Neither we nor Skinner claim that all reading proceeds phonetically. Assembly of minimal phonetic units probably occurs in pure form only when a student sounds out an unknown word, and even for unknown words other strategies are possible.

units. A *blend* is a frame that allows decoding of different sequences of phonemes. Teaching each of the 40 or fewer letter–sound relationships in any of these languages (i.e., teaching a language's minimal set), and teaching their frames for blending, allows correct decoding of more than 500,000 written words, a very favorable 10,000: 1 minimal-set to target-domain ratio of the use of resultant learning (Alessi, 1987).

In the case of teaching decoding by phonics, it might be imagined that teaching blending frames would be unnecessary, because students who are learning to read have learned to blend in the course of learning to speak. In other words, frames for blending speech sounds could be applied to phonetic reading, but they are not. Blending needs to be brought under the control of written stimuli, and that is the function of teaching blending frames when teaching phonics.

Each of the units in a minimal set is teachable as an elementary IF-THEN production, where each IF statement contains a unique stimulus element (or class of elements) from the set (Holyoak, 1985). When each element in the minimal set is unique, there is a regular point-to-point mapping between the minimal set and the target domain. There is no mystery about how to teach minimal sets nor the domains in which they will be used. The elements of a minimal set and frames can be taught directly, and they can be recombined to generate all untaught composites in their associated domain. Thus, a way to specify the relationships between what is taught, what is learned, and what is required by a range of target situations is to analyze the target domain into a unique minimal set of teachable units and frames. For example, Miller and Engelmann (1980) have so analyzed the writing of any English word in cursive, and Lane, Boyes-Braem, and Bellugi (1976) the spelling of any word in American Sign Language.

Even when the mapping of a minimal set onto a target domain involves some irregularities, minimal sets can still generate a large number of correct combination responses. The main accommodation that must be made for irregular sets is that separate units must be taught to account for exceptional cases. Thus, even though reading English involves many irregularities, a phonetic approach is not only possible, but can be highly efficient. For instructional analysis of irregular minimal sets in reading, see Carnine and Silbert (1979) and in mathematics see Silbert, Carnine, and Stein (1981, 1990).

The teaching of generative frames (e.g., sound blending) along with units of a minimal set (e.g., letter-sound correspondences) greatly increases the applicability of the units. One way generative frames do this is by giving students a strategy for generating portions of the mimimal set, thereby reducing the number of units to be learned. For example, the minimal set of basic, single-digit addition facts ($0 + 0 = 0$, $0 + 1 = 1$,...$9 + 8 = 17$, $9 + 9 = 18$) contains 100 units. This can be reduced to 55 by teaching the commutative frame "If A + B = C, Then B + A = C."[9] If another frame, "If A + B = C, then C − A = B and C − B = A," is taught as well, students can derive all the subtraction facts. Thus, with the use of two frames we can reduce the memorization load from 200 facts to 55 number families. The same relations hold for the basic multiplication/division facts.

Another kind of increase in applicability comes from teaching generative frames that multiply the domains to which a minimal set can be applied (i.e., expand the target domain). Metric measures of the domains of weights, distances, and volumes are an example. Once the basic prefixes for naming units (*deci, centi, milli, micro, kilo, mega, giga*) and the operations for converting from one unit to another (dividing or multiplying by 10, 100, 1000, etc.) have been taught for any one of these domains, only a new base word (*gram, meter, liter*) and the generative frame "Centigrams and milligrams are the same as centimeters and millimeters, except their base word is gram" need be taught for a person to be verbally proficient in another domain. Many important examples of rapid learning in a new domain may be due largely to transformation of previously learned minimal sets by generative frames, including learning to play a second musical instrument, to speak a second Romance language, and to write on a new word processor (cf. Alessi, 1987).

Although we have been considering teaching by example, our discussion of generative frames included some mention of teaching verbally by providing rules. That is the topic of the next section of this chapter. Here, we recap teaching by example. First, we argued that units of learning, be they called discriminated operants or productions, can be viewed as concepts, and we summarized rules for teaching concepts by example. Second, we argued that generative frames are also concepts and can be taught by example in the same way as simpler concepts. Third, we suggested that when a target domain can be derived from a minimal set of units, then teaching all of the elements and frames for combining produces learning of great generality and specificity. Fourth, we suggested that it is possible to teach generative frames that apply to whole minimal sets, multiplying the domains to which the learning of those minimal sets can be applied. Of course, most learning domains have not been reduced to minimal sets, but this does not diminish the importance of teaching by example, because any concept can be constrained precisely by exemplification.

Teaching by Rule. We have emphasized that the appropriate conditions for using any skill can be taught by example (Albin & Horner, 1988; Zhu & Simon, 1987), but pure exemplification is often slow and tedious. Control of behavior by appropriate rules and cues can sometimes be speeded up by verbally directing students' attention to the structural aspects of examples (Brown et al., 1986;

---

[9]This saves *almost* half the memorization, because there is no savings on facts with identical addends (e.g., 1 + 1 = 2, 2 + 2 = 4).

Catrambone & Holyoak, 1989; Crisafi & Brown, 1986). In addition, new units that subsume known units can sometimes be taught quickly by describing relations among the known and taught units. In some situations, learning is speeded by supplementing examples with discussions of hypothetical situations in which the strategy would or would not be appropriate (Pressley, Borkowski, & O'Sullivan, 1985) and by telling students which settings are and are not appropriate for taught strategies (Ghatala, Levin, Pressley, & Lodico, 1985; cf. Belmont & Butterfield, 1977). In cognitive terms, declarative-to-procedural learning can be more rapid than straight procedural learning. In behavioral terms, rule governance can generate behavior more efficiently than contingency shaping. (See pp. 00 and 00 for a discussion of rule-governed and declarative-to-proceduroal learning.)

Although teaching by pure exemplification can be needlessly slow, it is a thoroughly reliable way to secure stimulus control. Conversely, sole reliance on telling rules can produce rapid learning, but it often fails to create stimulus control (Hayes, Singley & Anderson, quoted on p. 00). Under what conditions are rule-governed and declarative-to-procedural learning reliable ways to secure contextual control of actions?

Behavioral and cognitive investigators agree on how to teach by rule, just as they agree about how to teach by example. They agree that rules are statements to be exemplified. For instance, to teach the simple rule "If the top and bottom of a fraction are the same, the fraction equals one," Engelmann and Carnine (1982, p. 102) recommend a sequence of examples (Table 7.5) that fulfills the

Table 7.5.   Teaching a rule by verbal instruction (From Engelmann & Carnine, 1982, p. 102)

	Example	Teacher Says
1.	$\frac{5}{4}$	My turn. Does the fraction equal one? No. How do you know? Because the top and bottom are not the same.
2.	$\frac{4}{4}$	My turn. Does the fraction equal one? Yes. How do you know? Because the top and bottom are the same.
3.	$\frac{98}{98}$	Your turn. Does the fraction equal one? How do you know?
4.	$\frac{7R}{7R}$	Your turn. Does the fraction equal one? How do you know?
5.	$\frac{7}{7R}$	Your turn. Does the fraction equal one? How do you know?
6.	$\frac{14}{8}$	Your turn. Does the fraction equal one? How do you know?
7.	$\frac{12}{12}$	Your turn. Does the fraction equal one? How do you know?
8.	$\frac{81}{5}$	Your turn. Does the fraction equal one? How do you know?
9.	$\frac{241P}{241P}$	Your turn. Does the fraction equal one? How do you know?

requirements of the five juxtaposition rules listed on page 000. For each example the student is asked "Does the fraction equal one?" then "How do you know?" Each example demonstrates application of the rule.

The cognitive case for using exemplification along with rules is shown in Parker's (1987, pp. 51–55) description of concept teaching:

In a concept-formation lesson, students are engaged in a logical sequence of thinking about examples of the concept:

1. studying three or more examples of the concept (data gathering);
2. reporting their findings (data retrieval);
3. noting differences among the examples (contrasting);
4. noting similarities among the examples (comparing);
5. summarizing the similarities into a single statement (concluding or summarizing);
6. giving the similarities a name (labeling);
7. deciding whether new items are examples or nonexamples and supporting these decisions (classifying).
8. creating new examples of the concept
9. Transforming negative examples into positive examples.

Parker argues that the main preparation for teaching concepts is careful selection of examples to represent each concept's full range of permissible diversity. In words that are reminiscent of Parker's on selecting examples and of Engelmann and Carnine's (1982) principles for teaching concepts, Zhu and Simon (1987, p. 141) attributed the success of their teaching of complex mathematical problems to careful sequencing of examples.

> a production system capable of performing the task was constructed to represent the skills that students would acquire in mastering the task.... Examples and problems were sequenced so that the initial problems could be handled with a small subset of the productions, and subsequent problems required additional productions for their solution. Thus, in accordance with the usual principles for shaping behavior, learners could attend to one or a few aspects of the problem situation at a time.

In sum, behavioral and cognitive workers agree that a most efficient way to teach is to tell students a rule and then exemplify it carefully. Without careful exemplification, learning is unreliable. Thus, investigators of such subject matters as physics (Larkin, McDermott, Simon, & Simon, 1980; Siegler, 1981) and mathematics (Kamii & DeClark, 1985; Schoenfeld, 1987) point out that students are often unable to match correct procedures with formal algorithms taught declaratively. Why?

One reason for the unreliability of declarative-to-procedural learning is that some students do not know how to respond to each clause in the rule and the relation it describes: They lack prerequisite learning. Alternatively, when attempting to map declarative knowledge onto the first examples encountered, students must discover which features of the example are structural (Cooper & Sweller, 1987; Forbus & Gentner, 1986; Holyoak & Thagard, 1989). In doing this, they necessarily attend to surface features as well as to structural ones, and until they have worked with enough examples to discriminate the two, learning will remain imprecise. In addition, it often requires many examples for necessary actions to become fluent or automatic, and the demands of attending to the components of required nonfluent actions can further distract students from critical contextual cues (Cooper & Sweller, 1987; Gick & Holyoak, 1987).[10] Supplementing rules with exemplification is a reliable way to overcome all of these problems.

Teaching Goals and Subgoals

some of the most widely decried failures of transfer—failures to apply knowledge learned in school to practical problems encountered in everyday life—may largely reflect the fact that material taught in school is often disconnected from any clear goal. (Gick & Holyoak, 1987, p. 31)

As Skinner put it, 'We observe the frequency of a selected response, . . . then make an event contingent upon it and observe any change in frequency. If there is a change, we classify the event as reinforcing to the organism under the existing circumstances' (1953, p. 73). [Thus] a child can be expected to anticipate what is coming and to have intentional ends in view. [But a response] becomes part of the child's standard repertoire only when it has achieved the child's anticipated goals repeatedly in a number of situations for which it was adequate. (J. McV. Hunt, 1969, pp. 20–21)

Behaviorally speaking, stimuli are discriminative for particular responses only when consequences that previously reinforced them are again reinforcing. In many situations, control by goals or establishing operations is more important than stimulus control. Looking for a coat when one is cold, going to the kitchen when one is hungry, filling in the answer blanks randomly so one won't be late for recess, and asking for an object that is not present are all responses that emphasize the importance of reinforcers and establishing operations.[11]

---

[10]There are also reasons for the vagaries of procedural-to-declarative learning. See Ericsson and Simon's (1980) "Verbal Reports as Data" and its fascinating behavioral translation by Hayes (1986).

[11]In most academic situations it is assumed that consequences associated with correct answers are generally reinforcing. In employment, the generalized reinforcement of money is said to be the ultimate consequence for many actions. But even when the reinforcing value of the result of a long sequence is assumed, establishing operations are necessary for linking of individual units into a sequence. The moment-to-moment behaviors that get things done are the result of specific establishing operations.

In cognitive terms, the condition side of a production can include stimuli, goals, or both. If the student's current goals do not match the goal statement of a production, it will not fire, even if the current stimuli are perceived as relevant. Holyoak (1985; Holyoak & Thagard, 1989) offers two reasons that insufficient attention to goals during teaching results in failure to apply learning in appropriate testing situations: (a) students see no reason to engage in the activity outside of the teaching context, and (b) goals present during opportunities to use prior learning are not perceived as similar to goals during teaching. Salomon and Perkins (1989) place goal-directed activity at the heart of strategic learning. They maintain that strategic behavior requires effort, and students will not exert the effort unless it is made worthwhile by their goals.

Behaviorists say that, during instruction, goals must be established, not just talked about. Cognitivists agree, which is why Soloway (1986), Carbonnell (1986), and Klahr and Carver (1988) argue for teaching manipulation of goals as well as code writing during instruction in computer programming. Soloway (1989) has built instructional software that allows novices to program computers by building goal structures.

Effective procedures for teaching goals are not as well understood or codified as techniques for optimizing stimulus control. A possible extension of stimulus control techniques to goals would be to teach the unit "Unfamiliar situations call for goal setting" and to teach goal setting procedures like those used by good problem solvers (cf. Pressley, Woloshyn, Lysynchuk, Martin, Wood, & Willoughby, 1989). Work by Hall and Sundberg (1987), described in row 8 of Table 7.3, suggests another approach. They began with the observation that it is relatively easy to teach mentally handicapped persons with limited verbal skills to say the names of objects, but teaching spontaneous requesting of objects that are not present has proved difficult. The problem is that spontaneous requests are mainly controlled by goals rather than by discriminative stimuli. To teach requesting disconnected from goals is absurd. Hall and Sundberg's used the following procedure to insure that students would have a relevant goal: (a) Teach a chain of behaviors; (b) arrange conditions so that the chain is started, (c) but an object necessary to complete the chain is absent; (d) when the student reaches the link in which he or she needs the missing object, teach requesting.

The potential of Hall and Sundberg's procedure lies in our ability to generalize it so that we will know what subgoals students have learned. Could it be generalized by a teacher of writing so that students establish the goal "make it cohesive" (Flower & Hayes, 1981, or by a math teacher so that students adopt the goal "check to see if there is another way to approach the problem" (Schoenfeld, 1987)? Answers to such questions are educationally critical.

One framework within which to seek answers to such questions has been provided by Klahr and Carver (1987). Their purpose was to increase the range of use of learning resulting from instruction in LOGO debugging. They analyzed LOGO debugging as a production system, and established the sufficiency of their analysis by building a computer simulation that successfully debugged both graphic and listing programs. They translated their analysis into LOGO debugging instructions, which they taught to children. Moreover, they used their analysis to construct tests of debugging outside the realm of programming. They found that 82% of their instructed subjects used some aspect of their instruction and 50% used the most sophisticated form of the instructed debugging procedures during their non-LOGO tests (Klahr & Carver, 1987, Figure 11).

Klahr and Carver argued that goal structures were the critical common elements of their teaching and test situations, but they taught both goals and procedures for implementing them. Therefore, it is impossible to tell which teaching was responsible for the observed broad use of learning. As they put it,

> in tasks like the ones studied in our work there is no principled way to allocate relative influence to [goals and their subordinate productions]...Thus, while we would expect a near perfect overlap between the production sets for generating goal trees (indeed, that was our intent in constructing the transfer tasks), it is not clear how to quantify the amount of [procedural] overlap between our [teaching] and transfer tasks. (Klahr & Carver, 1988, p. 402)

Although Klahr and Carver were left with interpretative uncertainties about the source of the "transfer" they observed, their thorough analysis of LOGO debugging provides an excellent framework for further experimentation on the teaching of goals. The challenges are (a) to sort out the relative contributions of goal structures and procedures for implementing them to broad use of learning and (b) to determine whether there are ways to separate the teaching of goal structures from the teaching of actions.

Conclusion. Cognitive and behavioral investigators agree on the importance of teaching goals, but the number of generally useful teaching procedures is limited. We suggest the possibilities of generalizing the procedures of Hall and Sundberg and refining the approach used by Klahr and Carver.

Teaching Chains of Operants or Production Systems

> *Designing cognitive routines is difficult....The reason is that there are many decisions that must be made in designing these routines. And at each decision point, there is more than one acceptable solution.* (Engelmann & Carnine, 1982, p. 195)

There are two kinds of chains or systems of units: (a) invariant sequences of productions or discriminated operants, called algorithms, and (b) sequences that are novel orderings of units.

Teaching Invariant. Chains. Teaching to create algorithms or invariant routines is described thoroughly in the behavioral literature (e.g., Cooper,

Heron, & Heward, 1987; Snell, 1987), which focuses on sequences of overt responses that accomplish a specific purpose such as tying a shoe, dressing, or making a meal. A task is analyzed into a series of individual units; then units are taught and linked together. Common instructional arrangements are forward chaining, backward chaining, and total task (Spooner & Spooner, 1984). These techniques are usually applied to instruction of students with learning difficulties, but they are applicable to any student.

Engelmann and Carnine (1982) have described the teaching of *cognitive routines,* which are chains of procedures for making complex discriminations or solving problems. Cognitive routines are needed if stimuli must be transformed in some way before a discriminative response is possible. For example, a cognitive routine could be constructed that would allow a student to distinguish prime numbers from nonprimes, or things that would float in a specific medium from those that would sink (see Table 7.6). They can also teach procedures for making a series of constructive responses such as factoring or solving fraction problems.

Teaching cognitive routines requires *analysis, externalization,* and *feedback.* Analysis identifies a sequence that yields a correct terminal response for every example in a target domain. It begins with specification of the range of examples constituting the domain to which learning should apply. Then, a descriptive rule is articulated to tell the learner exactly what to do with examples. A component task is designed to teach each unit, and sequences that walk the student through each component are designed. Each component task externalizes the required responses so that they can be taught explicitly and so the learner can be given feedback. According to Engelmann and Carnine (1982), cognitive routines are "a good vehicle for teaching the learner to solve a problem by chaining a series of steps together" (p. 195).

A large number of academic skills can be viewed as cognitive routines, which are particularly well taught as exemplified rules. Suppose we wanted to teach the concept of specific gravity. We could arrange a set of "objects" (cubes of some material), empty containers the same size as the objects, and a tank of "medium" (e.g., water). A completed cognitive routine for teaching the chain for calculating specific gravity might look like Table 7.6. The main weakness of cognitive routines is that they are difficult to teach with juxtaposition principles (see pp. 000), because they consist of several steps (Engelmann & Carnine, 1982).

Teaching Control Frames that Create Novel Chains.

metacognitive skills might be regarded as easy ones to instruct, or at least as the ones most likely to lead to transfer across task boundaries. (Campione, Brown, & Ferrara, 1982, p. 426)

Table 7.6.   Example of a cognitive routine to teach specific gravity (from Engelmann & Carnine, 1982, p. 211)

Teacher says	Student says
(Presents object) What do you do to figure out whether the blocks will float or sink in the medium? Do it.	Weigh a block and weigh a piece of the medium the same size. (Detaches one block from the object, fills second block with water from the tank, and places one object on either side of the scale. The block from the object goes up.)
What did the object do on the scale?	Went up.
So what will the object do in the medium?	Float.
How do you know?	Because it's lighter than a piece of medium the same size.
Let's see if you're right. (Places object on the medium.) What's it doing?	Floating.

Self-monitoring is a pivotal skill, in which "a child is taught to discriminate between correct and incorrect behavior....Next, the child is taught to self-observe, self-evaluate [for correctness and incorrectness], and then record [his behavior]. Finally, formal self-monitoring...is faded." (Koegel & Koegel, 1988, pp. 54–55)

A potentially important kind of learned unit changes subgoals or performs an action before an ongoing chain continues. Such units monitor the output of a unit in an ongoing chain and sometimes provide input for subsequent units, so they are called *metacognitive, control,* or *executive routines* in the cognitive literature and *self-management skills* (Meichenbaum, 1982) or *pivotal behaviors* (Koegel & Koegel, 1988) in the behavioral literature. The cognitive-behavioral teaching of Meichenbaum (1982) and verbal self-instruction of Gow, Ward, and Balla (1985) are intended to teach self-management routines, such as reminding oneself of current and long-term goals, attending to the accuracy and precision of responses, reinforcing oneself for completing components of tasks, and coping positively with errors.

In principle, the same stimulus control procedures that are used for concept instruction (e.g., General Case Instruction) could be used to teach self-management so that it is used in all appropriate situations. Behaviorists and cognitivists agree that teaching self-management is the same as teaching any other covert actions, such as those involved in reading. The desired behavior must be brought under the control of stimuli and establishing operations that will be present in the settings where the behavior is appropriate. If you want people to monitor routinely what they are doing or routinely check their goals when experiencing difficulty in novel contexts, then you should engineer novel teaching situations, induce chains of behavior, arrange for difficulties at various points in the chain, prompt "monitoring your behavior" and "checking goals" in the presence of difficulty, teach difficulty-reducing actions, and arrange for the students to experience the resulting benefits. Then, novel situations in which students are using chains of behavior that encounter difficulties should be discriminative for the units "monitor your behavior" and "check your goals," and students should do whatever appropriate "difficulty-reducing action" has been taught.

In practice, researchers have given too little attention to defining stimulus features of contexts in which self-management routines should occur. So far, attention has been paid almost exclusively to refining procedures for securing self-management in the contexts in which it has been taught. The closest investigators have come to analyzing the conditions under which self-management should occur has been to vary number of teachers, number of teaching settings, and number of tasks used as vehicles for training. Such indirectness amounts to what Stokes and Baer (1977) called "train and hope," which they found hopeless as a way to promote general learning.

Conclusion. Whether actual practice can be improved by application of the foregoing principles remains to be seen.

Teaching to Reduce Competition among Units

The diversity of human action complicates teaching. A naturally occurring opportunity to use what we have taught may suggest a wide variety of untaught actions to the learner. What is relevant or reinforcing in the eyes of a teacher may not be to a learner. Understanding students' actions requires that we remember that testing environments contain many salient features in addition to those that we view as related to teaching we have provided.

Horner and Billingsley (1988) pointed out that target contexts may include discriminative stimuli and establishing operations for responses not intended by a teacher. Even if the teacher's intended context statements do control an action, a student may have other actions to achieve the given goals in the given contexts.

Suppose we have flawlessly taught a student a strategy for solving ratio-based story problems. Our student recognizes situations in which the strategy is useful, she sets the appropriate subgoals, and she carries out the procedure accurately during teaching. But in the testing situation the student may have more pressing problems than demonstrating the breadth of our teaching. She may have just heard the bell for recess and set a goal of getting out the door as quickly as possible. Because her current goals do not include accuracy, the story problem we just gave her does not draw out any of the strategies that we taught. Instead the student quickly writes a guess and heads for the door. In behavioral terms, an establishing operation not present during teaching was responsible for behavior that was not taught. We may also watch our students in the supermarket for uses of our strategy for comparison shopping. But if being in a store has been associated with other comparison shopping strategies, our students will not use our well-taught ratio method. In behavioral terms, our student's response is controlled by discriminative stimuli in the market. In production terms, she had a specific production that matched the situation, and it wasn't the ratio method we taught.

To teach students with severe handicaps, Horner and Billingsley recommended ways to mitigate the problem of competing responses: (a) extend teaching into the target situations so that the cues in these situations will be associated with the target response, (b) artificially reduce the effectiveness of the competing responses in the target setting, and (c) temporarily eliminate the problematic stimuli from the target setting.

Competing behavior that interferes with use of what has been taught may be perfectly appropriate to the student's goals in a particular situation. In the above example, our student may have effective shopping strategies that preclude the need for our perhaps more effortful strategy. Siegler and Shrager (1984) demonstrated that young grade schoolers use a remarkably efficient mix of strategies when solving addition problems, the individual strategies being tagged to subtle differences in the characteristics of the particular problem.

Sometimes competing behaviors are a blessing. Two instances come to mind: (a) in some novel situations, the most appropriate learned action fails for a trivial reason, and it helps if the learner has "competing" operants that share some of the conditions of the failed one, so that second-best actions will be applied; and (b) individual differences in responses to test items from a target domain may reveal alternative response sequences that are more adaptive for some or all learners.

Teaching vs. Learning

Production systems are one kind of computer simulation of human behavior. A production system is a condition-action-outcome triad, but its resemblance to the S^D-R-S^R contingency is superficial. (Reese, 1989, p. 14)

Reese compared production systems and behavioral contingencies as organism–environment relations, and he rightly concluded that they are only superficially similar. Organism–environment interactions are dynamic descriptions; they concern learning. So, when Reese compared three-term contingencies and productions, he found no basis for claiming analogous treatments of learning by cognitive and behavioral theorists.

We compared individual productions and operants as descriptions of learned behavioral repertoires, and rightly concluded that they are analogous. Descriptions of behavioral repertoires are static characterizations of what a person will do at a particular moment in a particular environment. Behavioral repertoires are results of learning, not learning itself. We have not addressed the question of learning. Instead we addressed the question of how to teach. We conclude that behavioral and cognitive analyses are analogous with respect to what they say about how to teach. This is not the same as concluding that behavioral and cognitive theories of learning are the same.

It would require analogical reasoning that we have not done to decide whether behavioral and cognitive theories provide analogous accounts of learning. Part of our reason for postponing the required reasoning is that we are less interested in questions about learning than in questions about teaching. This parallels our greater interest in experimental than correlational tests of theory (see pp. 00-00).

Conclusion. There may be basic theoretical differences between operant and production and analyses of learning, but we doubt it, because they say analogous things about how to teach.

Summary

As a way of answering the question of how to teach so as to know what is learned, we spoke first about constraining contextual salience or stimulus control by teaching concepts with examples, including teaching of generative frames and minimal sets, and we spoke of supplementing examples by telling students rules. Second, we spoke of procedures for teaching goals and subgoals. Third, we spoke of teaching operant chains or production systems, including chains to be used invariantly and flexible modification of chains by control frames and pivotal behaviors. Fourth, we discussed ways of reducing competition from untaught procedures. Finally, we recognized the possibility that behavioral and cognitive theories may be shown to differ about how learning occurs, even though they now yield comparable prescriptions for how to teach.

QUESTION 3:
HOW DOES ONE KNOW THE RANGE OF USE OF WHAT IS TAUGHT?

Instead of just designing [a learning] activity or set of activities, hoping for the best, we should . . . have more precise expectations about what exactly students will learn from various contexts. (diSessa, 1988, p. 14)

When answering Question 2, we discussed minimal sets and cognitive routines. Identifying units of minimal sets and designing teachable cognitive routines are both task analyses whose function is to specify the range of use of what is taught. Here we consider such analyses in more detail, under the rubrics of *target domain* and *teaching task decomposition.* Identifying elements of minimal sets is an example of target domain decomposition. Identifying teachable cognitive routines is an example of teaching task decomposition.

We will use experiments by Butterfield and Nelson (1991) and Klahr and Carver (1988) to illustrate teaching task and target domain decomposition and to illustrate testing the range of use resulting from instruction based on decomposition. Klahr and Carver decomposed the teaching task LOGO debugging. Butterfield and Nelson decomposed the target domain of dimensional integration. We will compare instructional decisions based on pairs of decompositions written at different levels of analysis. We will argue that it makes no difference whether one's target of decomposition is a target domain or a teaching task. Implications for the range of use of what one teaches are the same.

Decomposition as a Way to Inform Teaching

> *[Knowing] what transfers to what necessarily calls for an analysis of the constituents of the 'whats.' For instance, the potential for studies in formal logic transferring to physics will depend on what component skills, key conceptual structures, pivotal procedures, or elements in some other sense of formal logic might contribute to physics.* (Salomon & Perkins, 1989, p. 137)

> *If a domain is properly analyzed, if instruction is based on the formal analysis, and if assessments of both what is learned in the base domain and what is transferred to the more remote domains are also grounded in formal analysis, then a powerful idea like debugging can be taught and can have an impact on general problem solving capacities.* (Klahr & Carver, 1988, p. 364)

A use of decomposition is to describe teachable contexts, goals, and actions, thereby specifying the range of use of what is taught. The extent to which this purpose is realized depends upon the levels of analysis used during decomposition.

Levels of Analysis.

Many decompositions of a cognitive skill are possible. (Singley & Anderson, 1989, p. 19)

The reason is that there are many decisions that must be made in designing [teaching] routines. And at each decision point, there is more than one acceptable solution. (Engelmann & Carnine, 1982, p. 195)

Three aspects of decompositions can differ in their level of analysis: (a) *specificity* of the stimulus or condition side of learned units, (b) *grain size* of the action or response side of units, and (c) *organization* (by goal or rote) of units into systems (cf. Singley & Anderson, 1989, pp. 257-269). In terms of our analogical mapping of productions onto discriminated operants (Table 7.1), specificity is a property of context statements or discriminative stimuli and of goals or current reinforcers, grain size is a property of goal setting or establishing operations and of actions or responses, and organization is a difference between alternative production systems or operant chains. Teaching is influenced by all three.

Specificity and Grain Size. Table 7.7 contains two productions (P1 and P2) that describe procedures for decomposing a teaching task. The teaching task is LOGO debugging. P1 is a hypothetical production designed to contrast sharply with P2, which is a description of decomposition procedures used by Klahr and Carver (1987). P2 is far less general than P1 with respect to both specificity and grain size. If these two productions were used as guides to teaching decomposition, P1 would constrain the selection of teaching examples less than P2, because its IF statements have less specificity. Comparing IFs of P1 and P2 shows that (a) more conditions per production, and (b) conditions with less generality both increase the specificity of a production (cf. Singley & Anderson, 1989), thereby more sharply constraining decisions about teaching contexts. P1 would constrain teaching very little. A teacher would receive no guidance about what teaching task to decompose from the IF statement in P1, so it is impossible to judge the range of applicability of what might be taught. The IF statement of P2 would constrain the teaching context to LOGO debugging, and the range of applicability of the teaching could be limited to LOGO debugging, rather than being applicable to the multitude of tasks and domains to which decomposition can be applied.

Another reason P1 would constrain teaching less than P2 is its larger grain size. Comparing the THENs in P1 and P2 shows that (a) more actions per production and (b) actions of less generality both decrease the grain size of a production, thereby more sharply constraining decisions about actions to teach. A teacher of decomposition would receive no guidance about what actions to teach from the THEN statement in P1. The THEN statement of P2 sharply constrains the actions to be taught. Those actions are very similar to the decomposition procedures of Klahr and Carver (1988).

Organization. Table 7.8 contains two productions (P1 and P2–P5) that describe procedures for testing a decomposition of a target domain. The domain is dimensional integration, a kind of formal reasoning. P1 and P2–P5 are different organizations of testing procedures that might have been used by Butterfield and Nelson (1991). P1 illustrates hierarchical organization by subgoals, and P2–P5 illustrate rote organization of a system of productions. The two organizations have the same specificity and grain size, but P1 is more general than P2–P5 because of its organization. Hierarchical organizations (P1) constrain teaching less than rote organizations, because they leave the order of acting on subgoals unspecified. Thus, if P1 were used to teach decomposition, a

Table 7.7. Two decompositions that differ in generality because of their specificities and grain sizes

More General	Less General
P1	**P2**
IF the goal is to teach for transfer	IF the goal is to teach for transfer and LOGO debugging is the teaching task
THEN decompose a teaching task	THEN break LOGO debugging into subtasks
	and call solving each subtask a goal
	and identify structural conditions presented by the subtasks
	and identify required actions of the goals and critical conditions
	and organize the goals, conditions, and actions into productions
	and organize the productions into a system
	and build a computer simulation of the system
	and determine that the computer stimulation solves LOGO debugging problems

teacher could vary the order of teaching selection of instructional examples (subgoal 1) and teaching design of instructional dialogues (subgoal 2), or he or she could teach them in tandem. If P2–P5 were used to guide teaching of testing a decomposition, the teacher would be constrained to teach selection of examples (P2) before and separately from designing instructional dialogues (P3), etc. In fact, Butterfield and Nelson tested their decomposition using procedures like those in P1. To the extent that different target domains require or allow different orders of the testing steps, P1 has a wider range of applicability.

Evaluating a Decomposition. Compared to Tables 7.7 and 7.8, the two columns of Table 7.9 are more detailed analyses of decomposing a teaching task (P1) and a target domain (P2) and evaluating those decompositions (P3–P8). They are cast at identical levels of specificity and grain size, and both have a rote organization. The left column of Table 7.9 is a hypothetical decomposition of the experiment by Klahr and Carver (1987), and the right column is a hypothetical decomposition of the experiment by Butterfield and Nelson (1991). The two columns differ from the experiments that inspired them primarily in the specification of General Case teaching and testing procedures (P7-P8). Table 7.9 says much about task decomposition, its uses to guide instruction, and how tests

Table 7.8.   Two decompositions that differ in generality because of their organizations

More General	Less General
P1 IF the goal is to teach for transfer to the domain of formal reasoning and balance scales, inclined planes, and shadow projectors are problems from that domain and decomposition of those problems has shown that they come in two types that require different solution methods and those methods are dimensional comparison and mathematical integration of values of the dimensions THEN set as subgoals to 1. select instructional examples for two of the problems 2. design instructional dialogues for teaching dimensional comparison and integration procedures 3. teach dimensional comparison and integration for two of the problems 4. test for transfer of the taught procedures to the third problem	**P2** IF the goal is to teach for transfer to the domain of formal reasoning and balance scales, inclined planes, and shadow projectors are problems from that domain and decomposition of those problems has shown that they come in two types that require different solution methods and those methods are dimensional comparison and mathematical integration of values of the dimensions THEN select instructional examples for two of the problems **P3** IF the goal is to teach for transfer to the domain of formal reasoning and instruction examples have been chosen for two problems from that domain THEN design instructional dialogues for teaching dimensional comparison and integration procedures **P4** IF the goal is to teach for transfer to the domain of formal reasoning and instructional dialogues have been designed THEN teach dimensional comparison and integration for two of the problems **P5** IF the goal is to teach for transfer to the domain of formal reasoning and dimensional comparison and integration have been taught for two of the problems THEN test for transfer of the taught procedures to the third problem

can be used to evaluate decompositions and their instructional implementation. We offer Table 7.9 for study of the extent to which decompositions can guide all of the instructional issues discussed under Question 2.

Table 7.9.   Comparison of decompositions of a teaching task and transfer domain

Teaching Task	Transfer Domain
P1 IF the goal is to teach for transfer and LOGO debugging is the teaching task	**P2** IF the goal is to teach for transfer to the domain of dimensional integration and balance scales, inclined planes, and shadow projectors are potential transfer tasks
THEN break LOGO debugging into subtasks and call solving each subtask a goal and identify structural conditions presented by the subtasks and identify required actions of the goals and critical conditions and organize the goals, conditions, and actions into productions and organize the productions into a system and build a computer simulation of the system and determine that the computer simulation solves LOGO debugging problems	THEN break balance scales, inclined planes, and shadow projectors into subtasks and call solving each subtask a goal and identify structural conditions presented by the subtasks and identify required actions of the goals and critical conditions and organize the goals, conditions, and actions into productions and organize the productions into a system and determine that the production systems for balance scales, inclined planes and shadow projectors are comparable
P3 IF the goal is to teach for transfer and the teaching task LOGO debugging has been decomposed	**P4** IF the goal is to teach for transfer to the domain of dimensional integration and the transfer tasks balance scales, inclined planes, and shadow projectors have comparable decompositions
THEN select teaching examples for units of the decomposition	THEN select teaching examples for units of the decompositions
P5 IF the goal is to teach for transfer and teaching examples have been selected for LOGO debugging	**P6** IF the goal is to teach for transfer to the domain of dimensional integration and teaching examples have been selected for balance scales, inclined planes, and shadow projects
THEN teach the examples using General Case Instruction's wording principle and its set up principle and its difference principle and its sameness principle	THEN use the examples to teach two of the tasks with General Case Instruction's wording principle and its set up principle and its difference principle and its sameness principle

Table 7.9.   (Continued)

Teaching Task	Transfer Domain
P7 IF the goal is to teach for transfer and examples for the units in the decomposition of LOGO debugging have been taught	**P8** IF the goal is to teach for transfer to the domain of dimensional integration and balance scales, inclined planes, and shadow projectors have been decomposed and two of the tasks have been taught
THEN select transfer problems from outside LOGO and administer tests of those problems according to General Case Instruction's testing principle	THEN use the examples from the third task to test for transfer according to General Case Instruction's testing principle

A Source of Uncertainty about Range of Use. Whether the object of decomposition is a target domain or a teaching task, using decompositions to constrain instructional decisions eliminates much uncertainty about the range of applicability of resultant learning. If one's method of teaching is sound, target domain decomposition is a dependable way to know much, if not all, of the learned range of applicability. It is the range of the decomposed domain. If one's methods of teaching and test selection are sound, teaching task decomposition is a dependable way to know much, if not all, of a range of applicability. It is the range of selected tests.

Regardless of which approach is used—decomposing a target domain or decomposing a teaching task—there remains some uncertainty (reflected in "if not all") about the range of applicability of what is taught. For target domain decomposition, the uncertainty stems from the possibility that some unconsidered domains have the same decomposition as the analyzed domain (P2 in Table 7.9). For teaching task decomposition, the uncertainty stems from the possibility that some unselected tests have the same decomposition as the teaching task (P7 in Table 7.9). We are convinced that these are the same sources of uncertainty. Teaching tasks or target domains are equivalent targets of decomposition, because experiments can determine whether teaching based on either has its intended range of applicability (see Table 7.9). Historically, such experiments depended on what were called "transfer" tests.

Conclusion. Methods of task decomposition used by behaviorists are analogous to methods used by cognitivists. Behavioral and cognitive decompositions constrain teaching to the extent that (a) their identified stimulus contexts have specificity, (b) their grain size of actions is smaller and less general, and (c) their organization is less hierarchical. More tightly constrained teaching allows more precise statements of the range of use of resultant learning.

Predictive vs. Instructional Uses of Decomposition and the Viability of Common Elements Theory

> *Thorndike and Woodworth's [1901] common elements theory holds that transfer happens when a new context or purpose shares elements with an old context or purpose, . . . Elements for current problems are selected by comparing representations of current situations to stored representations of past situations. . . . When representations of elements of past and present situations are the same, the past elements are selected, and if they are critical for the current situation, transfer should be highly positive.* (Butterfield & Nelson, 1989, pp. 7–19)

> *single productions are the units of cognitive skill, the elements that Thorndike was searching for.* (Singley & Anderson, 1989, p. 31)

> *We are in danger of having a vacuous theory because we may be able to accommodate any potentially embarrassing result by suitable assumptions about knowledge representation. . . . Without any representational assumptions, no predictions are possible.* (Singley & Anderson, 1989, p. 248)

When answering Question 3, we emphasized the use of task decompositions to constrain *instruction*. This emphasis is more typical of behaviorists than cognitivists, although it is not absent in the cognitive literature (e.g., Holzman, Glaser, & Pellegrino, 1976; Butterfield & Dickerson, 1976). Most cognitive authors have emphasized the use of task decomposition to *predict* use of learning resulting from instruction less or unconstrained by decomposition (e.g., Kieras & Bovair, 1986; Salomon & Perkins, 1989; Singley & Anderson, 1989).

We emphasized decomposition as a constraint on teaching because teaching is the only way to manipulate cognition with any precision. Teaching makes cognitive science experimental rather than correlational (cf. Holzman, Glaser, & Pellegrino, 1976; Butterfield & Dickerson, 1976). Emphasizing decomposition as a source of predictors underestimates the power of instructional techniques developed independently by behaviorists and cognitivists (see our treatment of Question 2), and it requires assumptions that unnecessarily weaken interpretation of even correlational findings on the range of applicability of learning (Singley & Anderson, 1989, pp. 251–255).

Singley and Anderson (1989) argued that using task decompositions as bases for predicting use of learning puts the modern student of transfer in the same embarrassing position as his forbears. Ever since Thorndike and Woodworth (1901a, b, c) first enunciated the theory of common elements, tests of the theory have been inconclusive because investigators lacked suitable ways to *measure* learners' representations of teaching and test settings. Therefore, investigators have not known the extent to which teaching and test settings shared common elements. Consequently, the temptation has been irresistible to conclude that unpredictability of test performance was due to inadequate measures of people's learned representations, rather than to inadequacies in the theory of common elements.

It is painfully obvious to Singley and Anderson (1984) that use of task decomposition does not avoid the vagaries of measuring learners' representations, even though identifying productions as elements of decompositions seems a better way than methods available to Thorndike and Woodworth or their behavioral descendents such as Gagné (1977). Singley and Anderson describe decomposition as model construction, and they observe in the end that "the kinds of evidence brought to bear on model construction are limited only by the ingenuity of the model builder" (p. 270).

It seems obvious to us that, when decompositions are used to guide teaching, learners' representations of situations, their goals, and their actions can be experimentally constrained so that there is less doubt what they have learned than when decompositions are used for predictive purposes alone. Consequently, experimental tests are possible of whether we can produce learning with known ranges of use. Notice, however, that common elements theory is not tested when decomposition is used instructionally rather than predictively. Rather, it is turned into an assumption of the instructional experiment. The question an instructional experiment can answer is whether assuming the correctness of common elements theory allows teaching for known uses of learning.

The loss in the instructional approach is the ability to test common elements theory. In the sense that an untestable theory is no theory at all, it is the loss of the theory itself. If the gain is increased confidence about the range of use produced by particular instructional sequences, the loss of common elements theory is acceptable to us. It may not be an acceptable loss to some, even though hanging onto common elements theory would leave to others experimental tests of how to promote transfer. We think that educationally relevant science can and must encompass experimental as well as predictive methods.

POSSIBILITIES FOR THE FUTURE

The experience of immersing yourself in and assimilating Piaget's work can alter in subtle but real and abiding ways the kind of research problems you select for study, the way you approach these problems, and the kind of interpretation you place on what you find. [These come] with no strings attached, . . . since science is in part a matter of the end game of one mind influencing the beginning and middle games of others. (Flavell, 1963, p. 425)

Like John Flavell after he immersed himself in Piaget's writings, we find that we have different views than we had before immersing ourselves in literatures bearing on the fundamental issue of the generality of learning. It is our judgment now that production-system cognitive answers are analogous to radical behavioral answers to our three questions on how to teach for general use of learning. It is our judgment now that arguments about the differences between behavioral and cognitive schools of thought have been overdrawn, which raises the possibility of a cognitive-behavioral collaboration on problems of teaching and learning. Most important, drawing the analogy between operant and production approaches suggests an agenda for future research that would not have occurred to us before. We conclude by mentioning future possibilities, which come, as Flavell observed, "with no strings attached," only potential to be realized.

Shared Understandings Between Radical Behaviorists and Production-System Cognitivists

Near the beginning of this chapter, we invited you to suspend any doubtsyou might have about our claims of similarities between operant and production analyses of learning. Since extending that invitation, we have argued that operant and production analyses are analogous in seven respects. First, both assume that current performance depends upon prior learning. Second, both justify the conclusion that it is unproductive to treat learning and transfer as different things. Rather, the fundamental question raised by both is the generality of the uses of learning. Third, operant and production theorists posit analogous units of learning. Thus, discriminative stimuli are analogous to context statements, current reinforcers to goal statements, establishing operations to subgoal setting, and responses to actions. Fourth, they posit analogous interactions among units. Thus, to account for complex performance, Skinnerians speak of chains of operants and theorists like Anderson, Klahr, and Simon speak of production systems. Chains and systems are analogous. To account for diversity of behavior in test situations, operant analysts speak of competition among discriminated operants and production theorists speak of similarity and associative strength of alternative productions. Competition among operants is analogous to competition among alternative productions. Fifth, operant and production theorists recommend the same approach to teaching so as to know what students learn. To produce known learning about conditions, goals, subgoals, and actions, both urge providing students with carefully sequenced positive and negative examples, and supplementing the examples with stated rules. Sixth, when teaching normally covert actions, both rely upon making the actions more overt so that instruction can work directly upon them. Seventh, both use task decomposition in ways that can constrain teaching so as to know the situations to which learning will apply.

Our primary claim is that the foregoing seven analogous relations indicate there are no basic differences between operant and production system answers to our three questions. There is no principled reason to continue the unproductive isolation of operant from production system analysts. They can read and understand each other's work if they will simply set themselves to doing so.

Conclusion. Radical behavioral and production-system cognitive researchers could share their research and theory about instruction. Can the same be said for other varieties of behavioral and cognitive theorists?

General Reconciliation of Behavioral and Cognitive Approaches

Cognitive psychology is often broken down into study of such subunits as perception, memory, language, and thought. . . . Behaviorism, on the other hand, takes an extreme molar view of the functioning of the organism as a whole. . . . The organism is empty in the behaviorist model, not because its contents are deemed unimportant, but because they are taken to be the subject of another discipline (neurophysiology primarily). About that, of course, the cognitivist who wants to fill the box with a mental design disagrees. But the behaviorist can be effectively agnostic vis-à-vis the program of the cognitivist. (Schnaitter, 1986, p. 309)

Our secondary claim is that differences between nonoperant behavioral and nonproduction cognitive modes of theoretical analysis have been exaggerated. One, it is incorrect to say that cognitive analyses assume represented events, but behavioral analyses assume real events. Behaviorists believe that environments have subjective characteristics, just as cognitivists believe that people's representations concern an objective reality. Like cognitive theorists, behaviorists believe that the effects of subjective characteristics depend on learning. Cognitive theorists put such subjective factors into goal and context statements and into goal-changing actions. Behavioral analysts put them in discriminative stimuli, reinforcers, and establishing operations. Two, it is incorrect to say that behavioral analyses account only for behavior and cognitive analyses account only for mental events. Cognitive and behavioral analyses both apply to overt and covert responses. Three, it is incorrect to say that cognitive theory makes all-or-none predictions, but behavioral theory makes probability statements. Both are probabilitistic, because both recognize that practice and feedback increase learning. Four, it is incorrect to say that cognitive theory has too little place for motivation, or that behavioral theory cannot encompass abstract establishing operations and reinforcers. Being analogous to reinforcers and establishing operations, goals and goal setting make plenty of room in cognitive theory for appetitive and abstract motivation. Five, it is incorrect to say that only cognitive theorists believe behavior is rule-governed in the sense that a person can sometimes acquire a new behavior by following a prescription for action. Both behavioral and cognitive investigators are actively investigating the determinants of rule-governed behavior. Six, it is incorrect to say that either behavioral or cognitive theory are inadequate because they have yet to analyze behaviors that seem especially flexible, dependent on richly structured knowledge, arational, and so on. A theory is impugned for not encompassing a phenomenon only when some other, nonanalogous theory does encompass it, which is not the case for behavioral or cognitive theory and any behavior identified so far. Seven, it is incorrect to say that either behavioral or cognitive theory has undesirable formal properties, for example, rigidity. Establishing that a theory has undesirable formal properties requires identification of a nonanalogous theory with desirable properties that applies to phenomena not encompassed by the accused theory.

Even though many unreal differences between behavioral and cognitive theory and research have been advanced as real, behavioral and cognitive approaches do differ. First, behaviorists play down mentalism and cognitivists play it up. At their best, the two are indifferent to the other's treatment of mentalism (Schnaitter, 1986), but their languages are mutually opaque because they are permeated with subtle ways of expressing their different stands on mentalism. Second, behaviorists are thoroughly functional in their style of explanation, and cognitivists are usually structural, which is also reflected in their language conventions and contributes to mutual incomprehensibility and misunderstanding. Despite these differences between behavioral and cognitive approaches, the shared ground between them stands out by viewing decompositions, which both use extensively, as guides to instructional design. Viewed this way, behaviorists can focus on instruction, which after all lies outside the box, and cognitivists can focus on the mental constraints resulting from instruction.[12] Viewing decomposition as a guide to instruction does not preclude viewing it as a way of mental modeling. Although we are not predicting it, both views could be adopted by behaviorists and cognitivists of all varieties.

Conclusion. Behaviorists and cognitivists of all stripes could read one another's instructional works and build them into their own "beginning, middle, and end games" (Flavell, 1963). The benefits to both could be great (cf. Butterfield & Dickerson, 1976; Skinner, 1977).

A Research Agenda

In theory (Gentner, 1989), an analogy does more than expose similarities between domains. It reveals possibilities that one would not see without it. Even when two domains are analogous, their different terminologies and organizations of concepts highlight different possibilities. In research domains, such as operant and production approaches to learning, this means that a useful analogy should not only allow translation of ideas between fields, it should suggest research questions. Drawing the analogy between operant and production systems suggested the following research questions to us.

Teaching Contextual Salience. About teaching to constrain contextual salience or stimulus control, unanswered questions concern (a) the effects of verbal

---

[12]We are indebted to Don Baer for showing us that a behaviorist could "accept" the ultimate cognitive concept *metacognition* simply by focusing on how it is taught.

instruction of rules which require declarative-to-procedural translations, (b) the use of procedural-to-declarative (introspective) reports as indices of what has been taught, (c) whether pivotal behaviors or executive routines can be brought under stimulus control, and (d) the relative efficacy of different ways of sequencing examples with and without supplemental verbal instruction.

Teaching Goals. Relatively little is known about teaching to constrain goals. The lack of such information seems to lie at the heart of our inability to teach complex, flexible behavior so that it is used in diverse contexts. In both the cognitive and behavioral views, flexibility and accuracy of complex behavioral–cognitive sequences stem in part from goals. Questions abound. (a) How satisfactorily can we externalize the diversity of goals that are used by effective problem solvers? (b) Having externalized and taught goals and goal setting, what must we do to insure that they are used covertly? (c) How much goal control can be secured from verbal instruction and how much exemplification is required? (d) How thoroughly must we decompose and teach goals in order to insure their use throughout a target domain? (e) Can we find teachable generative frames for uses of goals, or must we teach each and every sort of goal setting that benefits people?

Teaching Chains of Operants and Production Systems. Questions about teaching chains or systems blend into questions about teaching goal setting, unless one keeps firmly in mind the fact that units of learning are linked not only by goals, but also by changes in discriminative stimuli resulting from actions. In addition to setting goals, THEN statements contain actions that produce contexts for subsequent IF statements. Therefore, there are close parallels between unanswered questions about goals and unanswered questions about linking units into systems by action-created stimulus changes. (a) How satisfactorily can we externalize the diversity of actions used by effective problem solvers that produce covert contexts for subsequent productions in chains of cognition and behavior? (b) Having externalized them, what must we do to insure that contextual changes are used when they are covert? (c) How much control of covert actions can be secured from verbal instruction and how much exemplification is required? (d) How thoroughly must we decompose tasks used to teach use of action-produced contextual change in order to insure their use throughout a teaching domain? (e) Can we find teachable generative frames for uses of contextual changes, or must we teach each and every sort of response-generated contextual change that benefits students?

Reducing Competition Among Units. Reducing competition among units is perhaps the largest challenge remaining in the study of teaching for generalization. The difficulty is in knowing the kinds of competing stimuli and establishing operations to which our teaching must be immune. This suggests a kind of ecological research in which, following instruction, people are observed as they participate in contexts where their learning could be used. But this would capture only a small part of the complex relations among units that might occur over time in a given context. We discussed one corner of this vast territory under the rubric of *competing units* and suggested positive sides of the action of competing units. The richness and subtlety of interactions among units are perhaps the least explored frontier of research on teaching for generalization.

REFERENCES

Albin, R. W., & Horner, R. H. (1988). Generalization with precision. In R. H. Horner, G. Dunlap, & R. L. Koegel (Eds.), *Generalization and maintenance: Lifestyle changes in applied settings* (pp. 99–120). Baltimore: Paul Brookes.

Alessi, G. (1987). Generative strategies and teaching for generalization. *The Analysts of Verbal Behavior, 5,* 15–27.

Anderson, J. R. (1983). *The architecture of cognition.* Cambridge, MA: Harvard University Press.

Bassok, M., & Holyoak, K. J. (1989). Interdomain transfer between isomorphic topics in algebra and physics. *Journal of Educational Psychology: Learning, Memory, and Cognition, 15,* 153–166.

Bassok, M., & Holyoak, K. J. (1990, April). Pragmatic knowledge and conceptual structure: Determinants of transfer between quantitative domains. In D. Detterman (Chair), *Transfer on trial: Intelligence, cognition, and instruction.* Symposium conducted at the national meeting of the American Educational Research Association, Boston.

Belmont, J. M., & Butterfield, E. C. (1977). The instructional approach to developmental cognitive research. In R. Kail & J. Hagen (Eds.), *Perspectives on the development of memory and cognition* (pp. 437–481). Hillsdale, NJ: Erlbaum.

Bower, G. F., & Hilgard, E. R. (1981). *Theories of learning.* New York: Prentice-Hall.

Brown, A. L., Kane, M. J., & Echols, C. H. (1986). Young children's mental models determine analogical transfer across problems with a common goal structure. *Cognitive Development, 1, 103–121.*

Butterfield, E. C., & Dickerson, D. J. (1976). Cognitive theory and mental development. In N. R. Ellis (Ed.), *International review of research in mental retardation* (Vol. 8, pp. 105–137). New York: Academic.

Butterfield, E. C., & Nelson, G. D. (1989). Theory and practice of teaching for transfer. *Educational Technology Research and Development, 37,* 5–38.

Butterfield, E. C., & Nelson, G. D. (1991). Promoting positive transfer of different types. *Cognition and Instruction, 8,* 69–102.

Campione, J. C., Brown, A. L., & Ferrara, R. A. (1982). Mental retardation and intelligence. In R. J. Sternberg (Ed.), *Handbook of human intelligence* (pp. 392–490). New York: Cambridge University Press.

Carbonell, J. G. (1986). Derivational analogy: A theory of reconstructive problem solving and expertise acquisition. In R. S. Michalski, J. G. Carbonell, & T. M. Mitchell (Eds.), *Machine learning: An artificial intelligence approach* (pp. 371–392). Los Altos, CA: Kaufmann.

Carlson, R. A., & Schneider, W. (1989). Acquisition context and the use of causal rules. *Memory & Cognition, 17,* 240–248.

Carnine, D., & Silbert, J. (1979). *Direct instruction reading.* Columbus, OH: Charles E. Merrill Co.

Catrambone, R., & Holyoak, K. J. (1989). Overcoming contextual limitations on problem-solving transfer. *Journal of Experimental Psychology: Learning, Memory, and Cognition, 15,* 1147–1156.

Catania, A. C. (1984). *Learning* (2nd ed.). Englewood Cliffs, NJ: Prentice-Hall.

Catania, A. C., Shimoff, E., & Mathews, B. A. (1989). An experimental analysis of rule-governed behavior. In S. C. Hayes (Ed.), *Rule-governed behavior: Cognition, contingencies, and instructional control.* New York: Plenum.

Chomsky, N. (1959). A review of Skinner's *Verbal Behavior. Language, 35,* 26–58.

Cooper, G., & Sweller, J. (1987). Effects of schema acquisition and rule automation on mathematical problem-solving transfer. *Journal of Educational Psychology, 79,* 347–362.

Cooper, J. O., Heron, T. E., & Heward, W. Z. (1987). *Applied behavior analysis.* Columbus, OH: Merrill Publishing Co.

Cormier, S. M., & Hagman, J. D. (1987). *Transfer of learning: Contemporary research and applications.* San Diego: Academic Press.

Crisafi, M. A., & Brown, A. L. (1986). Analogical transfer in very young children: Combining two separately learned solutions to reach a goal. *Child Development, 57,* 953–968.

Detterman, D. (1990, April). The Case for the prosecution: Transfer as an epi-phenomenon. In D. Detterman (Chair), *Transfer on trial: Intelligence, cognition, and instruction.* Symposium conducted at the national meeting of the American Educational Research Association, Boston.

diSessa, A. A. (1988). Knowledge in pieces. In G. Forman & P. Pufall (Eds.), *Constructivism in the computer age.* Hillsdale, NJ: Erlbaum.

Dreyfus, H. L., & Dreyfus, S. E. (1986). *Mind over machine: The power of human intuition and expertise in the era of the computer.* New York: Free Press.

Ellis, H. C. (1965). *The transfer of learning.* New York: MacMillan.

Engelmann, S., & Carnine, D. (1982). *Theory of instruction: Principles and applications.* New York: Irvington Publishers.

Epstein, R. (1987). The spontaneous interconnection of four repertoires of behavior in a pigeon *(Columba livia). Journal of Comparative Psychology, 101,* 197–201.

Ericsson, K. A., & Simon, H. A. (1980). Verbal reports as data. *Psychological Review, 87,* 215–251.

Fagan, J. F. I., & Singer, L. T. (1983). Infant recognition memory as a measure of intelligence. In L. P. Lipsitt (Ed.), *Advances in infancy research* (Vol. 1, pp. 1–77). Norwood, NJ: Ablex Publishing Corp.

Flavell, J. H. (1963). *The developmental psychology of Jean Piaget.* Princeton, NJ: D. Van Nostrand & Company.

Flower, L., & Hayes, J. R. (1981). A cognitive process theory of writing. *College Composition and Communication, 32,* 365–387.

Forbus, K. D., & Gentner, D. (1986). Learning by analogy in the physical domains. In R. S. Michalski, J. G. Carbonell, & T. M. Mitchell (Eds.), *Machine learning: An artificial intelligence approach* (pp. 311–348). Los Altos, CA: Kaufmann.

Gagné, R. M. (1977). *The conditions of learning* (3rd ed.). New York: Holt, Rinehart, and Winston.

Gardner, H. (1985). *The mind's new science: A history of the cognitive revolution.* New York: Basic Books.

Gentner, D. (1988). Metaphor as structure mapping: The relational shift. *Child Development, 59,* 47–59.

Gentner, D. (1989). The mechanisms of analogical learning. In S. Vosniadou & A. Ortony (Eds.), *Similarity and analogical reasoning.*

Gentner, D., & Toupin, C. (1986). Systematicity and surface similarity in the development of analogy. *Cognitive Science, 10,* 277–300.

Ghatala, E. S., Levin, J. R., Pressley, M., & Lodico, M. G. (1985). Training cognitive strategy-monitoring in children. *American Educational Research Journal, 22,* 199–215.

Gick, M. L., & Holyoak, K. J. (1980). Analogical problem solving. *Cognitive Psychology, 12,* 306–355.

Gick, M. L., & Holyoak, K. J. (1983). Schema induction and analogical transfer. *Cognitive Psychology, 15,* 1–38.

Gick, M. L., & Holyoak, K. J. (1987). The cognitive basis of knowledge transfer. In S. M. Cormier & J. D. Hagman (Eds.), *Transfer of learning: Contemporary research and applications* (pp. 9–47). San Diego: Academic Press.

Gow, L., Ward, J., & Balla, J. (1985). The use of verbal self-instruction training (VSIT) to enhance learning in the mentally retarded: A study of techniques for improving acquisition, maintenance and generalization outcomes. *Educational Psychology, 5,* 115–134.

Greeno, J. (1989). Situations, mental models, and generative knowledge. In D. Klahr & K. Kotovsky (Eds.), *Complex information processing: The impact of Herbert A. Simon.* Hillsdale, NJ: Erlbaum.

Hall, G., & Sundberg, M. L. (1987). Teaching mands by manipulating conditioned establishing operations. *The Analysis of Verbal Behavior, 5,* 41–53.

Hall, R. P. (1989). Computational approaches to analogical reasoning: A comparative analysis. *Artificial Intelligence, 39,* 39–120.

Haring, T. G. (1985). Teaching between-class generalization of toy play behavior to handicapped children. *Journal of Applied Behavior Analysis, 18,* 127–139.

Hayes, S. C. (1986). The case of the silent dog—verbal reports and the analysis of rules: A review of Ericsson and Simon's *Protocol analysis: Verbal reports as data. Journal of the Experimental Analysis of Behavior, 45,* 351–363.

Hayes, S. C. (Ed.). (1989). *Rule-governed behavior: Cognition, contingencies, and instructional control.* New York: Plenum.

Herrnstein, R. J., Loveland, D. H., & Cable, C. (1976). Natural concepts in pigeons. *Journal of Experimental Psychology: Animal Behavior Processes, 2,* 285–302.

Holyoak, K. J. (1985). The pragmatics of analogical transfer. In G. H. Bower (Ed.), *The psychology of learning and motivation* (Vol. 19, pp. 59–87). New York: Academic Press.

Holyoak, K. J., & Thagard, P. (1989). A computational model of analogical problem solving. *Cognitive Science, 13,* 295–355.

Holzman, T. G., Glaser, R., & Pellegrino, J. W. (1976). Process training derived from a computer simulation. *Memory & Cognition, 4,* 349–356.

Horner, R. H., & Billingsley, F. F. (1988). The effect of competing behavior on the generalization and maintenance of adaptive behavior in applied settings. In R. H. Horner, G. Dunlap, & R. L. Koegel (Eds.), *Generalization and maintenance: Lifestyle changes in applied settings* (pp. 197–220). Baltimore: Paul Brookes.

Hunt, E. (1988). A case study of how a paper containing good ideas, presented by a distinguished scientist to an appropriate audience, had almost no influence at all. In A. C. Catania & S. Harnad (Eds.), *The selection of behavior.* New York: Cambridge University Press.

Hunt, J. McV. (1969). The impact and limitations of the giant of developmental psychology. In D. Elkind & J. H. Flavell (Eds.), *Studies in cognitive development* (pp. 3–66). New York: Oxford University Press.

Kamii, C., & DeClark, G. (1985). *Young children reinvent arithmetic: Implications of Piaget's theory.* New York: Teacher's College Press.

Kieras, D. E., & Bovair, S. (1986). The acquisition of procedures from text: A production-system analysis of transfer of training. *Journal of Memory and Language, 25,* 507–524.

Klahr, D., & Carver, S. M. (1988). Cognitive objectives in a LOGO debugging curriculum: Instruction, learning, and transfer. *Cognitive Psychology, 20,* 362–404.

Koegel, R. L., & Koegel, L. K. (1988). Generalized responsivity and pivotal behaviors. In R. H. Horner, G. Dunlap, & R. L. Koegel (Eds.), *Generalization and maintenance: Lifestyle changes in applied settings* (pp. 41–66). Baltimore: Paul Brookes.

Konarski, E. A., Crowell, C. R., & Duggan, L. M. (1985). The use of responsive deprivation to increase the academic performance of the EMR students. *Applied Research in Mental Retardation, 6,* 15–31.

Lachman, R., Lachman, J. L., & Butterfield, E. C. (1979). *Cognitive psychology and information processing: An introduction.* Hillsdale, NJ: Erlbaum.

Lane, H., Boyes-Braem, P., & Bellugi, U. (1976). Preliminaries to a distinctive feature analysis of handshapes in American Sign Language. *Cognitive Psychology, 8,* 263–289.

Larkin, J. H., McDermott, J., Simon, D., & Simon, H. A. (1980). Expert and novice performance in solving physics problems. *Science, 208,* 1335–1342.

Larkin, J. H., Reif, F., Carbonell, J., & Gugliotta, A. (1988). FERMI: A flexible expert reasoner with multi-domain inferencing. *Cognitive Science, 12,* 101–138.

Macphail, E. M., & Reilly, S. (1989). Rapid acquisition of a novelty versus familiarity concept by pigeons *(Columba livia). Journal of Experimental Psychology: Animal Behavior Processes, 15,* 242–252.

Medin, D., & Ortony, A. (1989). Psychological essentialism. In S. Vosniadou & A. Ortony (Eds.), *Similarity and analogical reasoning* (pp. 179–193) Cambridge: Cambridge University Press.

Meichenbaum, D. (1982). Teaching thinking: A cognitive-behavioral perspective. In S. Chipman, J. Segal, & R. Glaser (Eds.), *Thinking and learning skills* (pp. 407–426). Hillsdale, NJ: Erlbaum.

Michael, J. (1982). Distinguishing between discriminative and motivational functions of stimuli. *Journal of the Experimental Analysis of Behavior, 37,* 149–155.

Miller, S., & Engelmann, S. (1980). *Cursive writing program*. Tigard, OR: C. C. Publications.

Novick, L.R. (1988). Analogical transfer, problem similarity, and expertise. *Journal of Experimental Psychology: Learning, Memory, and Cognition, 14*, 1510–520.

Osgood, C. E. (1949). The similarity paradox in human learning: A resolution. *Psychological Review, 56*, 132-143.

Parker, W. C. (1987). Teaching thinking: The pervasive approach. *Journal of Teacher Education, 38*, 53–56.

Piaget, J. (1952). *The child's concept of number*. New York: W. W. Norton.

Pressley, M., Borkowski, J. G., & O'Sullivan, J. (1985). Children's metamemory and the teaching of memory strategies. In D. L. Forrest-Pressley, G. E. Mackinnon, & T. G. Waller (Eds.), *Metacognition, cognition, and human performance* (pp. 111–153). Orlando, FL: Academic Press.

Pressley, M., Woloshyn, V., Lysynchuk, L., Martin, V., Wood, E., & Willoughby, T. (1989). *Cognitive strategy instruction: The important issues and how to address them*. Unpublished manuscript.

Reed, S. K., Ernst, G. W., & Banerji, R. (1974). The role of analogy in transfer between similar problem states. *Cognitive Psychology, 6*, 436–450.

Reese, H. W. (1989). Rules and rule governance: Cognitive and behavioral views. In S. C. Hayes (Ed.), *Rule-governed behavior: Cognition, contingencies, and instructional control*. New York: Plenum.

Salomon, G., & Perkins, D. N. (1989). Rocky roads to transfer: Rethinking mechanisms of a neglected phenomenon. *Educational Psychologist, 24*, 113–142.

Schank, R. C., & Abelson, R. P. (1977). *Scripts, plans, goals, and understanding*. Hillsdale, NJ: Erlbaum.

Schnaitter, R. (1986). A coordination of differences: Behaviorism, mentalism, and the foundations of psychology. In T. R. Knapp & L. C. Robertson (Eds.), *Approaches to cognition: Contrasts and controversies* (pp. 291–315). Hillsdale, NJ: Erlbaum.

Schoenfeld, A. H. (1987). What's all the fuss about metacognition? In A. H. Schoenfeld (Ed.), *Cognitive science and mathematics education* (pp. 189–215). Hillsdale, NJ: Erlbaum.

Siegler, R. S. (1981). Developmental sequences within and between concepts. *Monographs of the Society for Research in Child Development, 46* (2, Serial No. 189).

Siegler, R. S. (1989). Mechanisms of cognitive development. *American Review of Psychology, 40*, 353–379.

Siegler, R. S., & Shrager, J. (1984). A model of strategy choice. In C. Sophian (Ed.), *Origins of cognitive skills* (pp. 229–294). Hillsdale, NJ: Erlbaum.

Silbert, J., Carnine, D., & Stein, M. (1981). *Direct instruction mathematics*. Columbus, OH: Merrill Publishing Co.

Silbert, J., Carnine, D., & Stein, M. (1990). *Direct instruction mathematics* (2nd ed.). Columbus, OH: Merrill Publishing Co.

Singley, M. K., & Anderson, J. R. (1989). *The transfer of cognitive skill*. Cambridge, MA: Harvard University Press.

Skinner, B. F. (1953). *Science and human behavior*. New York: MacMillan.

Skinner, B. F. (1957). *Verbal behavior*. New York: Appleton-Century-Crofts.

Skinner, B. F. (1966). An operant analysis of problem solving. In B. Klainmutz (Ed.), *Problem solving: Research, methods, and theory*. New York: Wiley.

Skinner, B. F. (1968). *The technology of teaching*. Englewood Cliffs, NJ: Prentice-Hall.

Skinner, B. F. (1977). Why I am not a cognitive psychologist. *Behaviorism, 5,* 1–10.

Slocum, T. A. (1990). *On situated cognition*. Unpublished manuscript, General Examination for Doctoral Degree, Department of Education, University of Washington, Seattle.

Snell, M. E. (1987). *Systematic instruction of persons with severe handicaps* (3rd ed.). Columbus, OH: Charles E. Merrill Publishing Co.

Soloway, E. (1986). Learning to program = learning to construct mechanisms and explanations. *Communications of the Association of Computing Machinery, 29,* 850–858.

Soloway, E. (1989, March). *What learning is all about: Confessions of a cloistered academic*. Paper presented at the Annual Meeting of the American Educational Research Association, San Francisco.

Spooner, F., & Spooner, D. (1984). A review of chaining techniques: Implications for future research and practice. *Education and Training of the Mentally Retarded, 10,* 114–124.

Stokes, T. F., & Baer, D. M. (1977). An implicit technology of generalization. *Journal of Applied Behavior Analysis, 10,* 349–367.

Suchman, L. (1987). *Plans and situated action*. New York: Cambridge University Press.

Thorndike, E. L. (1914). *The psychology of learning*. New York: Teacher's College.

Thorndike, E. L., & Woodworth, R. S. (1901a). The influence of improvement in one mental function upon the efficiency of other functions. (I). *Psychological Review, 8,* 247–261.

Thorndike, E. L., & Woodworth, R. S. (1901b). The influence of improvement in one mental function upon the efficiency of other functions. (II. The estimation of magnitudes). *Psychological Review, 8,* 384–395.

Thorndike, E. L., & Woodworth, R. S. (1901c). The influence of improvement in one mental function upon the efficiency of other functions. (III. Functions involving attention, observation and discrimination). *Psychological Review, 8,* 553–564.

Zhu, X., & Simon, H. A. (1987). Learning mathematics from examples and by doing. *Cognition and Instruction, 4,* 137–166.

Chapter 8

A Naturalistic Study of Transfer: Adaptive Expertise in Technical Domains*

Sherrie P. Gott, Ellen
Parker Hall, and Robert
A. Pokorny
Air Force Armstrong
Laboratory

Emily Dibble
University of Washington

Robert Glaser
LRDC, University of Pittsburgh

The rapidly advancing technologies that populate modern work environments demand considerable mental adaptiveness from human operators and maintainers. Workers in technical domains such as electronics must typically master a broad array of complex systems as well as adapt to a continuous stream of the latest "releases/generations/models" of those systems. Stated in psychological

_____

* This chapter is an extended version of a symposium presentation made at the annual conference of the American Educational Research Association in Boston, MA, April 17, 1990.

The authors wish to acknowledge the invaluable contributions made by Mr. Kurt Strobel, MSgt Gary Walker, and TSgt Ron Kane of the U.S. Air Force. Their avionics expertise and their insights into human learning and instruction have influenced every aspect of this work. We feel fortunate to count them as colleagues.

Requests for reprints should be sent to Sherrie Gott, Armstrong Laboratory, Human Resources Directorate (AL/HRMJ) Brooks AFT TX, 78235-5601.

The opinions reflected herein are those of the authors and do not necessarily reflect the opinions of the U.S. Air Force ArmstrongLaboratory or any other U.S. Air Force organization.

terms, to be effective the performer must be a good transferer of knowledge and skill.

The considerable demand for mental adaptiveness in Air Force workplaces has made it possible for us to undertake a rare naturalistic study of transfer. A consolidation of technical jobs has imposed a requirement for the transfer of knowledge and skill on hundreds of technicians who maintain avionics systems (airborne electronic devices). The merging of three avionics maintenance jobs into one has provided us a unique opportunity to examine transfer under authentic conditions of learning, away from the constrained conditions of the psychological laboratory. The questions that have guided our investigation are these: When the transfer of skill and knowledge occurs outside the laboratory, how is it done? What are the mechanisms by which transfer occurs? What are the levers that are used to access prior knowledge and utilize it productively? What is the content of the knowledge that is accessed and transferred? What features and/ or conditions associated with prior knowledge/skill appear to impede the acquisition process? This chapter represents an interim report of an ongoing study of transfer that addresses these questions.

There is a growing body of evidence that suggests that adaptiveness in generalizing one's knowledge—particularly in the context of complex problem solving tasks—is strongly influenced by the quality of the performer's knowledge representations (Brown & Burton, 1986; Brown & deKleer, 1985; Chi & Bassok, 1988; Chi, Feltovich, & Glaser, 1981; Clancey, 1986; Judd, 1908; Katona, 1940; Kieras, 1982; Kieras & Bovair, 1984; Wertheimer, 1945; White & Frederiksen, 1986, 1987). Adaptive expertise has in fact been posited as an advanced level of problem-solving performance that is characterized by principled representations of knowledge and skill as opposed to representations dominated by surface features (Hatano & Inagaki, 1984). For example, the procedural skills of adaptive experts are supported by reasons and other conceptual support knowledge that explain the steps of the procedure including the conditions of applicability. Understanding the rationales behind the procedures allows performers to be adaptive under altered conditions and to reconstruct procedures if they are forgotten. Further, in task domains where a device or system is the object of the problem solving, understanding why procedures work is directly tied to how-it-works knowledge of the device. Device knowledge organized as mental models provides an inference base that enables procedures to be inferred when exact procedural steps are either not accessible to follow, not previously known, or forgotten (Brown & Burton, 1986; Gentner & Stevens, 1983; Gott, 1989; Kieras & Bovair, 1984).

Even before procedural steps are taken, skilled performers appear to represent a problem in terms of some meaningful structure or functionality whereas less-skilled performers organize their representations around surface features and literal descriptive aspects (Chi, Feltovich, & Glaser, 1981; Glaser, 1988). This type of functional qualitative analysis often involves representing a problem in terms of a "runnable mental model," which specifies the main causal connections of the components of a situation. Running an internalized model can be thought of as invoking an explanatory theory to use in instantiating a given problem situation.

In sum, adaptive expertise in technical domains is grounded in understanding and is thereby generative. The robust performance is one in which procedural steps are not just naked, rule-based actions, but instead are supported by explanations that perform like theories to enable adaptiveness. This adaptive/ generative capability suggests that the performer not only knows the procedural steps for problem-solving tasks, but also understands when to deploy them and why they work. As a consequence, in knowledge-rich domains where ill-structured problems are plentiful (i.e., solution steps cannot be specified in advance) (Newell, 1969), a premium is placed on adaptive experts who have principle-based understanding that is rich with explanatory schemata.

THEORETICAL RATIONALE

The theoretical framework we have adopted in this effort is influenced by three dominant themes: (a) transfer and learning are viewed as functionally equivalent; (b) detailed cognitive models of performance are used as the basis for transfer predictions; and (c) the learner's perceptions of similarity in transfer-like tasks are believed to appreciably affect what is learned.

Transfer as Learning

Regarding the first theme, we view transfer as indistinguishable from learning in a general psychological sense. We share the position taken by Gick and Holyoak (1987, p. 10) that

> no empirical or theoretical chasm separates transfer from the general topic of learning. Rather, the consequences of prior learning can be measured for a continuum of subsequent tasks that range from those that are merely repetitions (self-transfer), to those that are highly similar (near transfer), to those that are very different (far transfer).

Our particular view of transfer addresses the question, "What is acquired during learning when it occurs in the context of expanding complex problem-solving capabilities?" We have formulated a number of expectations regarding the processes and content of transfer in this context.

First, in the technical domain of electronics problem solving, we expect transfer (as learning) to occur on many levels, such that a range of specific-to-general activities of either *transporting* or *transposing* prior knowledge takes place. For example, procedural skills such as the execution of standard electronic tests (e.g., ohms and voltage measurements) represent one of multiple types of knowledge that must be effectively coordinated to produce optimal levels of reasoning in a complex technical domain (Gott, 1989). The procedural steps of such standard electronic tests may be fairly constant across equipment systems. As a result, this rule-based knowledge may be transportable intact across job domains in a manner that suggests a common (or identical) elements form of transfer (Thorndike, 1903, 1906; Thorndike & Woodworth, 1901). Thus, transferring compact procedural subroutines such as the steps of an ohms test would represent an instance of specific procedural transfer (or self-transfer). By contrast, the transfer of abstract representations such as the goal structures and device schemata that are used to deploy and guide specific problem-solving steps would constitute transfer of a more general nature.

These and other expectations about the content of transfer are a consequence of the second theoretical theme that has influenced this study, namely, the use of detailed cognitive models of technical performances to investigate transfer.

Cognitive Models to Predict Transfer

For the past several years, the authors of this chapter have been engaged (in various capacities) in a large-scale research effort directed at examining the cognitive skills that allow individuals to interact adaptively with technologically complex systems (Glaser et al., 1985; Gott, 1989; Means & Gott, 1988). The goal is to develop an integrated cognitive task analysis/instructional development methodology to build training systems that foster adaptive expertise in complex domains. In particular, the task analysis component of the methodology has been designed to produce fine-grained cognitive models of diagnostic problem solving. The approach involves a structured, thinking-aloud interview with iterative rehashes of traces of solution steps that are designed to elicit the reasons that explain the organization of the task performance (Hall, Gott, & Pokorny, 1990; Means & Gott, 1988).

We have implemented this cognitive analysis approach to study dozens of maintenance technicians at varied proficiency levels. Our goal has been to produce detailed cognitive models of performance to use as targets in instruction. The abstracted cognitive skills architecture in Figure 8.1 has been derived from the fine-grained data yielded by the cognitive analyses.

To elaborate on the components of this architecture, consider the following description of a prototypical task where a human interacts with a machine of some type:

> Whether operating a word processor or diagnosing a faulty engine, the human performer is required to select and execute procedures to interact with an object to achieve a set of goals. The knowledge and processes that constitute that

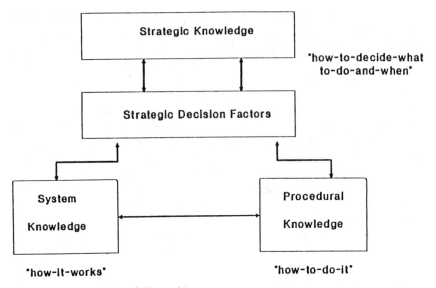

Figure 8.1.   Cognitive Skills Architecture

performance are (a) procedural (or how-to-do-it) knowledge; (b) declarative (domain) knowledge of the object, often called system or device knowledge (or how-it-works knowledge); and (c) strategic (or how-to-decide-what-to-do-and-when) knowledge. With this decomposition, it is assumed that procedural and device knowledge are organized and deployed by mechanisms such as the goals, plans, and decision rules that comprise strategic knowledge (Gott & Pokorny, 1987). This deployment capability serves a control function to enable what can be called dynamic, opportunistic reasoning. Ideally, this results in optimal solutions crafted in response to particular situations by applying just the right piece of knowledge at just the right time. (Gott, 1989, p. 100)

Detailed cognitive performance models, which represent instantiations of this abstracted model, have been generated for the three avionics maintenance jobs that are presently being consolidated and provide the foci for this transfer study. What follows is a brief description of these three models. They have provided us an independent basis for predictions about transfer. By comparing and contrasting these models, we can be explicit about the key objects of transfer to be studied.

In all three jobs, avionics technicians repair and maintain the components of electronic systems from F15 aircraft. When a component (or black box) is suspected as malfunctioning on a jet, the component is removed and sent to one of the three avionics repair shops. When it arrives in the shop, the unit is attached via connecting cables (or a similar apparatus) to a large piece of test equipment known as a test station (see Figure 8.2). It is then referred to as a unit

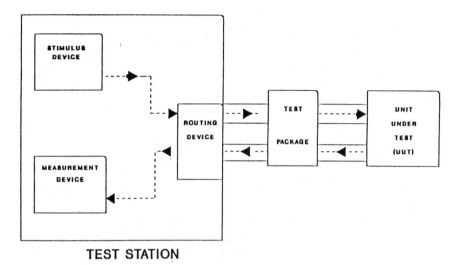

TEST STATION

Figure 8.2.   Top-Level Avionics Equipment Model

under test (or UUT). The functions of the test station are to simulate the electronic signals that the unit would receive if it were in an airplane and to measure the signals it produces. The test station tests the unit by sending every signal it is capable of receiving and then determining whether it is responding correctly. When one of these tests fails, the technician must identify the source of the problem and repair or replace the faulty element.

When the fault lies in the UUT, problem solving (i.e., troubleshooting) is relatively simple, because any given unit has a limited range of functions and components. When the fault lies in the test package (the cables and apparatus which serve as an interface between the unit and the test station), troubleshooting can also be achieved by routinized procedures. However, when the fault lies in the test station, troubleshooting is complicated by the size of the station— approximately 40 cubic feet of components; by the tremendous array of signal generation, signal measurement, and signal routing functions it serves; and by the fact that very little of what the test station does is visible to the technician. In effect, the complexity and opaqueness of the test station not only increases device knowledge demands on the performer but also heightens associated procedural and strategic knowledge requirements as well.

The transfer problem that we are studying involves the adaptiveness of technicians across the complex test station equipment used in the three avionics jobs that have been merged together. The nature of the test stations in fact defines the three domains. Although all stations serve the same general function, each works in different ways on different sets of units. As a result, each avionics job has unique types of test stations. For two of the three jobs (Automatics and Electronic Warfare Systems (EWS)), the station operation is computerized (i.e., software-driven); however, the configuration and external features of the two automated equipment systems are highly dissimilar despite the common functions that they share. In the third job (Manuals), the human technician manually operates the station.

The modeling of domain-specific diagnostic problem solving for the three avionics jobs has yielded performance models that are isomorphic at several levels of abstraction. In all domains, three general types of knowledge must be coordinated for troubleshooting to be effective: system or how-it-works knowledge of the equipment, procedural or how-to-do-it knowledge of troubleshooting operations, and strategic or how-to-decide-what-to-do-and-when knowledge that deploys the system and procedural knowledge. Skeletal cognitive models (at an intermediate level of representation) are shown in Figures 8.3a-c for the three jobs. For each type of knowledge, the adaptive expert appears to have access to elaborate hierarchical knowledge structures that range from specific knowledge instantiations to abstractly stated principles.

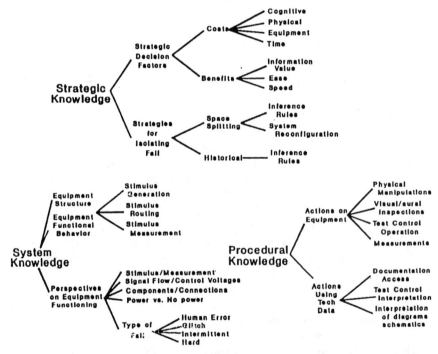

Figure 8.3a.   Cognitive Model for Manuals Avionics Equipment Troubleshooting

A comparative analysis of these three performance models reveals the dissimilarities that exist at this intermediate level of specificity. Dashed lines on Figures 8.3b and 8.3c denote the knowledge components that are demanded by

Figure 8.3b.   Cognitive Model for Autos Avionics Equipment Troubleshooting

the computerized test stations but not by the manually operated station (Figure 8.3a). At lower levels of specificity, similarities between the two automated jobs would also disappear. To elaborate on the computerized vs. manual station demands, technicians working on automated equipment need system knowledge about equipment structure and functioning that explains computer I/O functions and that differentiates hardware-related from software-related system behavior (see System Knowledge branches in Figures 8.3b and 8.3c). They also need procedural knowledge to know how to interact with the system's operating software and software diagnostics. Finally, they need fault isolation strategies (see Strategic Knowledge branches in Figures 8.3b and 8.3c) that are well suited to the more complex circuitry in the computerized stations, for example, a strategy where the results of multiple fails are integrated to narrow down the number of suspected sources of malfunction. We consider knowledge demands such as these to be objective properties of cognitive performance models. As such they provide plausible bases for predictions about transfer. For example, one might predict that technicians who work on automated equipment would find the other automated job easier to learn than the Manuals technicians, given the similar cognitive demands for software-related knowledge. While we believe cognitive models are useful in formulating hypotheses such as these, we also find them insufficient for predicting learning outcomes. They cannot tell us, for example, which of these similarities and differences are salient enough to affect

Figure 8.3c.   Cognitive Model for EWS Avionics Equipment Troubleshooting

the learning processes of experienced technicians. This proposition introduces the third theme of our study.

The Learner's Perceptions of Similarity in Transfer Tasks

Our preliminary views regarding the influence of *perceived* similarities on transfer arose from early interview data we collected during the hypothesis formation stage of this study (Glaser & Gott, 1988; Parker, Dibble, & Gott, 1989). We asked experienced technicians in one job about their learning experiences in one of the other jobs. Questions centered around their expectations regarding the relationship between their original job (Job 1) and the transfer or target job (Job 2) at the time they started the cross-training process. Expectations were elicited about the nature of the equipment, the approach to troubleshooting, the information available in technical manuals or from diagnostic software, and the more specific troubleshooting procedures.

The results of these early interviews suggested some interesting transfer-related differences across levels of technical proficiency in Job 1. Skilled performers appeared to use existing schemata from their source domain to build representations in the target domain. More specifically, their stated expectations revealed existing schemata of three general types: first, (mental) device models of the avionics equipment; second, general models of the task, in the form of a troubleshooting approach (or goal structure); and third, well-organized procedural knowledge that appeared to be adaptive to the conditions imposed by more and less complex equipment systems.

How-It-Works Knowledge. With respect to system knowledge, the better performers talked about the equipment in terms of an integrated device representation based on system functionality: "A test station is a test station. The same general functions are performed by every station—a stimulus is generated, routed, and measured. The electronic test process is the same. Most differences are in the physical aspects of the equipment" (Parker, Dibble, & Gott, 1989). Comments such as these suggest that the more able performers are working from an abstracted device schema or mental model such as the one depicted in Figure 8.2. By comparison, less proficient technicians were unable to represent such abstract functional similarities. "I treated the Autos stations as new equipment—unrelated to the Manuals stations." Other equipment-related expectations verbalized by the less-able performers were either rather global beliefs, such as "I expected the Autos stations to be more reliable, but they break down a lot," or in some cases, discrete component-to-component mappings, for example, "The Manual's digital multifunction meter (DMM) is the same as the EWS digital volt meter (DVM)."

How-to-Decide-What-to-Do-and-When Knowledge. Well-established knowledge structures were similarly used by better performers to predict other cognitive requirements in the target domain. For example, when queried about expectations regarding a general (strategic) troubleshooting approach that would apply in the new job, more proficient technicians talked in terms of a top-level, abstract goal structure (shown in Table 8.1), whereas less proficient technicians produced more specific procedural steps as a general approach, for example, "Use the external control panel to find out the role of particular drawers (of circuit cards) in the (electronic) test being run." The more abstractly stated goals from the skilled performers suggested the use of a troubleshooting plan schema that could be instantiated for any of the three domains. Even more general versions of the five abstract goals in Table 8.1 would resemble the following: (a) represent the problem in terms of the underlying functionality of

Table 8.1.   Top-Level Goal Structure for Avionics Troubleshooting (Interview Data)

1. Figure out what's going on in test being run (establish active signal path)
2. Verify fail
3. Isolate fail between UUT and Test Station
4. Verify that signal is good entering and leaving the routing device
5. Investigate remaining measurement circuitry

the equipment; (b) verify that the equipment failure is real; (c) eliminate the most suspect part of the equipment configuration first; and (d) focus attention on remaining equipment components having a high failure rate. The flexibility of a top-level plan such as this seems obvious. By comparison, the equipment-specific procedural steps produced by less proficient performers as a general approach suggest less flexible structures with limited generalizability. The performance that would be expected from these more localized representations would be unsystematic, that is, not informed by a top-level plan.

How-to-Do-It Knowledge. Finally, when asked about expectations regarding troubleshooting operations (procedural knowledge) in the target job, the more proficient technicians responded with statements that suggested the ways in which they were already adapting procedures from their source domain to the target domain. For example, proficient technicians working on the Manual's test stations recognized how the procedural options would change on the computerized test stations. "The more complicated circuitry in the automated stations demands the use of computerized self-tests (diagnostics) to do troubleshooting efficiently. So, the more complex stations elevate self-diagnostics in a list of useful procedures to consider." Notice how the change from manual to automatic equipment affects the procedural options and ascribed properties. This suggested interplay between system and procedural knowledge is consistent with the major premises that underlie the cognitive skills architecture depicted in Figure 8.1. The nature of the device (or system) that is the object of problem solving is believed to exert consequential influence on the procedures that are needed to investigate the system as well as on higher level plans and goals that provide strategic control knowledge. When system complexity increases, one expects to see corresponding changes in the complexity of procedural and strategic knowledge.

In sum, these initial interviews further informed our predictions about the content and mechanisms of knowledge/skill transfer across technical domains. More specifically, it became apparent to us that while cognitive models of performance may forecast in some objective way the difficulty and ease of transfer across domains, when in situ learning is examined, the learner's *perceptions* of similarities exert powerful influences on transfer processes as well. Further, in our initial data, the variability in learners' perceptions closely paralleled documented expert-novice differences in problem-solving tasks (Chi, Glaser, & Rees, 1982; Larkin, McDermott, Simon, & Simon, 1980). Technicians having high proficiency in their original job perceived device similarities in the target job in terms of deep functionality and causal components, whereas low-proficiency technicians tended to find the surface features of target devices more salient. Similarly, high performers perceived the structural commonalities of the troubleshooting task across domains in terms of standard yet flexible goal structures. Also, the coordination of system, procedural, and strategic knowledge was detected among high-proficiency technicians who often expressed their expectations about troubleshooting demands in terms of interrelated device, procedural, and strategic knowledge. This finding provides further affirmation of the cognitive skills architecture (Figure 8.1).

Collectively, these findings have informed the design of the transfer study that we have undertaken. Broadly stated, we have set out to establish authentic conditions of learning so that technicians can reveal their self-directed learning processes as well as their perceptions of similarity across domains.

DESCRIPTION OF STUDY METHODOLOGY

General Design

The study was divided into three phases, each serving a different purpose. Phase 1 was the Pretest Phase where technicians who had been identified by shop supervisors as skilled and experienced in their original job (either Manuals or Automatics Test Stations) were tested on their troubleshooting proficiency in that job and in the target or transfer job (Electronic Warfare Systems). The EWS job was selected as the target domain because the known differences between EWS troubleshooting demands and the other two jobs are greater than for any other pairings of the three jobs. In particular, in terms of the cognitive models presented in Figures 8.3a-c, considerable differences show up at lower levels of specificity between the EWS demands (Figure 8.3c) versus the other two models in these areas: the System Knowledge subcomponent "Equipment Structure" and the Procedural Knowledge subcomponent "Actions Using Tech Data." These more specific differences appear to impede transfer to this job from the other two jobs, even though one of the other two involves an automated test station (Figure 8.3b).

The purpose of Phase 1 was to use verbal troubleshooting tests to identify technicians who had sound Job 1 knowledge and enough Job 2 familiarity to benefit from the relatively short Learning Phase that was to follow. (The verbal troubleshooting testing procedures will be described in more detail later in this section.) In effect, this phase was used both to screen out technicians with insufficient Job 1 knowledge to transfer to Job 2 and to establish a baseline of prior knowledge (Job 1 and Job 2) for the selected technicians for use in later analytic comparisons. (The form of the verbal troubleshooting data will be illustrated later when the procedures are described in more detail.) Supervisors identified 10 technicians who met our stated criteria; six were ultimately selected for participation in later phases of the study.

Phase 2 was the Learning Phase where the six selected technicians were given the opportunity to work on a group of Job 2 troubleshooting problems with a Job 2 expert. Technicians were instructed to *direct their own learning,* using their best learning skills to interrogate the expert about the particular troubleshooting scenarios and about generally maintaining the Job 2 equipment. They were told that their goal should be to learn as much as possible in this phase in order to improve their troubleshooting performance on subsequent Phase 3 posttests. Improved performance was defined as becoming increasingly proficient in solving problems independent of assistance from the expert tutor.

This structured, self-directed learning activity was the principal cognitive task used in Phase 2. It is a variant of learning-from-examples tasks that have been used by other investigators to examine learning processes in situ (Chi & Bassok, 1989; Chi, Bassok, Lewis, Reimann, & Glaser, 1989). Two secondary cognitive tasks were also administered to the six subjects. One was designed to examine Job 1 and Job 2 system knowledge more directly and comparatively. The second was designed to achieve the same goal for Job 1 and Job 2 strategic knowledge.

Phase 3 was the Posttest Phase where subjects were tested on three new Job 2 problems that represented a range of near to far transfer tasks. The verbal troubleshooting test procedure was again used. Technicians were told in advance that only limited assistance would be available to them in this phase from the expert tutor. They were further informed that their performance on Phase 3 posttest problems would be compared to their Phase 1 performance to determine how effectively they had learned in Phase 2. This comparison would reveal the extent to which experienced Job 1 technicians could accelerate their Job 2 learning via self-directed tutorial sessions with a Job 2 expert. Next we describe each of the three phases in more detail.

Phase 1: Pretesting on Job 1 and Job 2 Problems

Verbal troubleshooting test procedures that were developed and implemented in earlier stages of our research project were used to administer Job 1 and Job 2 pretests (Gott, 1987; Pokorny, 1990). The verbal troubleshooting testing method is a structured, thinking-aloud dialogue procedure developed for the analysis and assessment of complex problem solving in real-world task environments. Execution of the method requires a domain expert, who poses an authentic problem to a subject, a problem solver (or subject) whose knowledge is being assessed, and a task analyst who documents the thinking-aloud processes in accordance with a particular interview format. The method is designed to reveal a technician's system, procedural, and strategic knowledge in the contexts of use, that is, tied to the varying task conditions of different problems.

The process begins with a detailed statement of an electronic test that has failed. The statement contains the same information the technician would have available under comparable conditions working on the actual equipment. The technician's role is to isolate the location of the fault by accessing technical data, deciding on an equipment component to investigate, and verbally selecting procedures to investigate the targeted component. The expert technician who poses the problem then provides the solver with information about the results of her or his proposed action. The solver interprets these results and specifies a suspect equipment component(s) to be targeted in the next action. A written record is created of this iterative process to capture the solver's troubleshooting goals, or *Precursors* to actions; the *Actions* taken by the solver; the *Results* or outcomes of the Actions, which are provided by the expert poser; and the solver's *Interpretations* of the Results. The task analyst who creates the record explicitly probes for each of these elements if they are not produced in a thinking-aloud mode. The analyst also asks the solver to draw a block diagram-level picture to illustrate the equipment being focused on at each solution step. The record of the completed solution is represented as a series of *Precursor, Action, Result*, and *Interpretation* nodes and is known as a PARI record, or PARI trace. A node from a PARI trace is shown in Table 8.2. Each trace is subsequently evaluated by several expert troubleshooters who judge the quality of the fault isolation process on the basis of an empirically derived scoring scheme (Pokorny, 1990).

The verbal troubleshooting task approach to testing is a form of work sample assessment. Tests of this type are generally viewed as a superior measure of job performance, because they provide a direct window to job proficiency (Pokorny, 1990). The PARI approach also has practical merit in a technical domain such as electronics because the proficiency evaluation is accomplished *away* from the actual equipment. Safety considerations, for example risk of harm to the technician and damage to the equipment, often make the use of actual equipment during assessment quite difficult. Also, the psychomotor skills demanded to manipulate the equipment are typically easy to learn though often quite time-consuming, a feature that could unnecessarily protract the testing process if done on the actual equipment.

In the Pretest Phase, subjects were given two Job 1 and three Job 2 problems to verbally troubleshoot. They had one hour to solve each of these problems. When solving Job 1 problems, the technicians were not allowed to ask for help of any kind from the expert. When solving Job 2 problems, the technicians were encouraged to work as independently as they could, but were allowed to ask questions if they got stuck and could not proceed with solving the problem. This type of "assisted" assessment was deemed necessary because of the intricate tech-data access procedures required in Job 2. This particular cognitive demand is one that involves procedural actions using tech data. It is a component of the cognitive performance models described earlier that accounts for some major dissimilarities between the target Job 2 and the two source jobs. None of the tested airmen showed even partial proficiency on these procedures during pretesting, and such performance gaps during verbal troubleshooting would block our access to other Job 2 knowledge which they might possess. As part of the PARI record, the task analyst recorded the amount and types of help a

Table 8.2   Example PARI Data

PRECURSOR: Want to see if the stimulus signal is
            good up to interface [test package] cable

ACTION: Measure signal at J14-28 with multimeter

RESULTS: 28 Volts

INTERPRETATION: This is the expected reading; this tells
                me that the stimulus is getting from the
                test station through the cable, so that
                part of the stimulus path is good

Technician's Drawing

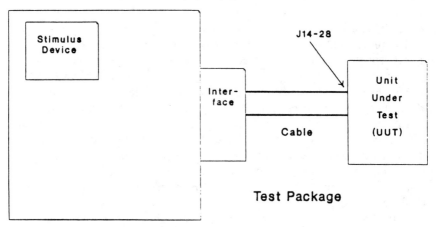

technician needed. If the technician failed to isolate the fault within the one hour allowed, the expert "moved" the fault close to where the technician was looking as time ran out. This was done to provide the technicians with an early Job 2 success experience, since most had limited practical experience working with the new test station. Moving the fault had no effect on the overall quality of the technician's solution to the problem, however, since the move did not occur until the last few minutes of the troubleshooting session.

Phase 2: Learning to Troubleshoot Job 2 Equipment

Our goal in this phase was to create authentic and challenging conditions of learning so that the technicians' learning processes and perceptions of similarity could be effectively elicited. In short, we wanted to observe transfer as it occurred. Our first attempt at this was modeled closely after a learning-from-examples paradigm reported by Chi and colleagues (Chi & Bassok, 1989; Chi et al., 1989). In this body of work, these investigators used worked-out solutions to mechanics problems to elicit elaborations from subjects who were instructed to think aloud about the solutions. In a later phase, subjects were given a range of related problems to solve on their own. Our approximation of this method consisted of (a) providing avionics technicians with worked-out troubleshooting solution traces (Action and Results) for Job 2 problems, (b) asking them to think aloud as they examined and studied the traces as preparation for subsequent problem solving of their own, and (c) posing new Job 2 problems to them to observe how the studying of example traces had enabled learning.

What we found clearly demonstrates how experimental procedures that are effective in the laboratory do not always move smoothly into real-world inquiries. Experienced Air Force technicians at varying levels of proficiency repeatedly failed to generate informative elaborations. Instead, they were quite passive in their examination of the exemplar solutions. Predictably, when required to solve Job 2 problems on their own, they required a great deal of expert assistance. As a consequence, this method was not effective in inducing learning, making our initial attempt to observe transfer unsuccessful. We believe this occurred for several reasons.

First of all, the demand characteristics of this method are quite different for students who are volunteers for a psychology experiment than they are for young adults with real-world work experience and technical training. Students will be compliant, presumably because they view compliance as part of their agreement to participate in an experiment. Further, revealing their lack of knowledge in the domain under study does not cause any loss of esteem or status. In fact, they probably qualified as subjects because of their domain naivete. Conversely, in a naturalistic study of transfer with adult members of a labor force, both noncompliance—or more accurately, failure to engage with the task—and ego defenses are formidable barriers in a learning study such as this. All of the technicians whom we encountered had completed some level of Job 2 training and were experienced Job 1 technicians; therefore, it seems reasonable to assume that they had certain self-expectations about their avionics capabilities in general as well as their Job 2 proficiency. They were reluctant to reveal that there were questions about troubleshooting that they could not answer for themselves. Further, the subculture of aircraft maintenance and repair has a decidedly "macho" character to it. The independent capability of the individual is highly regarded despite the fact that work is typically accomplished in teams. It is not generally considered appropriate behavior to ask for help because of a lack of knowledge, especially if you have years of experience in a related domain. What we learned from this informed our present design.

To neutralize the technicians' tendency to passively review worked-out solution traces, we extracted the top-level goals from each of the three Job 2

Learning Phase problems and used the abstracted goal structures as examples to learn from. This procedural manipulation shifted a considerable cognition burden onto the individual technicians. They could no longer be passive and satisfactorily meet the demands of the task. Their role was now substantially expanded because they had to specify actions that would achieve each goal in the exemplar structure and then interpret the results (see Table 8.3 for a set of illustrative goals). To do that and to preserve the naturalistic character of the study, we instructed the technicians to direct their own learning, using their best learning skills to improve their troubleshooting capabilities. They were encouraged to ask questions of the Job 2 expert tutor, and were told he would only provide information in response to questions.

Each technician was provided the ordered set of goals, one at a time. They had two hours per problem for a total of six hours of learning sessions. At the end of each problem session, technicians were given the option to reorder the goals or to propose alternative goals if they believed they could improve upon the goal structure. This option was considered important to include in order to give credence to the notion that troubleshooting is an ill-structured activity; therefore, there are always equivalent alternative solutions to any given problem.

To overcome the ego barriers associated with revealing one's lack of knowledge by the act of questioning, technicians were told that the highest level management in their organization was questioning the value of the months of resident training in Job 2 that was presently being provided to them. Further, they were told that our research laboratory was assisting their top-level management in investigating this question by conducting the present study. (These statements are true.) We then issued what amounted to a challenge to them to show everyone how much they could learn about Job 2 if they had practical problem-solving instruction with one-on-one coaching from a Job 2 expert. In this way we hoped to sanction their questioning behavior so that it was not viewed as an indication of ignorance. At the same time we believed that establishing these conditions for learning would create the right climate for transfer to occur and be observed.

Table 8.3.   Goal Structure for Learning Phase Problem (Job 2)

Goal No.	Goal
1	Analyze all available information about the fail
2	Verify the IF [interface or test package] stimulus through the cables.
3	Run OA/FI [software diagnostics] on the Noise Source
4	Analyze available information resulting from OA/FI [software diagnostics]
5	Identify signal routing from the second stimulus source to the Noise Source
6	Verify the second stimulus to the Noise Source
7	Verify the signal flow through the Interface Adapter Unit [circuitry in Test Package]
8	Determine where the signal is being lost and why

Phase 3: Posttesting on Job 2 Problems

The Posttest Phase was designed to realize two major goals. First, we wanted to remove the scaffolding that subjects had been provided to assist their learning in the previous phase. For posttest problems, no goal structures were provide to guide their solution paths. Further, the expert tutors were instructed to give assistance only when a subject explicitly stated, "I need to know   x   ." Tutors were cautioned not to provide unsolicited help in response to student impasses. Secondly, we wanted the problems selected for this phase to span a rather lengthy transfer continuum so that we could be reasonably sure we were allowing for a full range of acquired skills to be displayed. Accordingly, the near-transfer problem was almost a mirror image of a problem from an earlier phase. The slight variation involved relocating the fault; however, the cognitive demands of the problem were so similar to an earlier problem that it almost represented self-transfer. The far-transfer problem, by comparison, shared few similarities with earlier problems or with Job 1 problem demands. The third posttest problem fell somewhere between these two extremes.

Technicians were again tested using verbal troubleshooting procedures. In addition, the task analyst recorded incidents where information was requested from the experts. Subjects were given one hour to solve each problem. The expert did not "move" the fault when the time was close to expiring as was done in the pretest.

PRELIMINARY RESULTS

In this section we report preliminary findings from the three-phase study just described. Presentation of the data will be guided by (a) the cognitive skills architecture described earlier where the coordination of system, procedural, and strategic knowledge produces a model for effective technical problem solving (see Figure 8.1), and (b) the transfer questions posed earlier that have given focus to our investigation. Those questions are repeated here in Table 8.4. Comparisons will be made between stronger and weaker performers based on their demonstrated improvements in troubleshooting from pretest to posttest problems. Possible reasons for performance gains will be proposed, generally with

Table 8.4. Focusing Questions for Naturalistic Study of Transfer

- What are the mechanisms by which transfer occurs?
- What are the levers that are used to access prior knowledge and utilize it productively?
- What is the content of the knowledge that is accessed and transferred?
- What features and/or conditions associated with prior knowledge/skill appear to impede the acquisition process?

reference to the intervening Learning Phase. The first findings of interest address how prior knowledge influences learning in a related domain.

Use of Prior System Knowledge in Learning

Better learners[1] appeared to use existing device model schemata and available functional representations of electronic test processes to instantiate new Job 2 situations. This adaptation showed the better performers to be flexible in tuning and extending their existing models when necessary. Poorer learners, by comparison, appeared unable to extend their existing mental models of the equipment in response to novel Job 2 situations.

To illustrate, on one of the Learning Phase problems, Technician AT drew an illustrative Job 2 diagram (Figure 8.4) that constitutes an instantiation of the general avionics device model (see Figure 8.2). This Job 2 representation is predictable from both the general device model (Figure 8.2) and the Job 1 specific models he displayed in Job 1 pretests. A diagram that AT drew as part of a Job 1 pretest problem is shown in Figure 8.5. This drawing illustrates the mental model of the avionics equipment with which AT entered our study. Notice that the Job 1 device model in this figure is a partial instantiation of the general avionics model shown in Figure 8.2. What has been instantiated is the circuit path from the Unit Under Test to the Test Package through the Routing Device (here called the RAG or Relay Assembly Group) to a Measurement Device (here, the DMM or Digital Multifunction Meter). We've termed this a partial instantiation because the Stimulus Device and UUT are not made specific in the diagram. In AT's Job 2 diagram (Figure 8.4), notice the very similar partial instantiation of the general avionics device model. The path from a UUT (here, UUT #3) to a Measurement Device (here, the DTU or Digital Test Unit) is made specific. The consistent use of this device model across equipment systems suggests a level of understanding that "a test station is a test station" having common functions of generating, routing, and measuring stimuli.

An interesting bit of learning occurred as AT attempted to use his Figure 8.4 model to solve the Learning Phase problem. The feedback he got from the expert who was tutoring him caused him to adjust his representation to incorporate the unusual situation where the UUT sends a signal to a *Stimulus* Device as well as to a Measurement Device. The more standard mental model of an electronic test on this equipment involves a signal originating in a Stimulus Device, being routed through a Routing Device, being received by the UUT, which in turn sends a signal back through the Routing Device to be measured by a Measurement Device (see Figures 8.2 and 8.5). AT's adjusted diagram for the Job 2 problem is depicted in Figure 8.6. Now, the UUT is sending a signal to a Stimulus Device

---

[1] As measured by pre- to posttest gains on Job 2 problems.

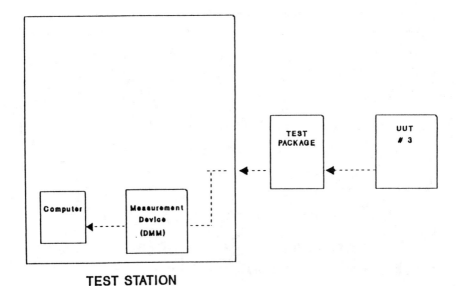

TEST STATION

Figure 8.4.   AT's Initial Diagram (Job 2 Problem)

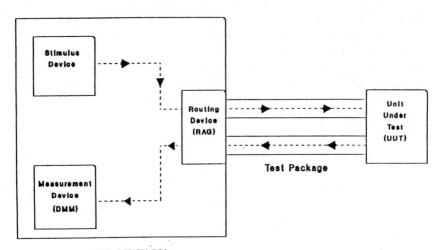

TEST STATION

Figure 8.5.   AT's Job 1 Device Model

(here, the Pulse Generator or PG) as well as along the expected path to a Measurement Device (here, the Digital Test Unit or DTU). The change in AT's drawing from Figure 8.4 to Figure 8.6 illustrates how he adjusted his prior model to accommodate this novel situation in Job 2. Other good performers also

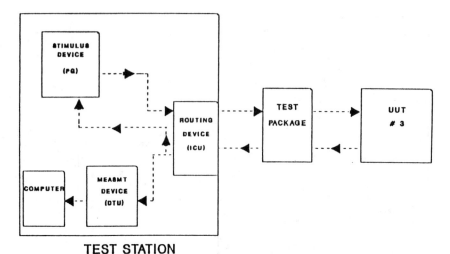

TEST STATION

Figure 8.6.   AT's Adjusted Diagram (Job 2 Problem)

showed evidence of invoking an existing device model and then flexibly adapting that model to accommodate the rather unusual electronic test situation encountered in this problem.

By comparison, two weaker performers, WN and JH, who appeared to have sound, standard test station device models from their Job 1 experience, did not appear to be instantiating a general model in responding to Job 2 electronic test situations. Job 1 diagrams from WN and JH are shown as Figures 8.7 and 8.8. WN's diagram for the same Job 2 problem illustrated above in Figure 8.6 is

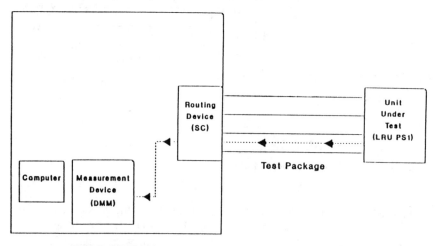

TEST STATION

Figure 8.7.   WN's Job 1 Device Model

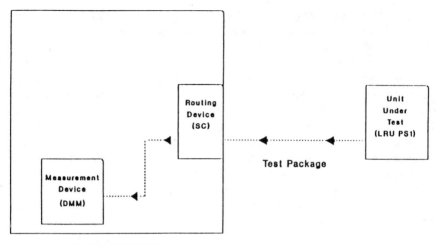

TEST STATION

Figure 8.8.   JH's Job 1 Device Model

shown in Figure 8.9, but is difficult to interpret. It shows some influence of a
standard equipment representation, but is incomplete. In particular, the routing
and measurement devices are not specified in this diagram. Further, although
the diagram accurately depicts the unusual situation of the UUT sending a signal
to a stimulus device, there is reason to believe this functional relationship is not

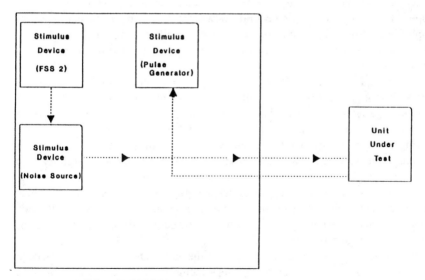

TEST STATION

Figure 8.9.   WN's Device Model for Job 2 Learning Phase Problem

meaningfully understood by Technician WN. His verbalizations and troubleshooting actions on this problem are generally detached from, not guided by, his depicted model.

We can draw some tentative conclusions about transfer from these particular results. The better performers appeared to access old device schemata—or mental models of the equipment and the electronic test process—and use them in interpreting new Job 2 problem situations. Further, they flexibly used the Job 1 schemata that they invoked as building blocks for learning novel aspects of Job 2. They neither ignored nor rigidly held to their prior mental models. They subsequently used the adapted Job 2 models to give focus and direction to their problem solving. The abstracted device schemata that provide the content for this instance of transfer illustrate transfer at a general level. A second set of findings illustrates transfer at a more specific level.

Use of Prior Procedural Knowledge

As expected, all technicians showed evidence of transporting intact procedural subroutines (or clusters of procedural steps) from Job 1 to use in Job 2 situations. The steps required to execute standard electronic tests (namely, ohm, voltage, and waveform measurements) as well as the interpretive processes that are needed to respond to test results were displayed by all performers across equipment contexts, that is, on both Job 1 and Job 2 problems. Interesting differences among performers were manifested, however. Better performers appear to access existing procedural knowledge and then interrogate it for its applicability to Job 2 problem conditions. Conversely, weaker performers appear to access the same procedural knowledge but fail to adapt it to fit the altered problem-solving demands.

For example, weaker performer WN showed some procedural inflexibility by not acting on the guidance from his tutor to amend his procedural steps for measuring a relay. He was advised to add a step to determine if the logic (data bits) needed as input to set the relay was present. His procedural subroutine for testing a relay was restricted to measuring continuity through the relay by taking an ohms measurement. It is unclear whether WN's procedural rigidity is a function of highly compiled procedural knowledge or whether the source of the difficulty is a system or strategic knowledge gap. He could have a weak relay device model that fails to incorporate logic input, or he could have weak strategic knowledge that does not include a rationale that would justify in efficiency terms why the added step is worthwhile.

Better performers appeared to transfer the more abstract goals associated with procedural steps, as well as the steps themselves. For example, several of the better learners asked the expert tutors about the existence of procedures to accomplish the rerouting of signals. They wanted to see if a reconfigured signal path would affect the test failure they had encountered. Instead of transporting specific procedural knowledge to do this, they anticipated that any existing procedures might have to be transposed. So, they accessed the goal of such procedures and used the goal as a means to interrogate the expert.

In sum, in the case of skill transfer at the more specific level of procedural operations, we find evidence of the transportability of test-step sequences across domains. Also, the goals achieved by the procedures are transferred by better learners as levers to acquire appropriate Job 2 procedures. Weaker performers, by comparison, appear to be welded to more specific procedural steps, sometimes persistently so.

Learning Processes that Affect Transfer

Other early data suggest an interesting finding about the learning processes by which both general and specific transfer is achieved. A positive relationship appears to exist between active learning behavior and subsequent improved troubleshooting performance. The culminating Job 2 posttest problems provided an objective criterion by which to establish better and poorer learners. The better performers solved all three posttest problems in the allotted time. Conversely, one of the weaker performers was unable to solve two of the posttest problems at all and another required 25% more time per problem to solve two of the three problems. In general, all of the technicians who showed improved performance on the posttests actively interrogated the expert tutors during the Learning Phase as they constructed their own understanding of the problems. They asked more questions, and they also produced more self-explanations, often generating additional questions from their elaborations. By comparison, weaker performers tended to ask fewer questions, showed little evidence of self-explanation, and often engaged in unproductive actions and questioning tactics.

To elaborate on the nature of the active learning behavior of the better performers, they showed evidence of spending considerable time in constructing a deep functional representation of the causal components of a problem before and during problem solving. This provided them a mental model which they then used to guide their problem-solving performance. For example, in a Learning Phase problem (see Figure 8.10), Technician CF asked questions in order to understand the role of the stimulus and measurement path associated with a particular measurement device being used (in this case, the Digital Test Unit or DTU). This line of questioning is noteworthy because that segment of the circuitry was eliminated as a source of the fault in the introductory problem statement. (This simplification was used to make an especially difficult problem more tractable.) Nonetheless, Technician CF appeared to want to understand the role of the DTU in the test being run in order to have a complete representation of the problem—even though he did not have to concern himself with testing that component.

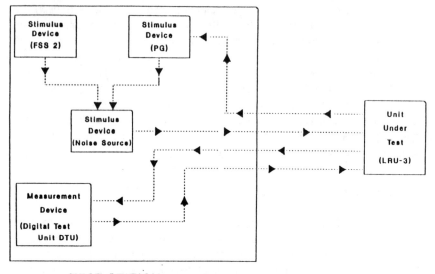

TEST STATION

Figure 8.10.   CF's Device Model for Job 2 Learning Phase Problem

On this particular problem, other improved performers like CF also included the DTU in their diagrams. All of them indicated a desire to initially depict all the functional interrelationships in a complete problem representation. Then, they focused on the relevant aspects of the device models they had generated (i.e., they excluded the DTU from their focus) and used the constrained model as a plan for their actions to investigate the equipment. With this guiding mental model, these technicians never strayed off the actual signal path during the solution process. What is of special interest is that they appeared unwilling to ignore a functional component that had been ruled out in the problem statement (the DTU) until they understood its role in the circuit.

By comparison, weaker performer WN did not include the DTU in his diagram for this problem (see Figure 8.9), but he wanted to take steps to measure areas of the signal path affected by the DTU. In his case, performance is clearly detached from—not guided by—the model he generates. Further, the exclusion of the DTU as a suspect in the problem statement does not appear to be salient to him, since he ignores that piece of information and takes steps to investigate this irrelevant component. Overall his performance suggests an uninformed mode of investigation where his failure to initially build an adequate device model results in unnecessary and thus unproductive procedural steps. He often strayed off the active circuit path during the solution process, whereas the better learners did not.

While Technician WN was generally taciturn during most problem-solving sessions, Technician JH was not. Examining his performance addresses the question of whether active problem solving means something more than being highly veral. On the same Learning Problem depicted above, JH generated elaborations in response to the goal, "Analyze all available information about the fail." The quality of his elaborations is noticeably different from those of better learners AT and CF. JH typically restated information about the failed test using the tech data he was in the process of reading. He made few inferences, but drew several faulty conclusions. Feedback from the expert tutor was ineffective in either fostering JH's comprehension or eliminating his misconceptions. Moreover, he displayed no signs of monitoring his own comprehension. Perhaps the most distinctive characteristic of his troubleshooting is the lack of systematicity in his action sequences. His actions are not predictable from either his sketchy, often misguided representations of the problems or from his restatements of problem conditions. This complete disconnection between what he said and what he did suggests that his verbalizations were not meaningful to him and that his actions were probably guesses. This discontinuity further suggests that while JH performed satisfactorily in Job 1, he did not possess robust enough knowledge structures to use to interpret novel Job 2 information (in contrast to AT and CF). He also displayed deficiencies in the learning skills one needs to build and bolster such structures.

One final piece of evidence provides additional support for the relationship between active learning behavior and improved troubleshooting performance. Better performers actively monitored their comprehension processes during learning. They appeared to know when their understanding was incomplete and took steps to remedy the condition. They knew when to ask questions because of the self-monitoring in which they seemed continuously engaged. Weaker performers tended not to manifest any such self-regulatory processes.

To illustrate this point, the posttest problem that occupied the farthest spot on our transfer continuum had a particularly interesting feature in common with a problem the subjects encountered in earlier phases. Like the Learning Phase problem discussed above (see Figure 8.10), the far-transfer posttest problem incorporated the situation where a stimulus device receives a signal from another source. In the Learning Phase problem, one Stimulus Device (the Pulse Generator) is sending a signal to trigger another Stimulus Device (the Noise Source). In the far-transfer posttest problem, one stimulus device similarly provides the trigger for a second stimulus. All the better performers showed no difficulty in representing this dual stimulus condition and were successful in solving the far-transfer problem. This occurred despite the fact that these same subjects, save one, expressed confusion in the Learning Phase when this unusual situation was encountered. One illustrative elaboration from a better performer was, "I'm confused. I don't know if the signal is coming or going." Better performers showed awareness of their confusion, as this comment illustrates, and subsequently asked questions and produced self-explanations until they could generate an accurate device model. This model appeared to be responsible for their subsequent on-target troubleshooting actions.

In contrast, weaker performers WN and JH did not appear to comprehend the use of two stimulus devices in the Learning Phase problem and never appeared to achieve a tight correspondence between their models of the equipment and their procedural steps. On the far-transfer posttest problem, they fared much worse than the other group. JH failed to isolate the fault in the allotted time and WN needed 15 additional minutes to solve the problem. The difference in the subjects' earlier learning behavior appears to explain this performance difference under far-transfer conditions.

Comprehension Monitoring During Learning. As noted above, elaborations and self-explanations (as active learning behavior) often took the form of comprehension monitoring for the better learners. In the monitoring process, they attended in particular to conditions of applicability associated with Job 2 procedures. They also engaged in various processes intended to reduce their working memory load and in turn to enhance their comprehension. Poorer learners, by comparison, tended to reduce their cognitive load through inappropriate overgeneralization and oversimplification activities.

Technician CF illustrates the comprehension monitoring of better learners. He noticed procedural repetitions (or self-transfer) when they occurred during solution searches, making comments such as, "I remember [how to do] this from before." He also attended to altered conditions of applicability when he contemplated using some recently learned procedure or higher level strategy.

"This [situation] is different from what we had before."

"I don't know if I would have thought about logically eliminating relays from known data [information available in various test results]. This might be a waste of time if you only had a few relays, but if you had 15 [a large number], it could be good."

The second comment above also illustrates how the better learners were both receptive and evaluative when novel strategies were proposed by the expert tutors to reduce the cognitive load of interpreting multiple complex findings. On several occasions during the Learning Phase, technicians were presented goals that called for them to integrate and correlate information derived from multiple equipment failures. Better performers learned and sometimes commented on the intent of such a strategy, as illustrated in CF's second comment above. When implemented in one of the learning problems, the strategy involved comparing the signal paths and results of several failed tests to reduce the number of suspect relays from four to two. Better performers learned and used this approach to simplify the information arrays that they encountered.

Technician CF demonstrated another form of effectively reducing his cognitive load as well. When exposed to a complicated procedure for using technical data in a Job 2 pretest, he asked questions in order to elicit explanations of how the procedure worked and why it took the form it did. In this way he appeared to acquire conceptual support knowledge that enabled him to simplify the procedure. This conclusion is based on the fact that CF was able to produce a clever simplification of the complex procedure in the Posttest Phase even though in the intervening Learning Phase sessions there had been no occasion to practice or otherwise become more familiar with the procedure. In other words, he not only transferred the procedure, he made it more elegant.

Less able performers exhibited a range of alternative behaviors instead of comprehension monitoring and appropriate simplification strategies. When they encountered novel or overwhelming Job 2 situations, they often displayed poor comprehension and overgeneralization in the form of schema fixation, hypothesis bias, and localized treatment of information arrays.

For example, Technician WN seemed to oversimplify problem characteristics in order to fit new Job 2 situations into his existing Job 1 structures. He appeared more comfortable with force-fitting novel input into available schemata (schema fixation) than interrogating his current structures, interrogating the expert, and ultimately transposing old structures into enhanced ones. This practice repeatedly resulted in the exclusion of critical problem components from WN's mental models. In turn, he frequently took unnecessary actions or inefficiently strayed off the active signal path, apparently because of his earlier faulty comprehension and incomplete modeling of problem components. When making decisions about procedural options to deploy, WN similarly tended to overgeneralize his old Job 1 procedures. For example, an instance of negative transfer of diagnostic self-tests resulted in hypothesis bias during one of his solution searches. Self-tests are software diagnostics that can be run on the test station to assist in isolating test station fails. WN resisted using them in Job 2, even when recommended by the expert tutor. His reasoning was that he found them generally uninformative and incomplete on his Job 1 equipment and therefore believed they would be of little use in Job 2. This predisposition against the use of self-tests influenced WN's reasoning on one of the rare occasions when he actually used self-diagnostics in Job 2 troubleshooting. In the problem involving the Noise Source (see Figures 8.9 and 8.10 above), the goal structure that was given to each subject to follow included the goal of running diagnostics on the Noise Source. WN highly suspected the Noise Source, and so he expressed surprise when told that that component checked out all right on the diagnostics. His interpretation of the result amounted to an indictment of the self-test: "It (self-test) didn't check out the problem I'm having." He continued to suspect the Noise Source even in the face of mounting evidence that the fail was located elsewhere. This unfounded bias toward a particular hypothesis appears to be partially due to negative transfer of a procedural subroutine.

In general, it was not uncommon for poorer performers to appear over-whelmed by the Job 2 information they were presented. Their maladaptive response was often a violation of a widely held troubleshooting dictum, namely, "Breadth before depth." Good troubleshooters typically represent problems and in turn investigate equipment in breadth-first fashion. This means they mentally model the major components of a problem and attempt to eliminate some of these major components before going in depth into any particular component. Novices, by comparison, often operate on too localized a level too soon. The poorer learners in this study thus resembled novices when they failed to incorporate major problem components in their mental models and instead narrowly focused on specific subcomponents before investigating the equipment more broadly. Interestingly, procedural deficiencies such as these can be traced to the quality of the mental model the technician is using to reason about the equipment.

COMMENTARY

The investigation of transfer that we have undertaken involves processes of *intentional* transfer, meaning the need to transfer is apparent to learners. Since the requirement to transfer one's existing knowledge is not disguised, what we see when we observe intentional transfer is the presence of a range of adaptive to maladaptive behaviors. The question of interest is not *whether* subjects will attempt to transfer prior knowledge and skills (since the requirements to transfer is transparent) but rather *how* they attempt to do so. We believe an explication of the processes of intentional transfer is of scientific interest because the undisguised need for mental adaptiveness is often the trigger for knowledge and skill generality in the real world.

Perhaps the most interesting theoretical dimension of our preliminary data is the strong influence exerted by mental models on both knowledge access and subsequent reasoning. Our results show that in this domain the primary content of transfer takes the form of abstract knowledge representations. Time and again we observed good learners access their existing mental models of equipment structure and function and of the troubleshooting task itself. They then used these models to guide their performance as they crafted solutions to new problems. Their prior models became interpretive structures, and when these models were inadequate, better learners flexibly used them to interrogate the expert and as the basis for transposed and elaborated structures that could accommodate the novel situations.

Less able performers devised ways to avoid this experience of learning. They displayed maladaptive behaviors as they oversimplified new problems and overgeneralized existing structures. As a result, their performance in the new domain appeared novice-like, without the benefit of abstract plans and adapted models. They were wedded to their old structures, unable to perceive that the functional variations in the target devices were plausible extensions of their current understanding.

As we continue to collect and study this type of learning data, we expect to enhance our early profile of the "adaptive expert" in ways that will eventually lead to instruction that fosters its growth.

REFERENCES

Brown, J.S., & Burton, R.R. (1986). Reactive learning environments for teaching electronic troubleshooting. In W.B. Rouse (Ed.), *Advances in man-machine systems research* (pp. 65–98). Greenwich, CT: JAI Press.

Brown, J.S., & deKleer, J. (1985). A qualitative physics based upon confluences. In D.G. Bobrow (Ed.), *Qualitative reasoning about physical systems.* Cambridge, MA: MIT Press.

Chi, M.T.H., & Bassok, M. (1989). Learning from examples via self-explanations. In L.B. Resnick (Ed.), *Knowing, learning, and instruction: Essays in honor of Robert Glaser* (pp. 251–282). Hillsdale, NJ: Erlbaum.

Chi, M.T.H., Bassok, M., Lewis, R., Reimann, P., & Glaser, R. (1989). Self-explanations: How students study and use examples in learning to solve problems. *Cognitive Science, 13,* 145–182.

Chi, M.T.H., Feltovich, P.J., & Glaser, R. (1981). Categorization and representation of physics problems by experts and novices. *Cognitive Science, 5,* 121–152.

Clancey, W.J. (1986). Qualitative student models. *Annual Review of Computer Science, 1,* 381–450.

Gentner, D., & Stevens, A.L. (Eds.). (1983). *Mental models.* Hillsdale, NJ: Erlbaum.

Gick, M.L., & Holyoak, K.J. (1987). The cognitive basis of knowledge transfer. In S.M. Cormier & J.D. Hagman (Eds.). *Transfer of learning: Contemporary research and applications* (pp. 9–46). San Diego, CA: Academic Press.

Glaser, R. (1988, January). *Expert knowledge and processes of thinking.* Paper presented at the American Association for the Advancement of Science Meeting, San Francisco, CA.

Glaser, R., & Gott, S. (1988). [Interview data from avionics cross-trainees]. Unpublished raw data.

Glaser, R., Lesgold, A., Lajoie, S., Eastman, R., Greenberg, L., Logan, D., Magone, M., Weiner, A., Wolf, R., & Yengo, L. (1985). *Cognitive task analysis to enhance technical skills training and assessment* (Contract No. F41689-83-C-0029). Brooks AFB, TX: Air Force Human Resources Laboratory.

Gott, S.P. (1989). Apprenticeship instruction for real-world tasks: The coordination of procedures, mental models, and strategies. In E.Z. Rothkopf (Ed.), *Review of research in education* (Vol. 15, pp. 97–169). Washington, DC: American Education Research Assn.

Hall, E.P., Gott, S.P., & Pokorny, R.A. (in press). *A procedural guide to cognitive task analysis: The PARI methodology* (Tech. Rep.) Brooks AFB, TX: Air Force Human Resources Laboratory.

Hatano, G., & Inagaki, K. (1984). *Two courses of expertise*. In the annual report of the Research and Clinical Center for Child Development. Sapporo, Japan: Hokkaido University.

Judd, C.H. (1908). The relation of special training and general intelligence. *Educational Review, 36,* 28–42.

Katona, G. (1940). *Organizing and memorizing*. New York: Columbia University Press.

Kieras, D.E. (1982). *What people know about electronic devices: A descriptive study* (Tech. Rep. No. 12 UARZ/DP/TR-82/ONR-12). Phoenix: University of Arizona, Department of Psychology.

Kieras, D.E., & Bovair, S. (1984). The role of a mental model in learning to operate a device. *Cognitive Science, 8,* 255–273.

Larkin, J.H., McDermott, J., Simon, D.P., & Simon, H.A. (1980). Expert and novice performance in solving physics problems. *Science, 208,* 1335–1342.

Means, B., & Gott, S.P. (1988). Cognitive task analysis as a basis for tutor development: Articulating abstract knowledge representations. In J. Psotka, L.D. Massey, & S.A. Mutter (Eds.), *Intelligent tutoring systems: Lessons learned.* Hillsdale NJ: Erlbaum.

Newell, A. (1969). Heuristic programming: Ill-structured problems. In J. Aronowsky (Ed.), *Progress in operations research* (Vol. III, pp. 360–414). New York: Wiley.

Parker, E., Dibble, E., & Gott, S.P. (1989, July). *An investigation of transfer of technical knowledge and skill.* Paper presented at the AF Basic Job Skills Scientific Progress Review. Brooks AFB, TX: AF Human Resources Laboratory.

Pokorny, R.A. (in press). *The evaluation of a real-world instructional system: Using technical experts as raters* (Tech. Rep.). Brooks AFB, TX: Air Force Human Resources Laboratory.

Thorndike, E.L. (1903). *Educational psychology*. New York: Lemke & Buechner.

Thorndike, E.L. (1906). *Principles of teaching*. New York: A.G. Seiler.

Thorndike, E.L., & Woodworth, R.S. (1901). The influence of improvement in one mental function upon the efficiency of other functions. *Psychological Review, 8,* 247–261.

Wertheimer, M. (1945). *Productive thinking*. New York: Harper & Row.

White, B.Y., & Frederiksen, J.R. (1986). *Progressions of qualitative models as foundations for intelligent learning environments* (BBN Report No. 6277). Cambridge, MA: BBN Laboratories Inc.

White, B.Y., & Frederiksen, J.R. (1987). *Causal model progressions as a foundation for intelligent learning environments* (BBN Report No. 6686). Cambridge, MA: BBN Laboratories Inc.

Author Index

Subject Index